Shojo Beat

# Skip·Beat!

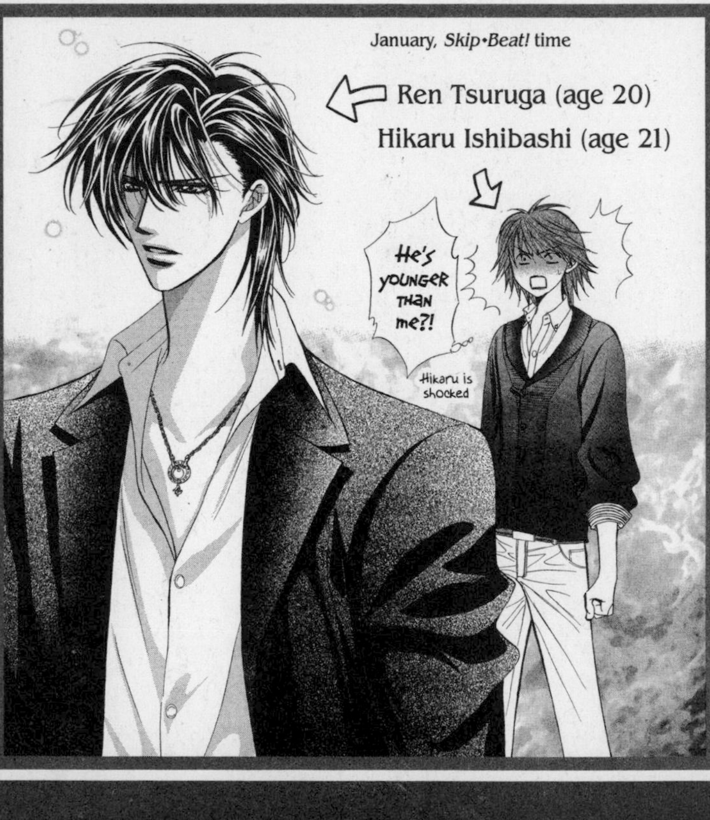
January, *Skip•Beat!* time
Ren Tsuruga (age 20)
Hikaru Ishibashi (age 21)
He's younger than me?!
Hikaru is shocked

22

Story & Art by Yoshiki Nakamura

# Skip·Beat!
## Volume 22

## CONTENTS

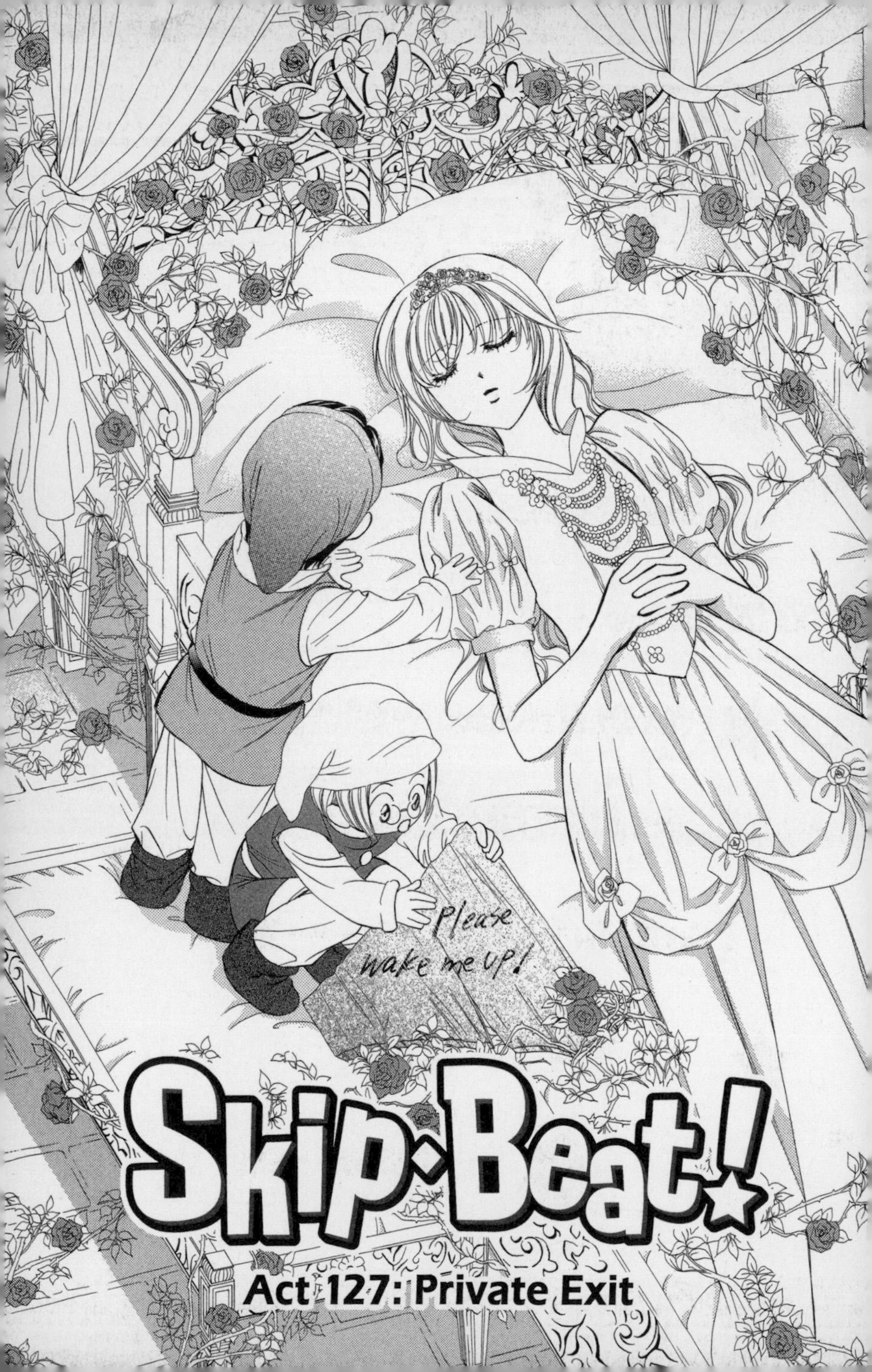
Please wake me up!
Skip·Beat!
Act 127: Private Exit

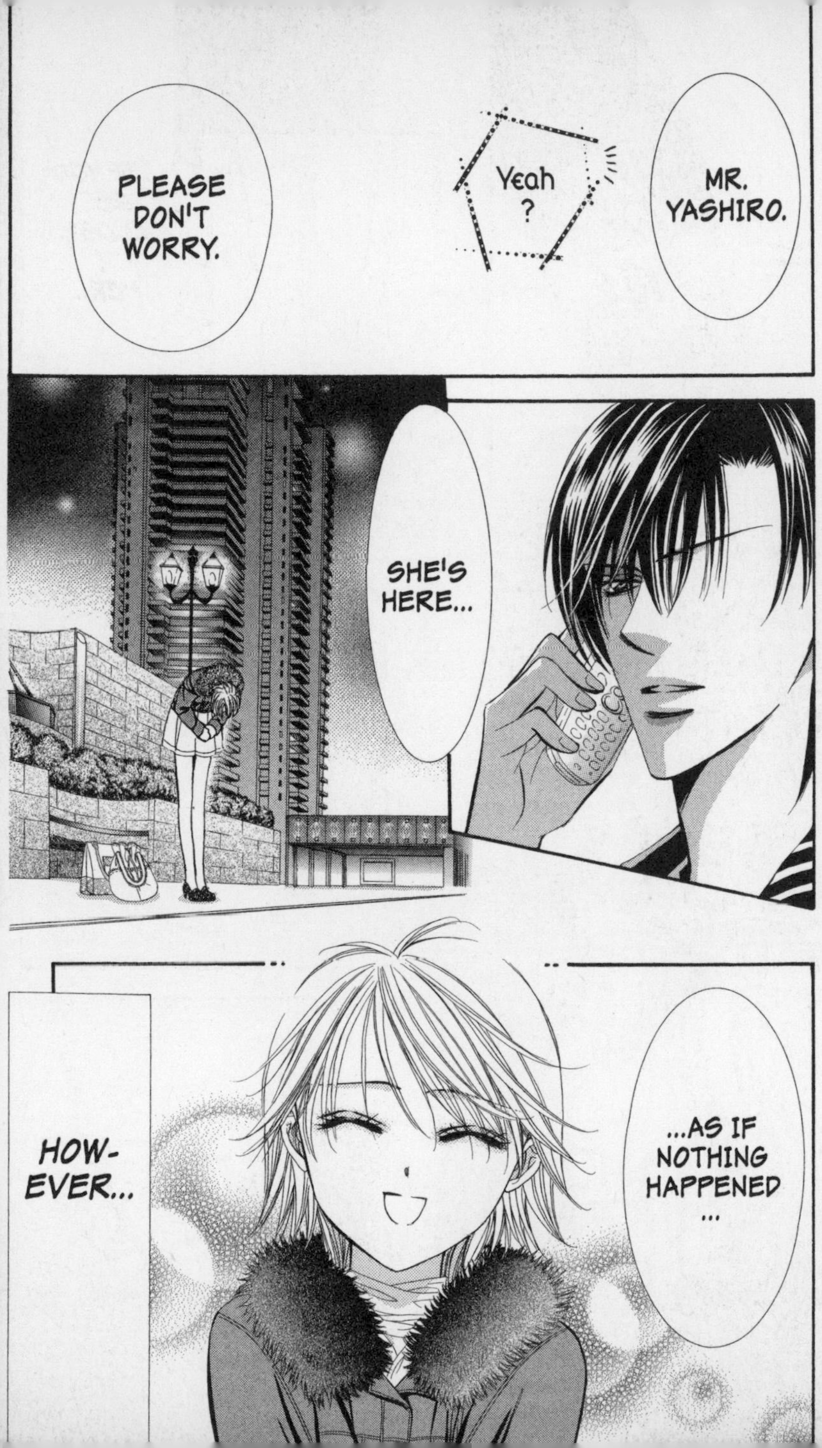
MR. YASHIRO.
Yeah ?
PLEASE DON'T WORRY.
SHE'S HERE...
...AS IF NOTHING HAPPENED ...
HOW-EVER...

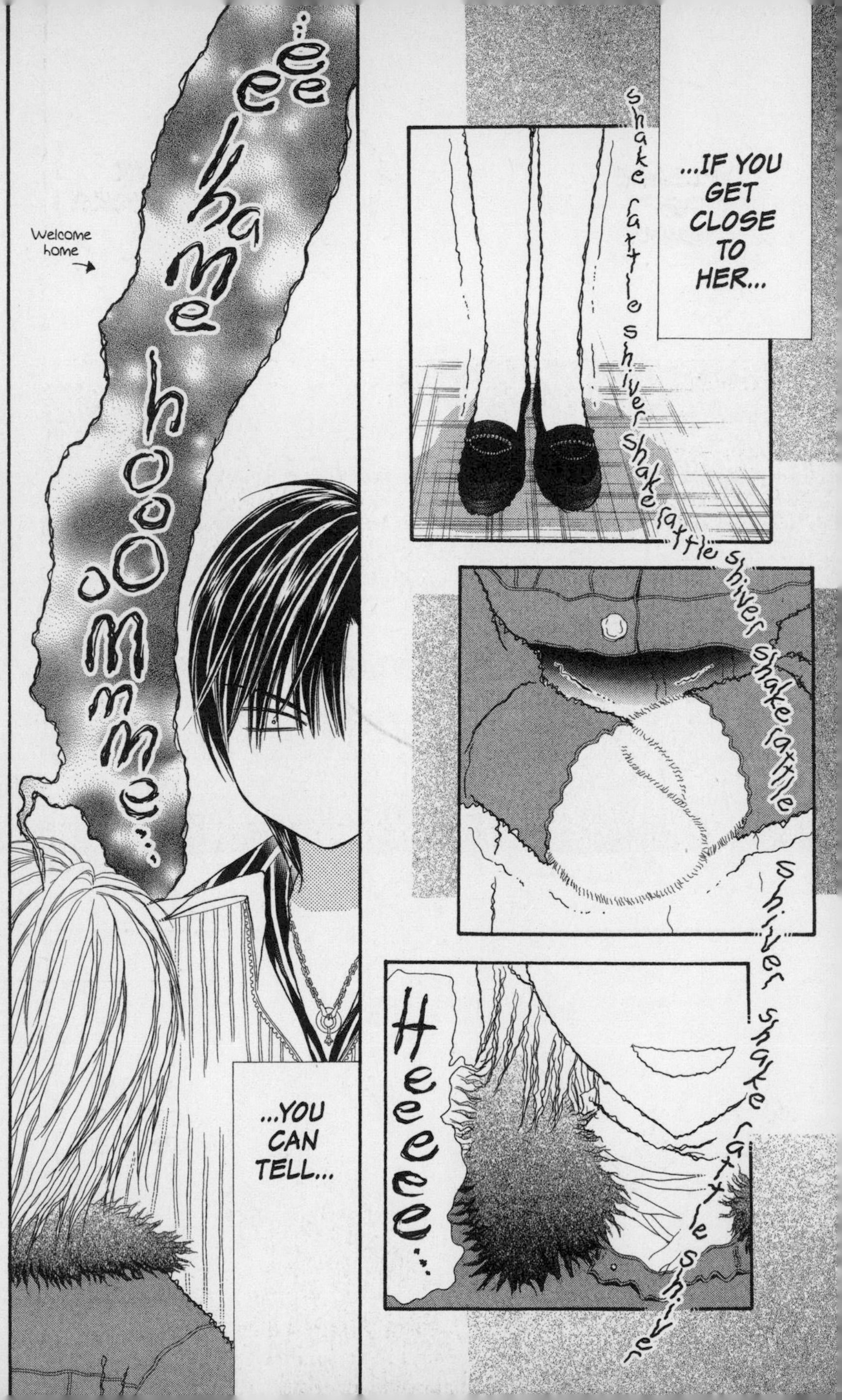
...IF YOU GET CLOSE TO HER...
shake rattle shiver shake rattle shiver shake rattle shiver shake rattle shiver
Heeeee...
Eeehame hooommme...
Welcome home
...YOU CAN TELL...

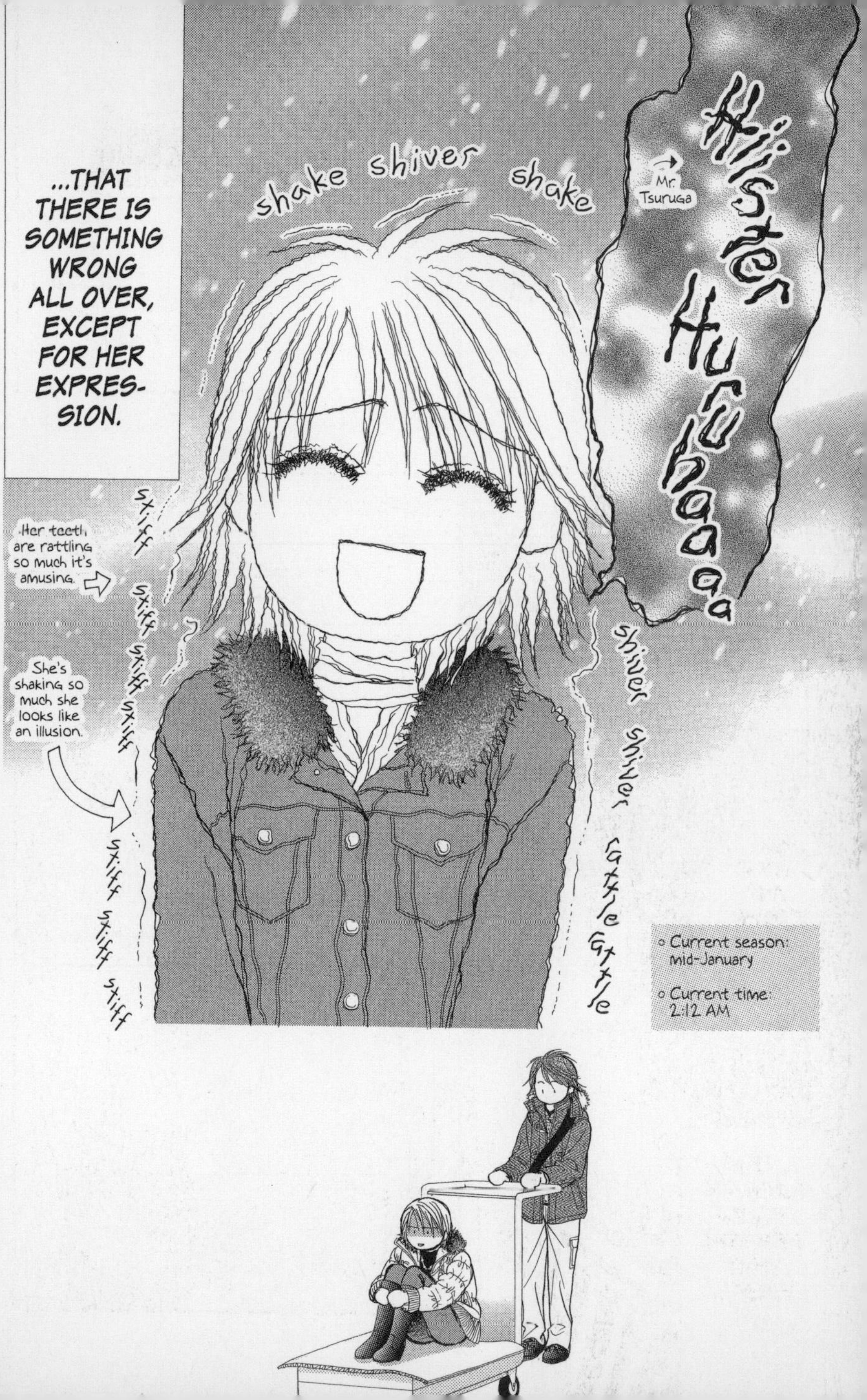
Hiister Hucuhaaaa
Mr. Tsuruga
shake shiver shake
...THAT THERE IS SOMETHING WRONG ALL OVER, EXCEPT FOR HER EXPRESSION.
shiver shiver rattle rattle
stiff stiff stiff stiff stiff stiff stiff stiff
Her teeth are rattling so much it's amusing.
She's shaking so much she looks like an illusion.
Current season: mid-January
Current time: 2:12 AM

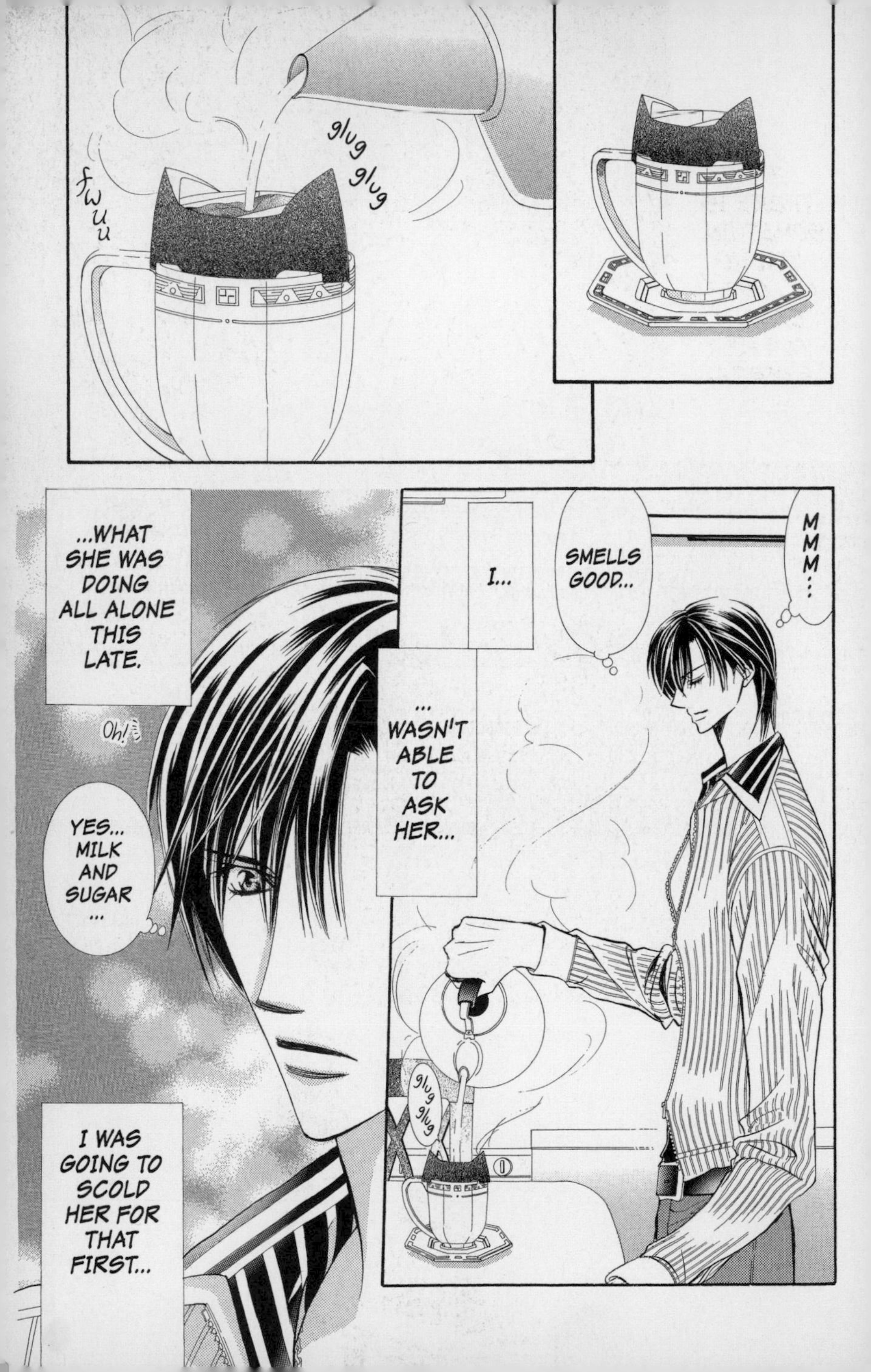
glug glug
fwuu
MMM...
SMELLS GOOD...
I...
...WASN'T ABLE TO ASK HER...
glug glug
...WHAT SHE WAS DOING ALL ALONE THIS LATE.
Oh!
YES... MILK AND SUGAR...
I WAS GOING TO SCOLD HER FOR THAT FIRST...

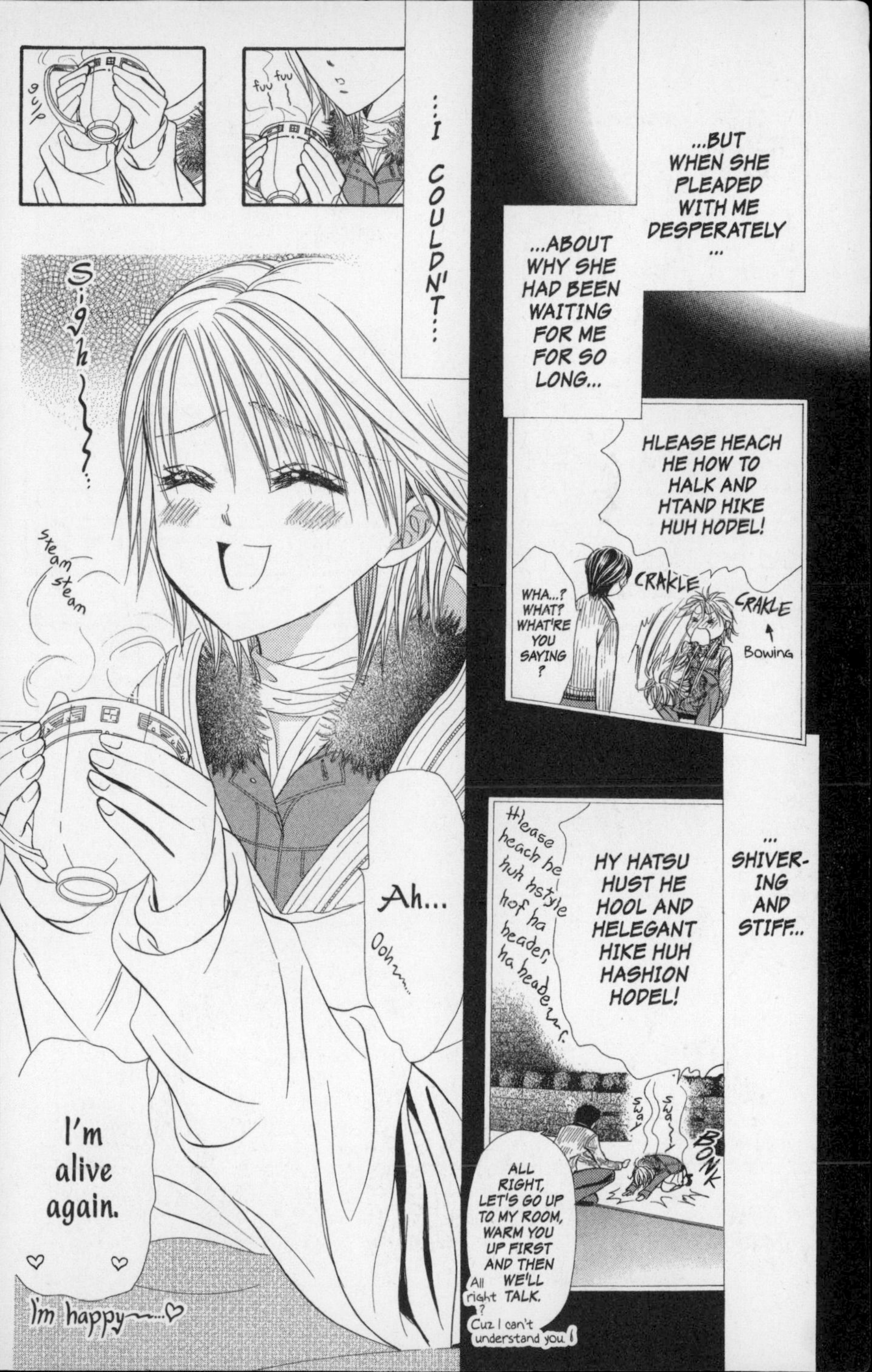
...BUT WHEN SHE PLEADED WITH ME DESPERATELY ...
...ABOUT WHY SHE HAD BEEN WAITING FOR ME FOR SO LONG...
HLEASE HEACH HE HOW TO HALK AND HTAND HIKE HUH HODEL!
CRAKLE
CRAKLE
Bowing
WHA...? WHAT? WHAT'RE YOU SAYING ?
...SHIVERING AND STIFF...
HY HATSU HUST HE HOOL AND HELEGANT HIKE HUH HASHION HODEL!
Hlease heach he huh hstyle hof ha header, ha headerr.
SWAY
SWAY
BONK
ALL RIGHT, LET'S GO UP TO MY ROOM, WARM YOU UP FIRST AND THEN WE'LL TALK.
All right ?
Cuz I can't understand you!
...I COULDN'T...
fuu fuu
gulp
Sigh.....
steam steam
Ah...
Ooh....
I'm alive again.
I'm happy....

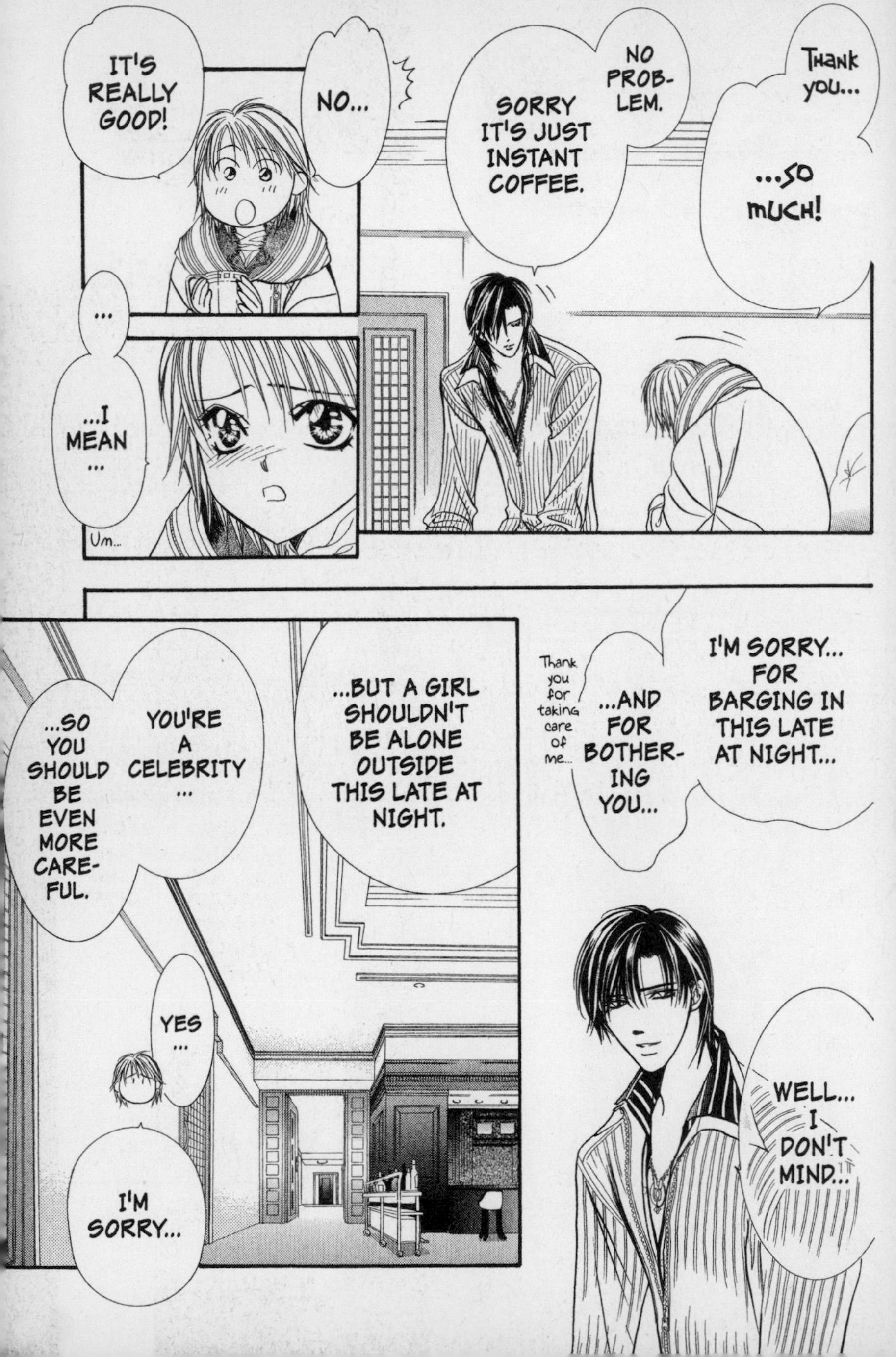
Thank you...
...SO MUCH!
NO PROB-LEM.
SORRY IT'S JUST INSTANT COFFEE.
NO...
IT'S REALLY GOOD!
...
...I MEAN...
Um...
I'M SORRY... FOR BARGING IN THIS LATE AT NIGHT...
...AND FOR BOTHER-ING YOU...
Thank you for taking care of me...
WELL... I DON'T MIND...
...BUT A GIRL SHOULDN'T BE ALONE OUTSIDE THIS LATE AT NIGHT.
YOU'RE A CELEBRITY...
...SO YOU SHOULD BE EVEN MORE CARE-FUL.
YES...
I'M SORRY...

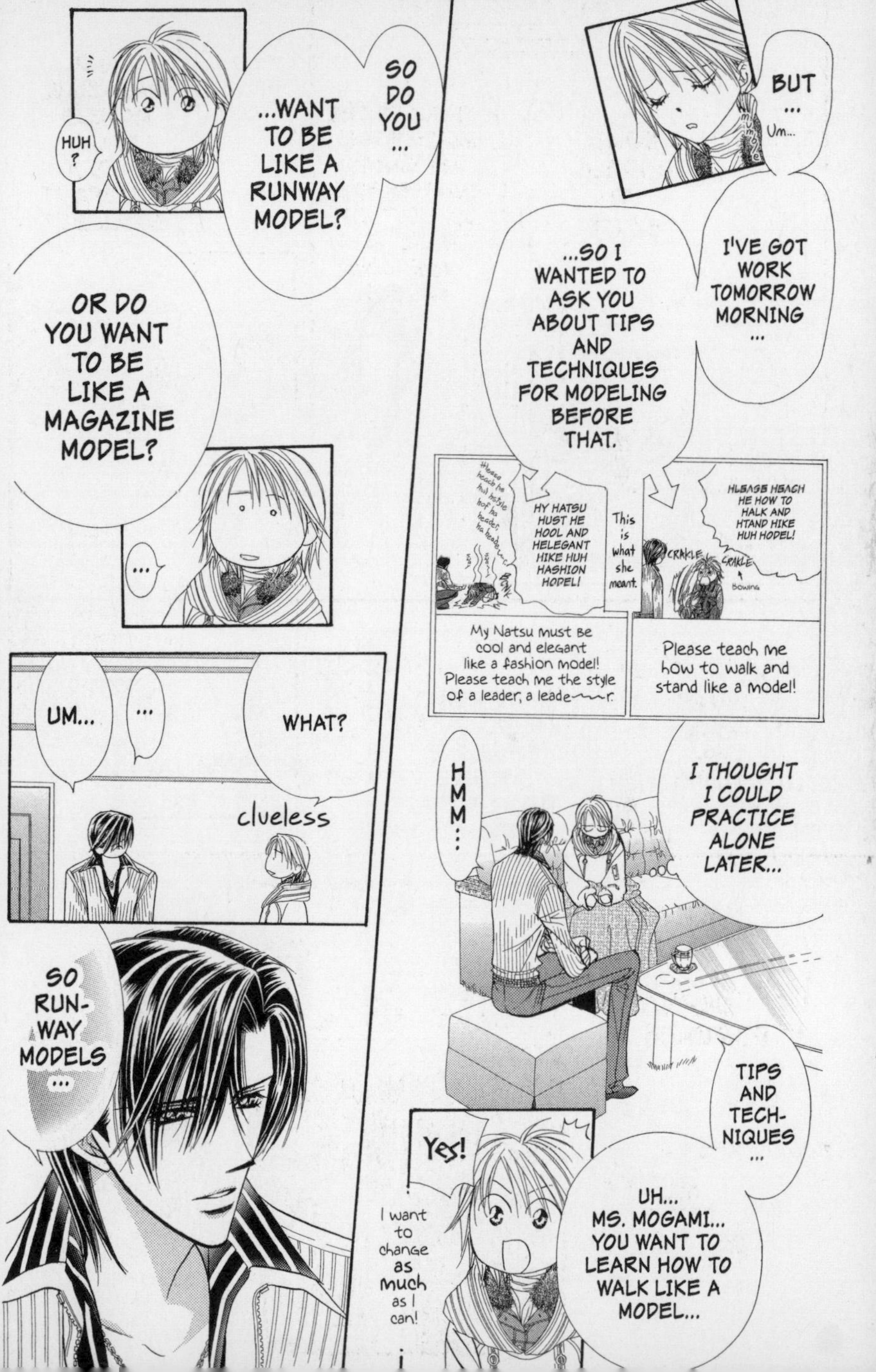
BUT ...
Um...
I'VE GOT WORK TOMORROW MORNING ...
...SO I WANTED TO ASK YOU ABOUT TIPS AND TECHNIQUES FOR MODELING BEFORE THAT.
HLEASE HEACH HE HOW TO HALK AND HTAND HIKE HUH HODEL!
CRAKLE
CRAKLE
Bowing
Please teach me how to walk and stand like a model!
This is what she meant.
HY HATSU HUST HE HOOL AND HELEGANT HIKE HUH HASHION HODEL!
My Natsu must be cool and elegant like a fashion model! Please teach me the style of a leader, a leade~~r.
I THOUGHT I COULD PRACTICE ALONE LATER...
HMM...
TIPS AND TECH-NIQUES ...
UH... MS. MOGAMI... YOU WANT TO LEARN HOW TO WALK LIKE A MODEL...
Yes!
I want to change as much as I can!
SO DO YOU ...
...WANT TO BE LIKE A RUNWAY MODEL?
HUH ?
OR DO YOU WANT TO BE LIKE A MAGAZINE MODEL?
...
WHAT?
...
UM...
clueless
SO RUN-WAY MODELS ...

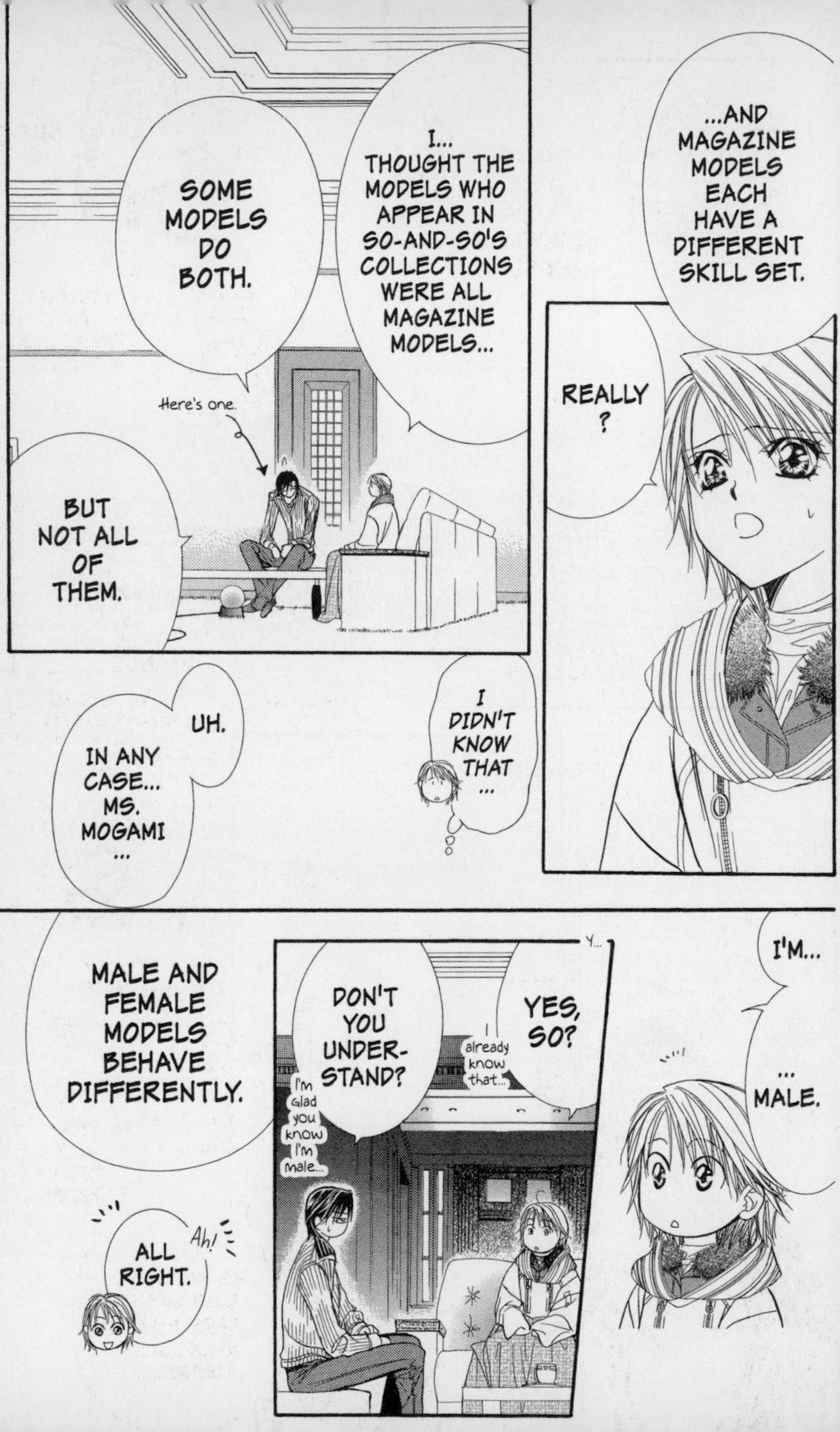
...AND MAGAZINE MODELS EACH HAVE A DIFFERENT SKILL SET.
REALLY?
I... THOUGHT THE MODELS WHO APPEAR IN SO-AND-SO'S COLLECTIONS WERE ALL MAGAZINE MODELS...
SOME MODELS DO BOTH.
Here's one.
BUT NOT ALL OF THEM.
I DIDN'T KNOW THAT...
UH.
IN ANY CASE... MS. MOGAMI...
I'M...
...MALE.
Y...
YES, SO?
I already know that...
DON'T YOU UNDER-STAND?
I'm Glad you know I'm male...
MALE AND FEMALE MODELS BEHAVE DIFFERENTLY.
Ah!
ALL RIGHT.

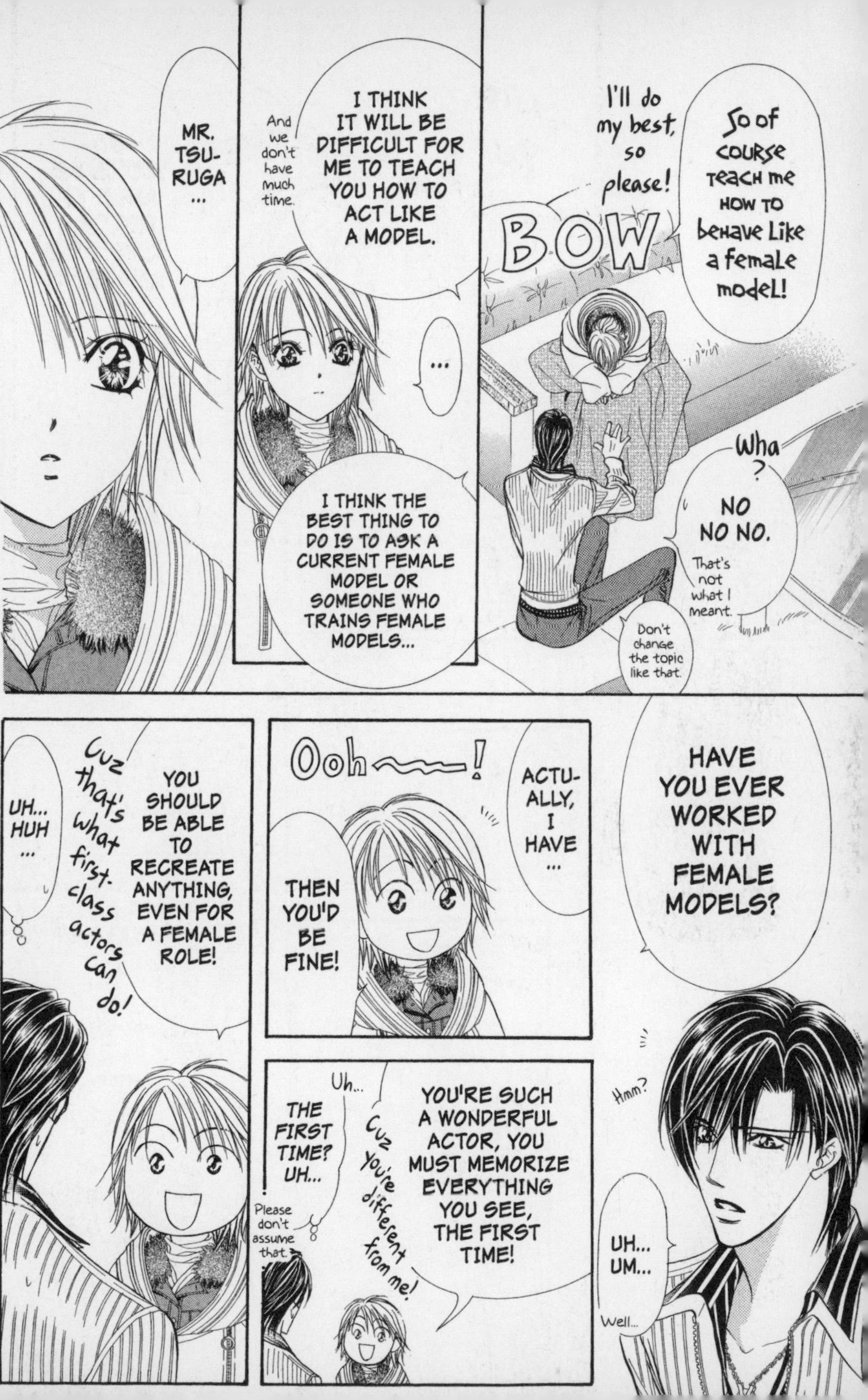
So of course teach me how to behave like a female model!
I'll do my best, so please!
BOW
Wha?
NO NO NO.
That's not what I meant.
Don't change the topic like that.
I THINK IT WILL BE DIFFICULT FOR ME TO TEACH YOU HOW TO ACT LIKE A MODEL.
And we don't have much time.
...
I THINK THE BEST THING TO DO IS TO ASK A CURRENT FEMALE MODEL OR SOMEONE WHO TRAINS FEMALE MODELS...
MR. TSURUGA...
HAVE YOU EVER WORKED WITH FEMALE MODELS?
Hmm?
UH... UM...
Well...
ACTUALLY, I HAVE...
Ooh~!
THEN YOU'D BE FINE!
YOU'RE SUCH A WONDERFUL ACTOR, YOU MUST MEMORIZE EVERYTHING YOU SEE, THE FIRST TIME!
Cuz you're different from me!
Uh...
THE FIRST TIME? UH...
Please don't assume that.
YOU SHOULD BE ABLE TO RECREATE ANYTHING, EVEN FOR A FEMALE ROLE!
Cuz that's what first-class actors can do!
UH... HUH...

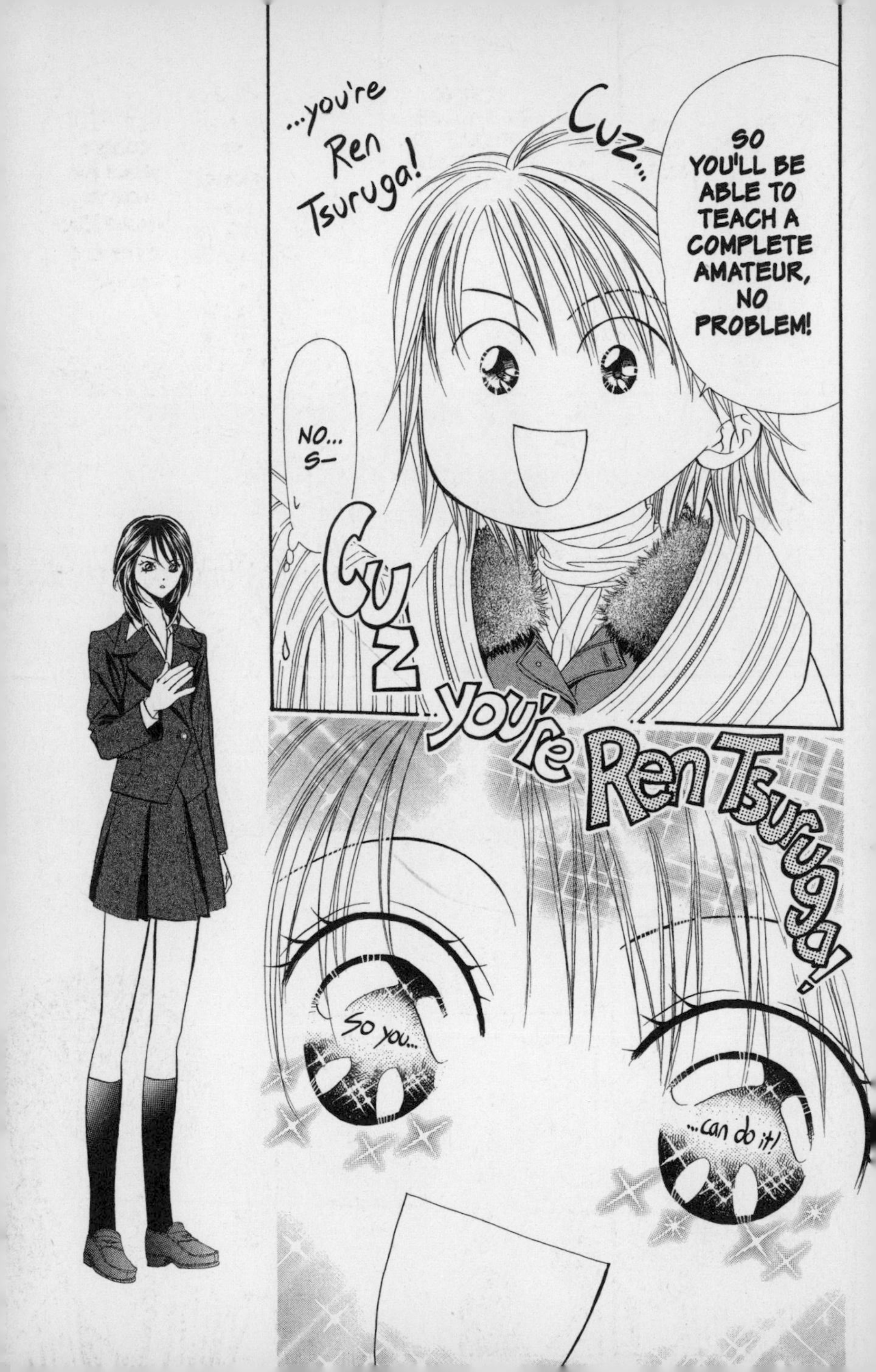
SO YOU'LL BE ABLE TO TEACH A COMPLETE AMATEUR, NO PROBLEM!
Cuz...
...you're Ren Tsuruga!
NO... S–
CUZ
...you're Ren Tsuruga!
So you...
...can do it!

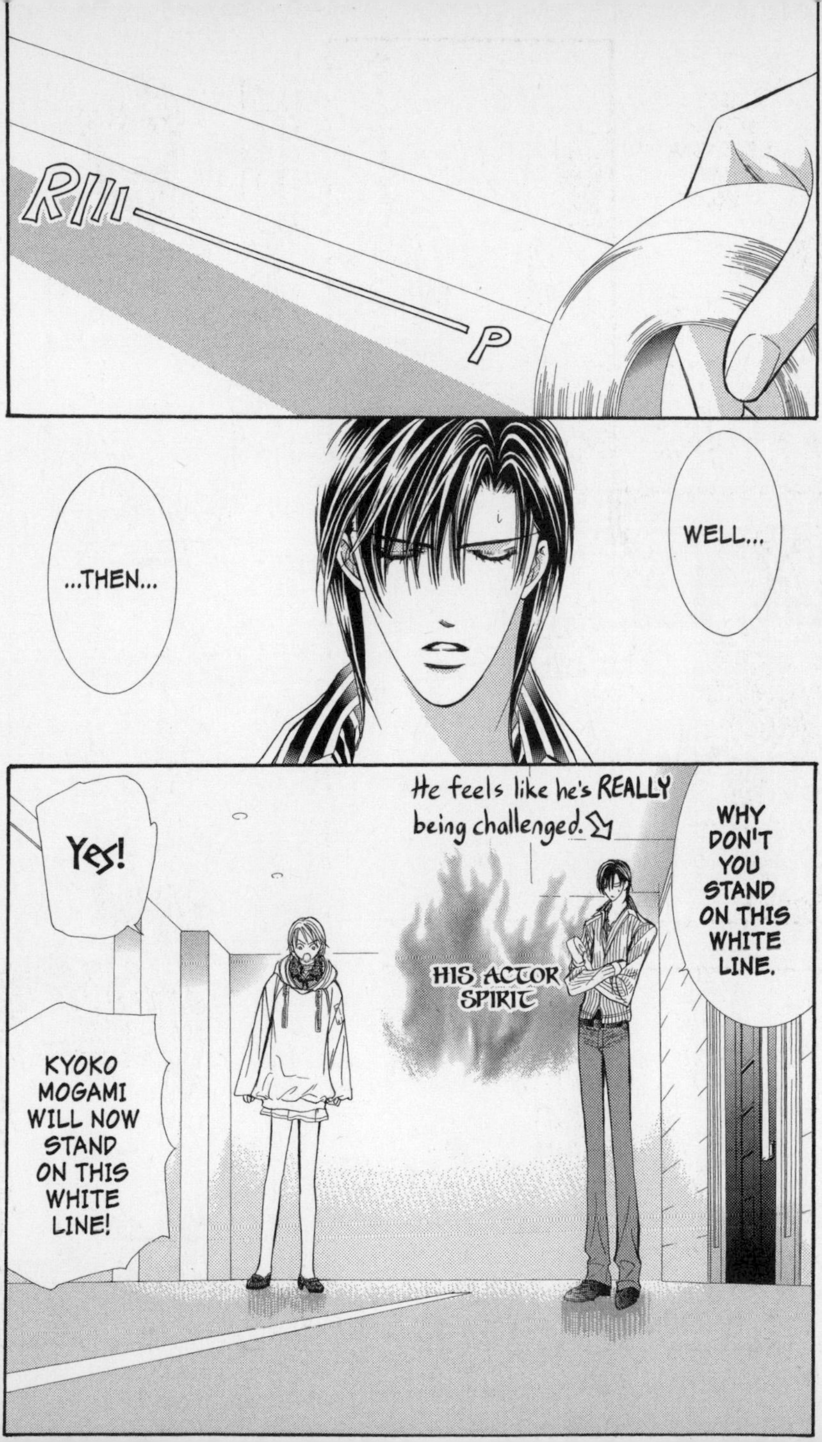
RIII—P
WELL...
...THEN...
WHY DON'T YOU STAND ON THIS WHITE LINE.
He feels like he's REALLY being challenged.
HIS ACTOR SPIRIT
Yes!
KYOKO MOGAMI WILL NOW STAND ON THIS WHITE LINE!

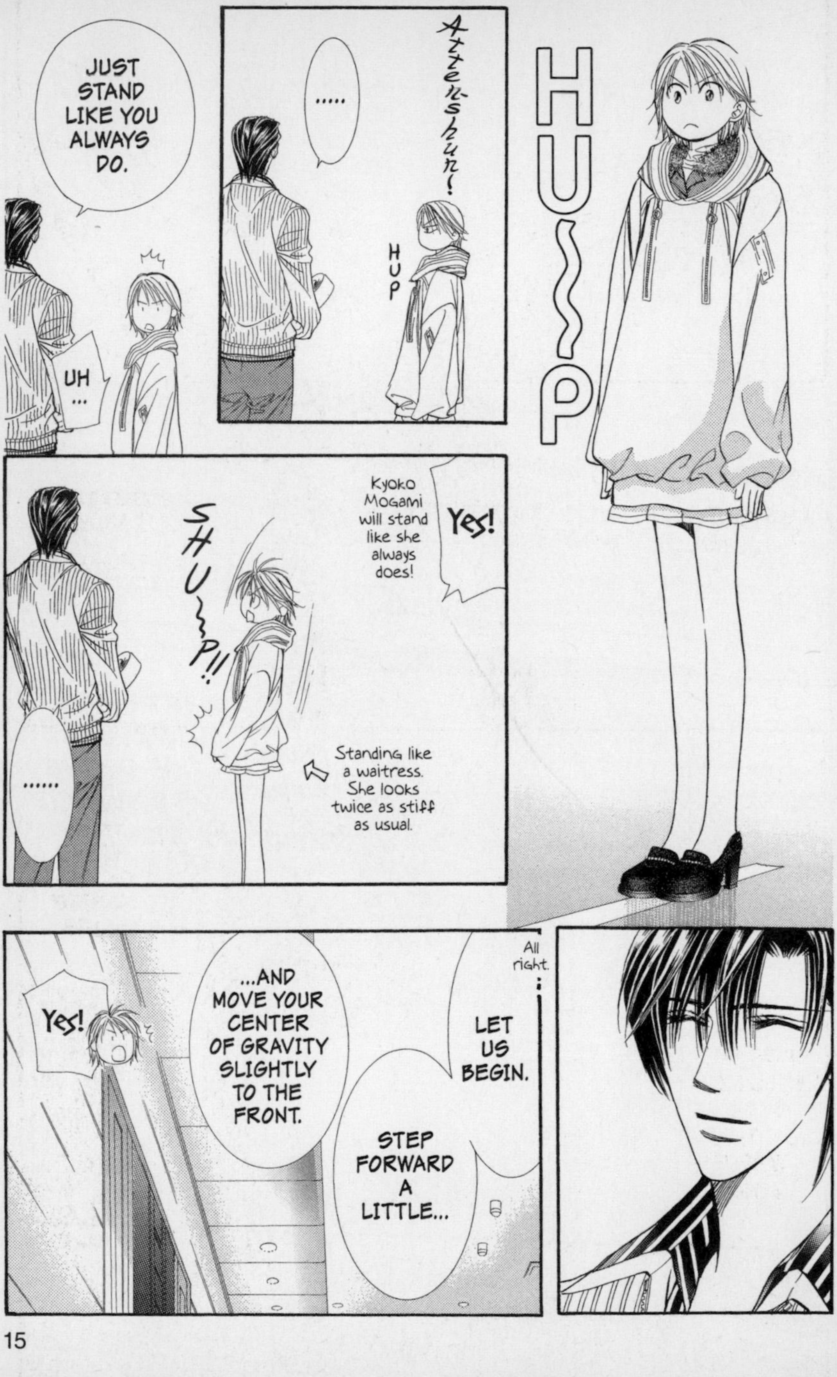
HU~P
.....
Attenshun!
HUP
JUST STAND LIKE YOU ALWAYS DO.
UH ...
Yes!
Kyoko Mogami will stand like she always does!
SHU~P!!
Standing like a waitress. She looks twice as stiff as usual.
......
All right.
LET US BEGIN.
STEP FORWARD A LITTLE...
...AND MOVE YOUR CENTER OF GRAVITY SLIGHTLY TO THE FRONT.
Yes!

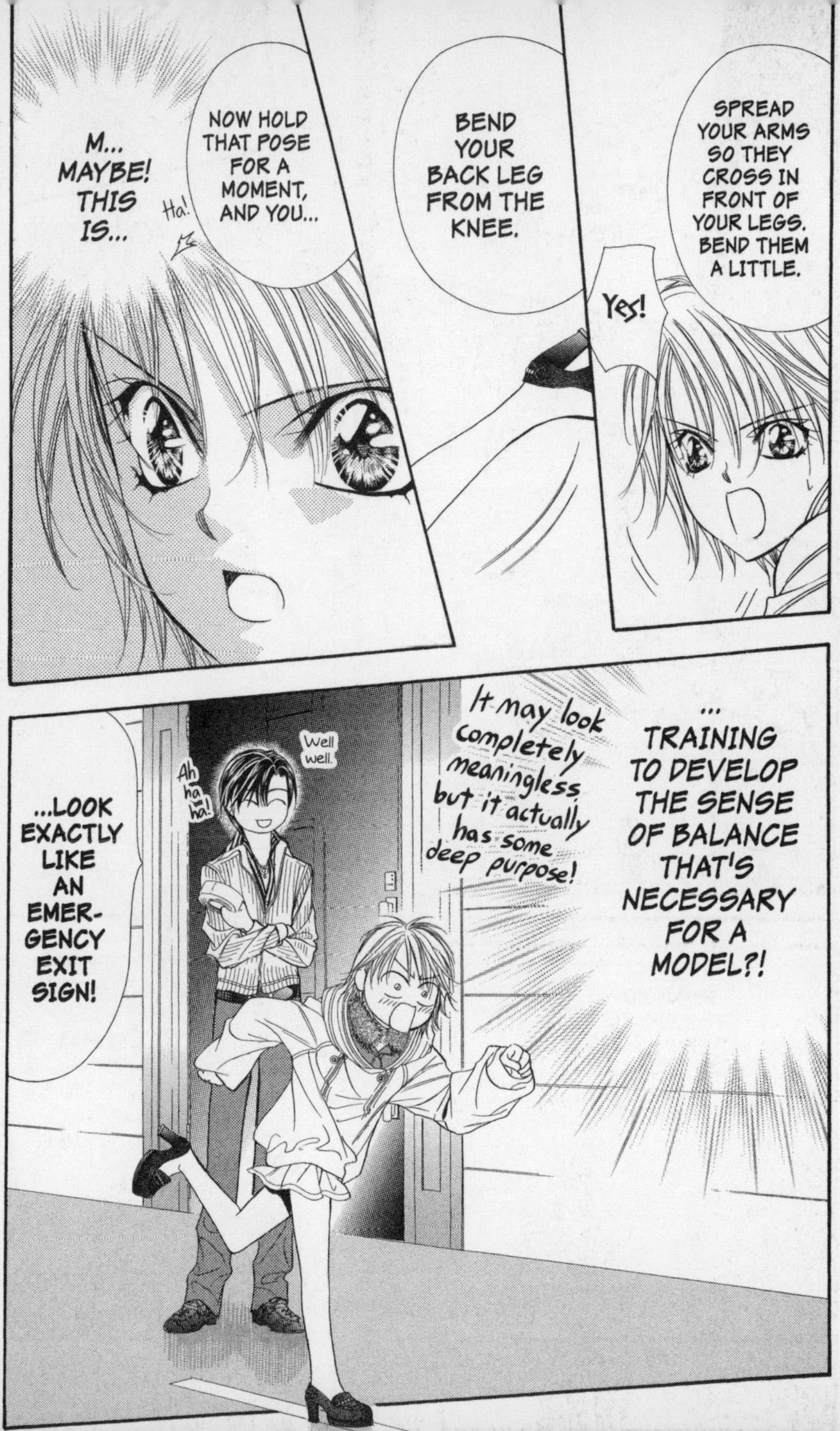
SPREAD YOUR ARMS SO THEY CROSS IN FRONT OF YOUR LEGS. BEND THEM A LITTLE.
Yes!
BEND YOUR BACK LEG FROM THE KNEE.
NOW HOLD THAT POSE FOR A MOMENT, AND YOU...
Ha!
M... MAYBE! THIS IS...
... TRAINING TO DEVELOP THE SENSE OF BALANCE THAT'S NECESSARY FOR A MODEL?!
It may look completely meaningless but it actually has some deep purpose!
Well well.
Ah ha ha ha!
...LOOK EXACTLY LIKE AN EMERGENCY EXIT SIGN!

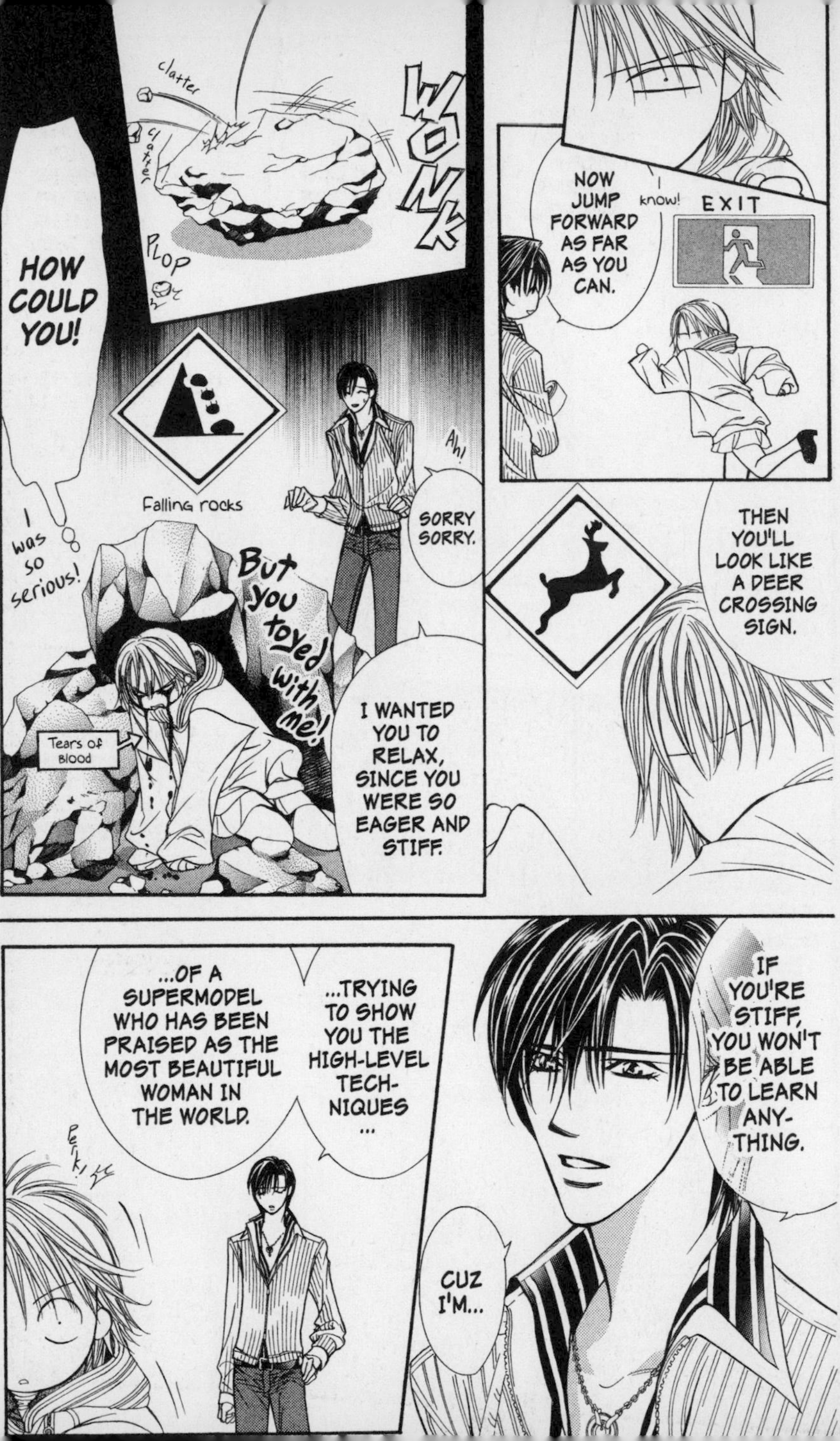

NOW JUMP FORWARD AS FAR AS YOU CAN.
I know!
EXIT
THEN YOU'LL LOOK LIKE A DEER CROSSING SIGN.
WONK
clatter
clatter
PLOP
HOW COULD YOU!
I was so serious!
Falling rocks
Ah!
SORRY SORRY.
But you toyed with me!
I WANTED YOU TO RELAX, SINCE YOU WERE SO EAGER AND STIFF.
Tears of blood
IF YOU'RE STIFF, YOU WON'T BE ABLE TO LEARN ANY-THING.
CUZ I'M...
...TRYING TO SHOW YOU THE HIGH-LEVEL TECH-NIQUES ...
...OF A SUPERMODEL WHO HAS BEEN PRAISED AS THE MOST BEAUTIFUL WOMAN IN THE WORLD.
Perk!

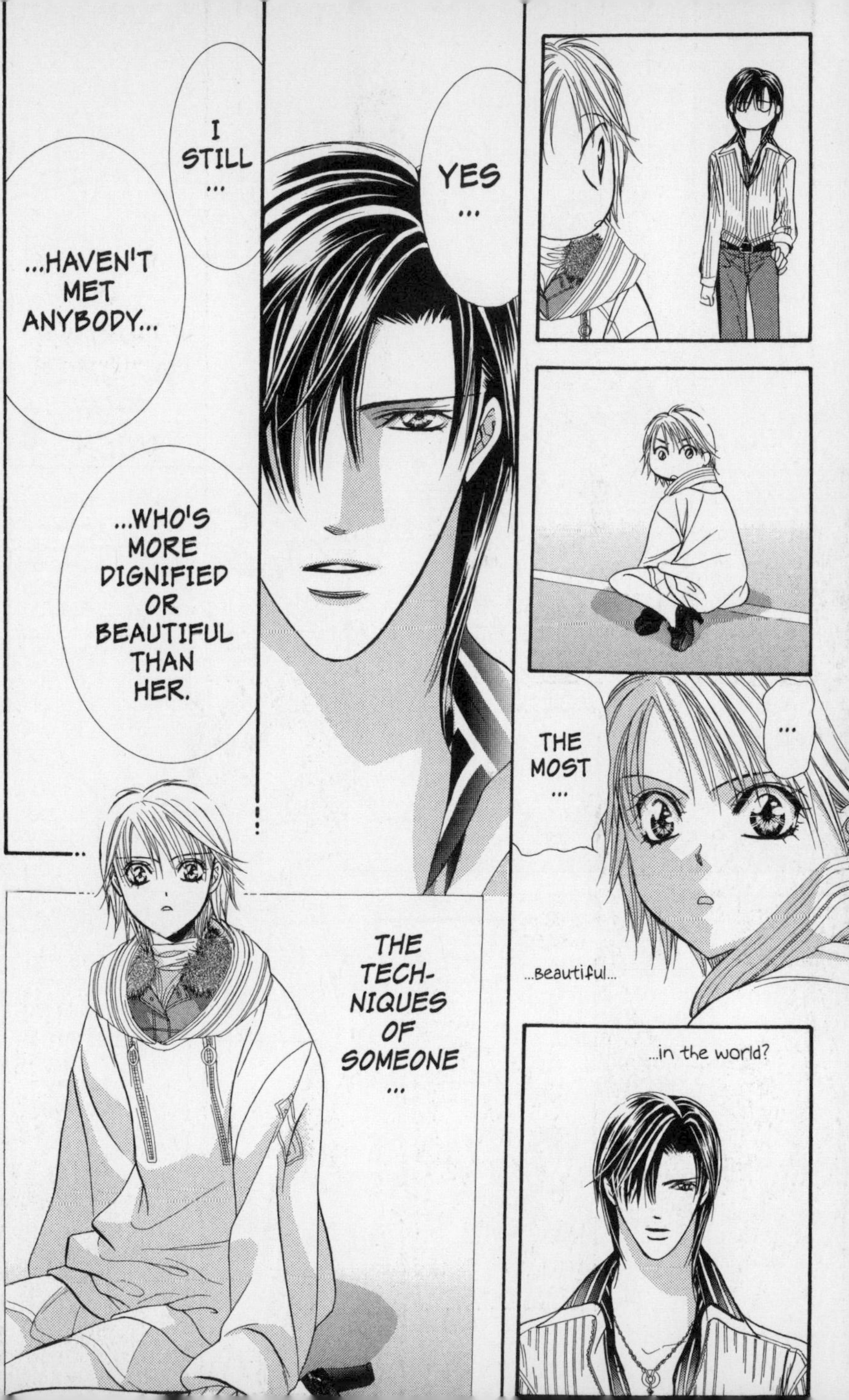
YES ...
I STILL ...
...HAVEN'T MET ANYBODY...
...WHO'S MORE DIGNIFIED OR BEAUTIFUL THAN HER.
THE TECHNIQUES OF SOMEONE ...
THE MOST ...
...
...beautiful...
...in the world?

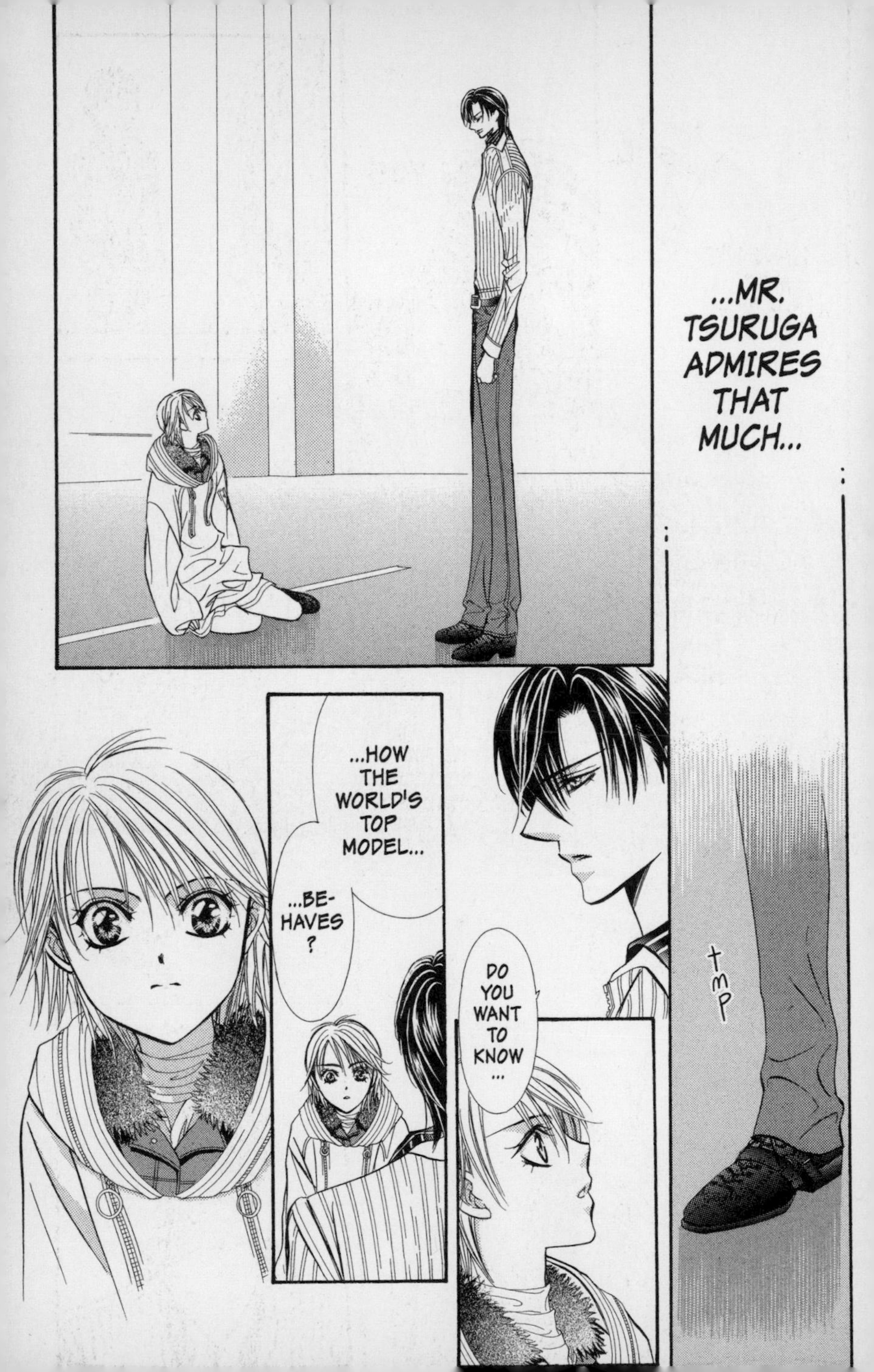
...MR. TSURUGA ADMIRES THAT MUCH...
TMP
DO YOU WANT TO KNOW...
...HOW THE WORLD'S TOP MODEL...
...BE-HAVES?

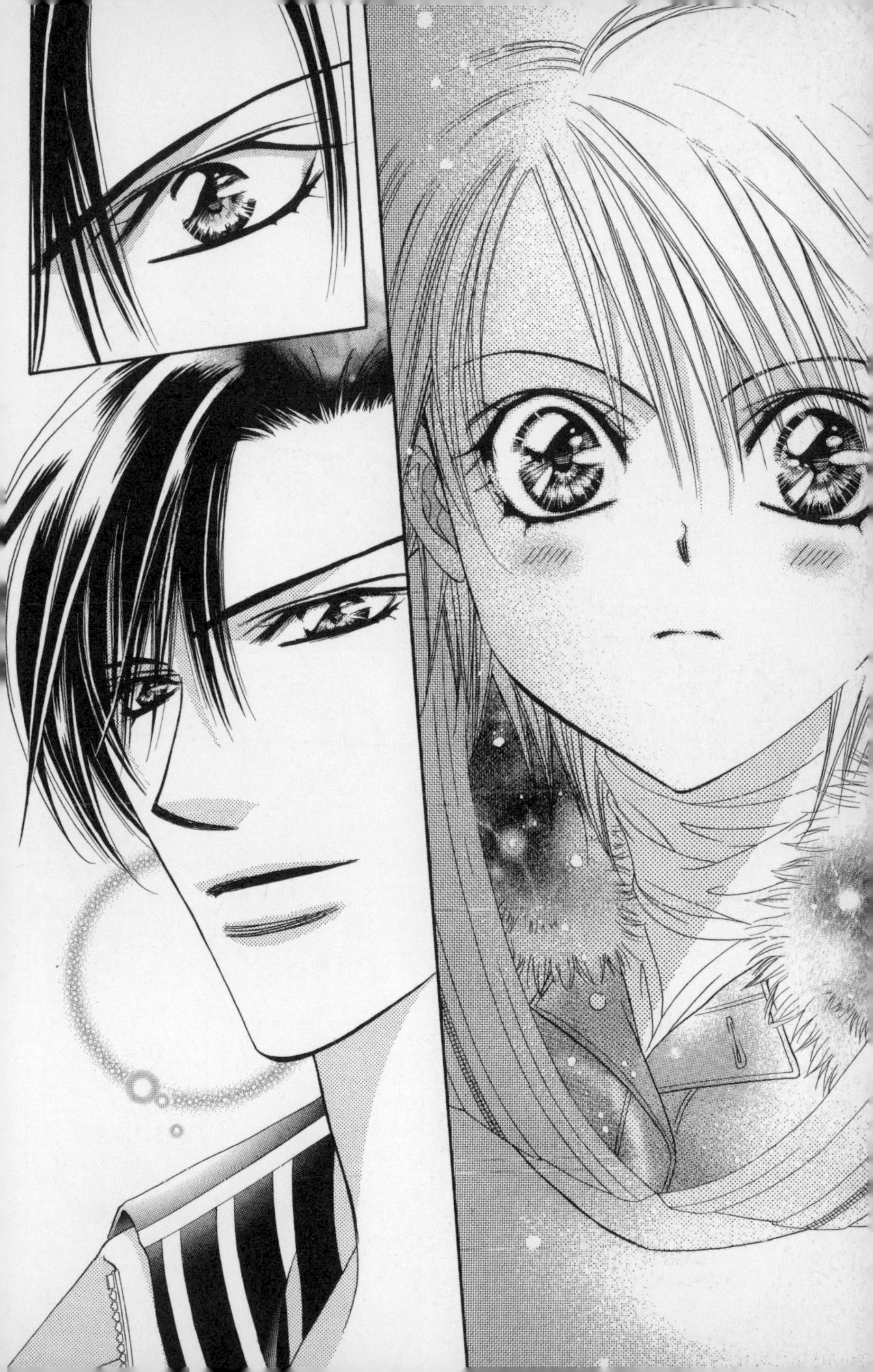

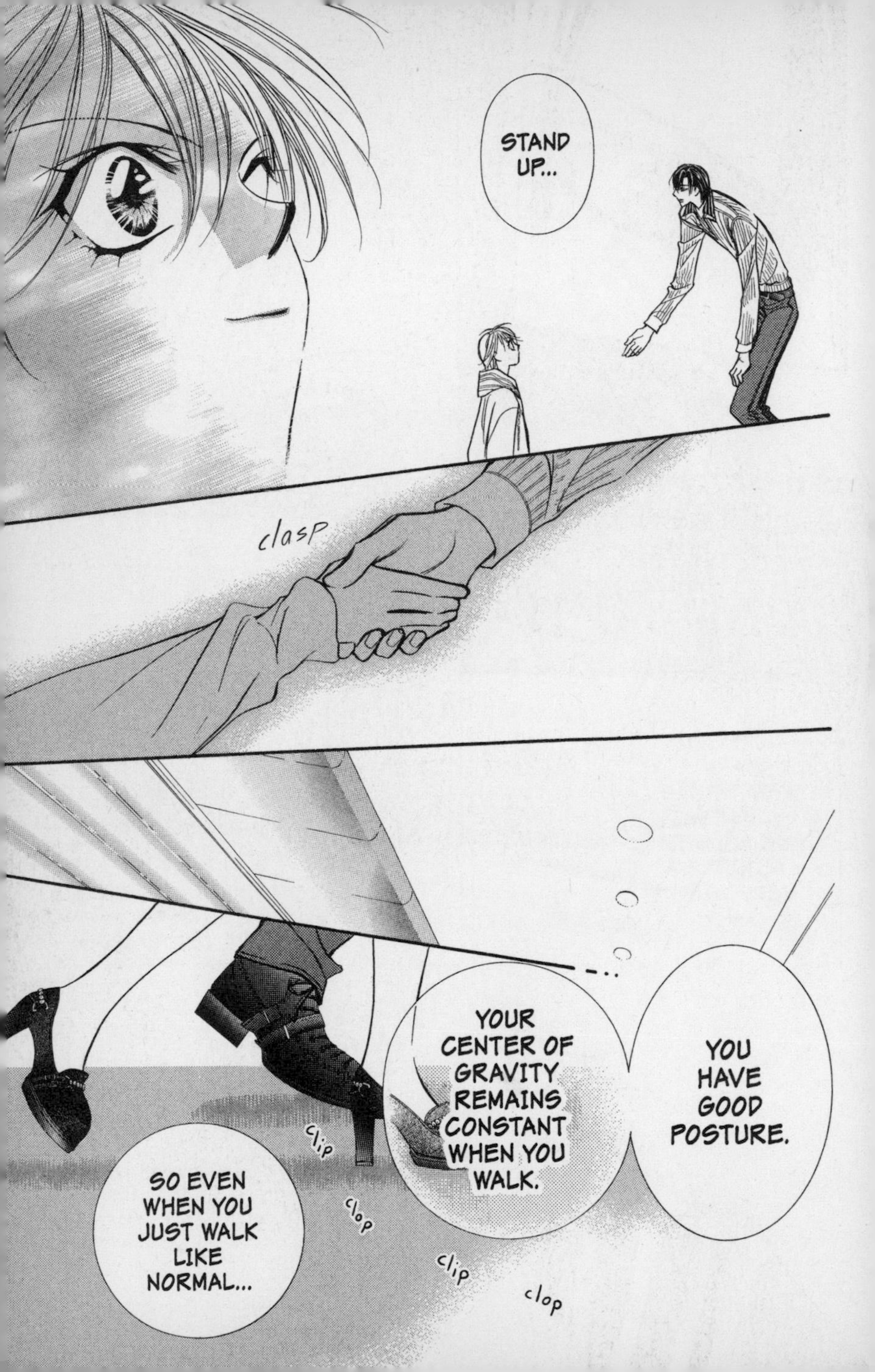
STAND UP...
clasp
YOU HAVE GOOD POSTURE.
YOUR CENTER OF GRAVITY REMAINS CONSTANT WHEN YOU WALK.
clip
clop
SO EVEN WHEN YOU JUST WALK LIKE NORMAL...
clip
clop

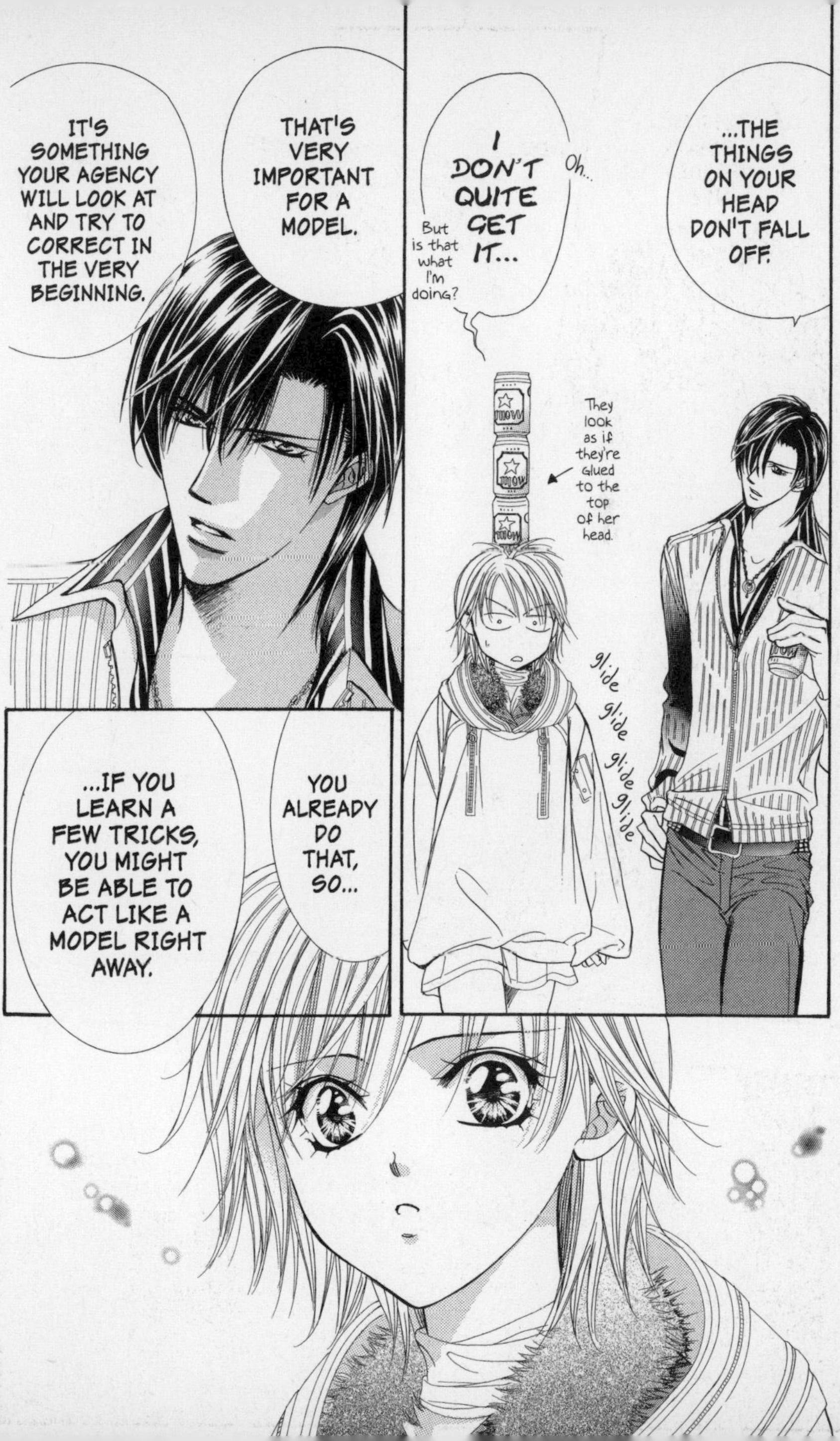
...THE THINGS ON YOUR HEAD DON'T FALL OFF.
I DON'T QUITE GET IT...
Oh...
But is that what I'm doing?
They look as if they're glued to the top of her head.
glide glide glide glide
THAT'S VERY IMPORTANT FOR A MODEL.
IT'S SOMETHING YOUR AGENCY WILL LOOK AT AND TRY TO CORRECT IN THE VERY BEGINNING.
YOU ALREADY DO THAT, SO...
...IF YOU LEARN A FEW TRICKS, YOU MIGHT BE ABLE TO ACT LIKE A MODEL RIGHT AWAY.

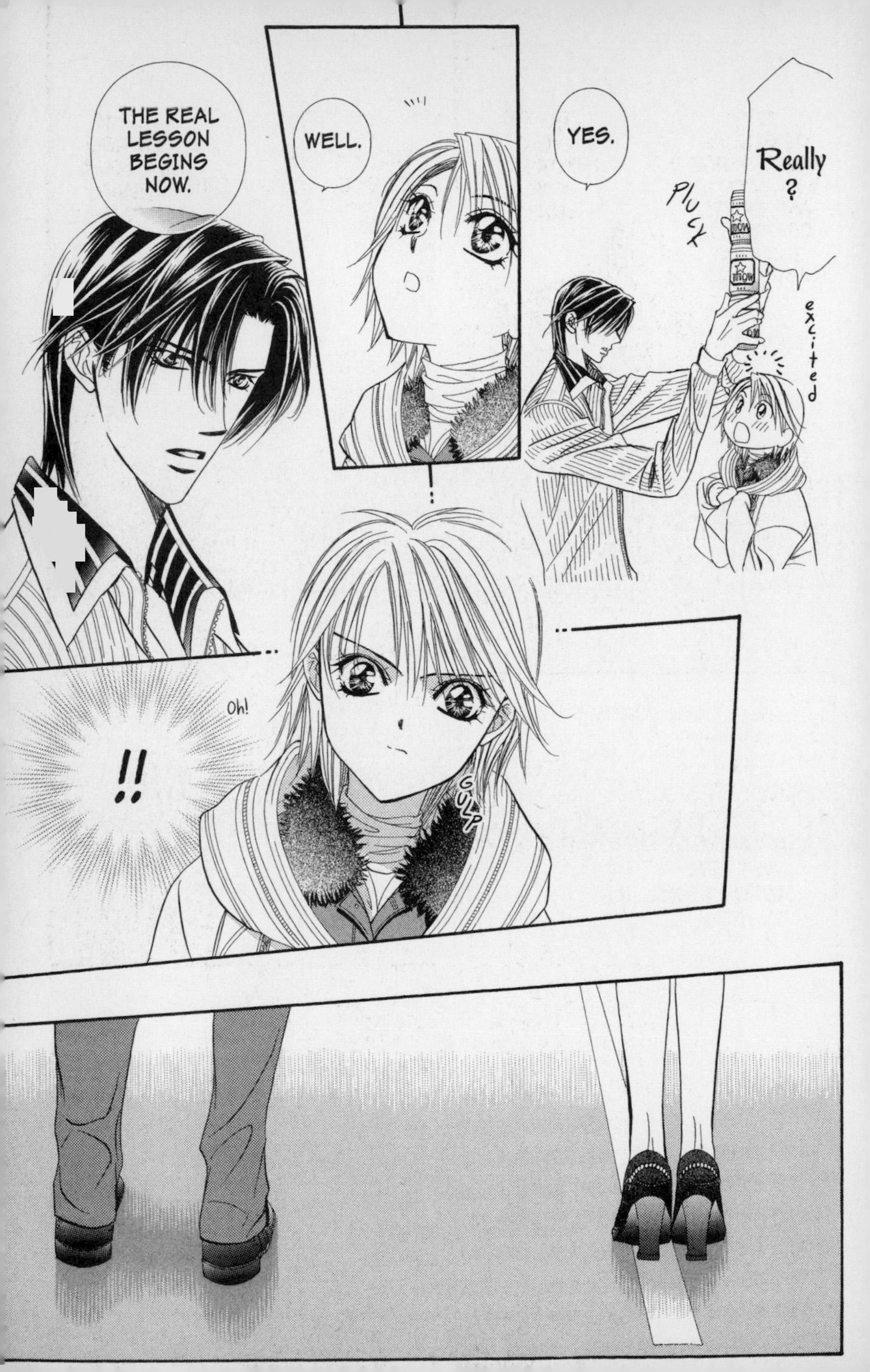
Really ?
YES.
PLUCK
excited
WELL.
THE REAL LESSON BEGINS NOW.
...
GULP
Oh!
!!

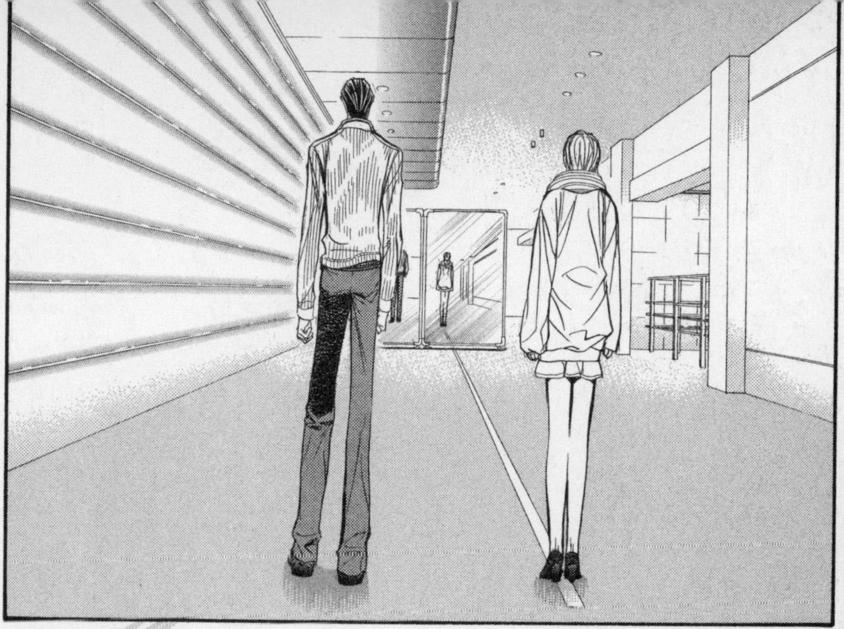

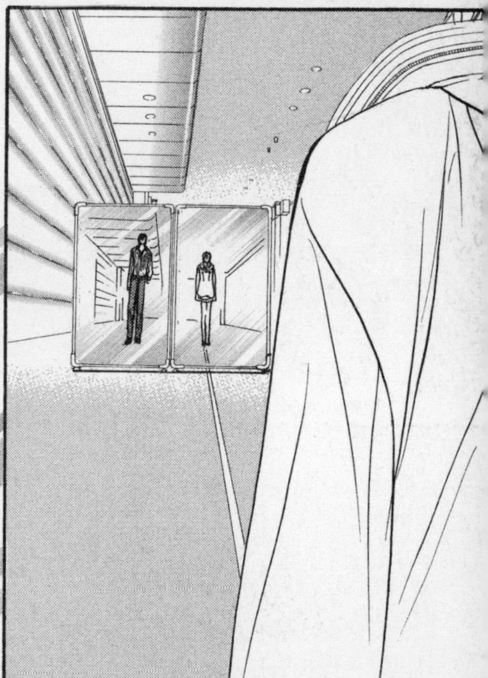

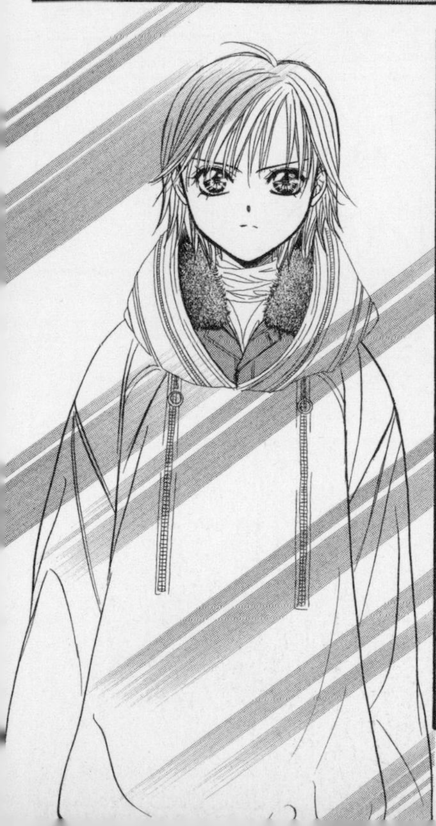

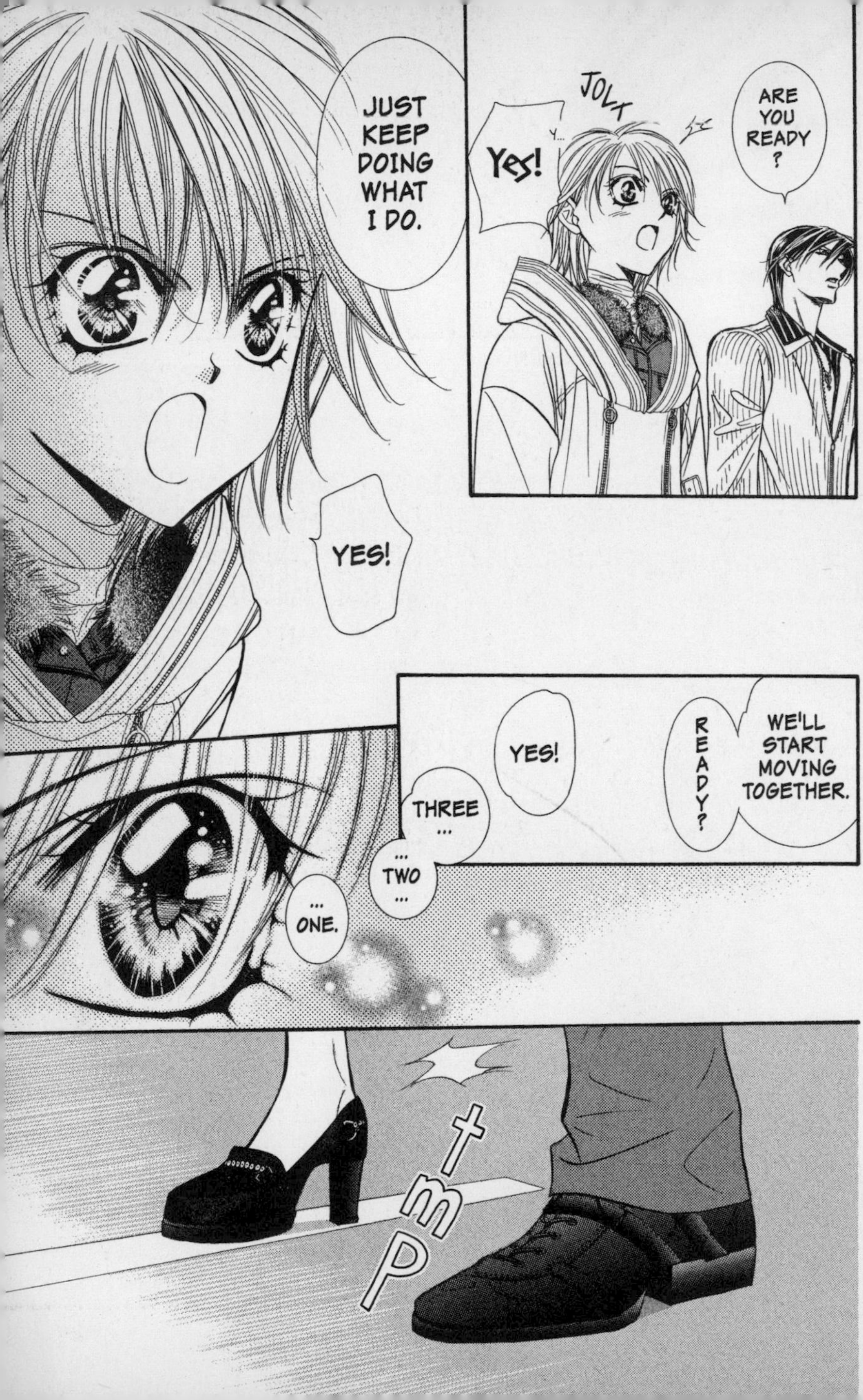
ARE YOU READY?
JOLT
Y...
Yes!
JUST KEEP DOING WHAT I DO.
YES!
WE'LL START MOVING TOGETHER.
READY?
YES!
THREE...
...TWO...
...ONE.
tmp

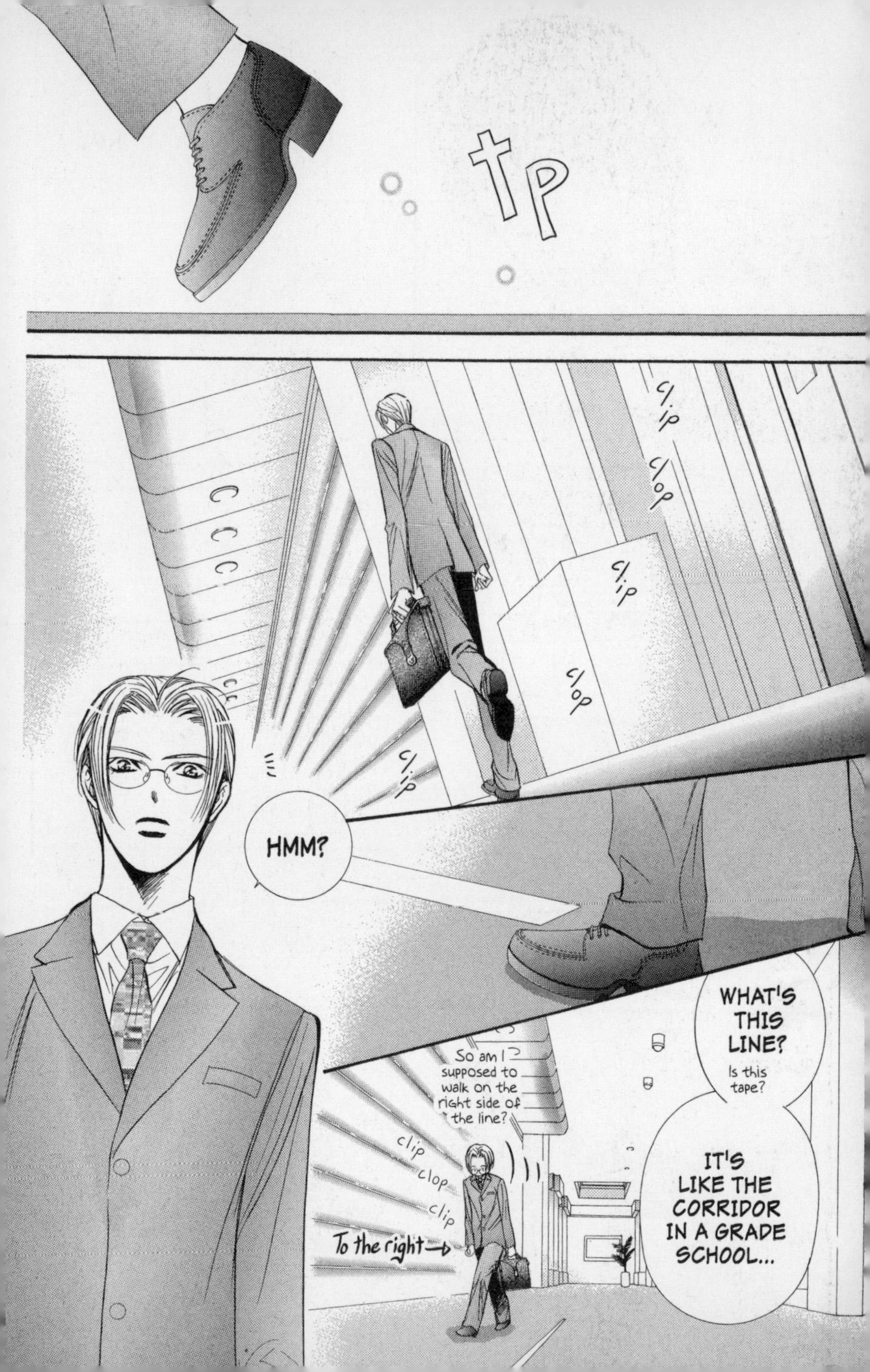
tp
clip
clop
clip
clop
clip
HMM?
WHAT'S THIS LINE?
Is this tape?
IT'S LIKE THE CORRIDOR IN A GRADE SCHOOL...
So am I supposed to walk on the right side of the line?
clip
clop
clip
To the right→

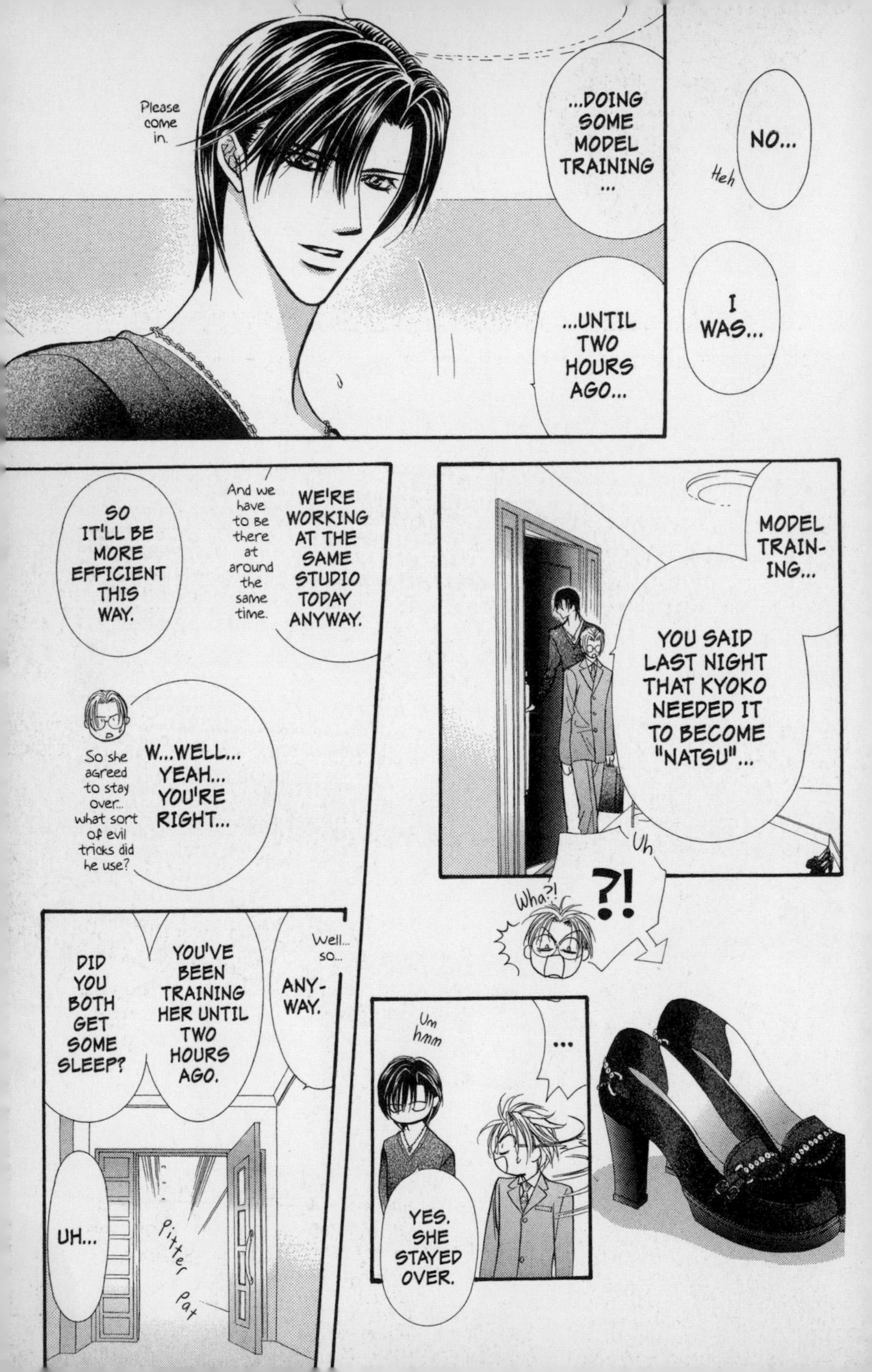
NO...
Heh
I WAS...
...DOING SOME MODEL TRAINING ...
...UNTIL TWO HOURS AGO...
Please come in.
MODEL TRAIN-ING...
YOU SAID LAST NIGHT THAT KYOKO NEEDED IT TO BECOME "NATSU"...
Uh
?!
Wha?!
WE'RE WORKING AT THE SAME STUDIO TODAY ANYWAY.
And we have to be there at around the same time.
SO IT'LL BE MORE EFFICIENT THIS WAY.
W...WELL... YEAH... YOU'RE RIGHT...
So she agreed to stay over... what sort of evil tricks did he use?
...
Um hmm
YES. SHE STAYED OVER.
Well... so...
ANY-WAY.
YOU'VE BEEN TRAINING HER UNTIL TWO HOURS AGO.
DID YOU BOTH GET SOME SLEEP?
UH...
Pitter Pat

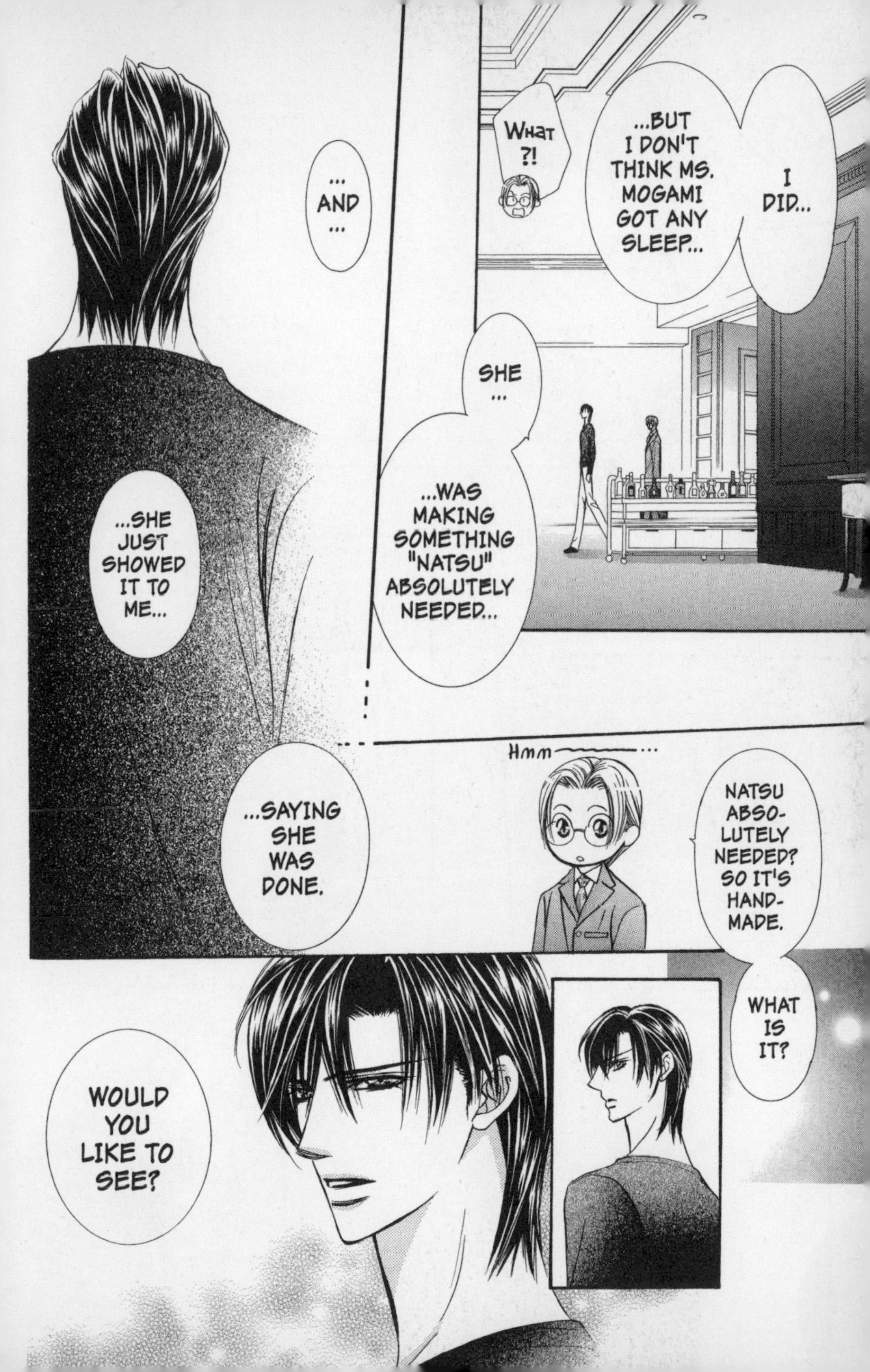
I DID...
...BUT I DON'T THINK MS. MOGAMI GOT ANY SLEEP...
WHAT ?!
SHE ...
...WAS MAKING SOMETHING "NATSU" ABSOLUTELY NEEDED...
... AND ...
...SHE JUST SHOWED IT TO ME...
...SAYING SHE WAS DONE.
Hmm...
NATSU ABSO-LUTELY NEEDED? SO IT'S HAND-MADE.
WHAT IS IT?
WOULD YOU LIKE TO SEE?

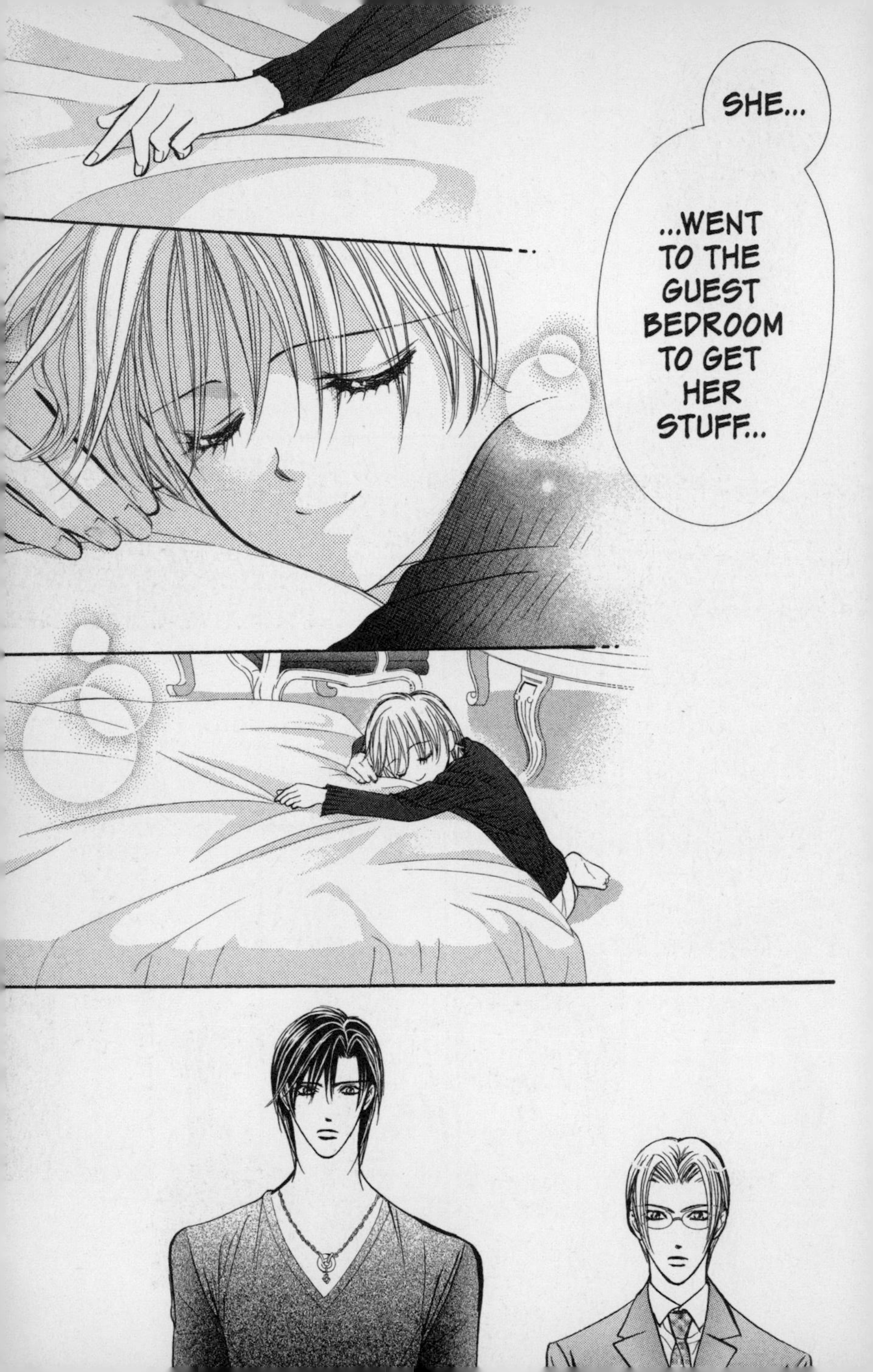
SHE...
...WENT TO THE GUEST BEDROOM TO GET HER STUFF...

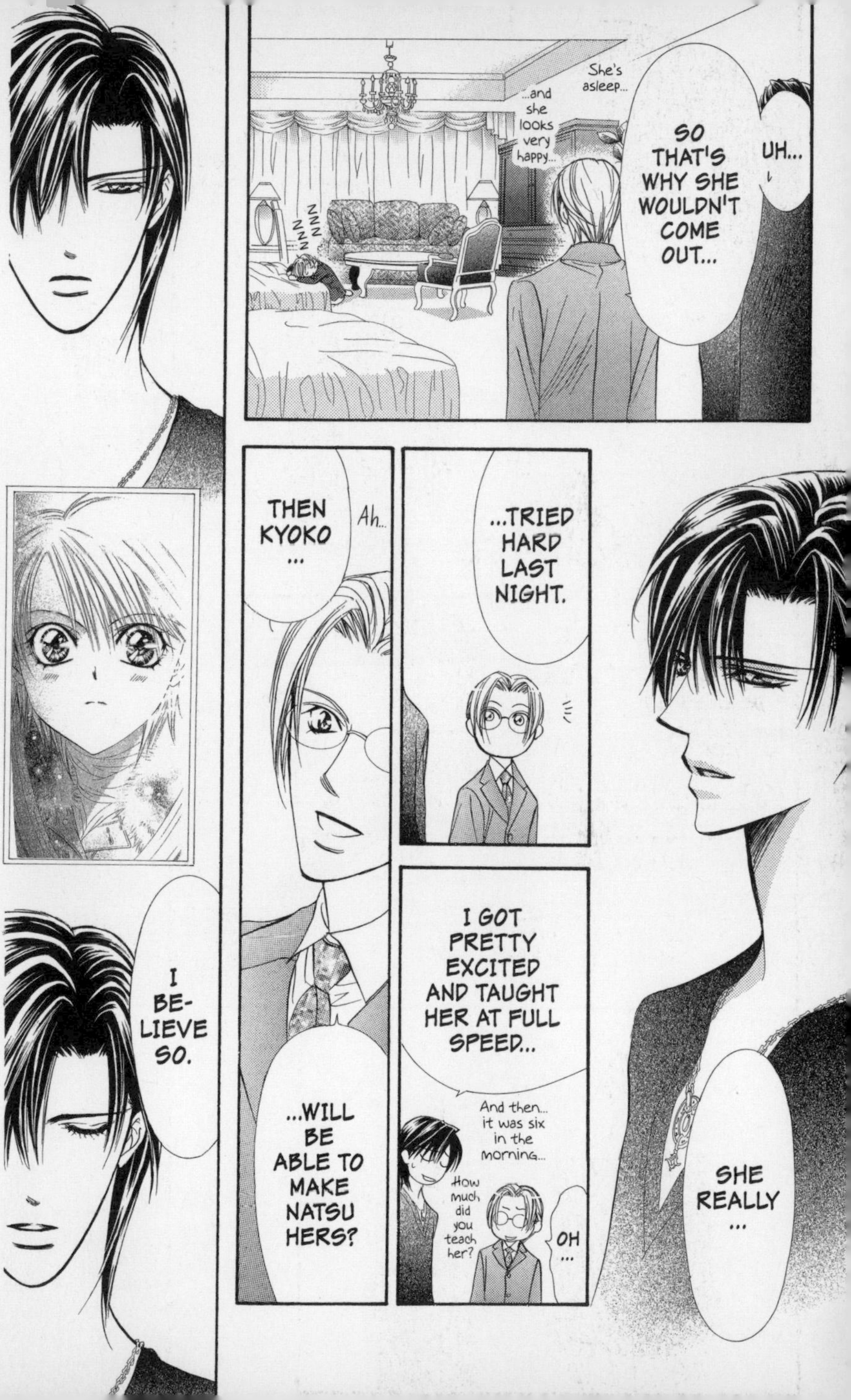
UH...
SO THAT'S WHY SHE WOULDN'T COME OUT...
She's asleep...
...and she looks very happy...
SHE REALLY ...
...TRIED HARD LAST NIGHT.
I GOT PRETTY EXCITED AND TAUGHT HER AT FULL SPEED...
And then... it was six in the morning...
OH ...
How much did you teach her?
Ah...
THEN KYOKO ...
...WILL BE ABLE TO MAKE NATSU HERS?
I BE-LIEVE SO.

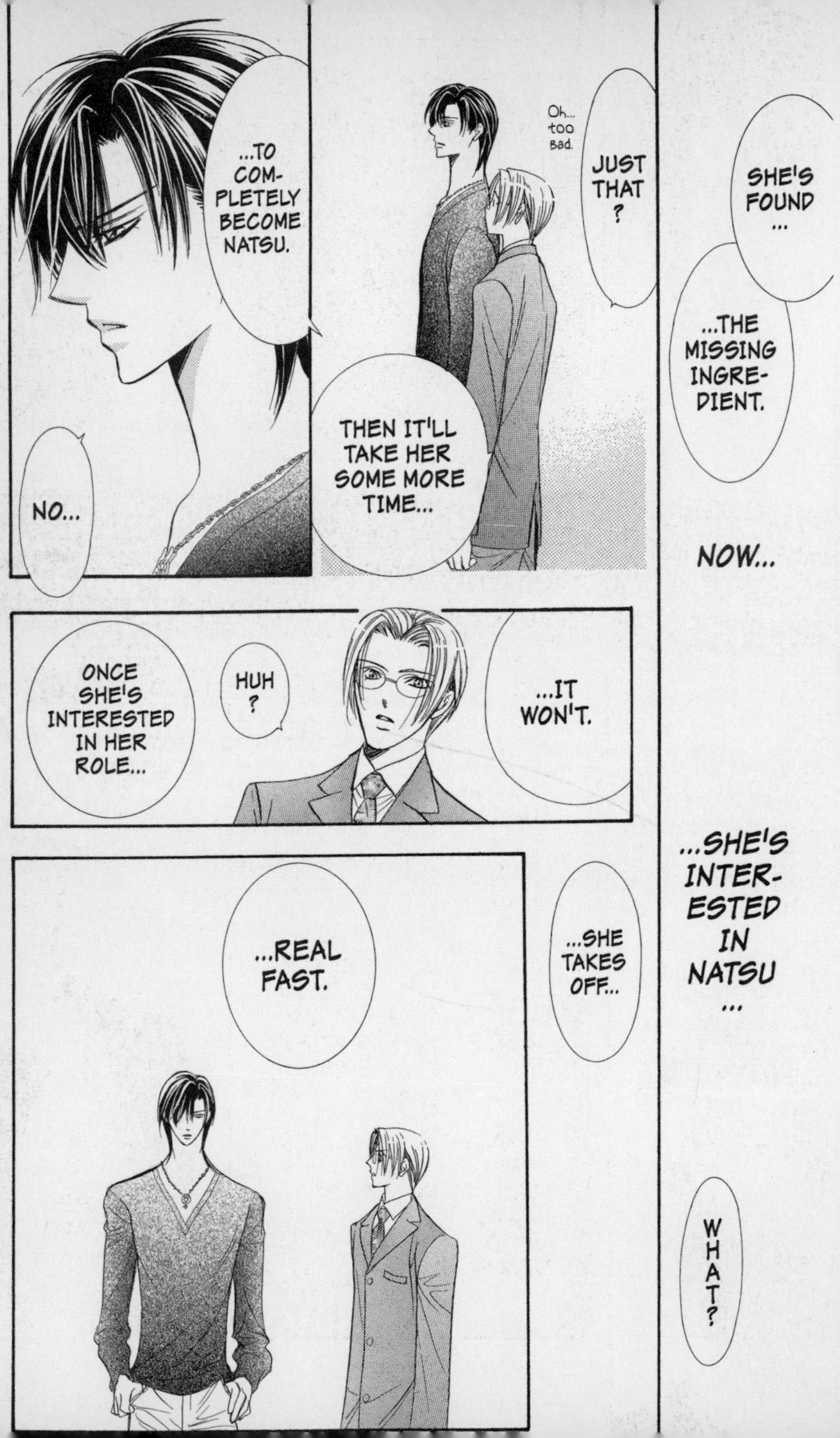
SHE'S FOUND...
...THE MISSING INGREDIENT.
NOW...
...SHE'S INTERESTED IN NATSU...
WHAT?
JUST THAT?
Oh... too bad.
THEN IT'LL TAKE HER SOME MORE TIME...
...TO COMPLETELY BECOME NATSU.
NO...
...IT WON'T.
HUH?
ONCE SHE'S INTERESTED IN HER ROLE...
...SHE TAKES OFF...
...REAL FAST.

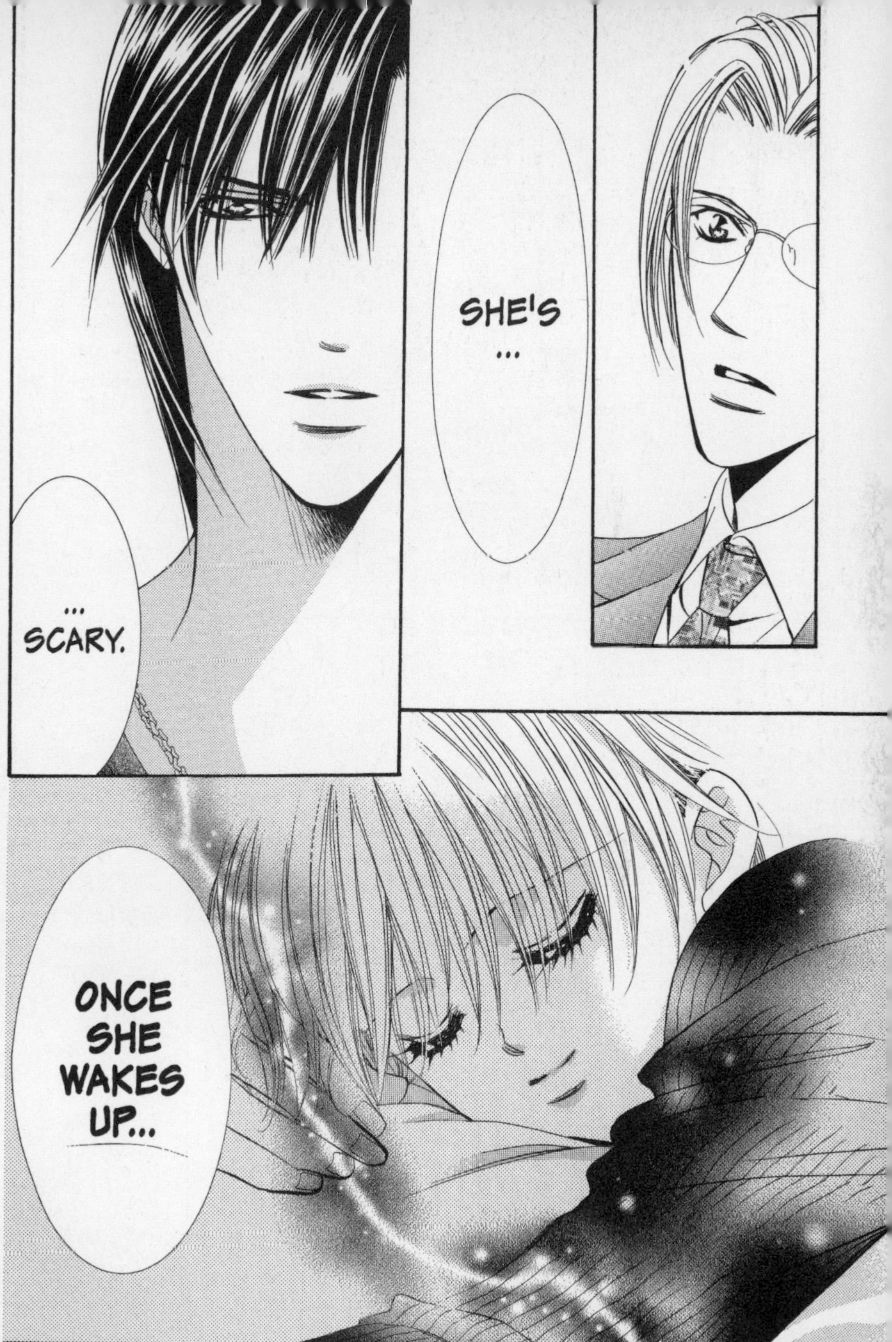
SHE'S ...
... SCARY.
ONCE SHE WAKES UP...

End of Act 127

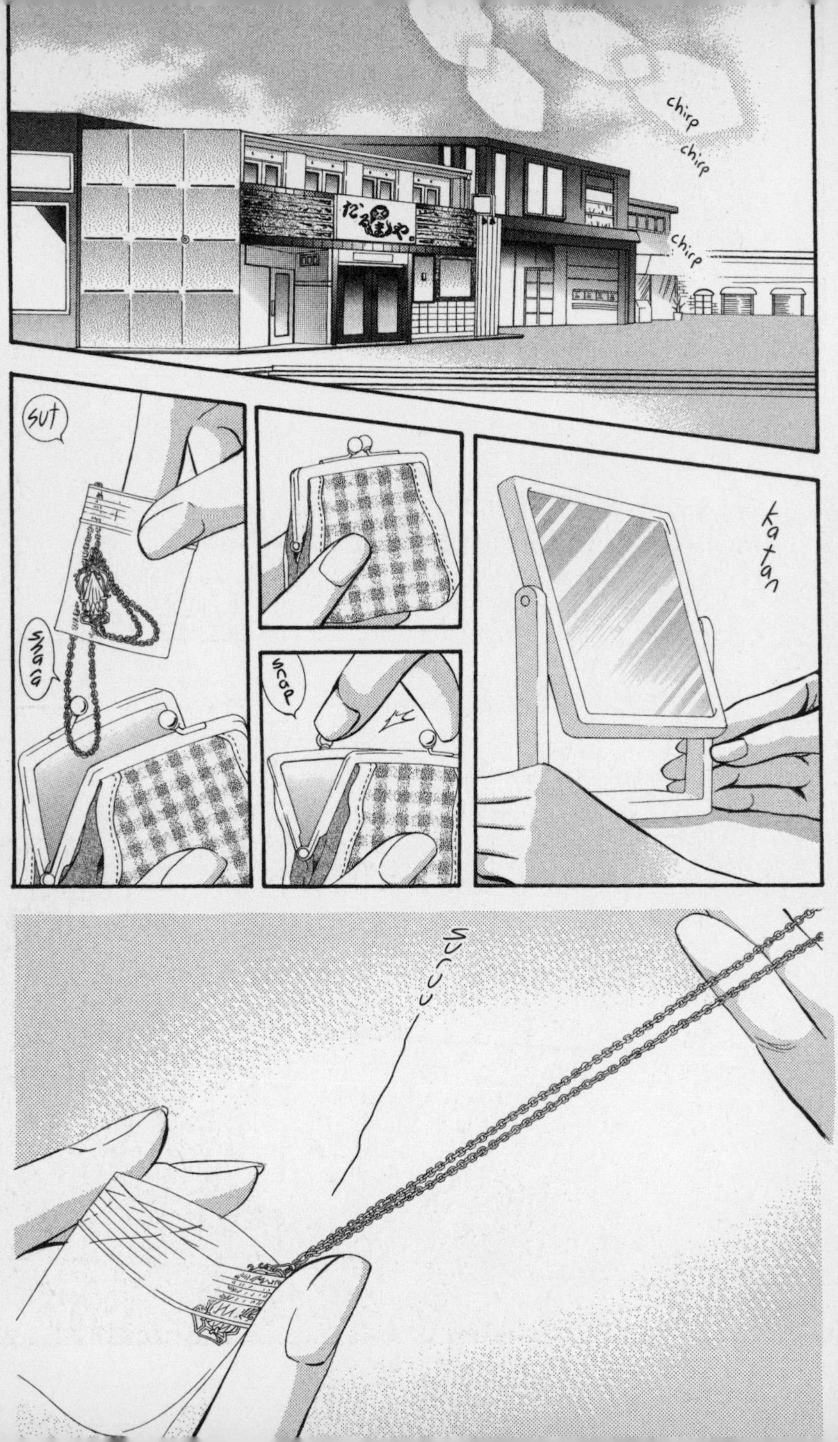
chirp
chirp
chirp
katan
snap
sut
shara
suruuu

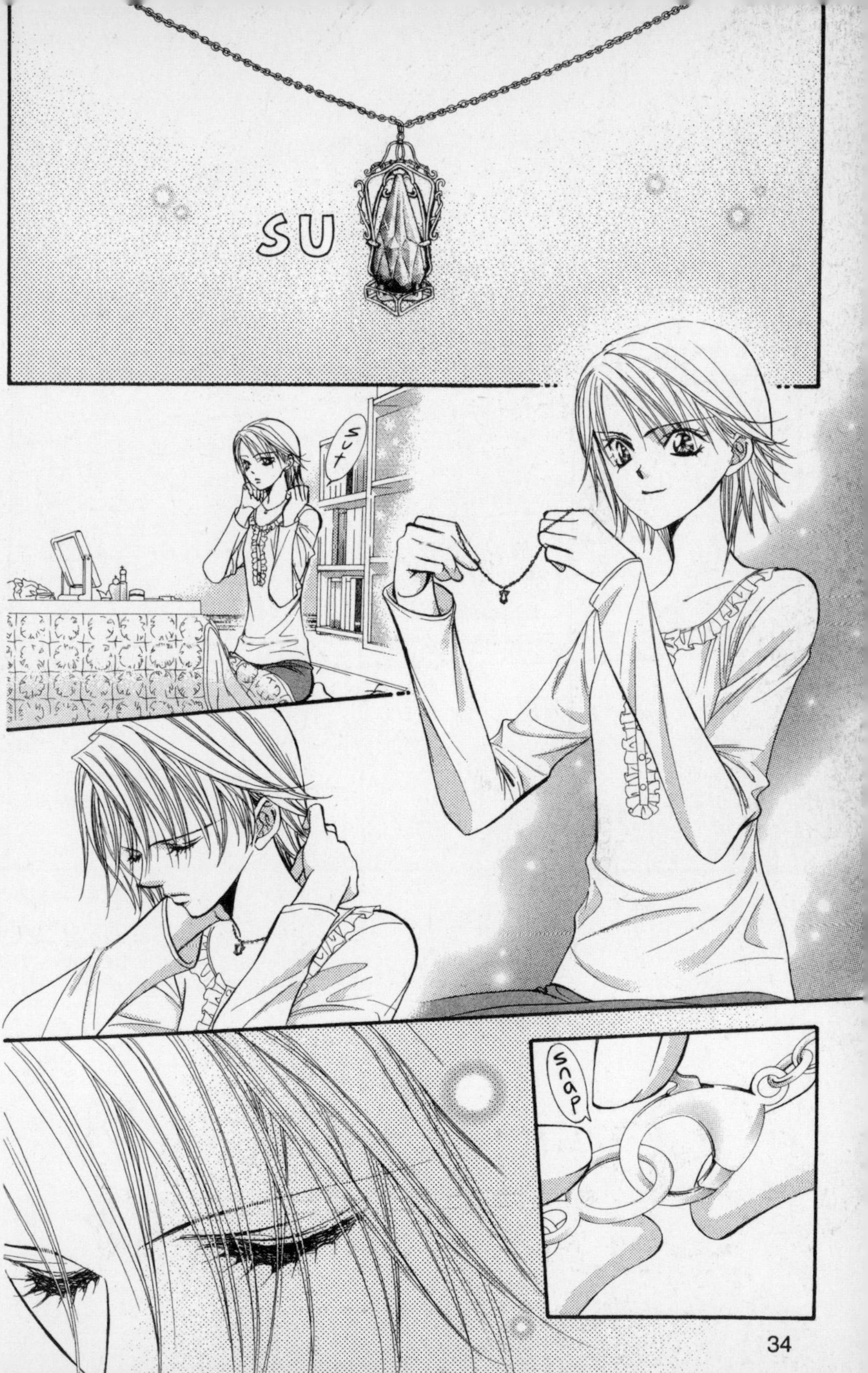
SU
SUT
snap

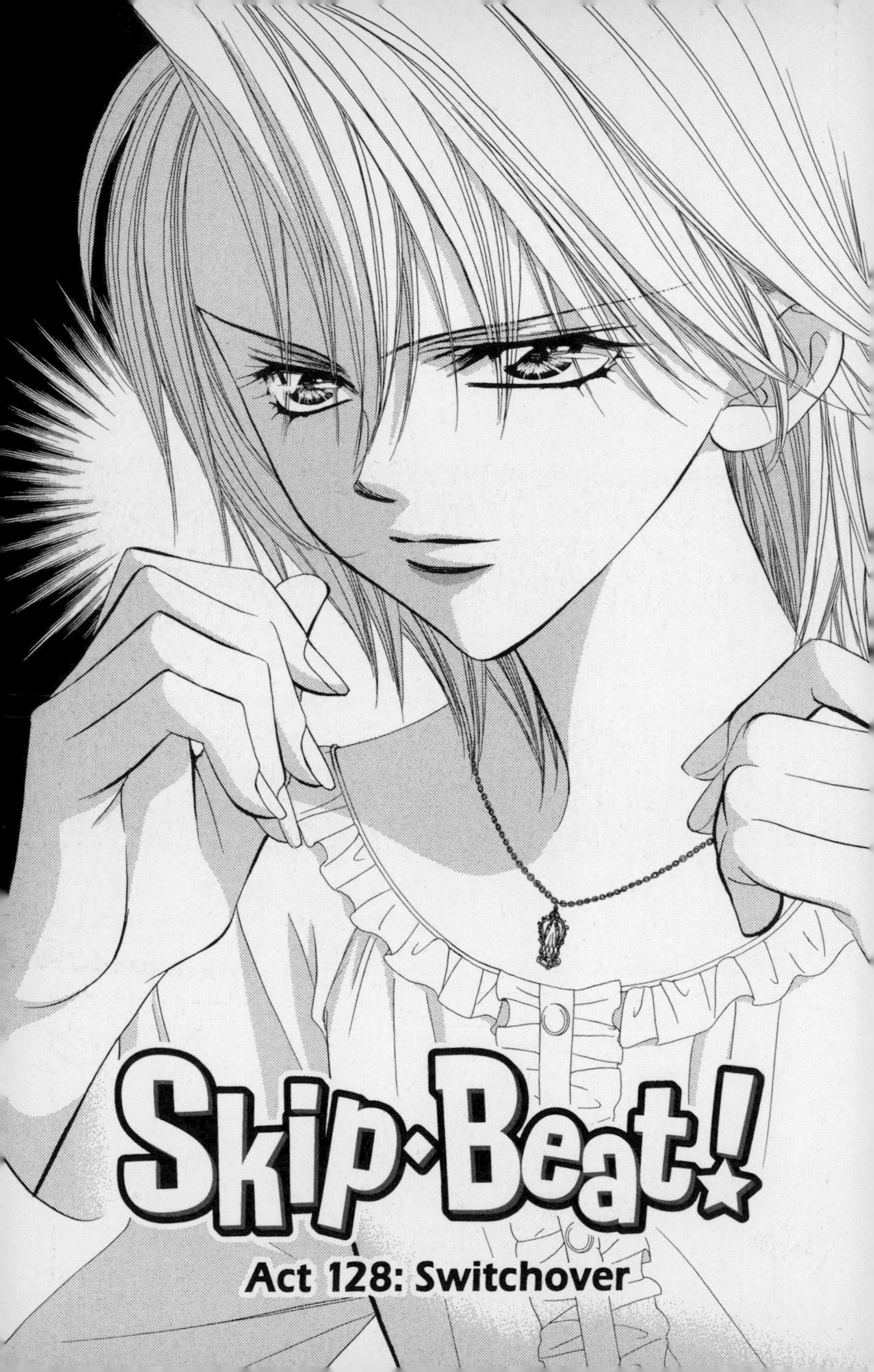
Skip·Beat!
Act 128: Switchover

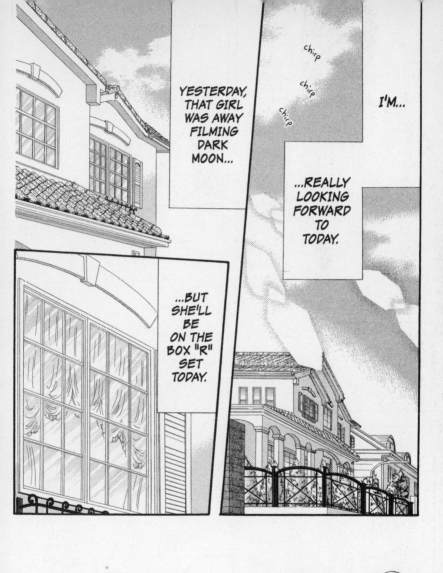

chirp
chirp
chirp
I'M...
...REALLY LOOKING FORWARD TO TODAY.
YESTERDAY, THAT GIRL WAS AWAY FILMING DARK MOON...
...BUT SHE'LL BE ON THE BOX "R" SET TODAY.

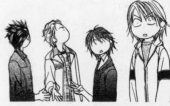

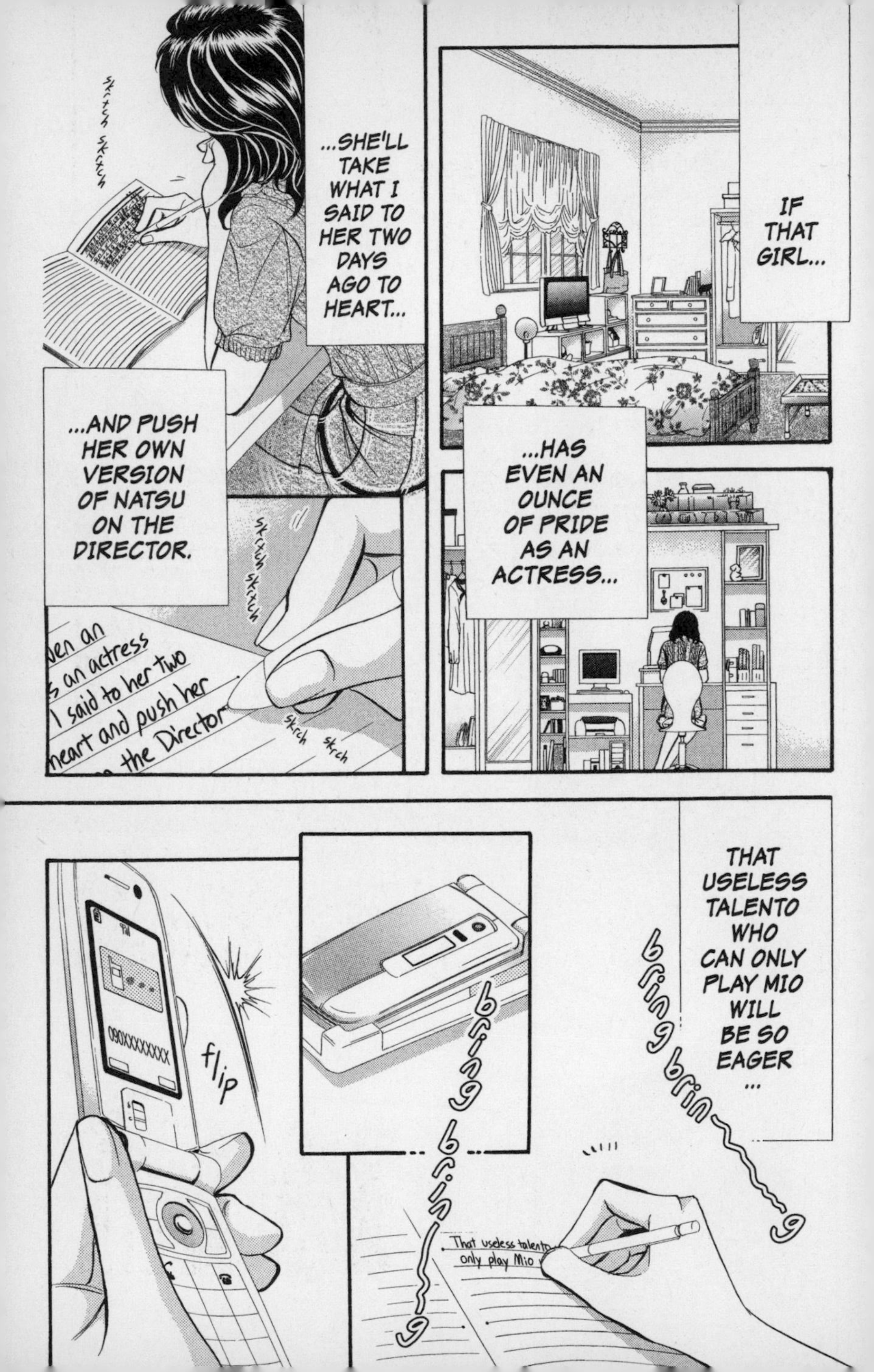
IF THAT GIRL...
...HAS EVEN AN OUNCE OF PRIDE AS AN ACTRESS...
...SHE'LL TAKE WHAT I SAID TO HER TWO DAYS AGO TO HEART...
skrtch skrtch
...AND PUSH HER OWN VERSION OF NATSU ON THE DIRECTOR.
skrtch skrtch
ven an
s an actress
I said to her two
heart and push her
the Director
skrch skrch
THAT USELESS TALENTO WHO CAN ONLY PLAY MIO WILL BE SO EAGER ...
bring brin~~g
That useless talento
only play Mio
bring bring brin~~g
090XXXXXXXX
flip

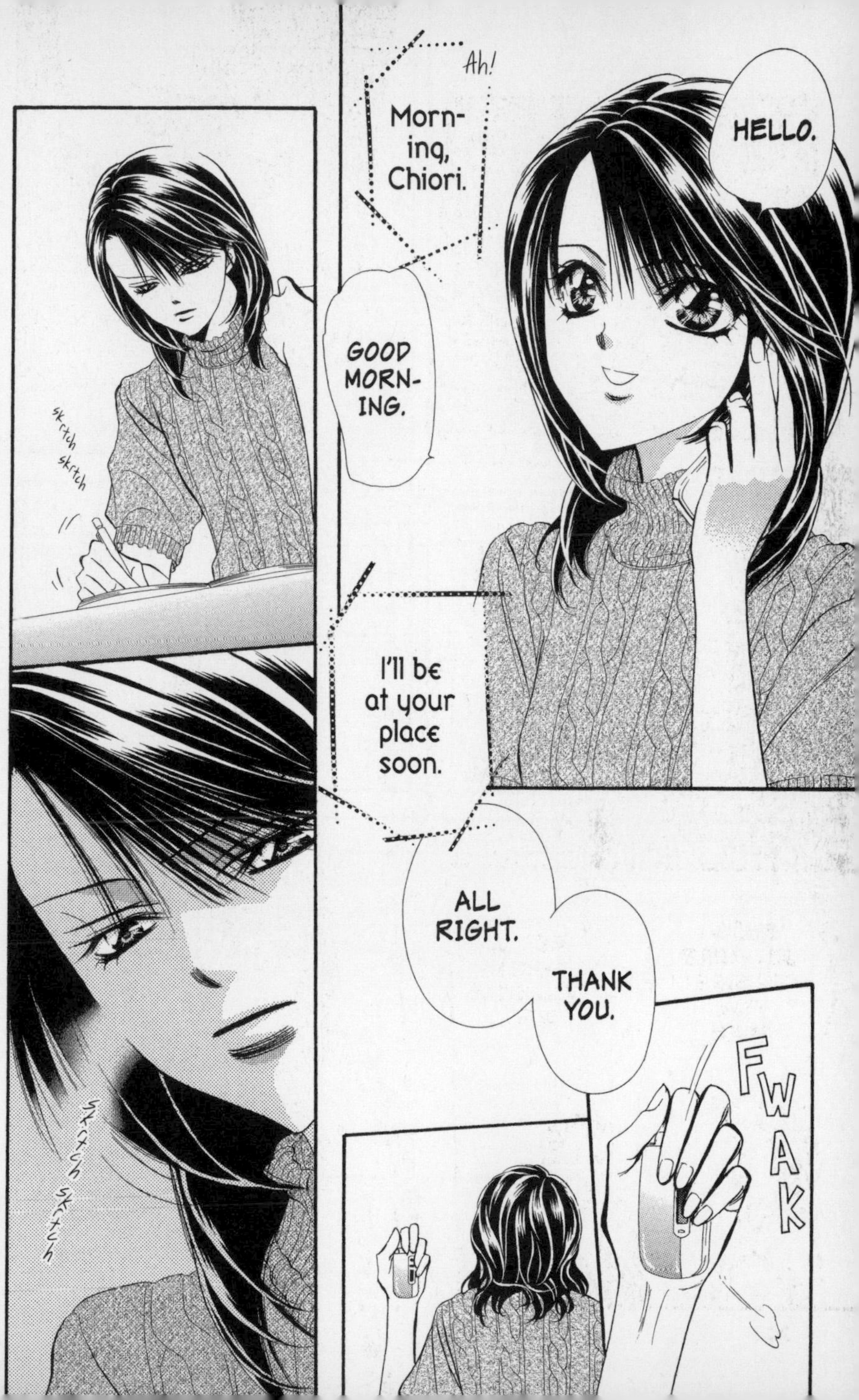

HELLO.
Ah!
Morning, Chiori.
GOOD MORNING.
I'll be at your place soon.
ALL RIGHT.
THANK YOU.
FWAK
skrtch skrtch
skrtch skrtch

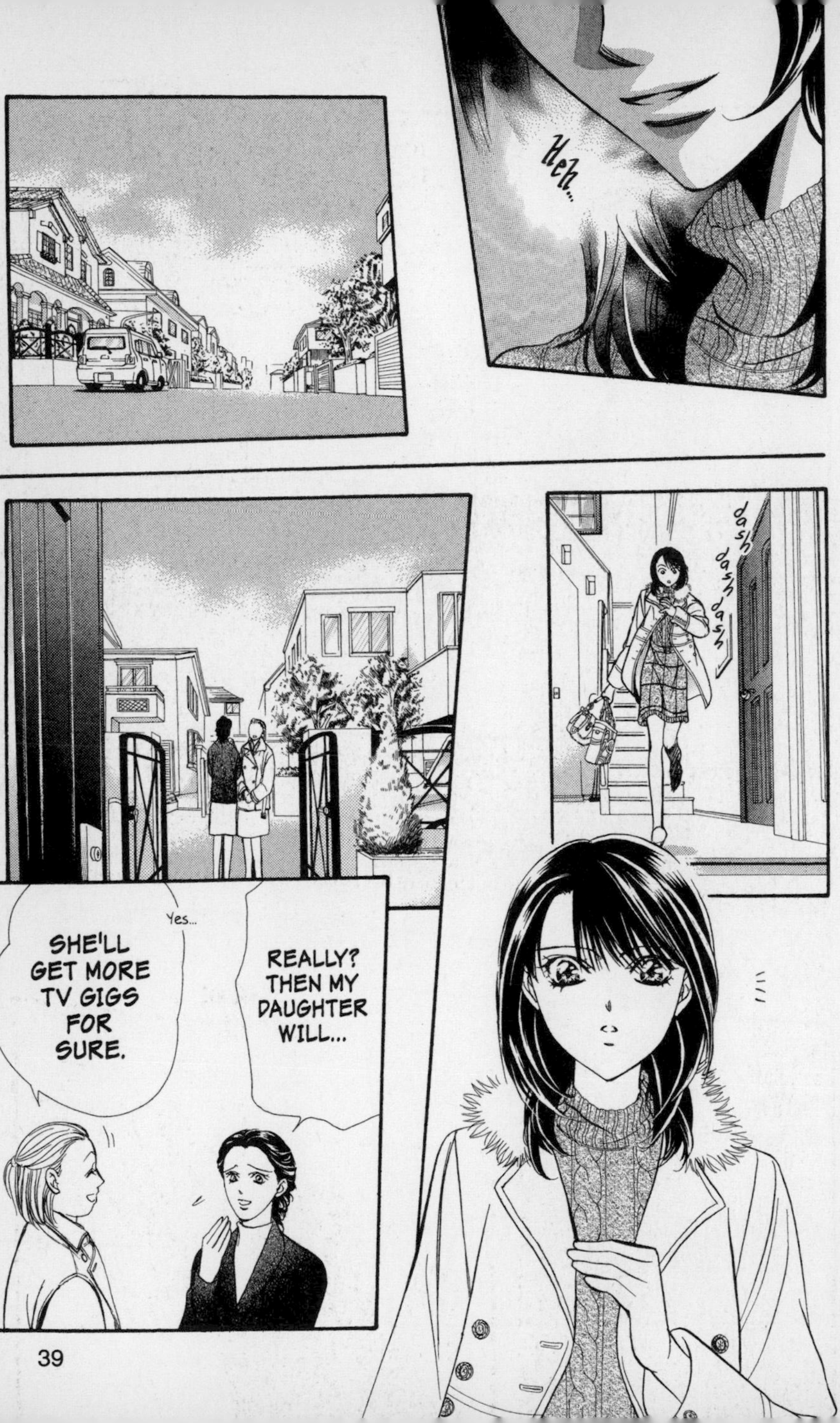
Heh...
dash dash dash
REALLY? THEN MY DAUGHTER WILL...
Yes...
SHE'LL GET MORE TV GIGS FOR SURE.

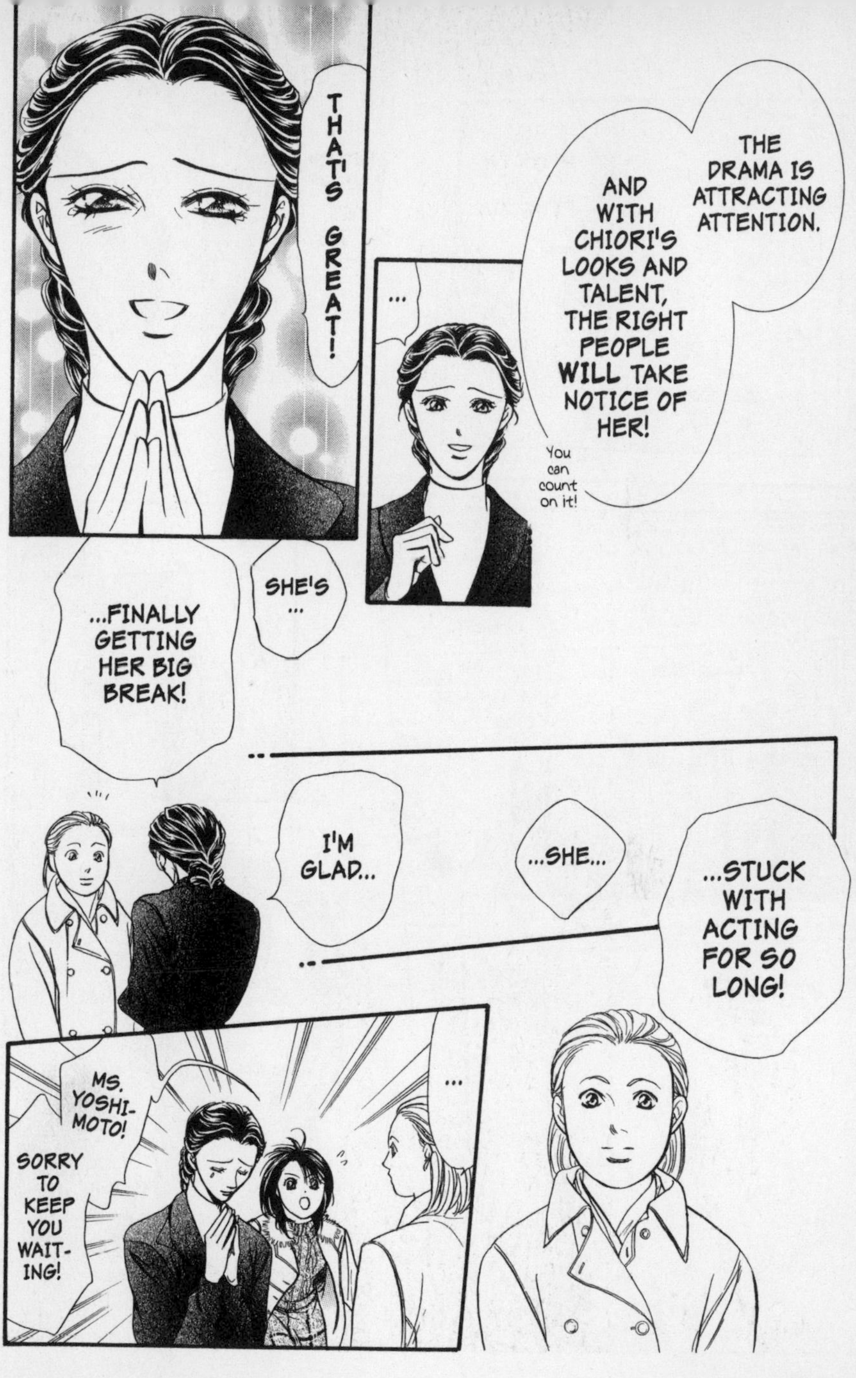
THE DRAMA IS ATTRACTING ATTENTION.
AND WITH CHIORI'S LOOKS AND TALENT, THE RIGHT PEOPLE WILL TAKE NOTICE OF HER!
You can count on it!
...
THAT'S GREAT!
SHE'S ...
...FINALLY GETTING HER BIG BREAK!
I'M GLAD...
...SHE...
...STUCK WITH ACTING FOR SO LONG!
...
MS. YOSHIMOTO!
SORRY TO KEEP YOU WAITING!

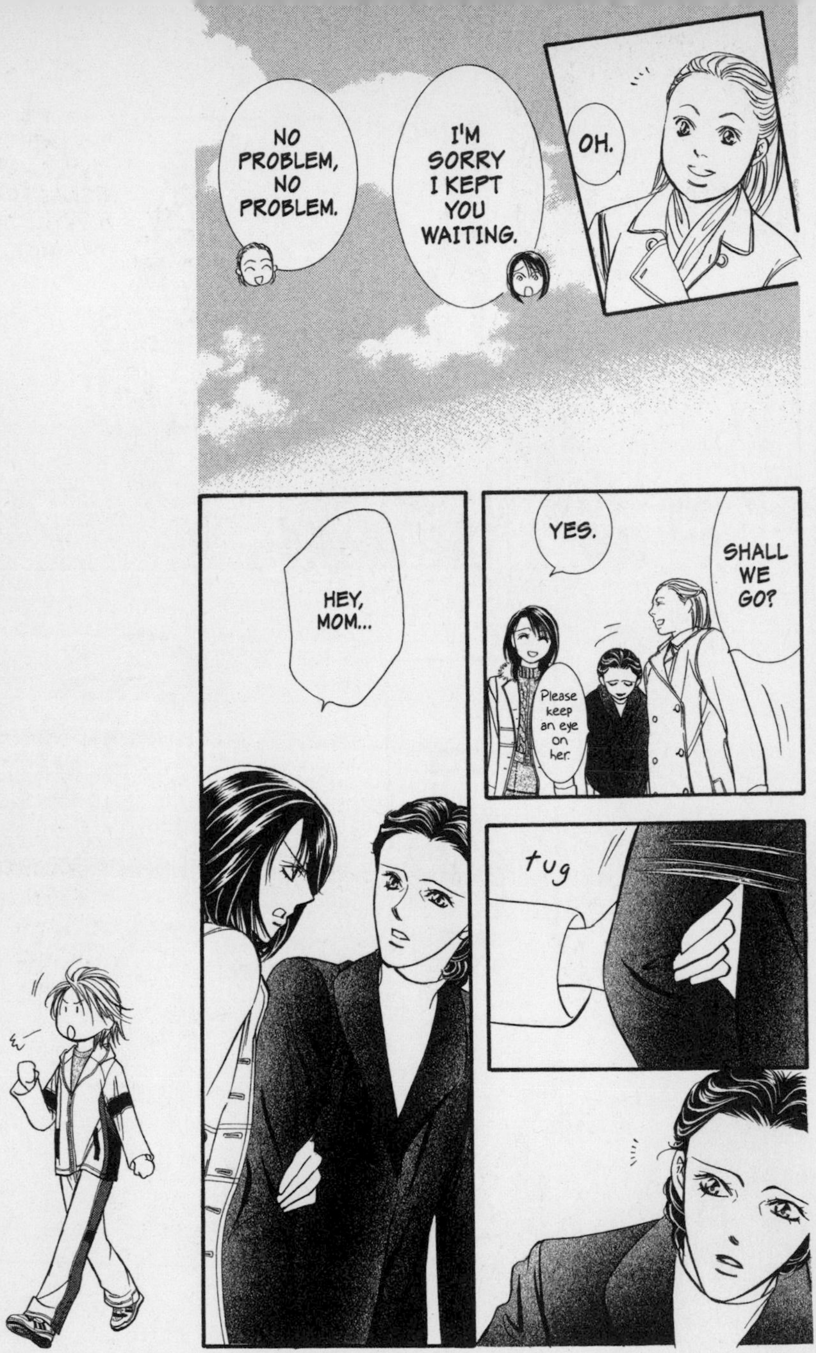
OH.
I'M SORRY I KEPT YOU WAITING.
NO PROBLEM, NO PROBLEM.
SHALL WE GO?
YES.
Please keep an eye on her.
tug
HEY, MOM...

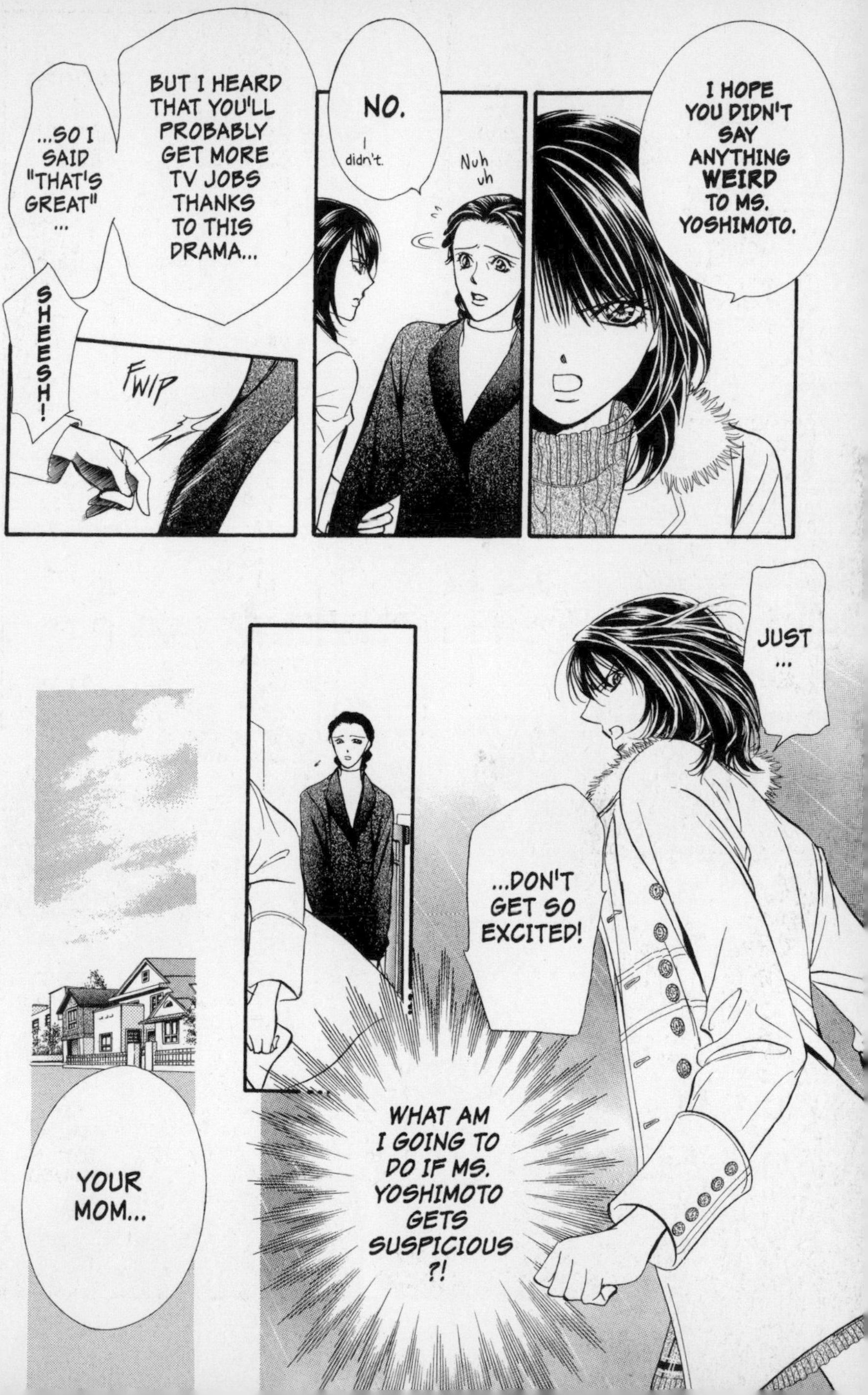
I HOPE YOU DIDN'T SAY ANYTHING WEIRD TO MS. YOSHIMOTO.
NO.
I didn't.
Nuh uh
BUT I HEARD THAT YOU'LL PROBABLY GET MORE TV JOBS THANKS TO THIS DRAMA...
...SO I SAID "THAT'S GREAT" ...
SHEESH!
FWIP
JUST ...
...DON'T GET SO EXCITED!
WHAT AM I GOING TO DO IF MS. YOSHIMOTO GETS SUSPICIOUS ?!
YOUR MOM...

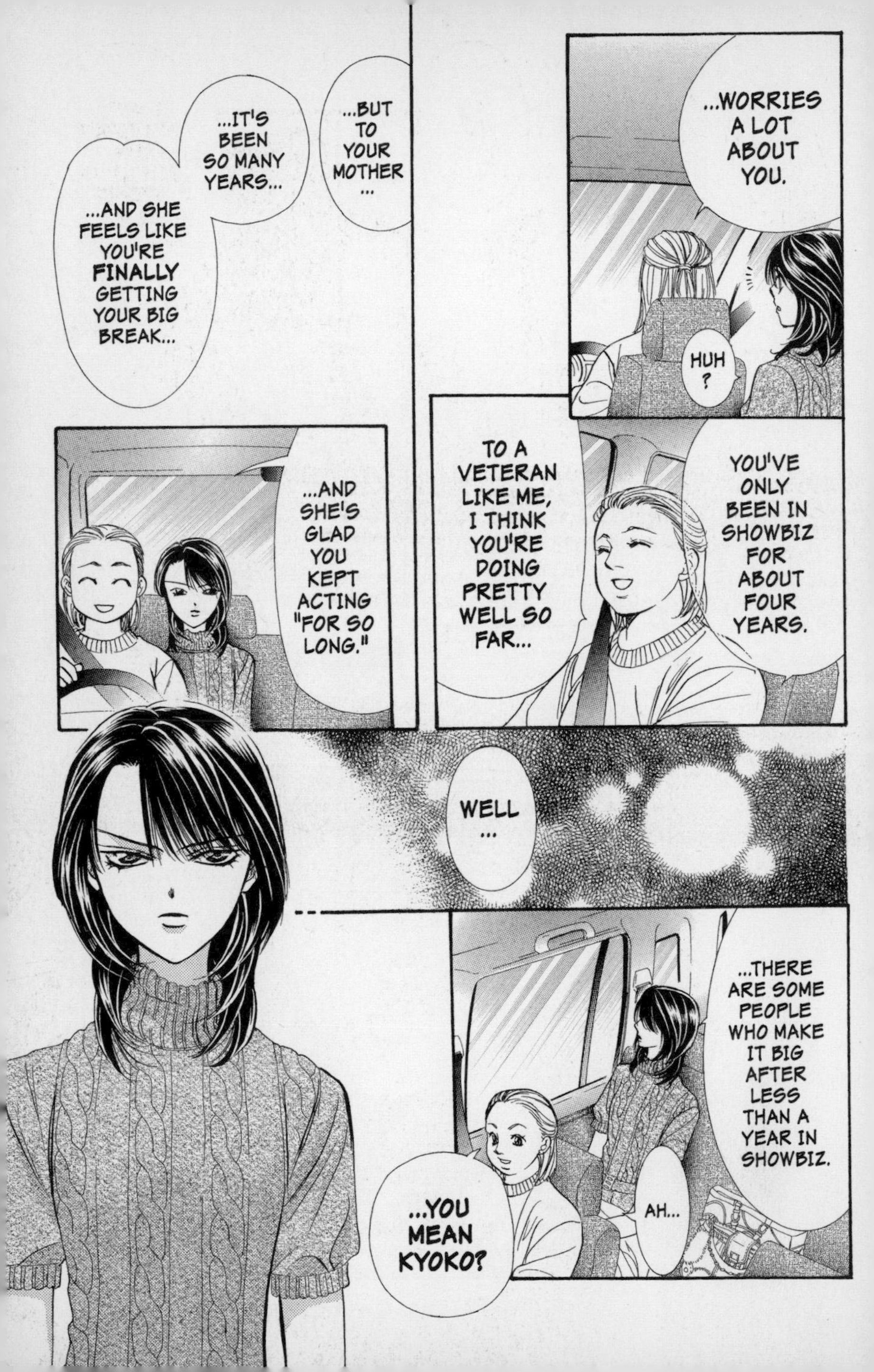
...WORRIES A LOT ABOUT YOU.
HUH?
...BUT TO YOUR MOTHER...
...IT'S BEEN SO MANY YEARS...
...AND SHE FEELS LIKE YOU'RE FINALLY GETTING YOUR BIG BREAK...
YOU'VE ONLY BEEN IN SHOWBIZ FOR ABOUT FOUR YEARS.
TO A VETERAN LIKE ME, I THINK YOU'RE DOING PRETTY WELL SO FAR...
...AND SHE'S GLAD YOU KEPT ACTING "FOR SO LONG."
WELL...
...THERE ARE SOME PEOPLE WHO MAKE IT BIG AFTER LESS THAN A YEAR IN SHOWBIZ.
AH...
...YOU MEAN KYOKO?

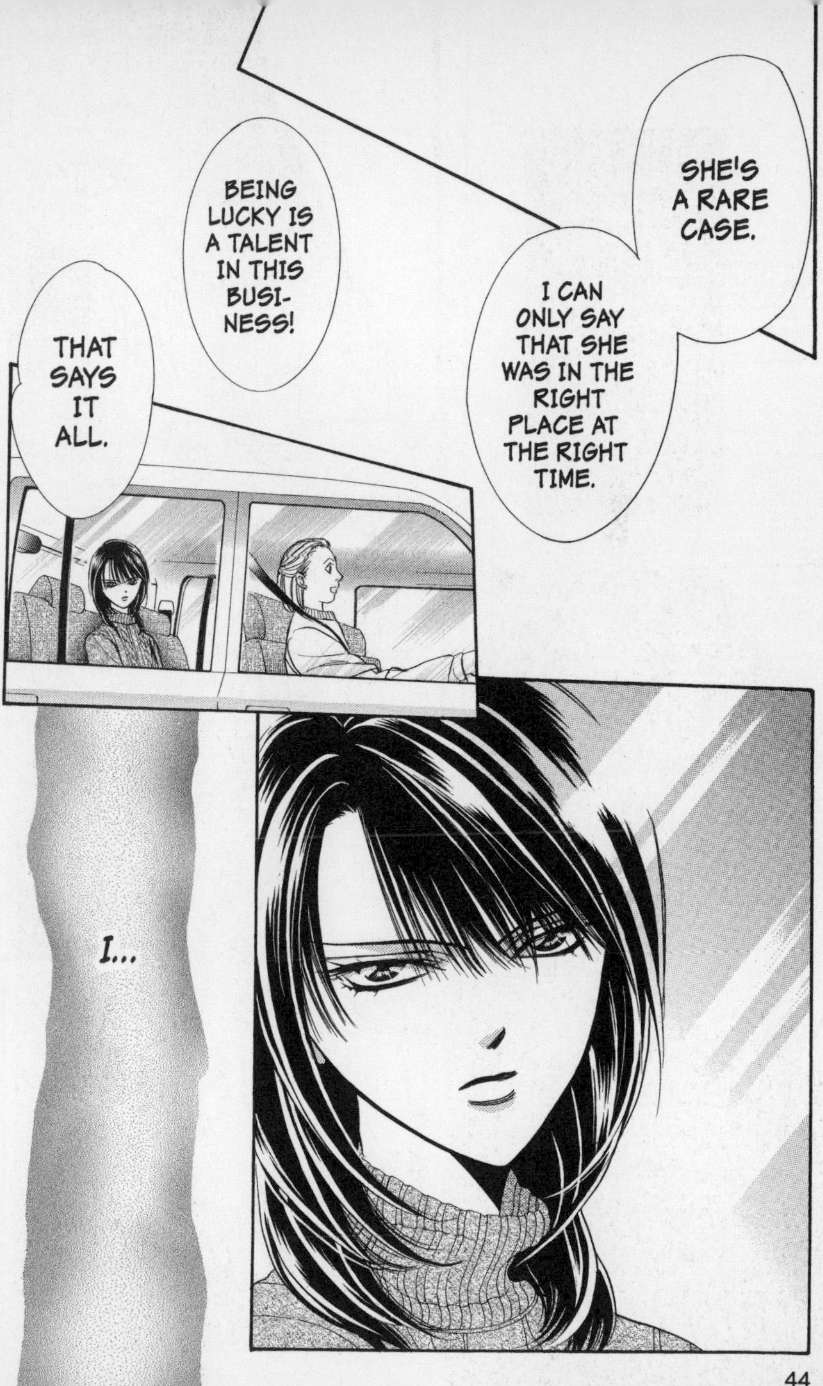
SHE'S A RARE CASE.
I CAN ONLY SAY THAT SHE WAS IN THE RIGHT PLACE AT THE RIGHT TIME.
BEING LUCKY IS A TALENT IN THIS BUSI-NESS!
THAT SAYS IT ALL.
I...

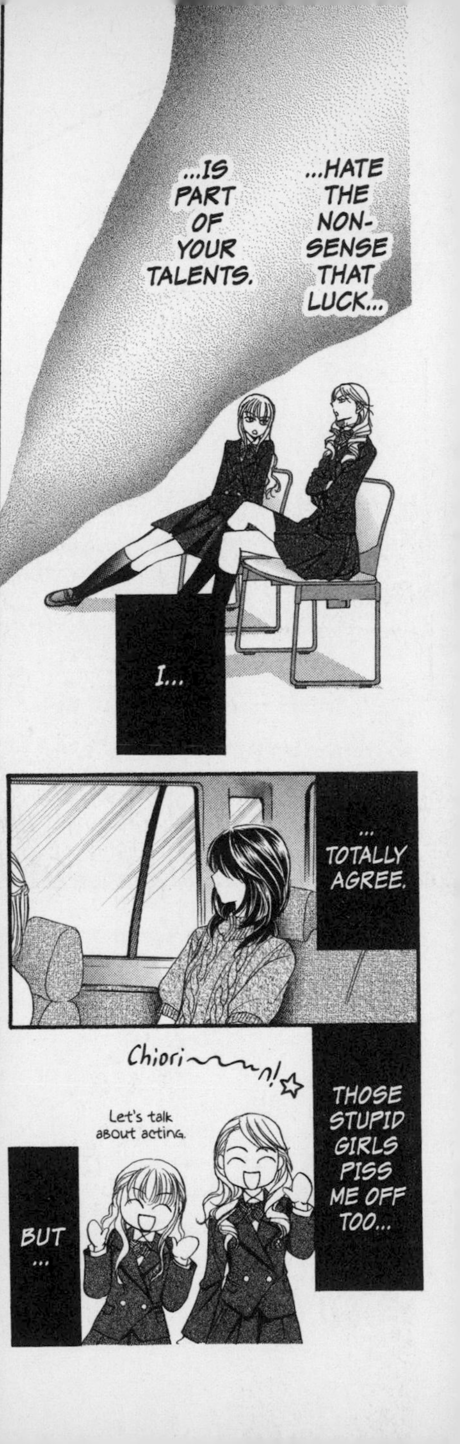
...HATE THE NON-SENSE THAT LUCK...
...IS PART OF YOUR TALENTS.
I...
...TOTALLY AGREE.
THOSE STUPID GIRLS PISS ME OFF TOO...
Chiori~~n!
Let's talk about acting.
BUT ...

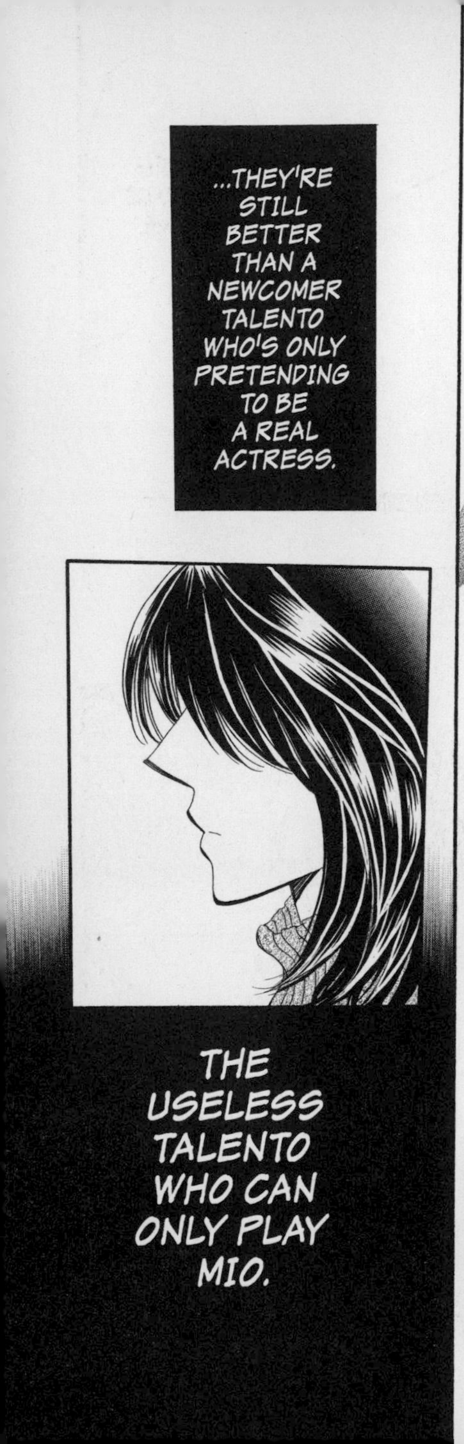
...THEY'RE STILL BETTER THAN A NEWCOMER TALENTO WHO'S ONLY PRETENDING TO BE A REAL ACTRESS.
THE USELESS TALENTO WHO CAN ONLY PLAY MIO.

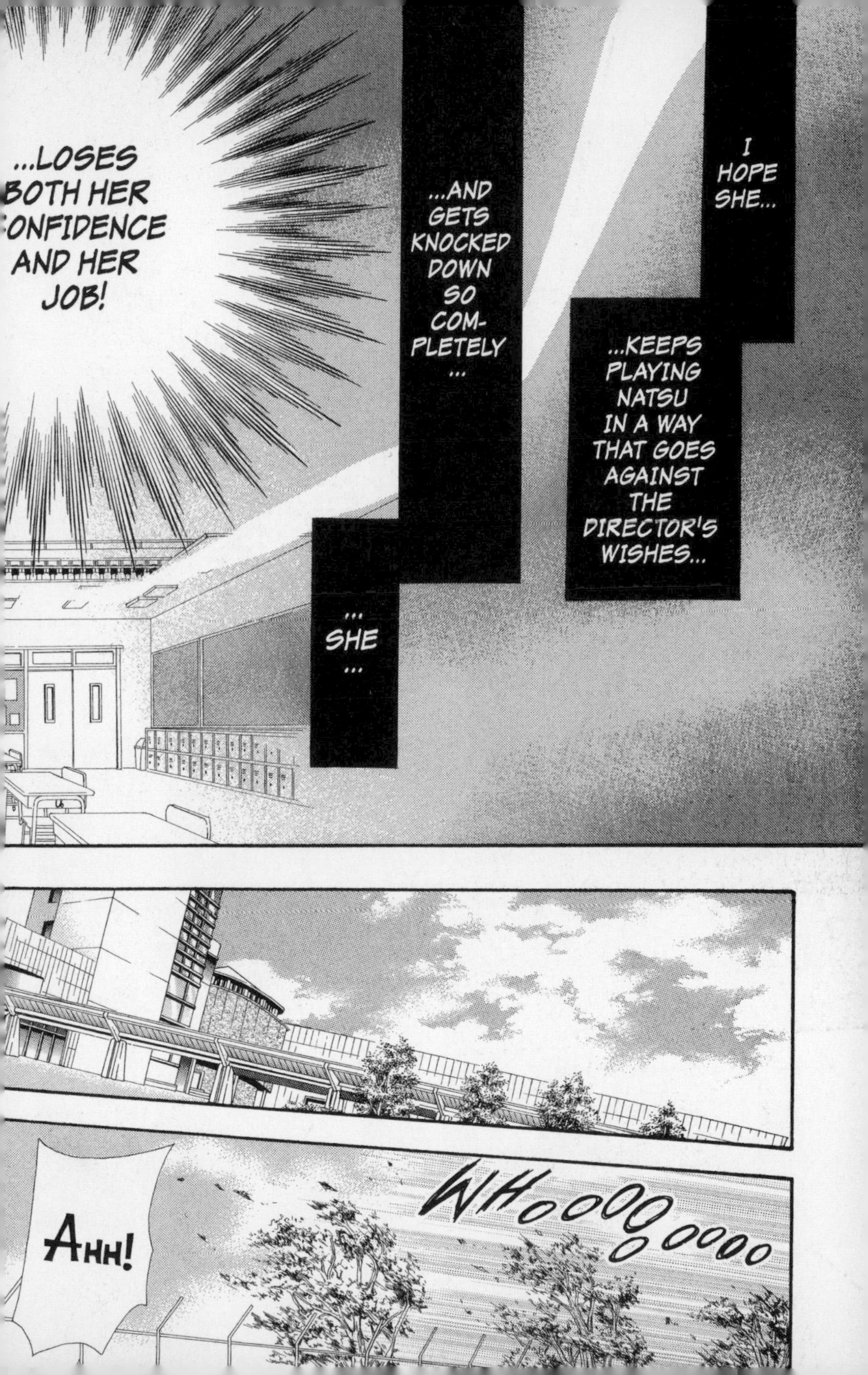
I HOPE SHE...
...KEEPS PLAYING NATSU IN A WAY THAT GOES AGAINST THE DIRECTOR'S WISHES...
...AND GETS KNOCKED DOWN SO COM-PLETELY...
...SHE...
...LOSES BOTH HER CONFIDENCE AND HER JOB!
WHOOOOOOOOOO
AHH!

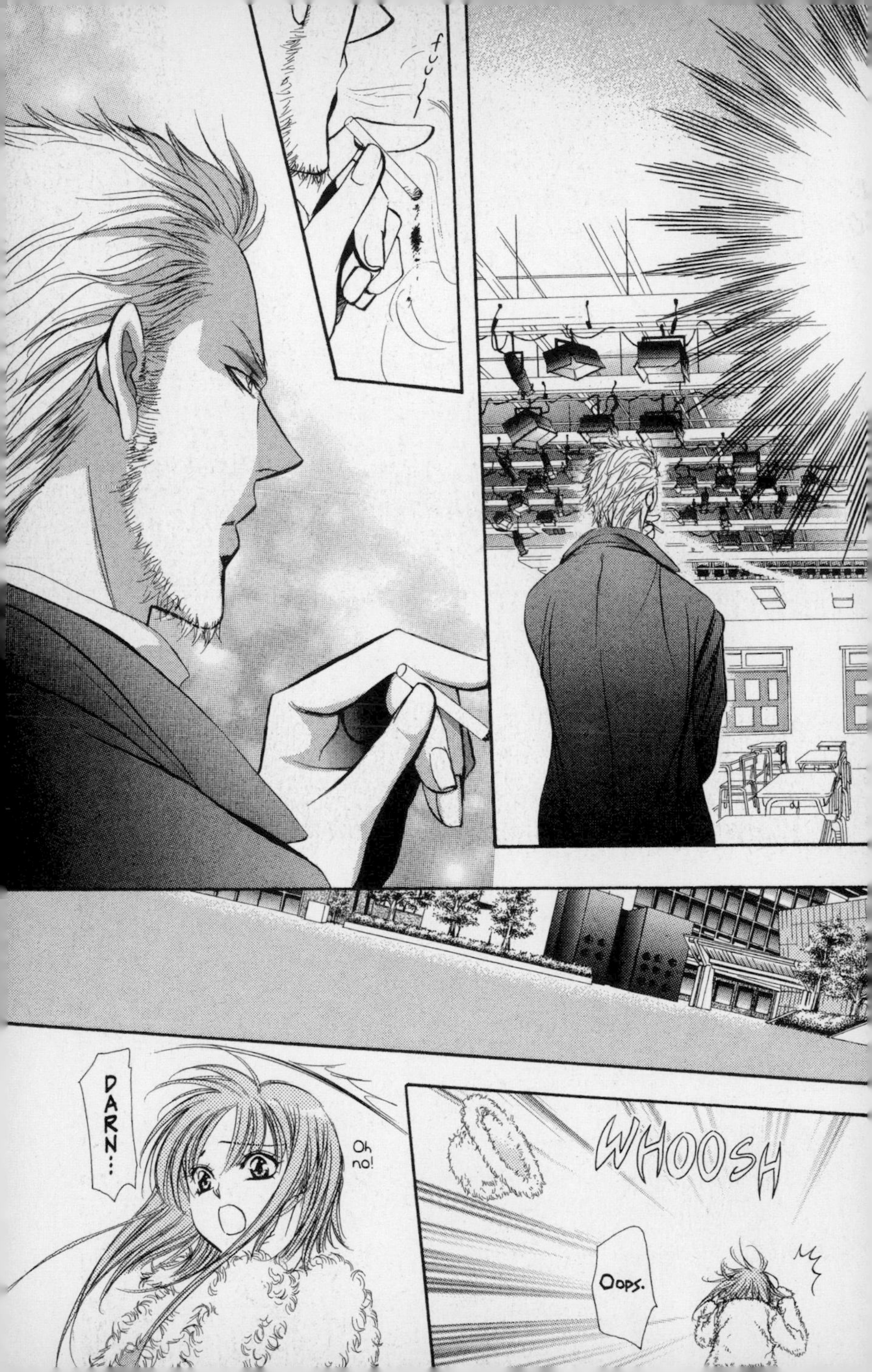
fuu
WHOOSH
Oops.
Oh no!
DARN...

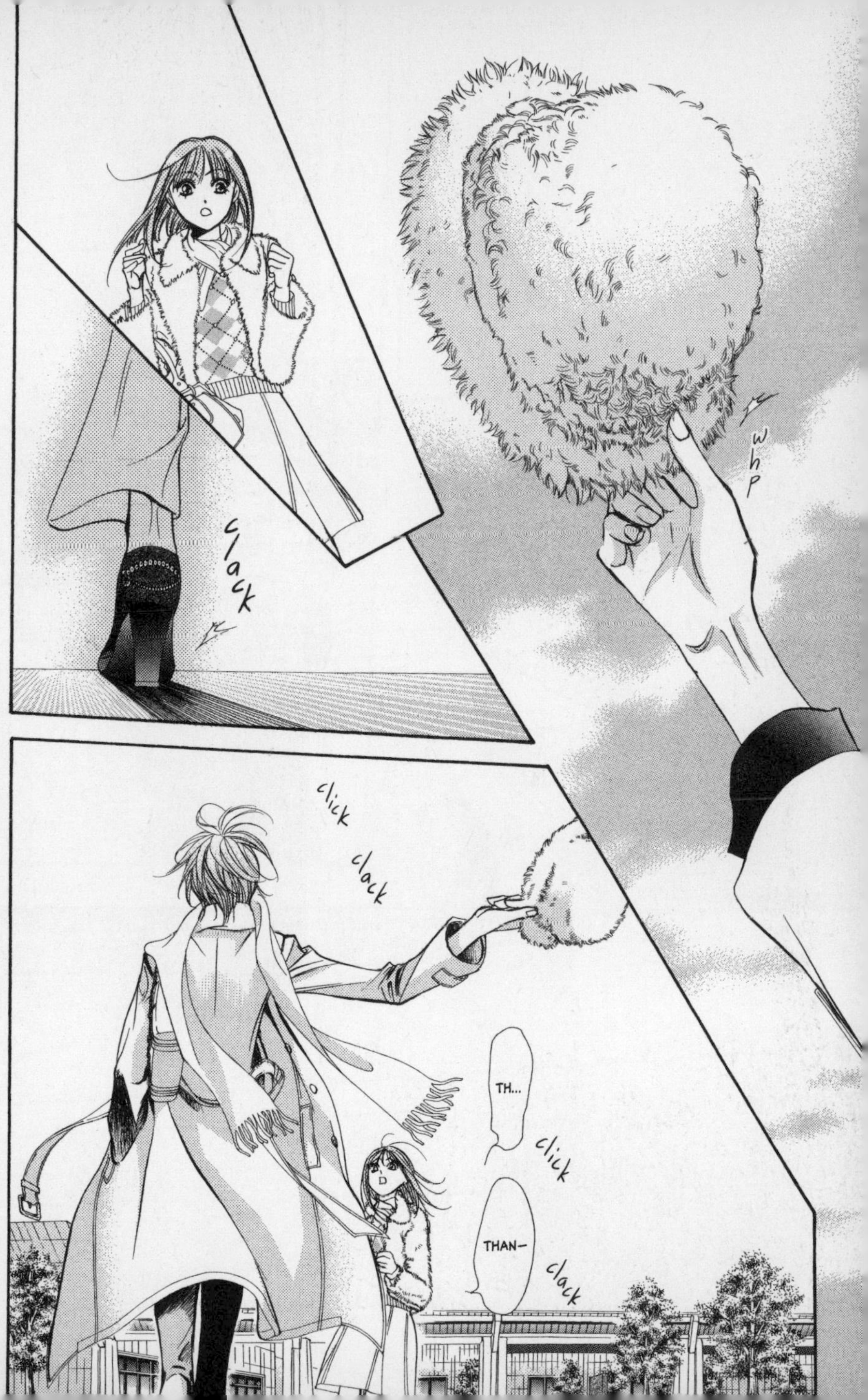
whp
clack
click
clack
TH...
click
THAN—
clack

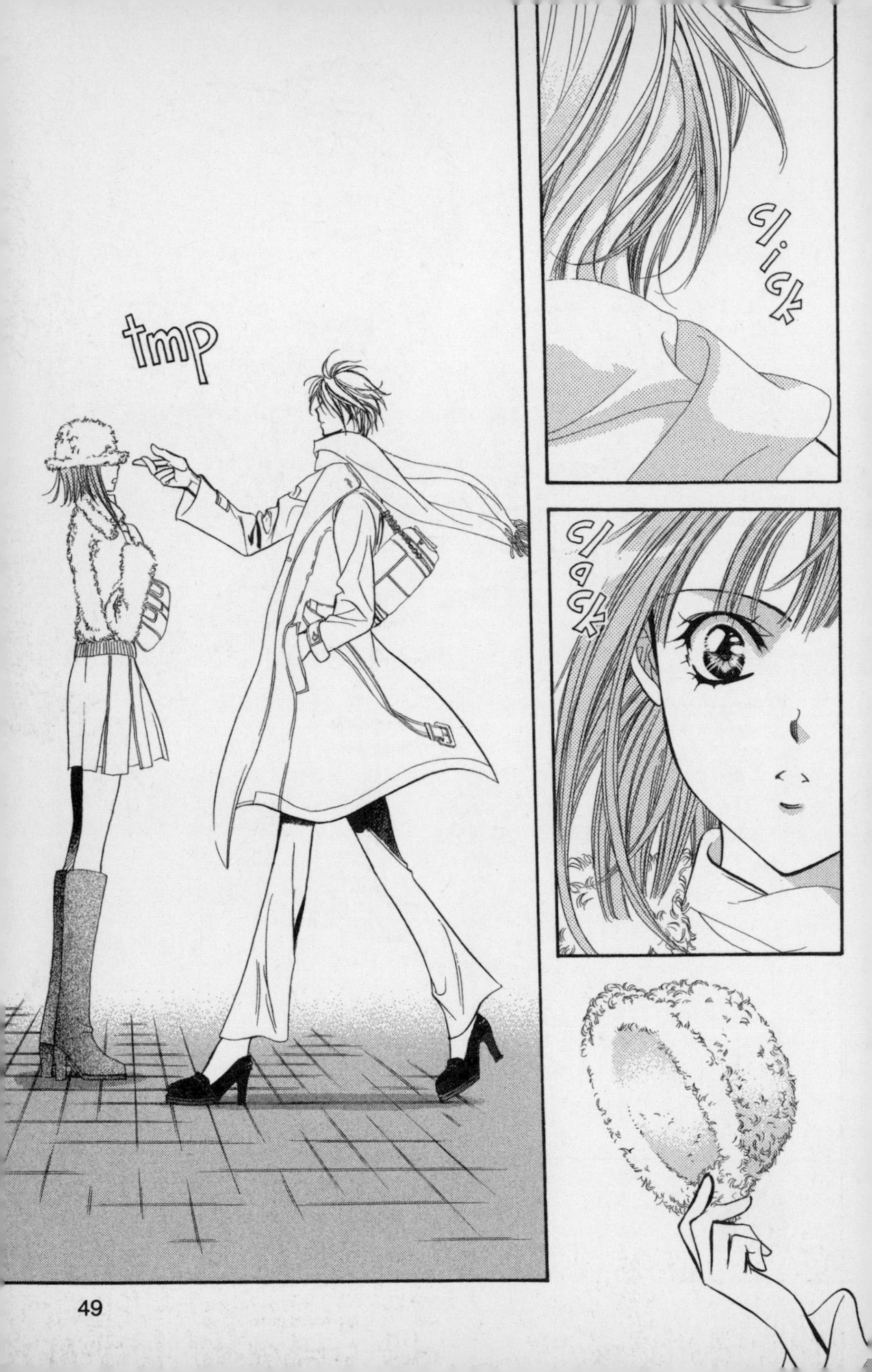
click
clack
tmp

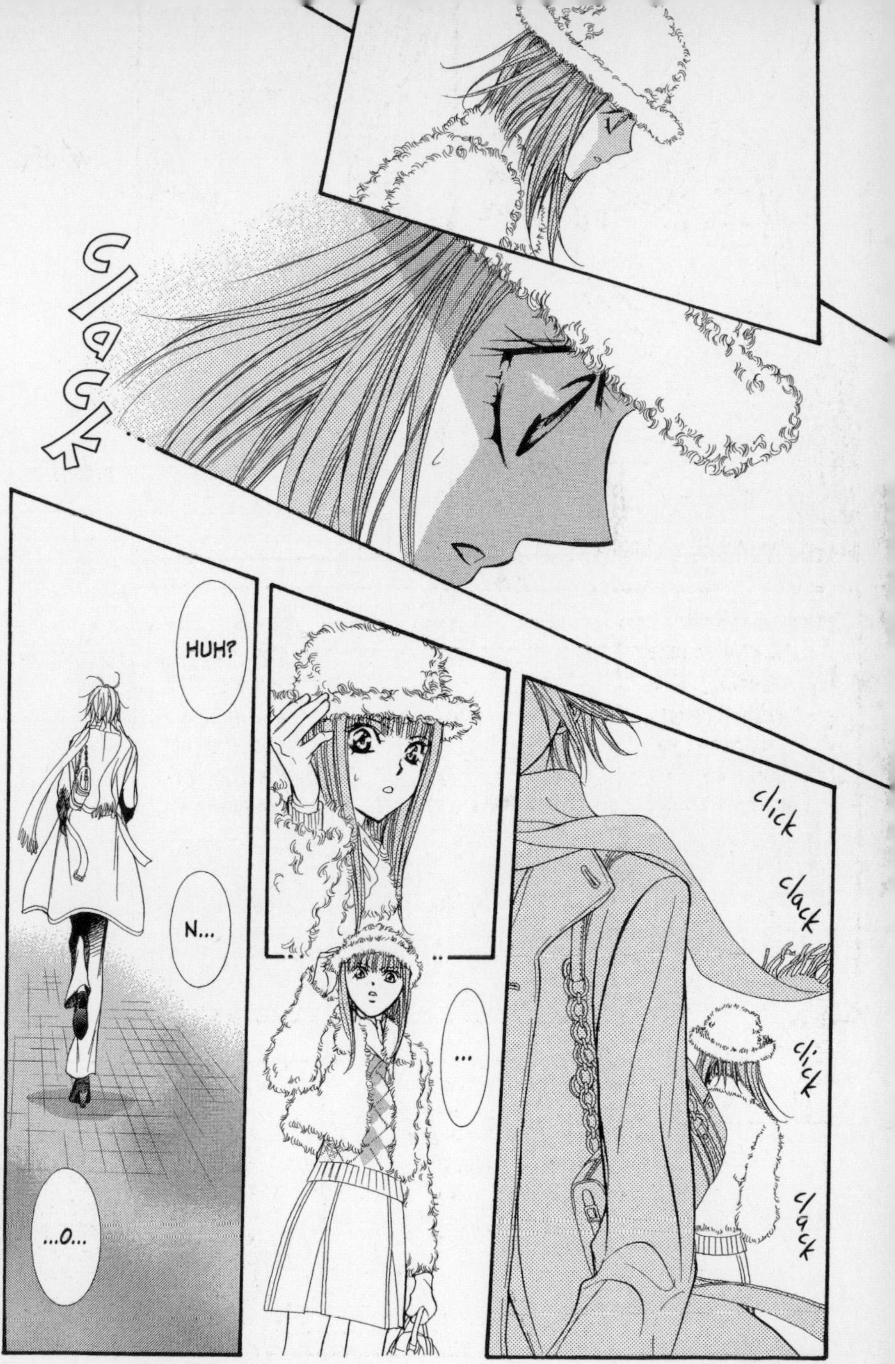
clack...
click
clack
click
clack
...
HUH?
N...
...O...

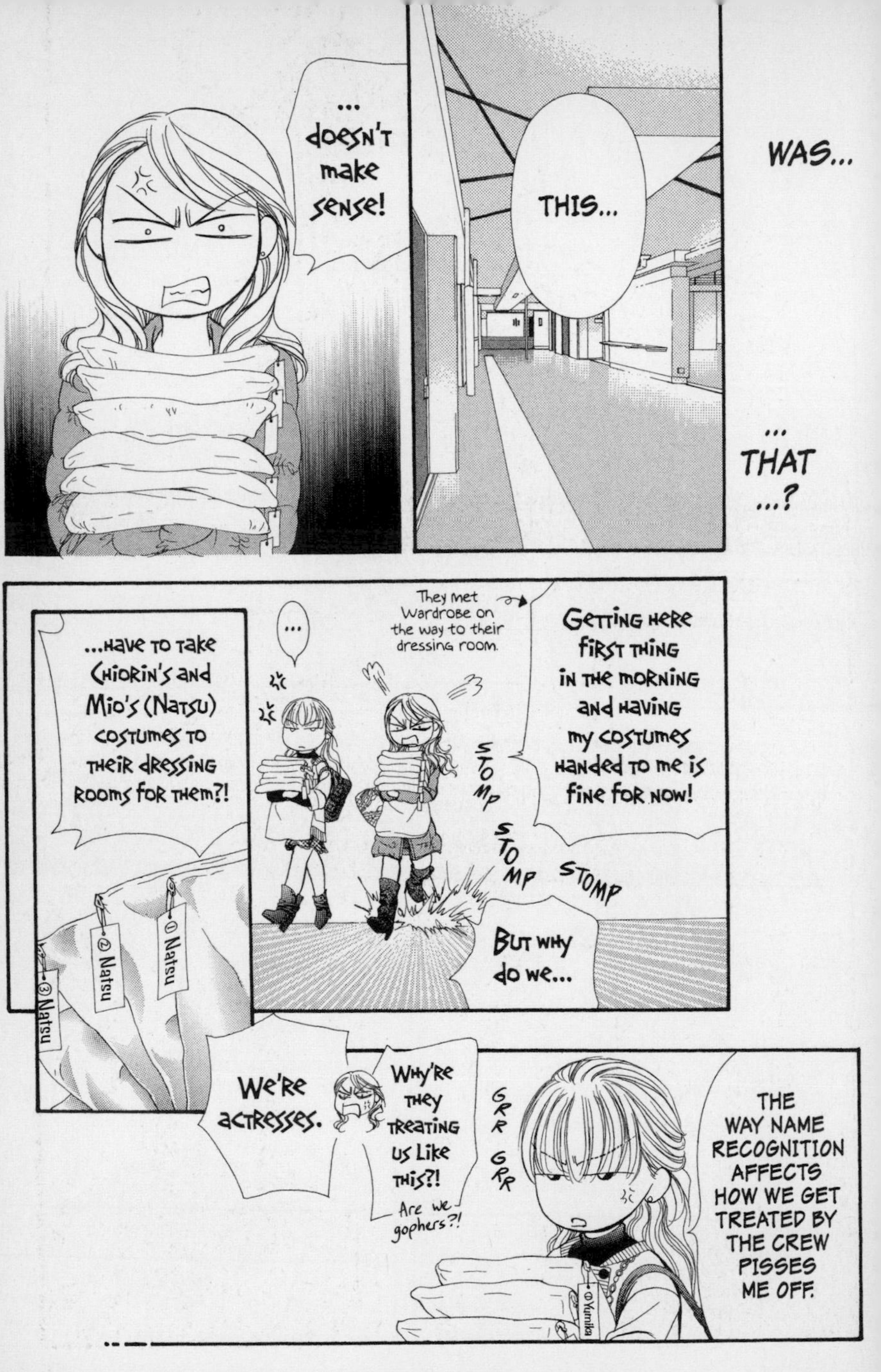
WAS...
THIS...
...THAT...?
...doesn't make sense!
They met Wardrobe on the way to their dressing room.
Getting here first thing in the morning and having my costumes handed to me is fine for now!
STOMP
STOMP
STOMP
But why do we...
...have to take Chiorin's and Mio's (Natsu) costumes to their dressing rooms for them?!
...
① Natsu
② Natsu
③ Natsu
THE WAY NAME RECOGNITION AFFECTS HOW WE GET TREATED BY THE CREW PISSES ME OFF.
① Yumika
GRR GRR
Why're they treating us like this?!
Are we gophers?!
We're actresses.

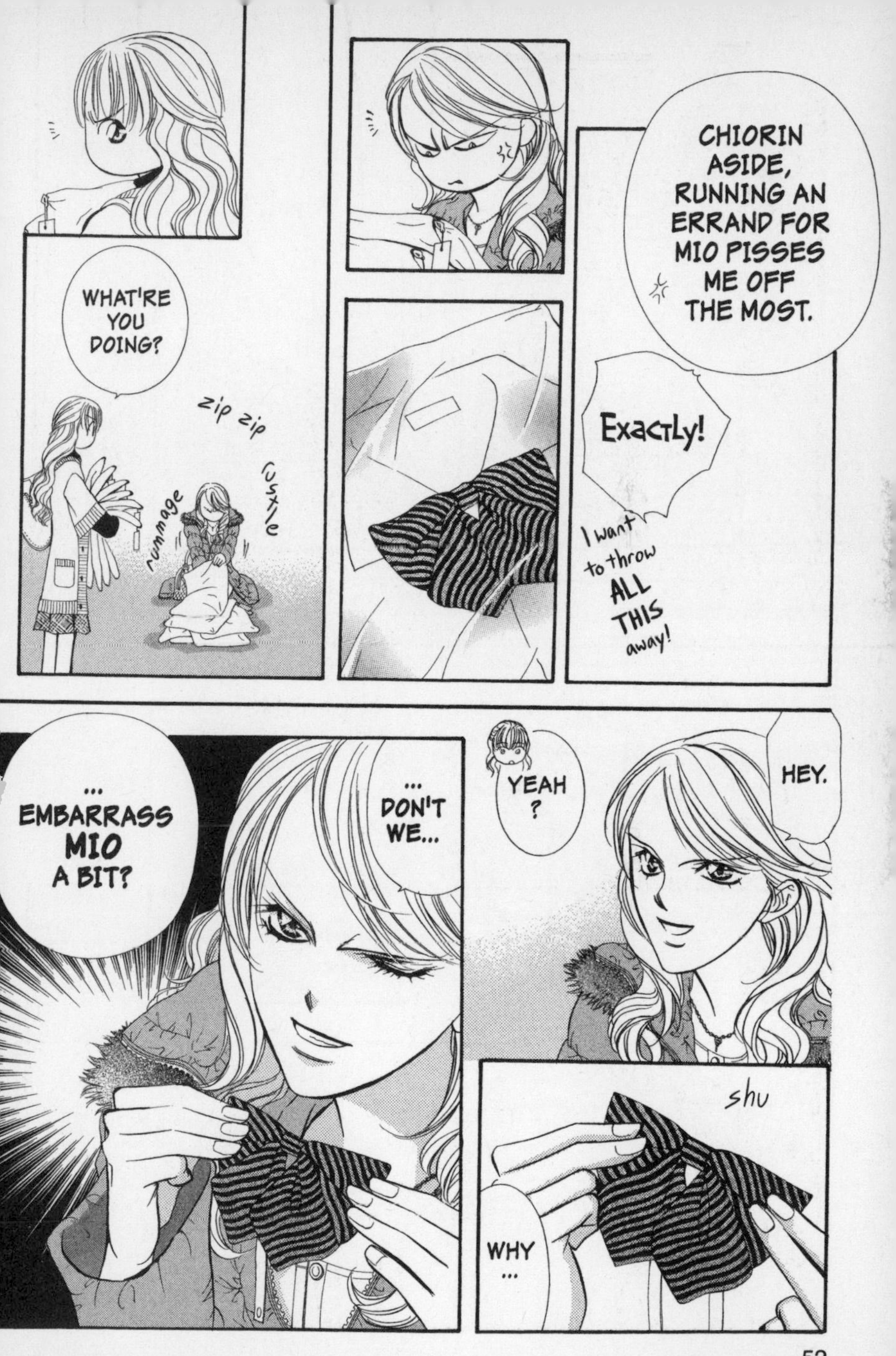
CHIORIN ASIDE, RUNNING AN ERRAND FOR MIO PISSES ME OFF THE MOST.
Exactly!
I want to throw ALL THIS away!
WHAT'RE YOU DOING?
zip zip
rustle
rummage
HEY.
YEAH?
shu
WHY...
...DON'T WE...
...EMBARRASS MIO A BIT?

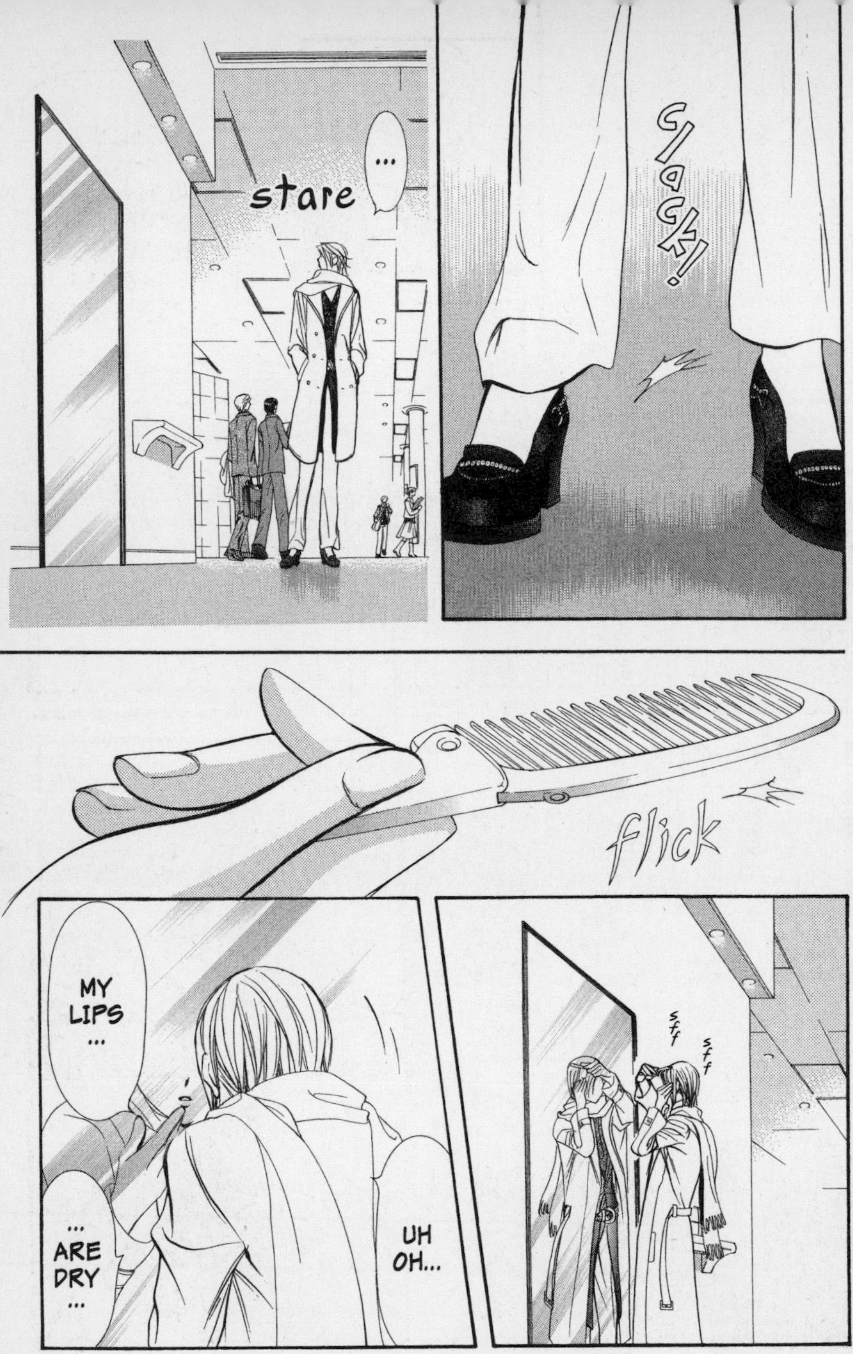
clack!
...
stare
flick
sff
sff
MY LIPS ...
... ARE DRY ...
UH OH...

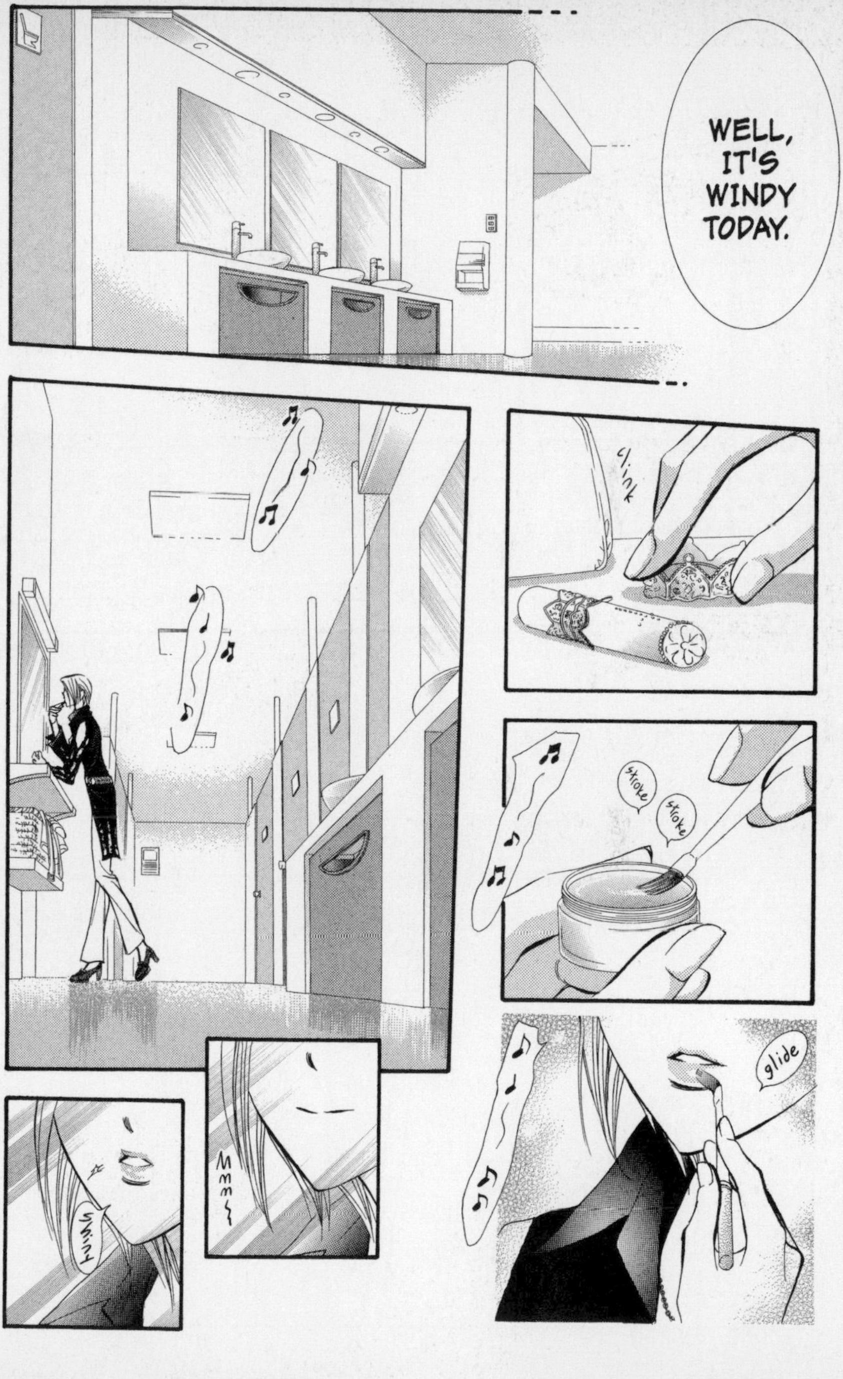
WELL, IT'S WINDY TODAY.
clink
stroke
stroke
glide
Mmm~
shiny

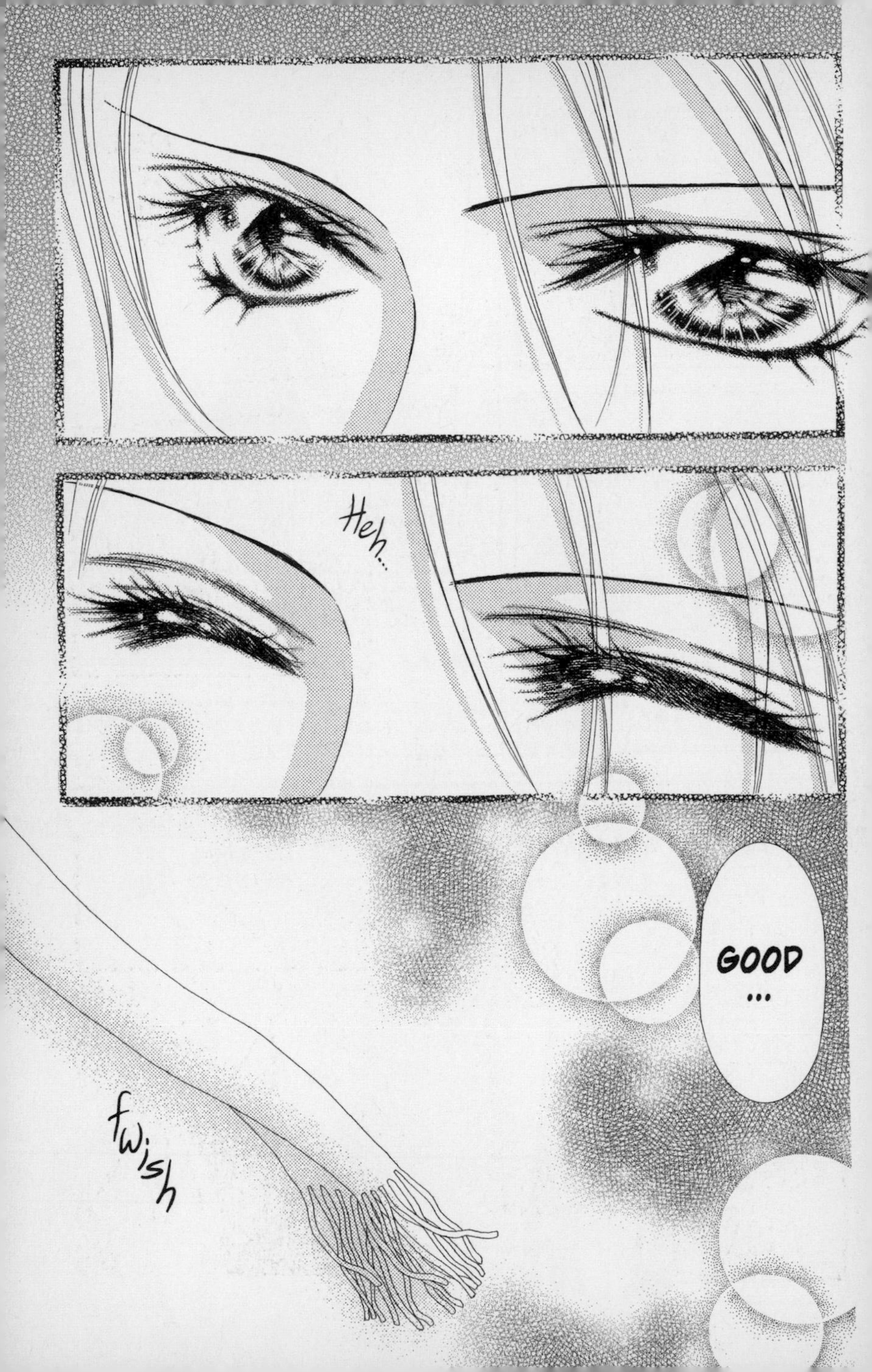
Heh...
GOOD ...
fwish

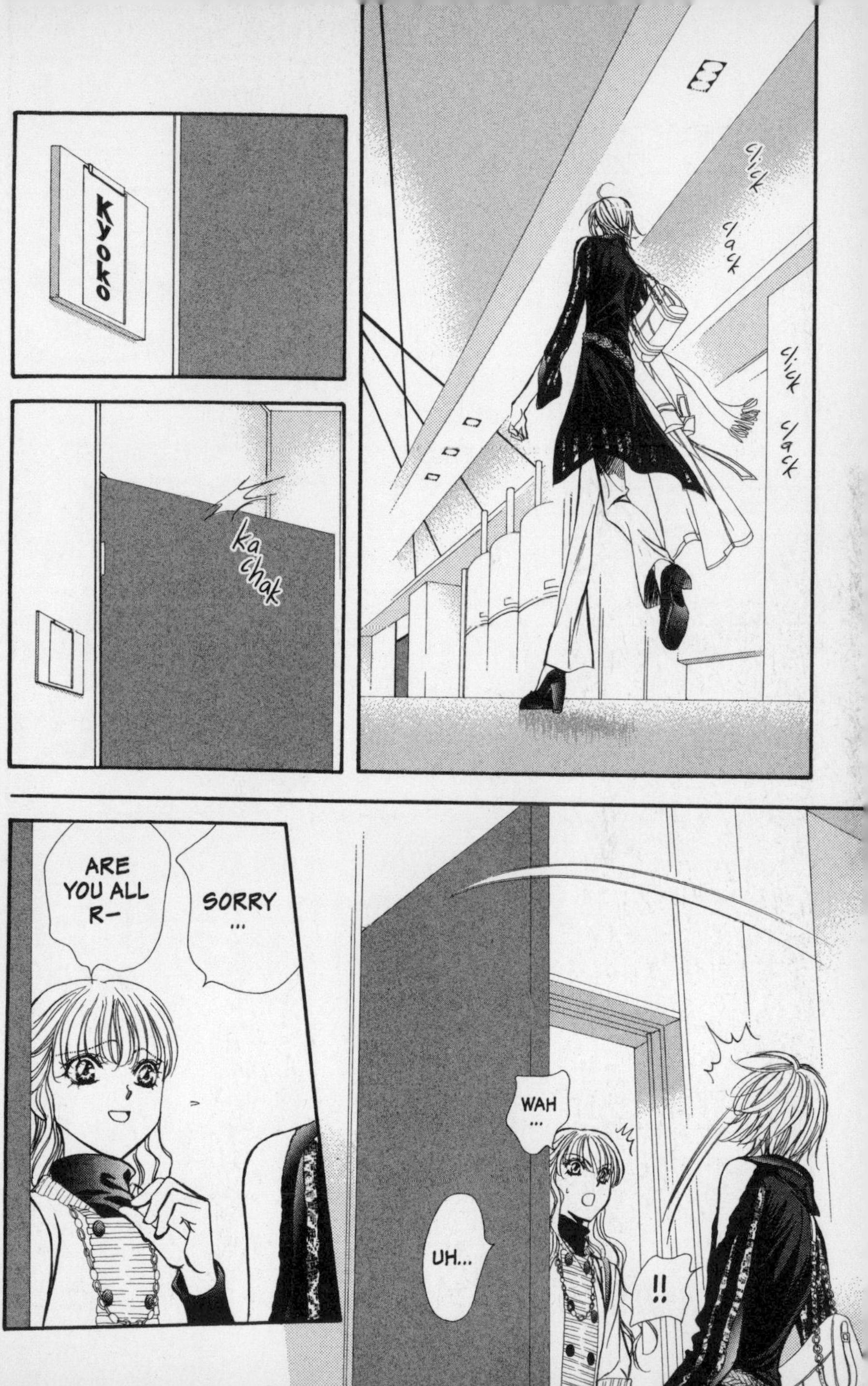
click
clack
click
clack
KYOKO
ka chak
WAH...
UH...
!!
ARE YOU ALL R—
SORRY...

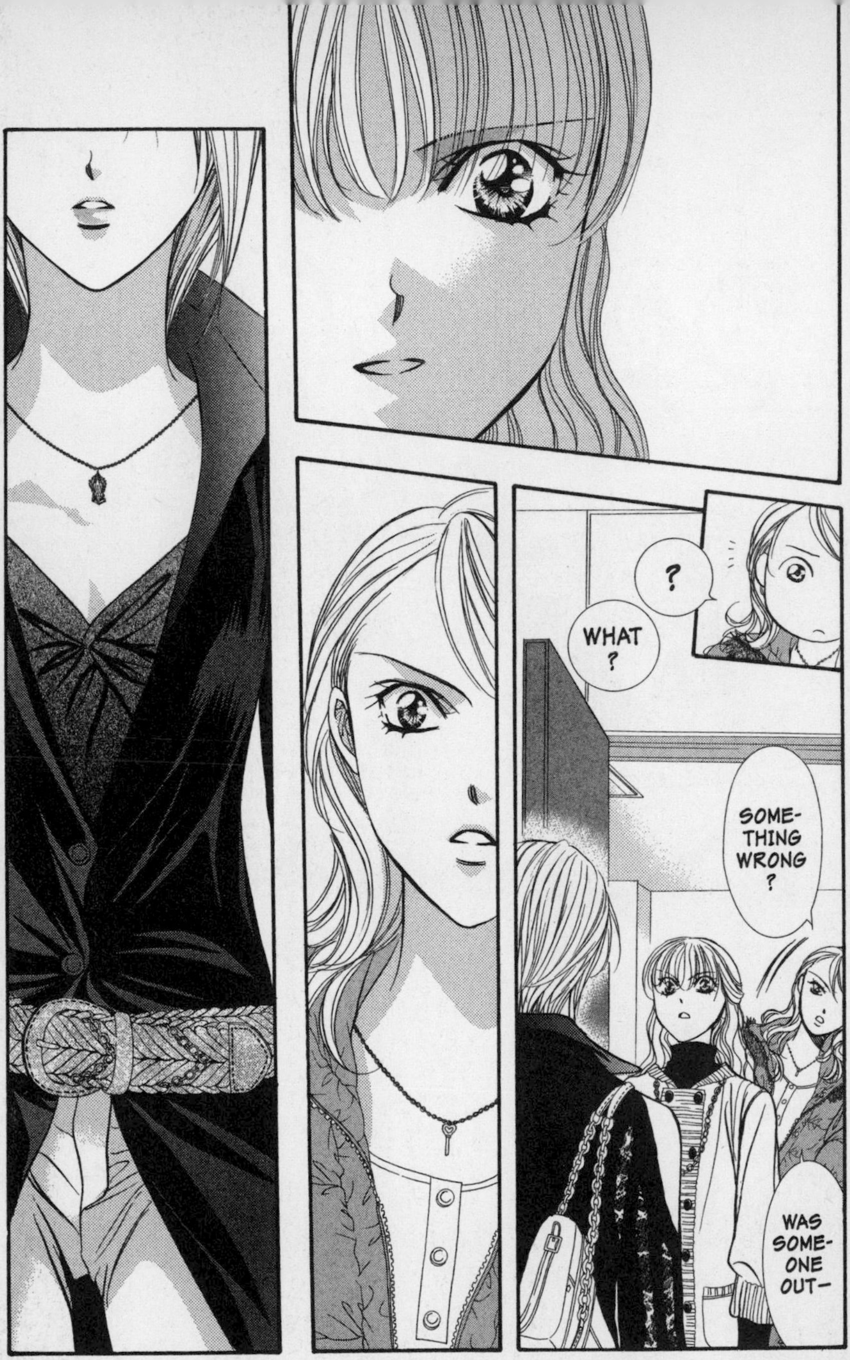
?
WHAT?
SOME-THING WRONG?
WAS SOME-ONE OUT-

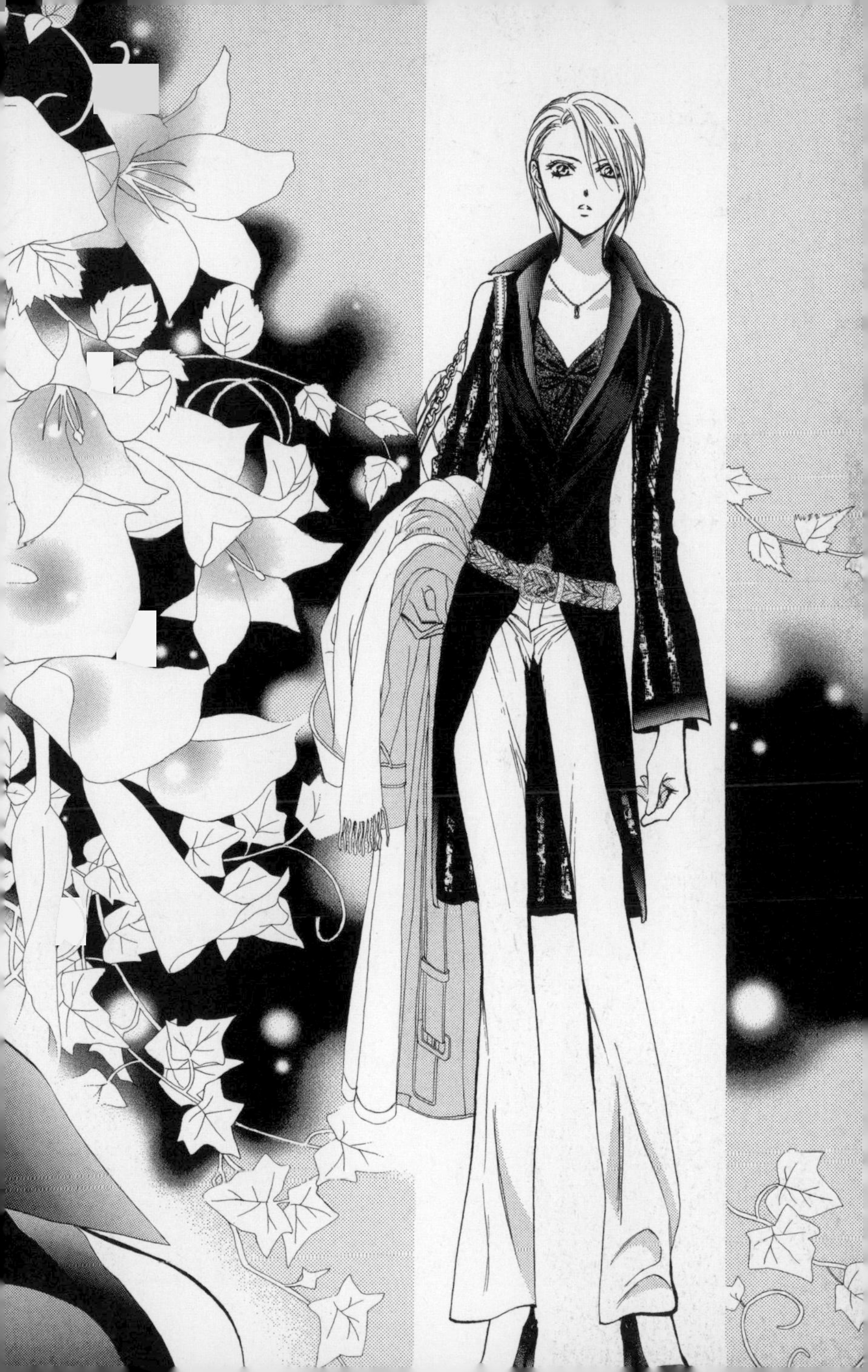

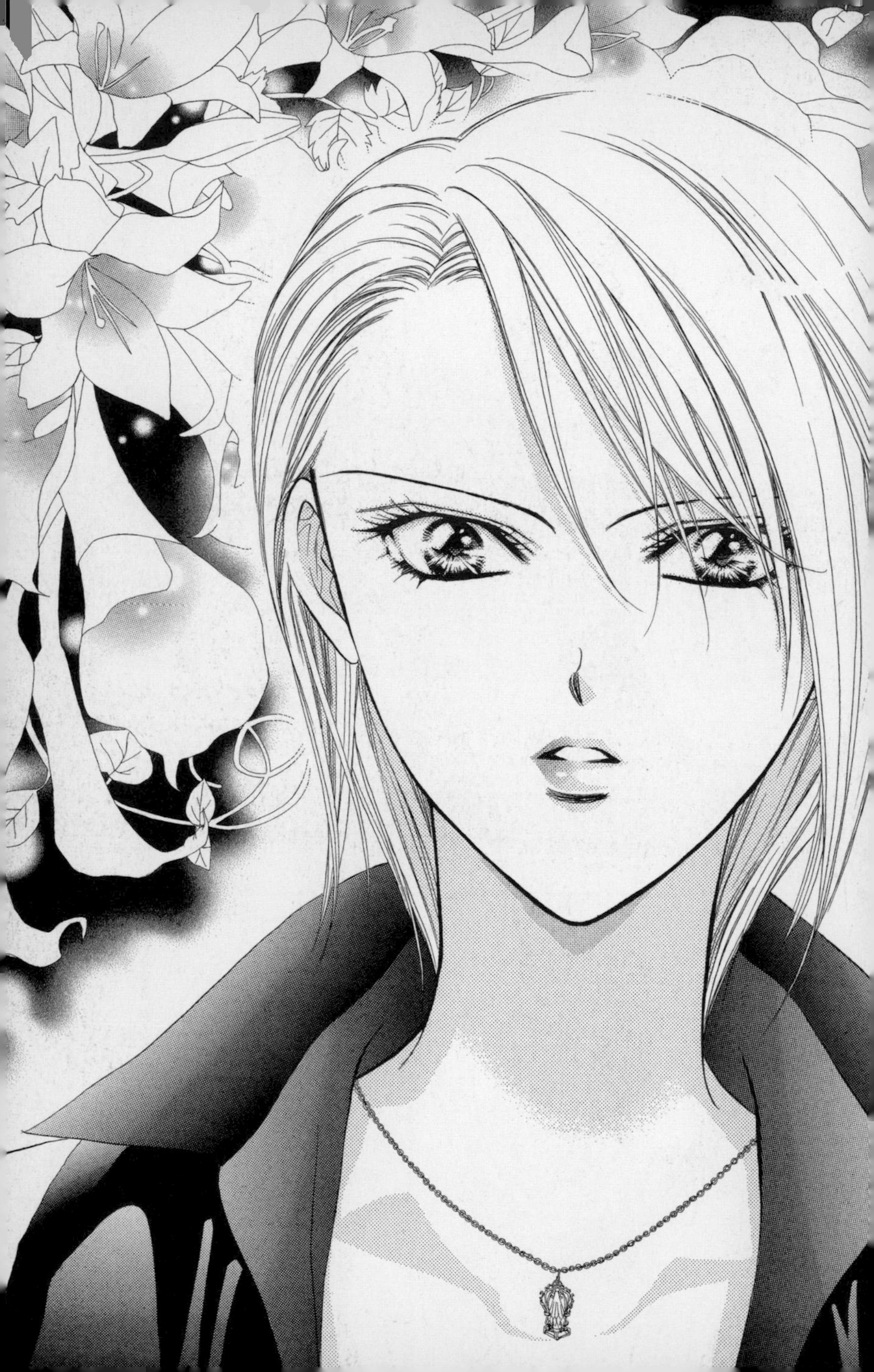

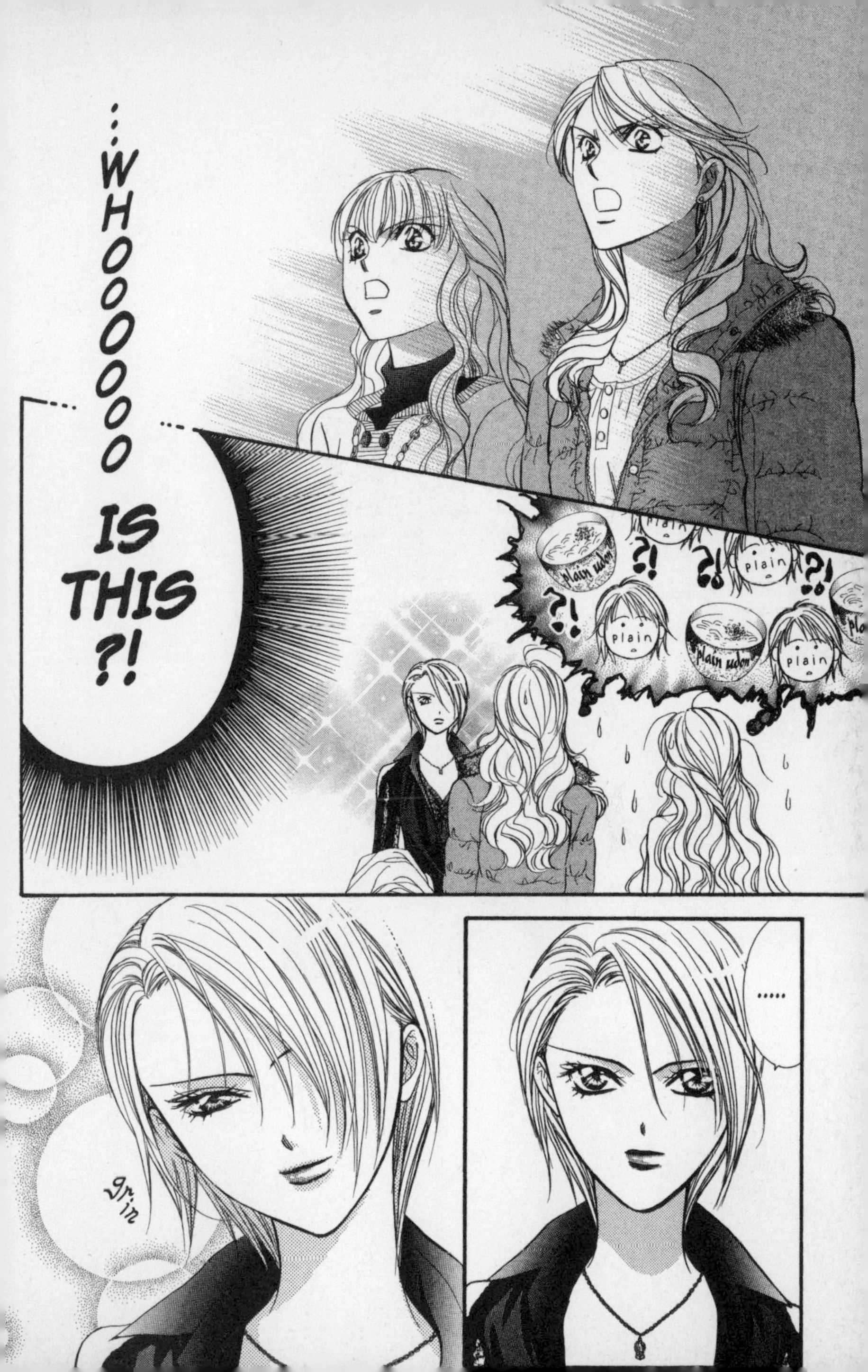
...WHOOOOOOO
IS THIS?!
plain udon
plain
?!
plain udon
.....
grin

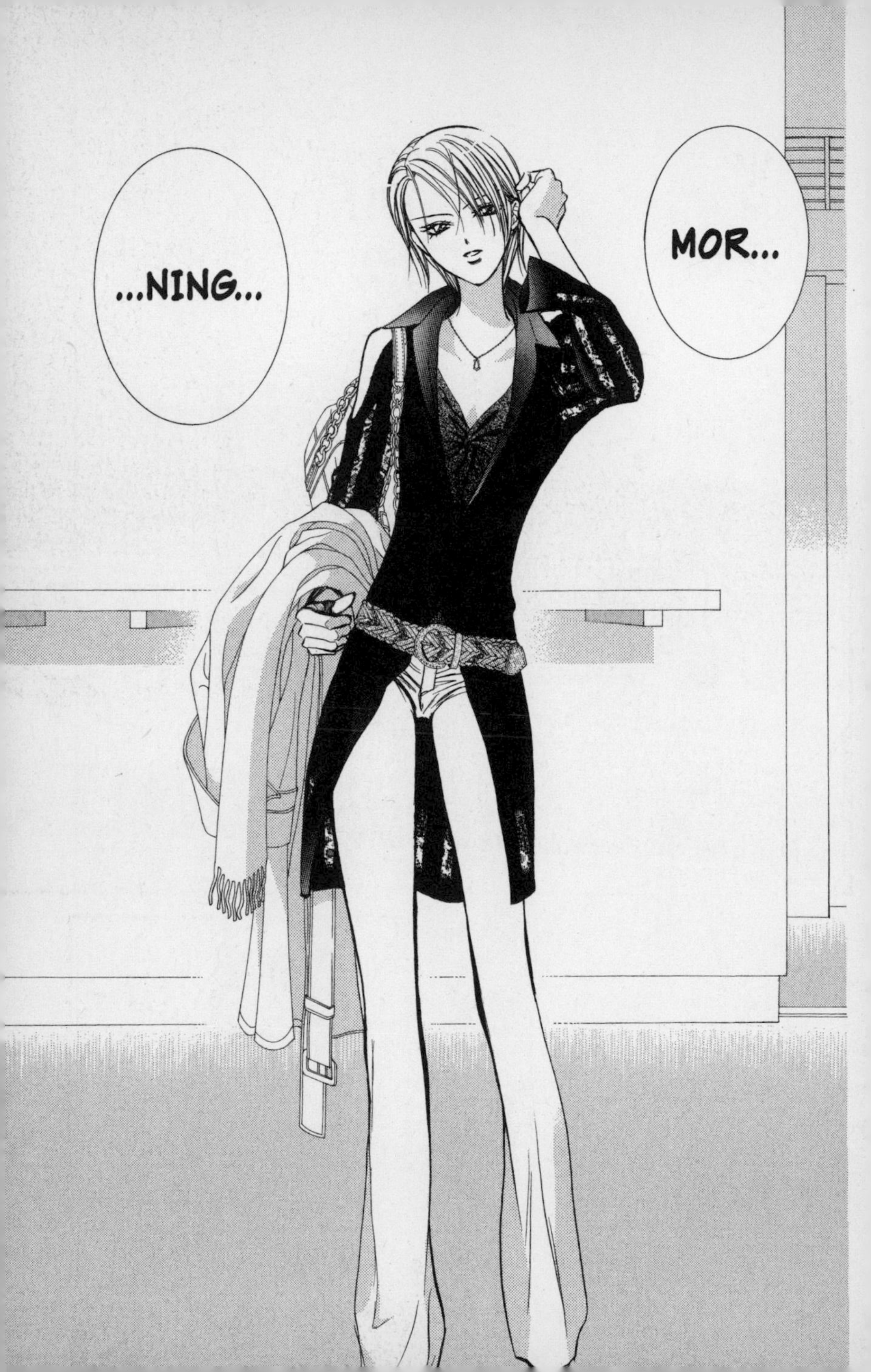
MOR...
...NING...

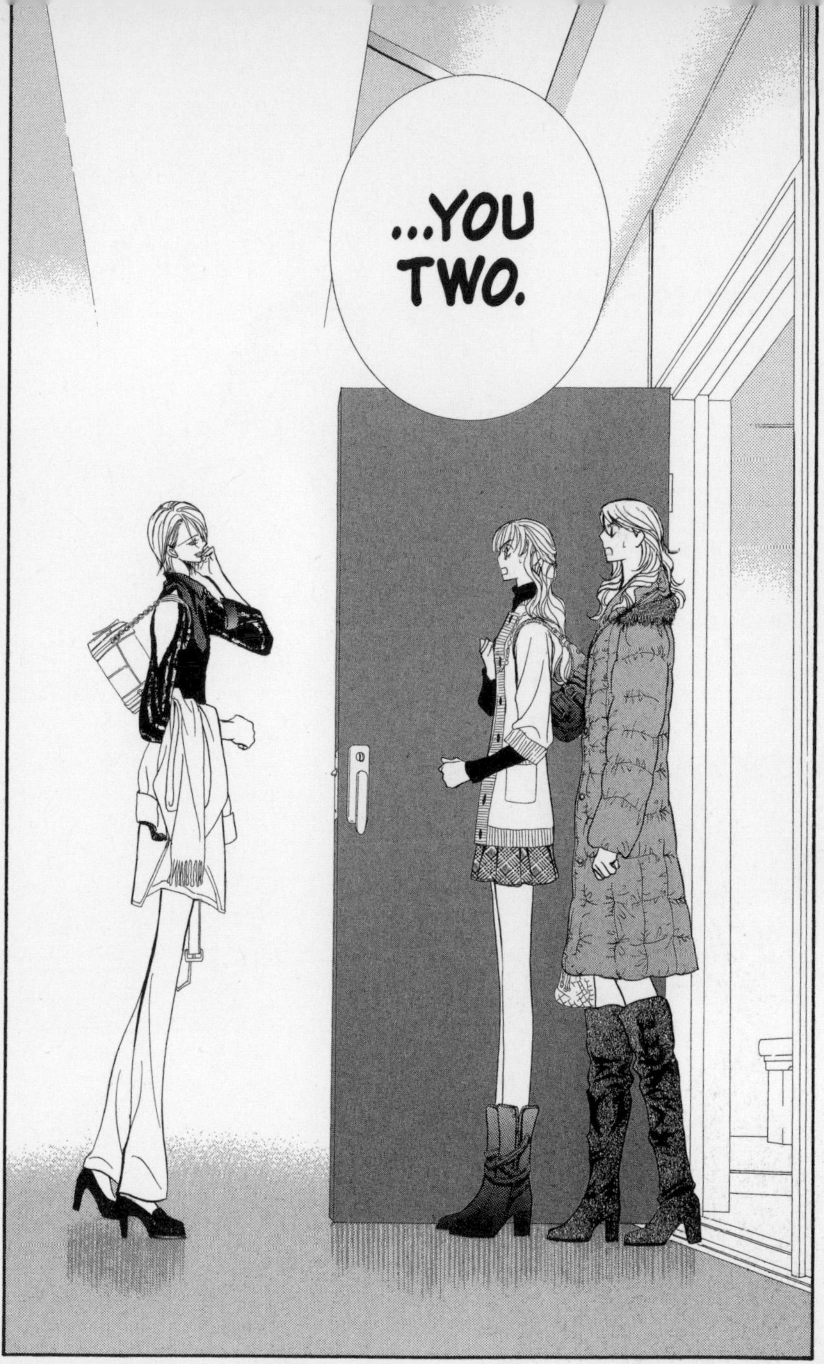
...YOU TWO.

End of Act 128

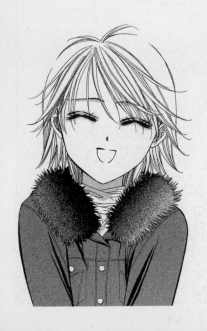

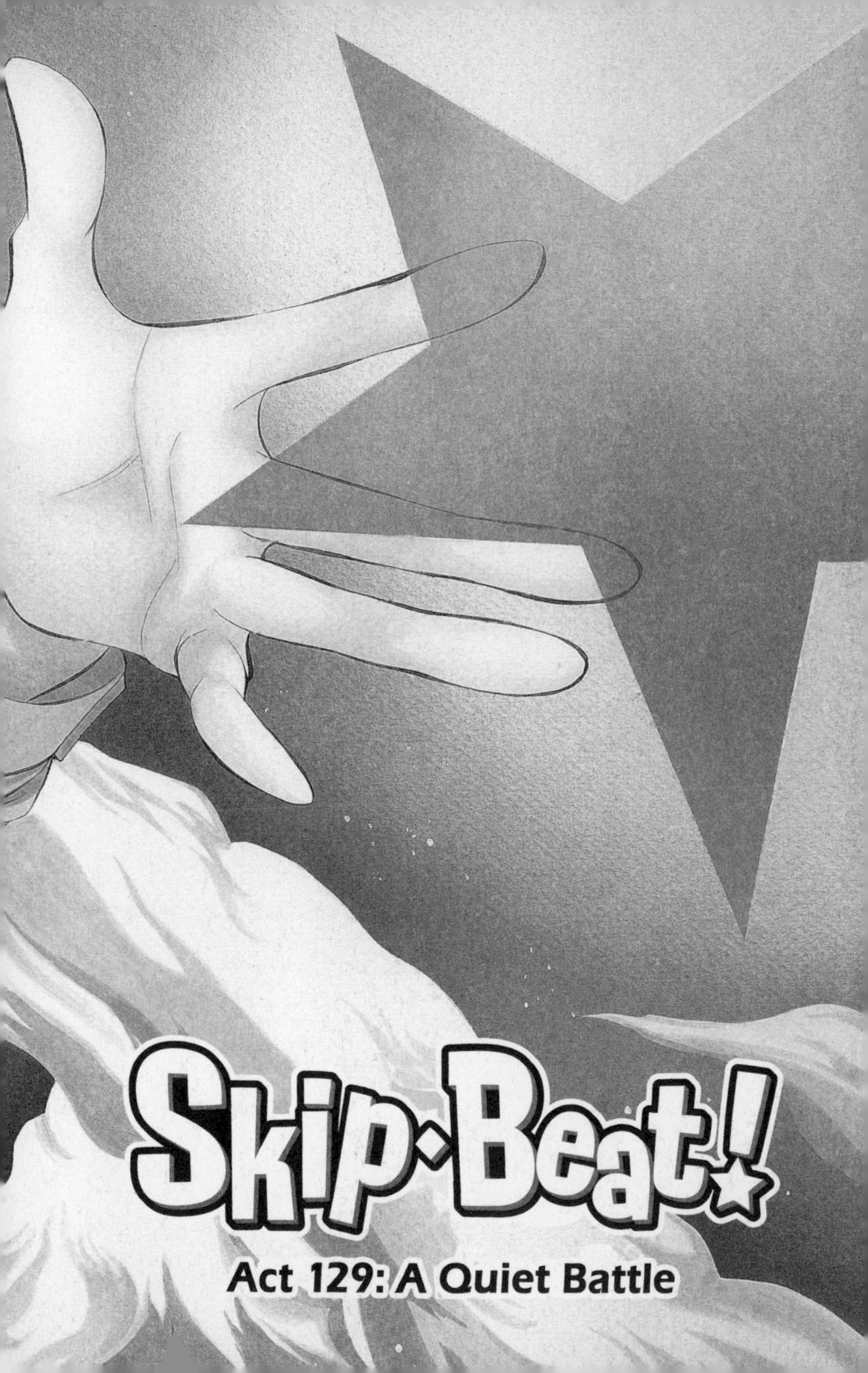
Skip·Beat!
Act 129: A Quiet Battle

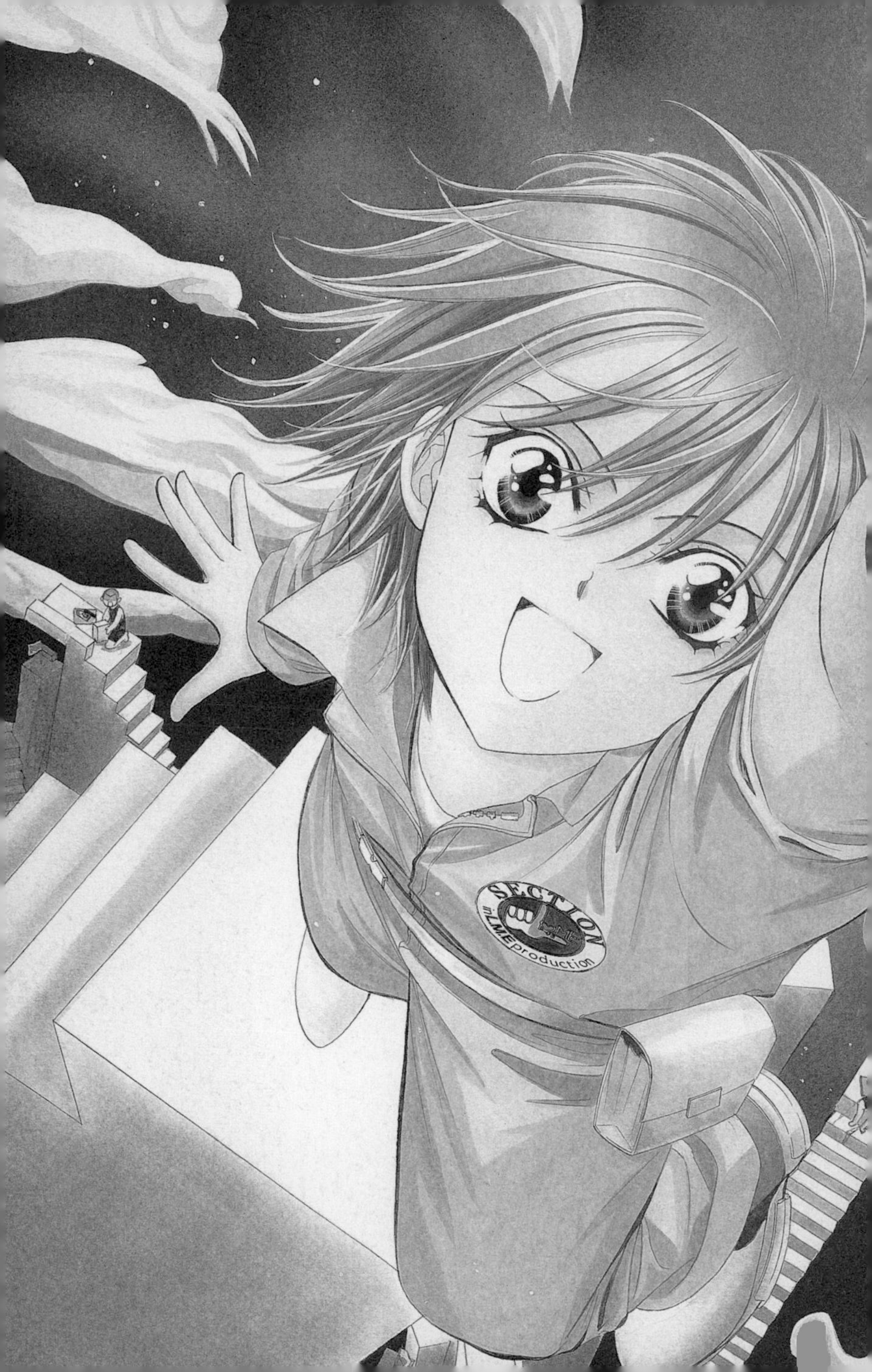
SECTION
in L.M.E production

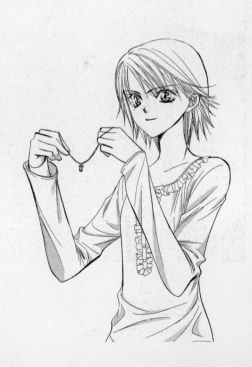

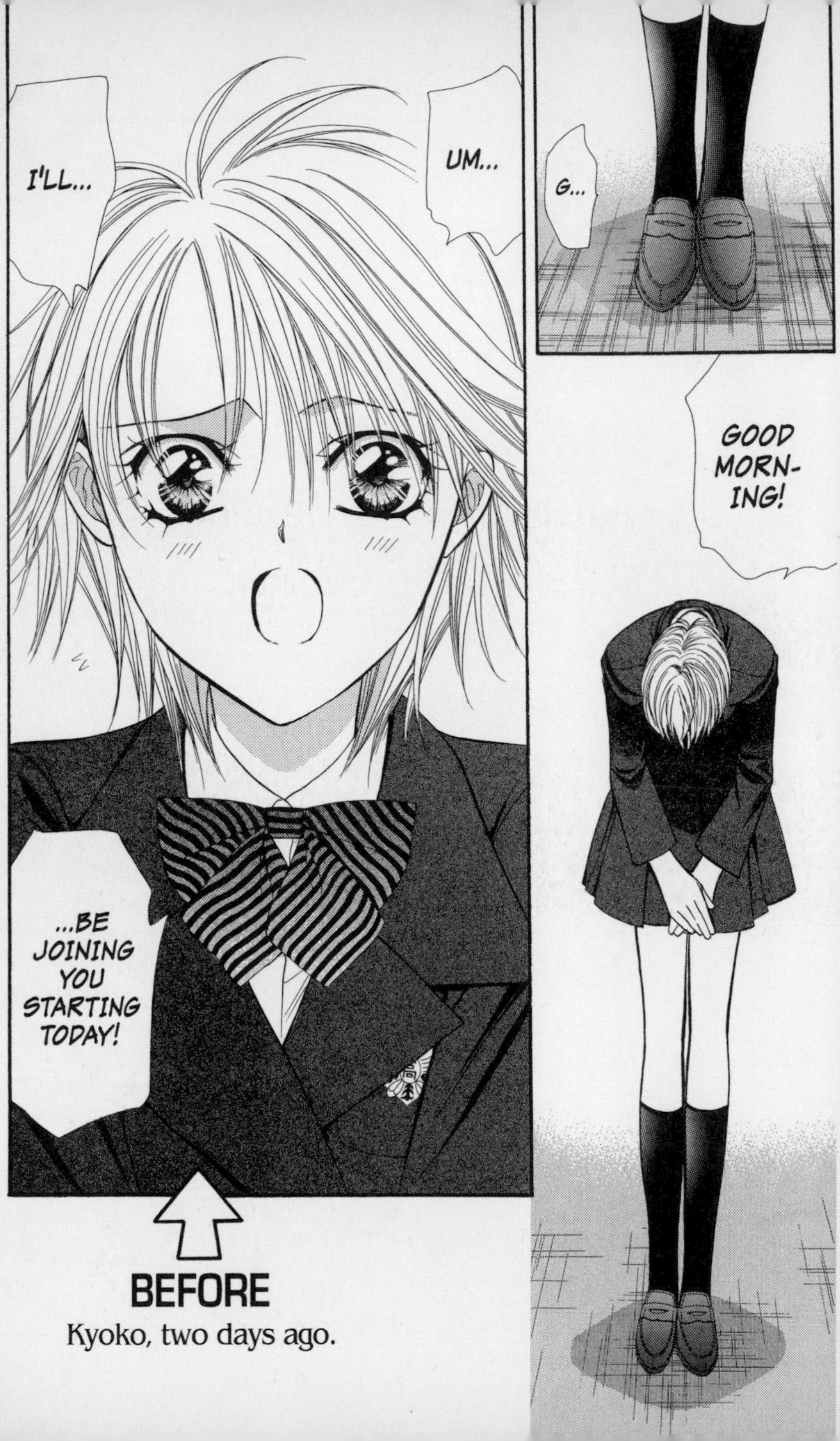
G...
GOOD MORNING!
UM...
I'LL...
...BE JOINING YOU STARTING TODAY!

**BEFORE**
Kyoko, two days ago.

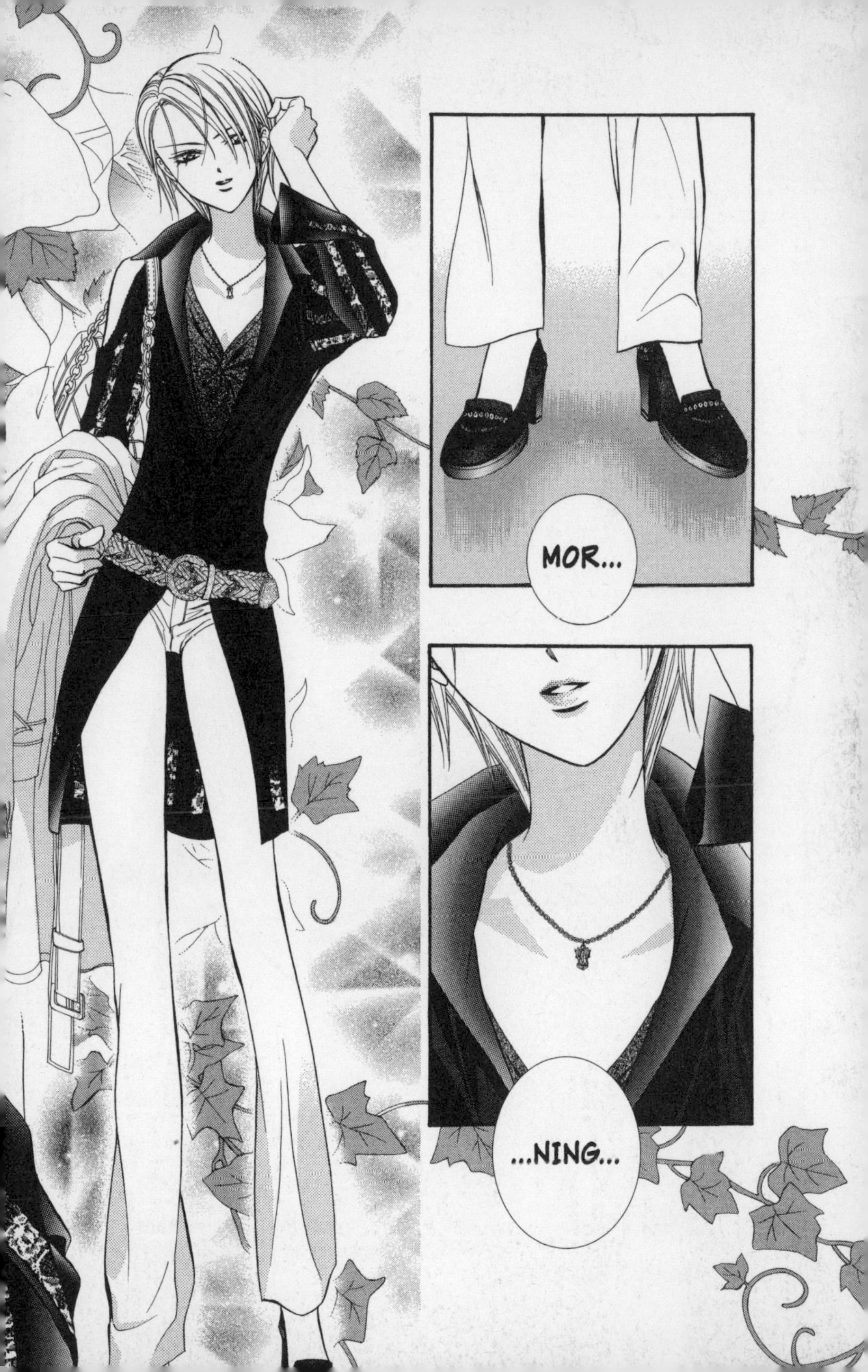
MOR...
...NING...

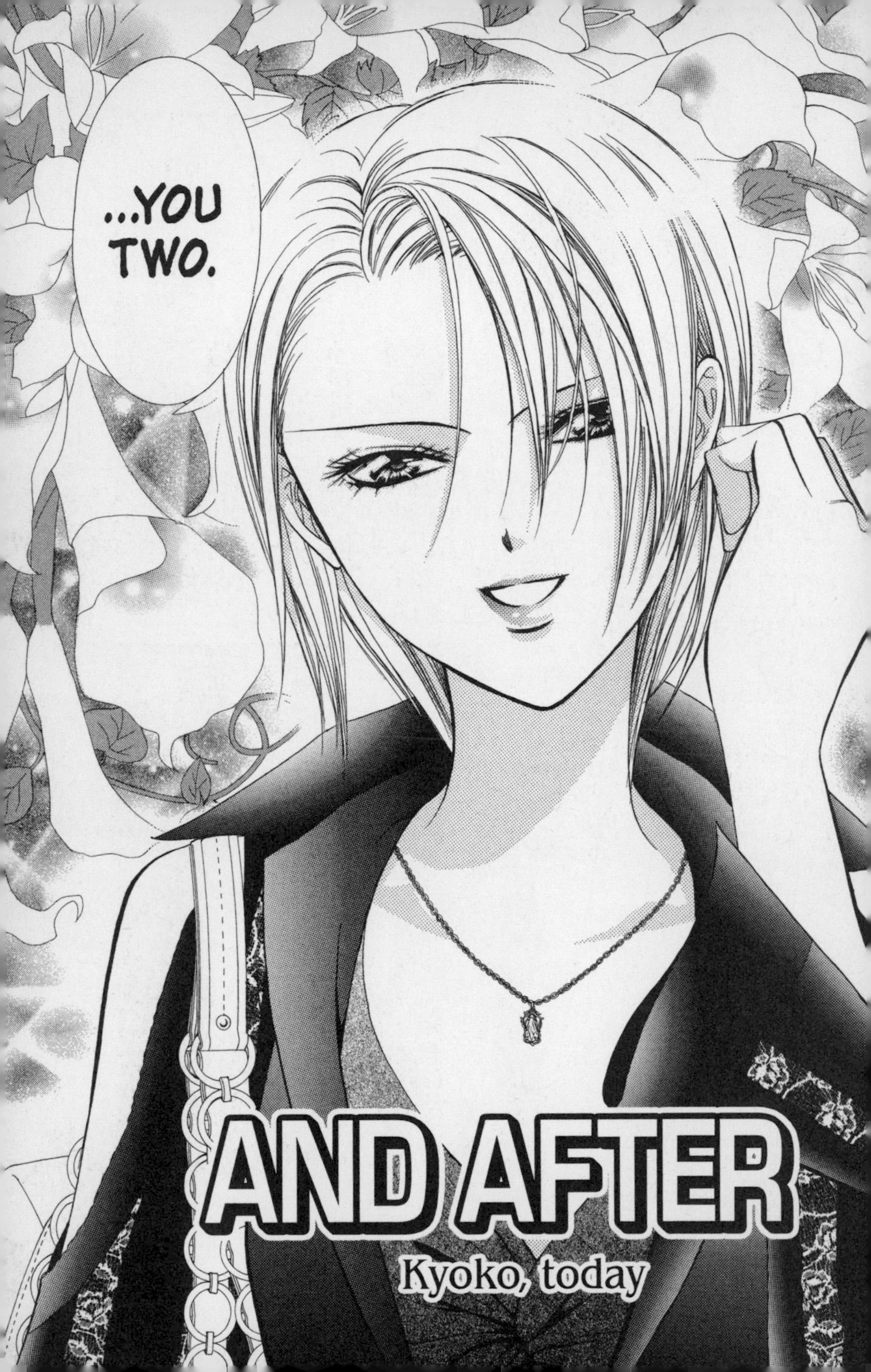
...YOU TWO.
AND AFTER
Kyoko, today

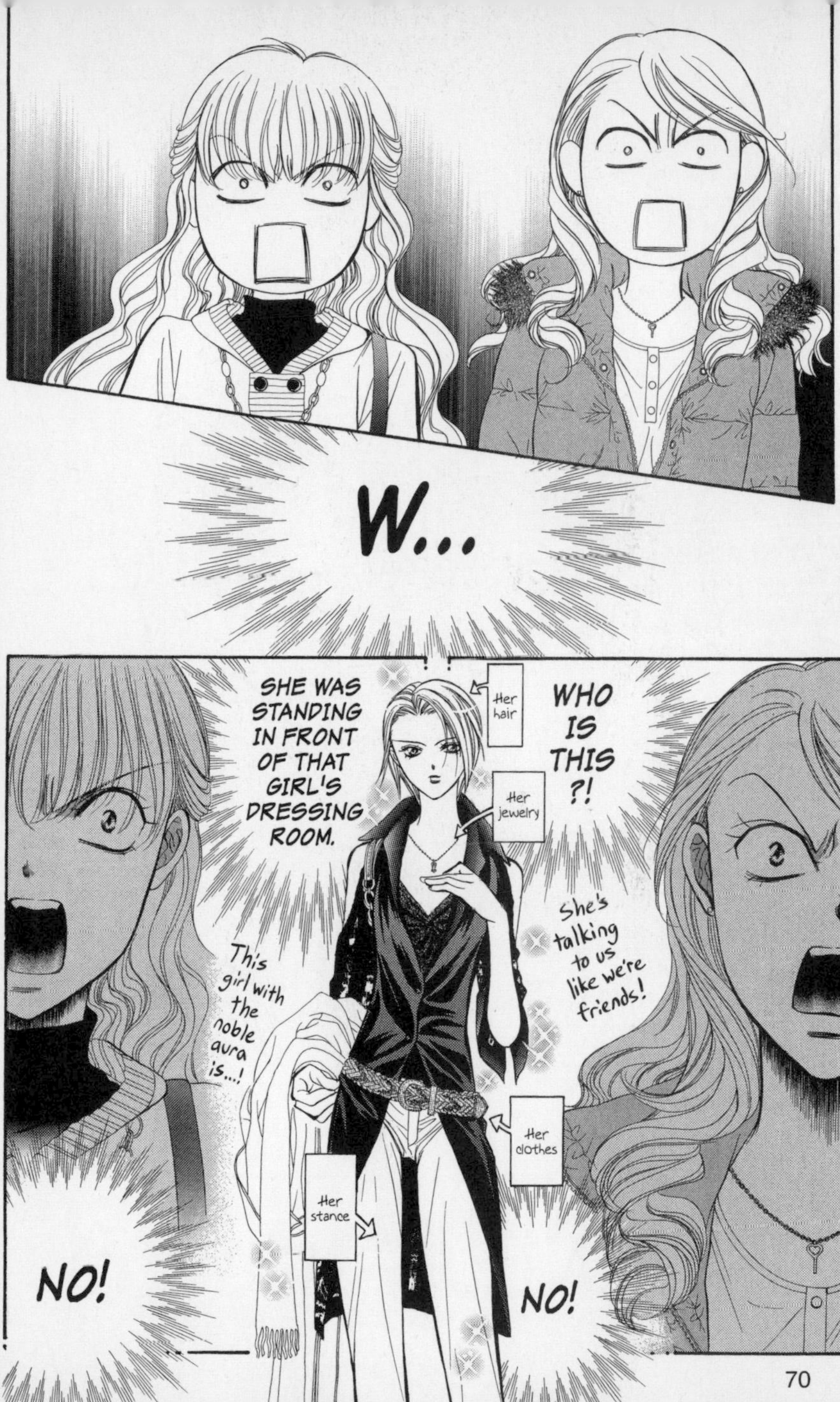
W...
WHO IS THIS ?!
Her hair
SHE WAS STANDING IN FRONT OF THAT GIRL'S DRESSING ROOM.
Her jewelry
She's talking to us like we're friends!
This girl with the noble aura is...!
Her clothes
Her stance
NO!
NO!

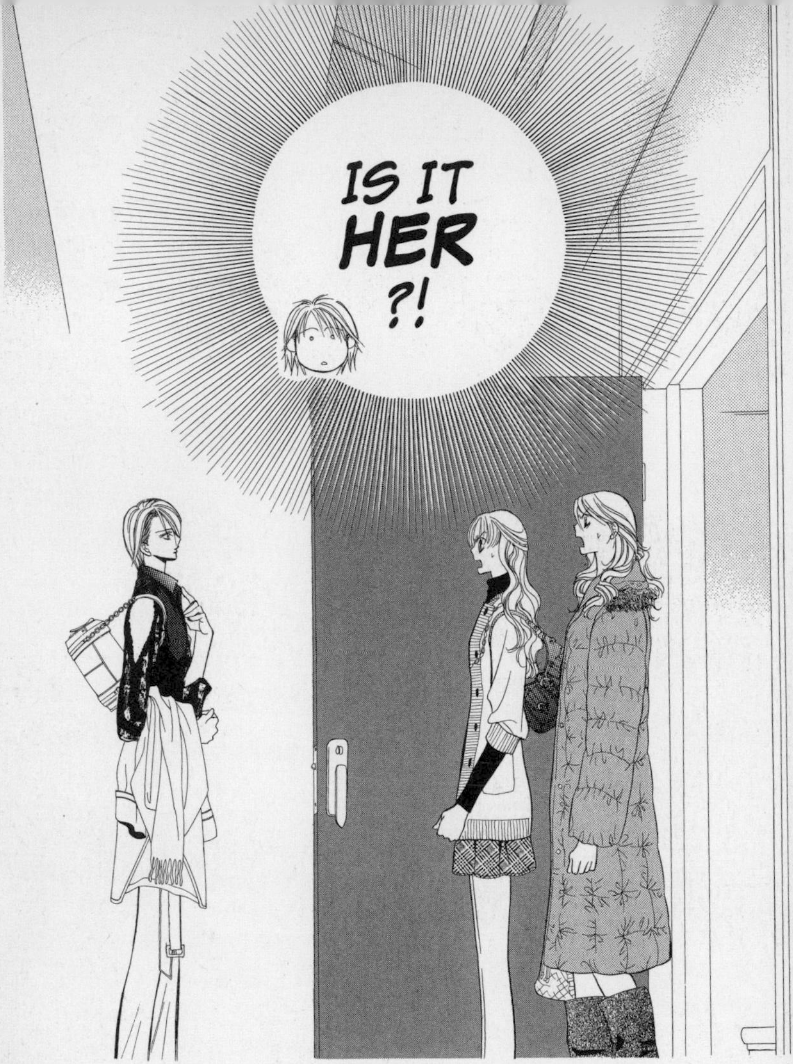
IS IT HER ?!

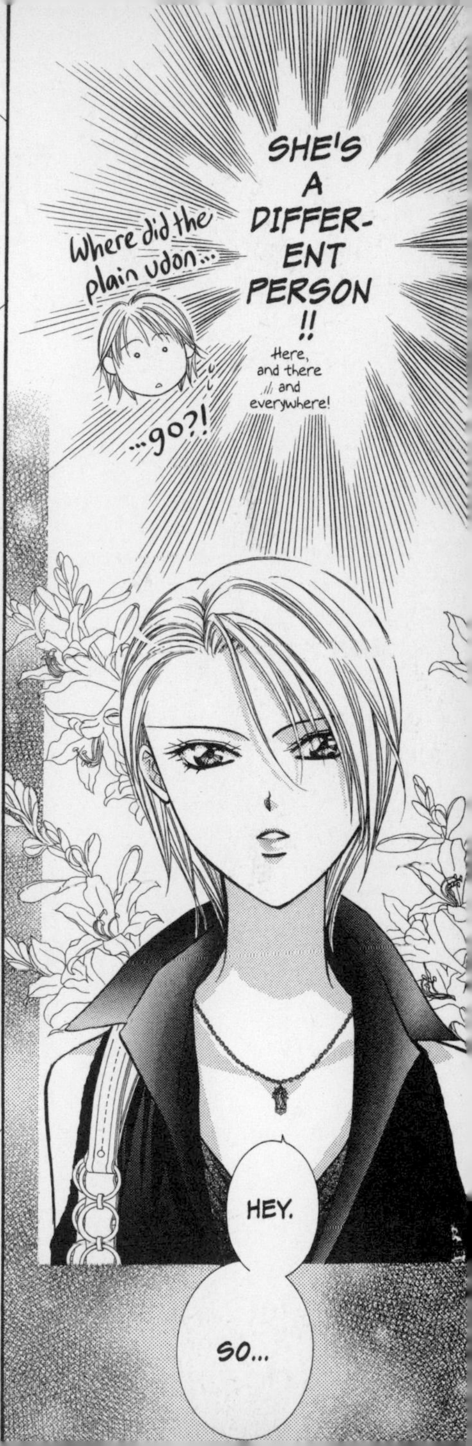
SHE'S A DIFFERENT PERSON!!
Where did the plain udon...
...go?!
Here, and there and everywhere!
HEY.
SO...

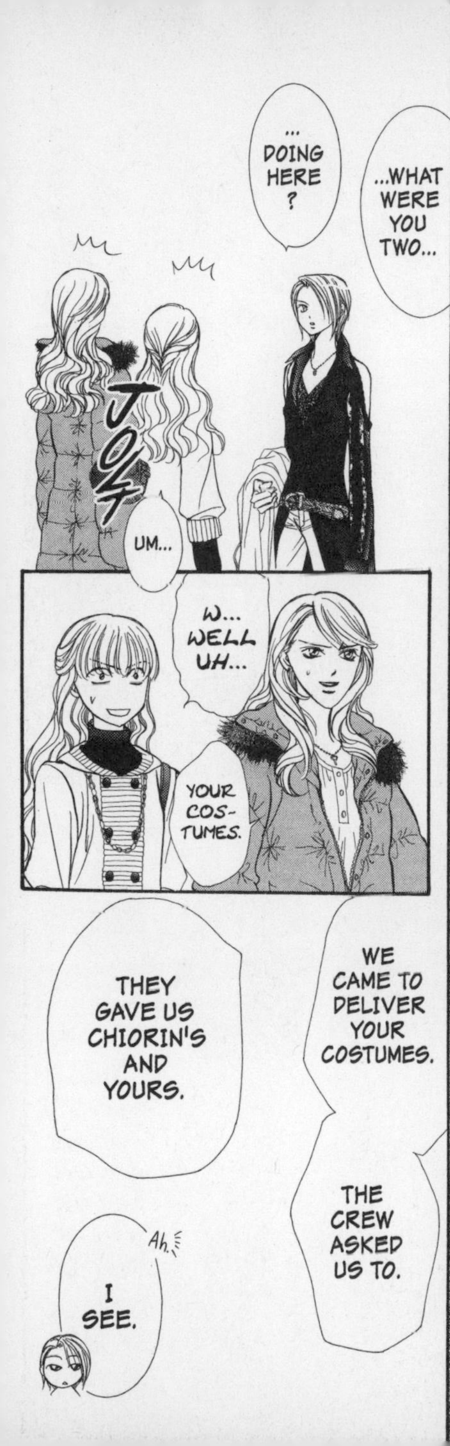
...WHAT WERE YOU TWO...
...DOING HERE?
JOLT
UM...
W... WELL UH...
YOUR COSTUMES.
WE CAME TO DELIVER YOUR COSTUMES.
THEY GAVE US CHIORIN'S AND YOURS.
THE CREW ASKED US TO.
Ah.
I SEE.

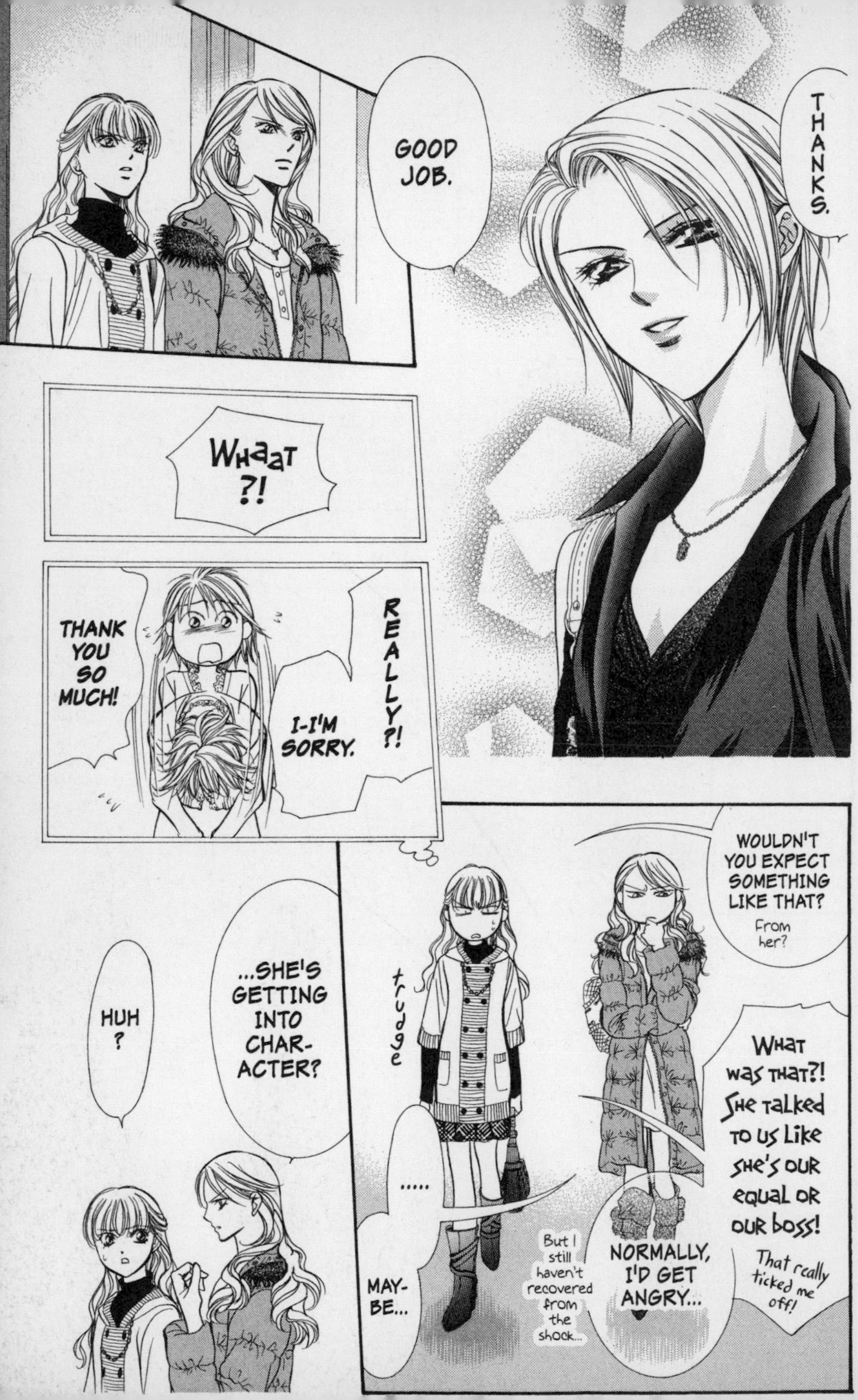
THANKS.
GOOD JOB.
Whaat?!
REALLY?!
THANK YOU SO MUCH!
I-I'M SORRY.
WOULDN'T YOU EXPECT SOMETHING LIKE THAT?
From her?
What was that?! She talked to us like she's our equal or our boss!
That really ticked me off!
NORMALLY, I'D GET ANGRY...
But I still haven't recovered from the shock...
trudge
.....
MAY-BE...
...SHE'S GETTING INTO CHAR-ACTER?
HUH?

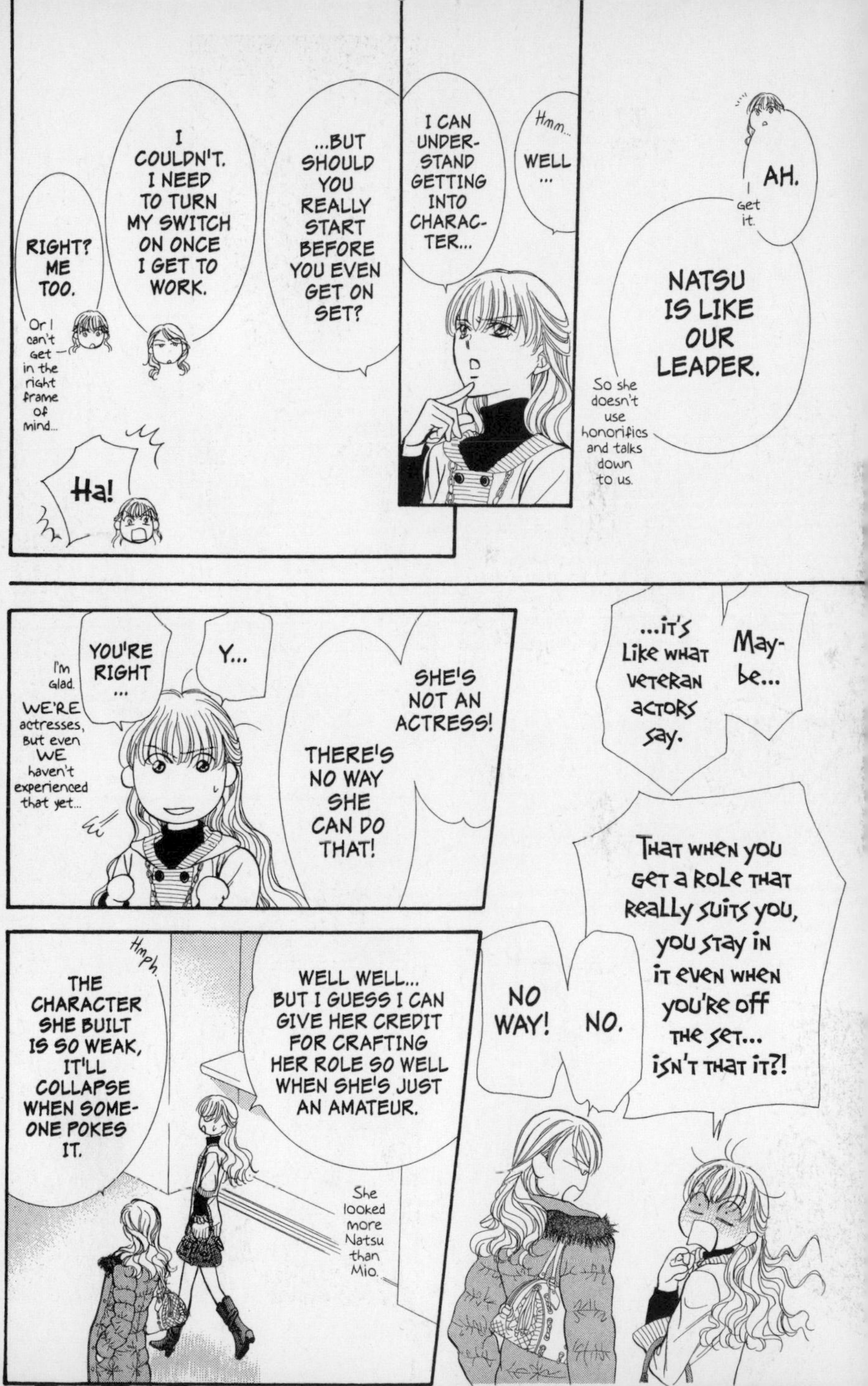
AH.
I get it.
NATSU IS LIKE OUR LEADER.
So she doesn't use honorifics and talks down to us.
Hmm...
WELL...
I CAN UNDER-STAND GETTING INTO CHARAC-TER...
...BUT SHOULD YOU REALLY START BEFORE YOU EVEN GET ON SET?
I COULDN'T. I NEED TO TURN MY SWITCH ON ONCE I GET TO WORK.
RIGHT? ME TOO.
Or I can't get in the right frame of mind...
Ha!
May-be...
...it's like what veteran actors say.
That when you get a role that really suits you, you stay in it even when you're off the set... isn't that it?!
NO.
NO WAY!
SHE'S NOT AN ACTRESS!
THERE'S NO WAY SHE CAN DO THAT!
Y...
YOU'RE RIGHT...
I'm glad. WE'RE actresses, but even WE haven't experienced that yet...
WELL WELL... BUT I GUESS I CAN GIVE HER CREDIT FOR CRAFTING HER ROLE SO WELL WHEN SHE'S JUST AN AMATEUR.
Hmph.
THE CHARACTER SHE BUILT IS SO WEAK, IT'LL COLLAPSE WHEN SOME-ONE POKES IT.
She looked more Natsu than Mio.

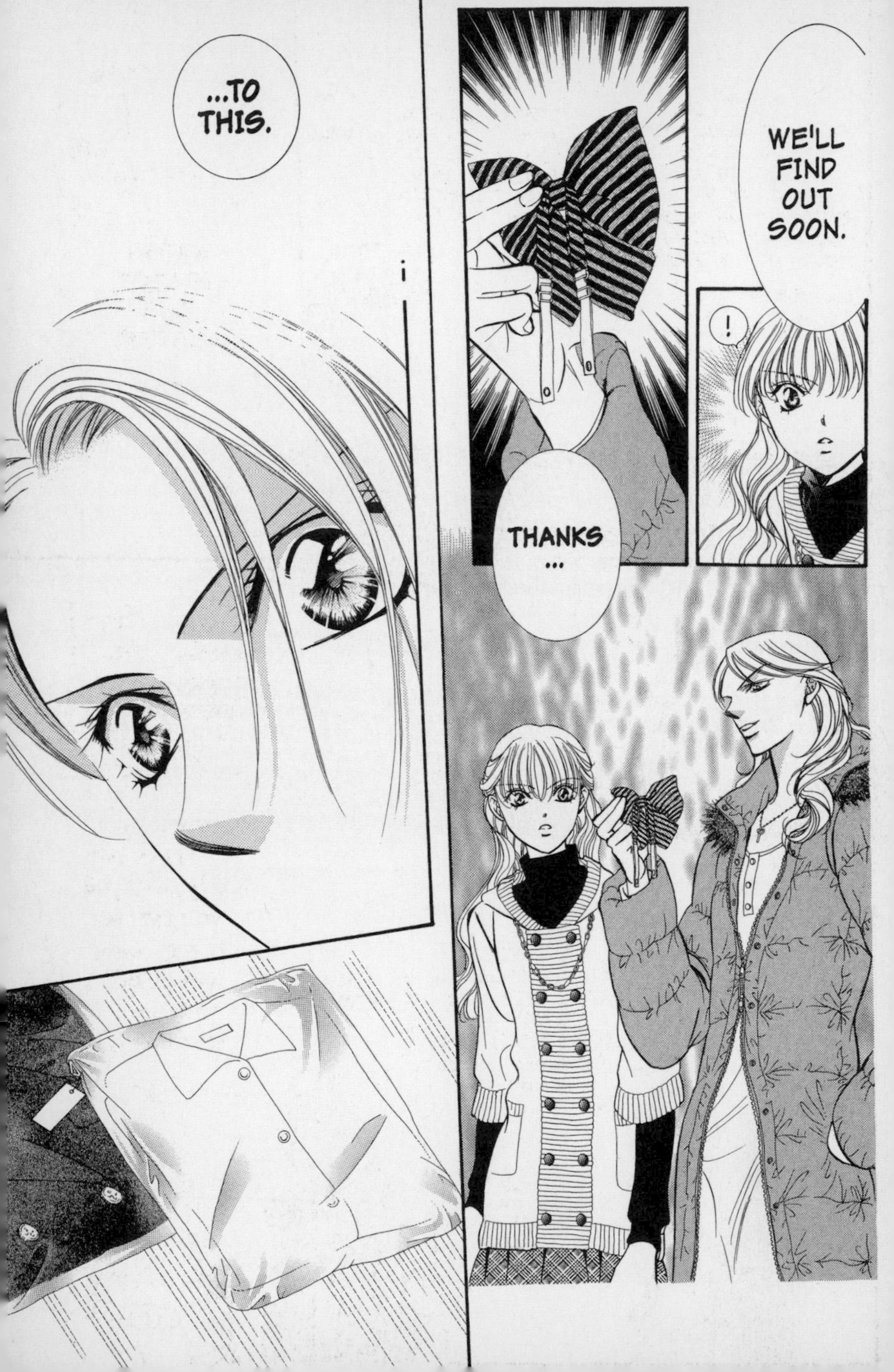
WE'LL FIND OUT SOON.
!
THANKS ...
...TO THIS.

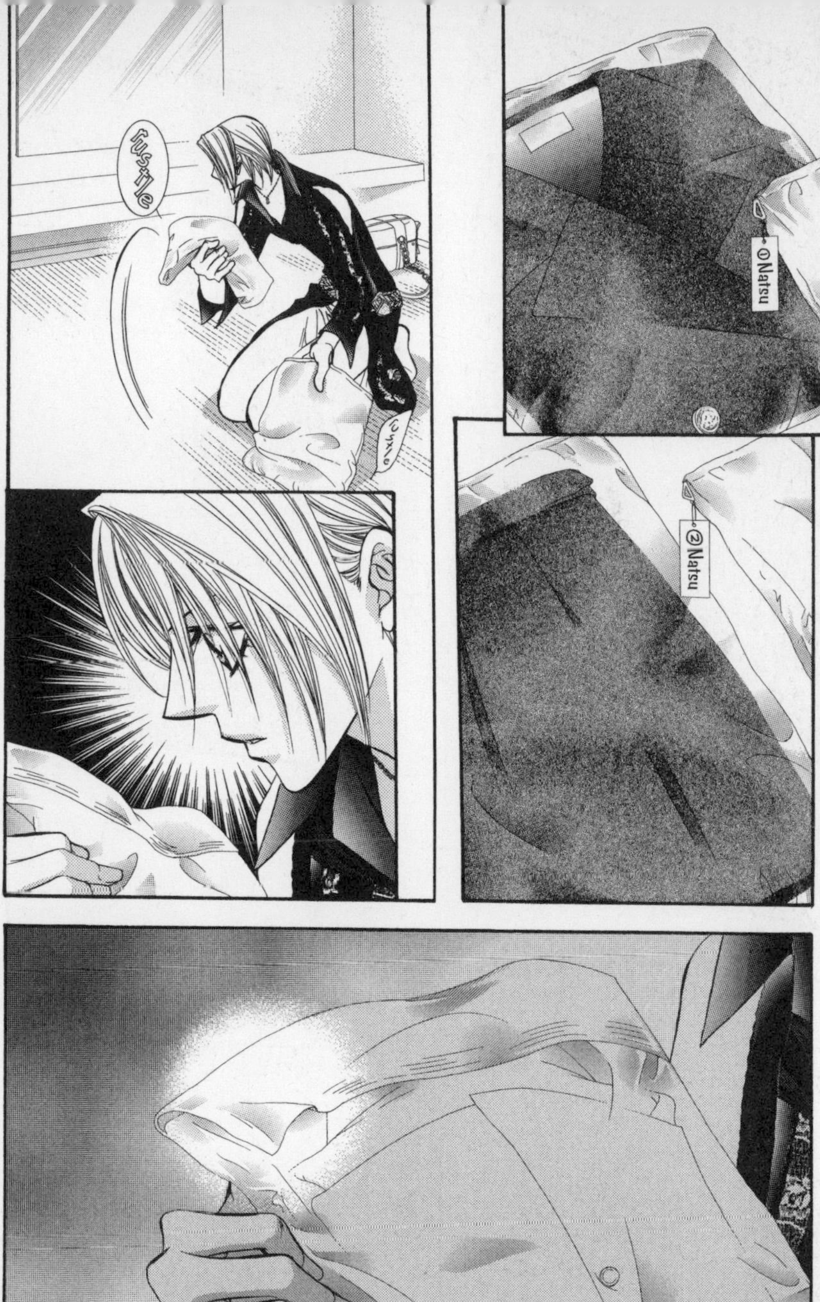
①Natsu
rustle
rustle
②Natsu

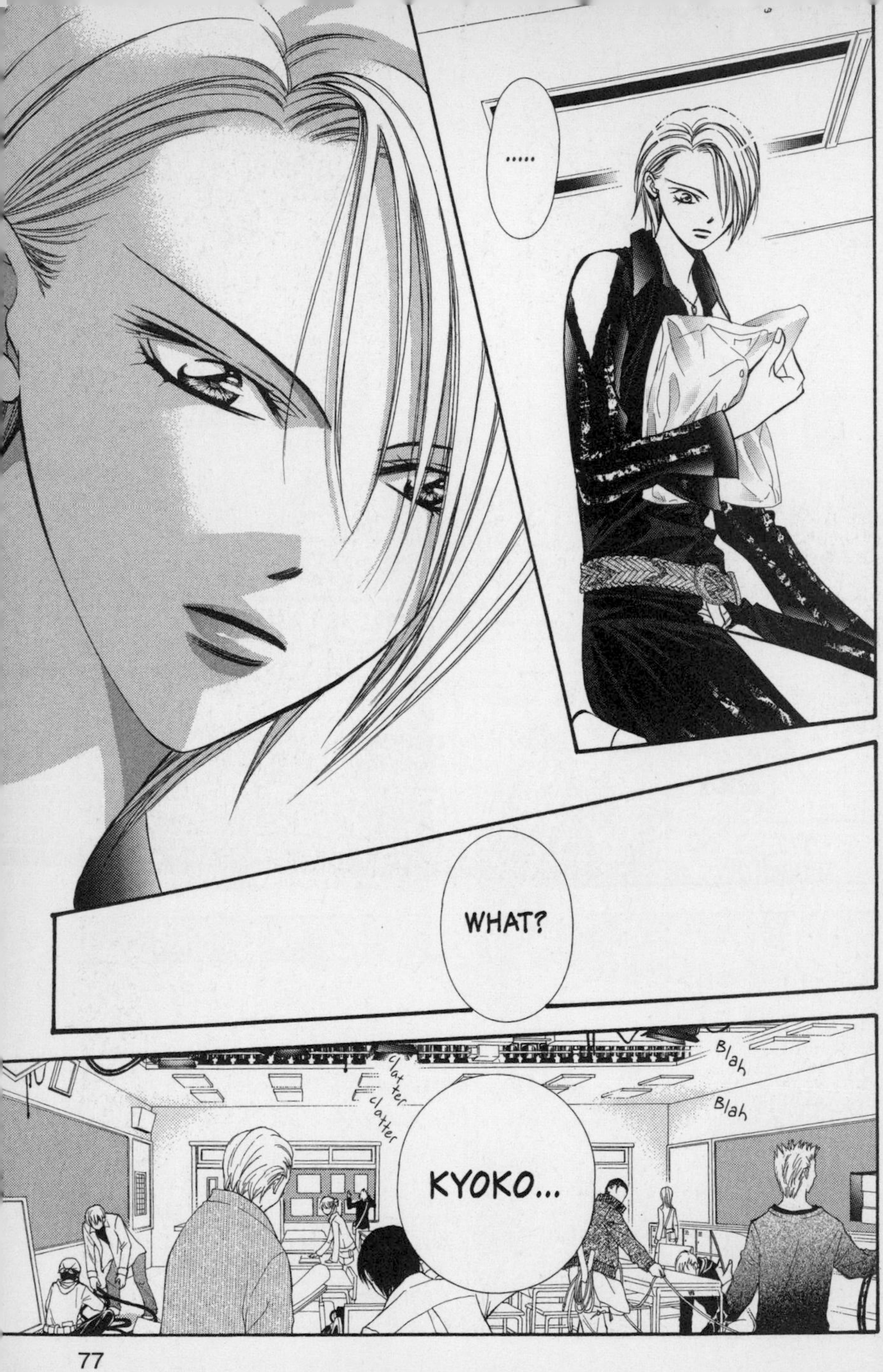
.....
WHAT?
Blah
Blah
clatter
clatter
KYOKO...

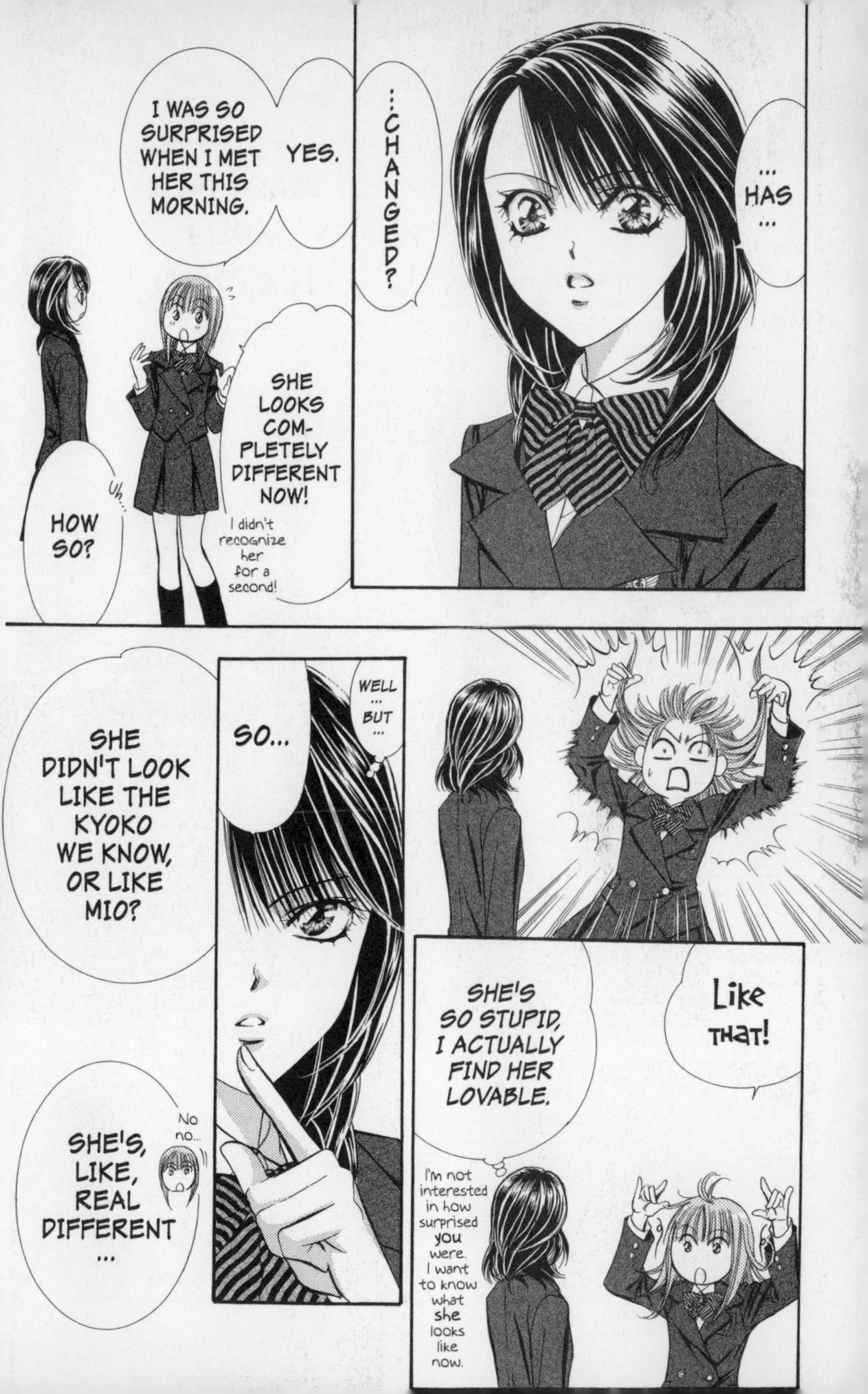
... HAS ...
...CHANGED?
YES.
I WAS SO SURPRISED WHEN I MET HER THIS MORNING.
SHE LOOKS COM-PLETELY DIFFERENT NOW!
I didn't recognize her for a second!
Uh...
HOW SO?
Like THAT!
SHE'S SO STUPID, I ACTUALLY FIND HER LOVABLE.
I'm not interested in how surprised you were. I want to know what she looks like now.
WELL ... BUT ...
SO...
SHE DIDN'T LOOK LIKE THE KYOKO WE KNOW, OR LIKE MIO?
SHE'S, LIKE, REAL DIFFERENT ...
No no...

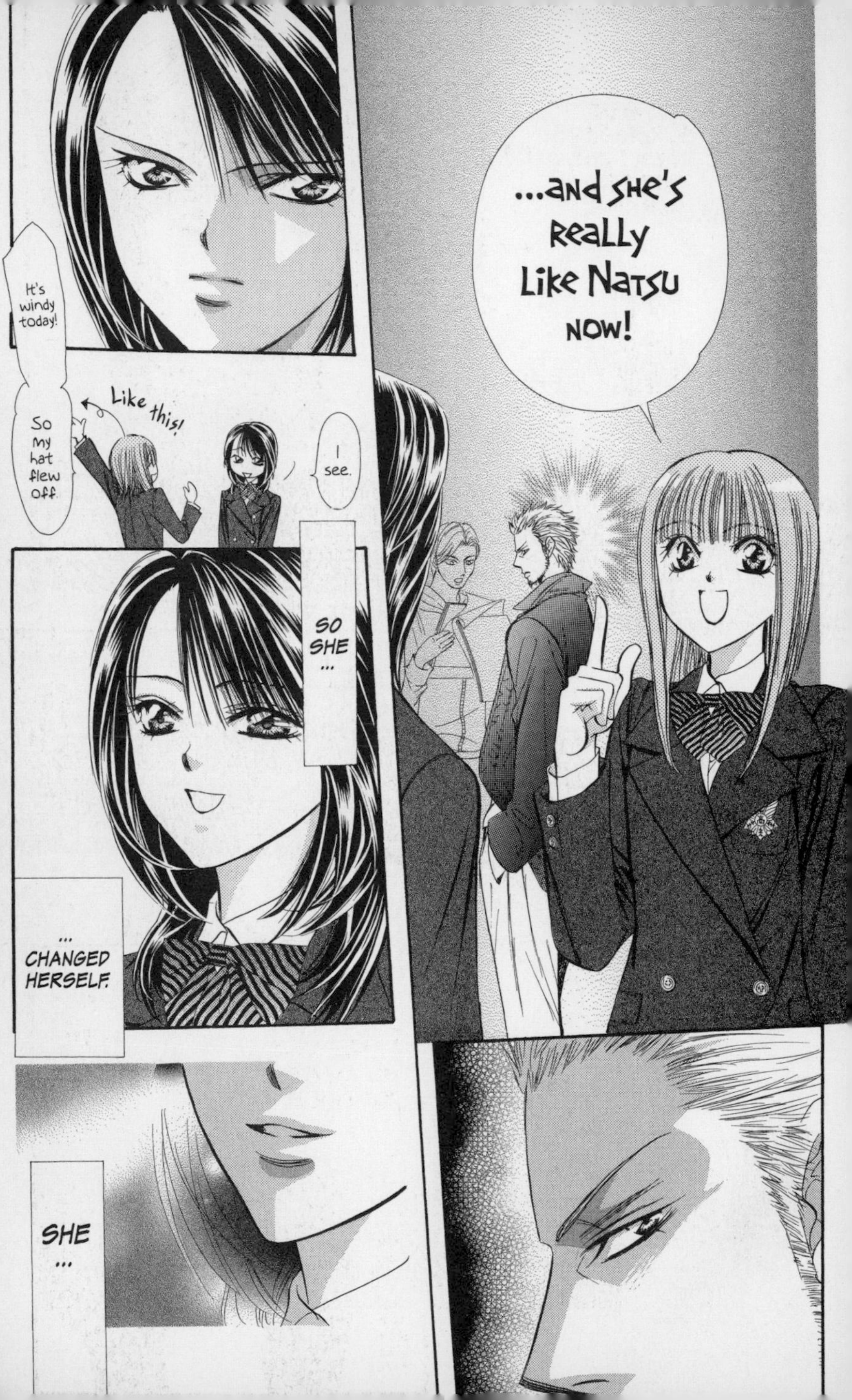
...and she's really like Natsu now!
It's windy today!
So my hat flew off.
Like this!
I see.
So she ...
... changed herself.
She ...

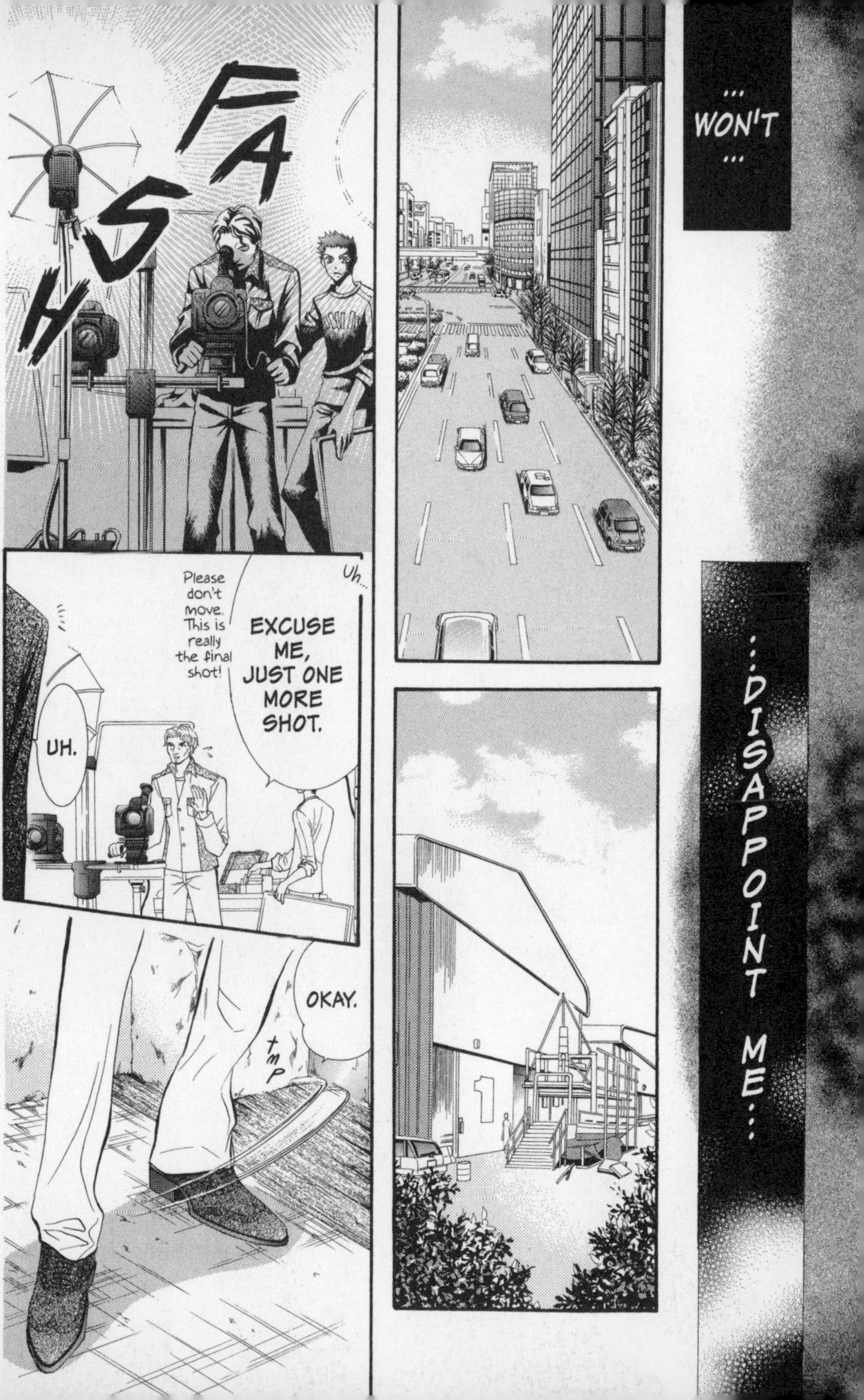
...WON'T...
...DISAPPOINT ME...
FASH
Uh...
EXCUSE ME, JUST ONE MORE SHOT.
Please don't move. This is really the final shot!
UH.
OKAY.
tmp

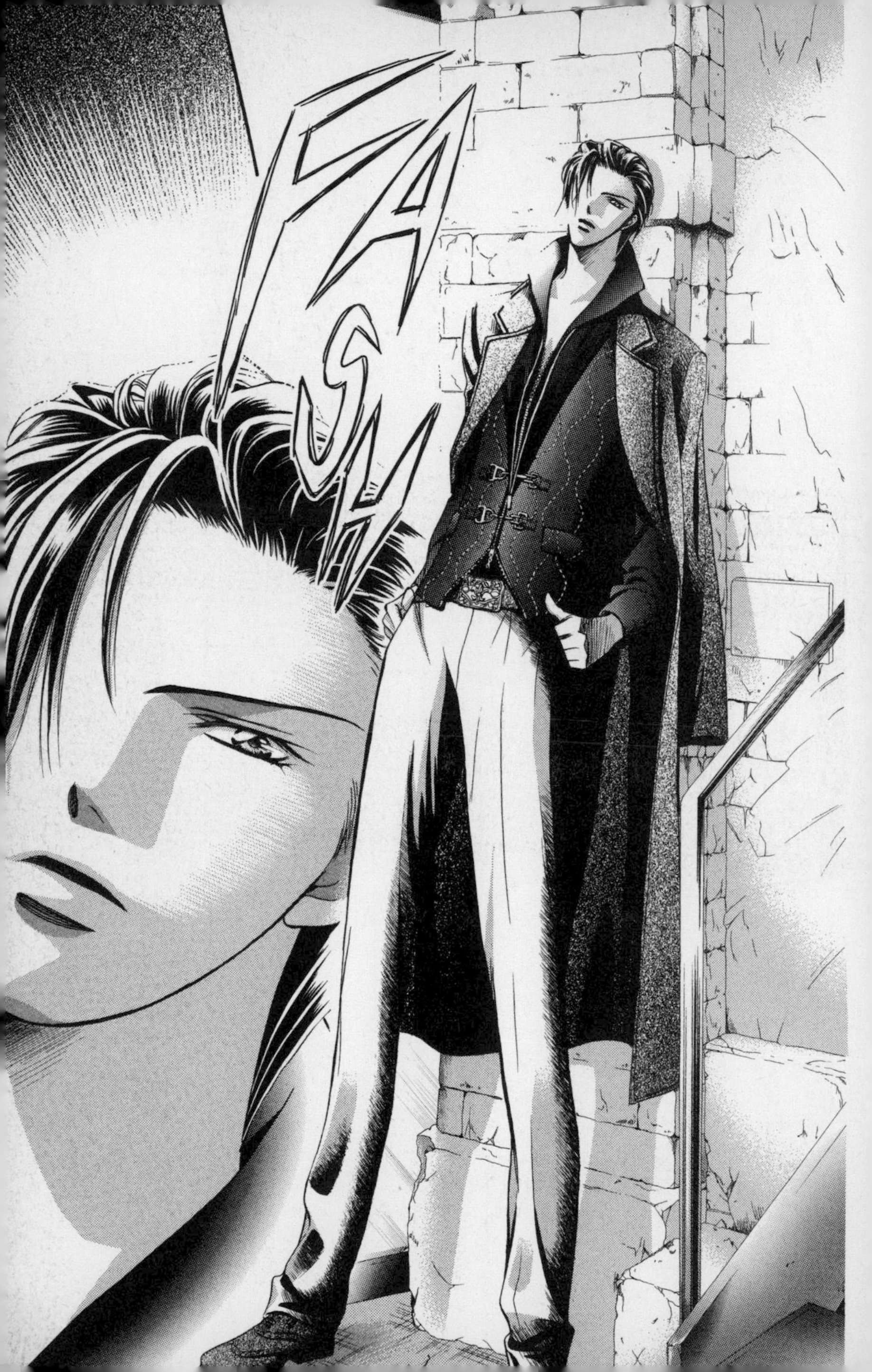
FASH

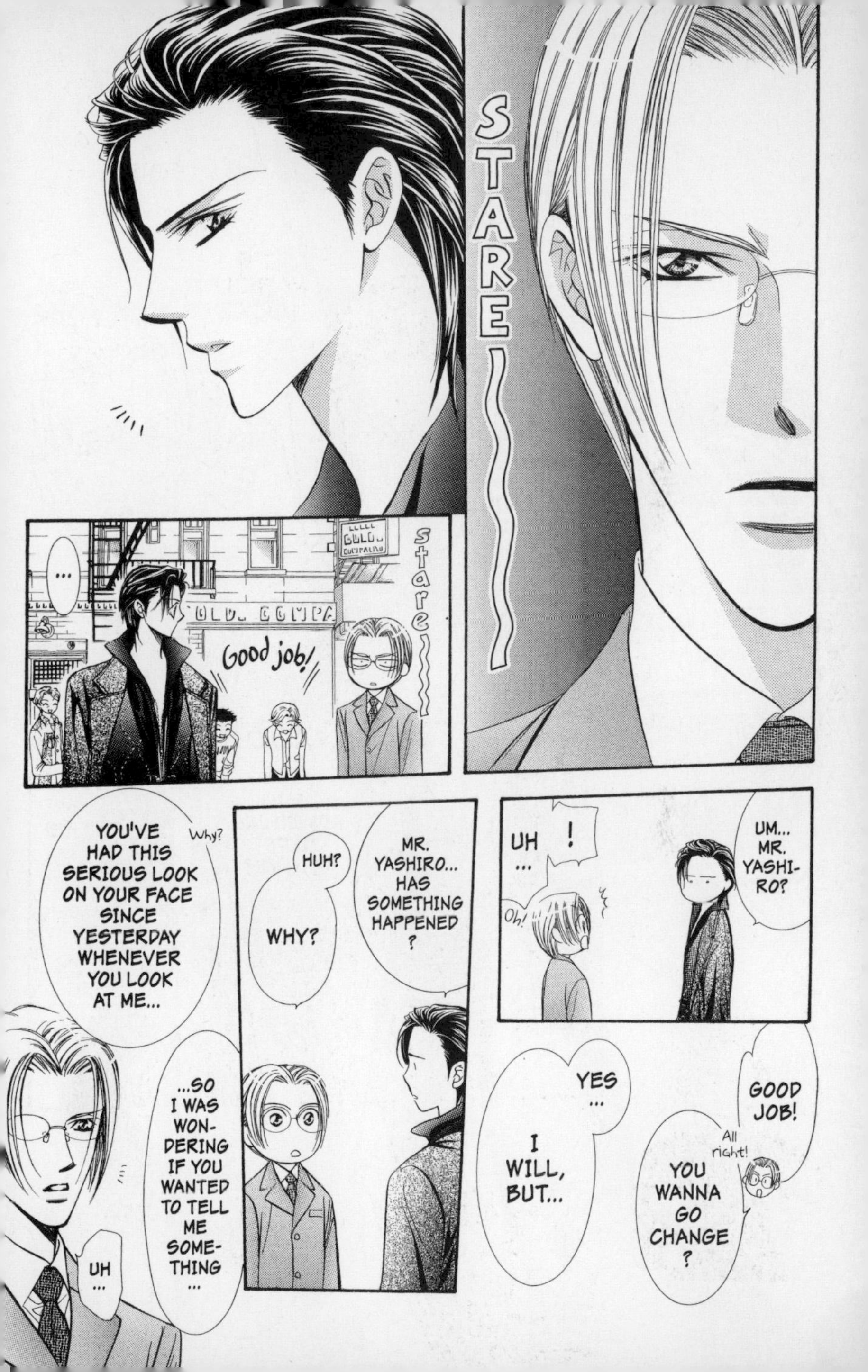
STARE~
...
Good job!
stare~
UM... MR. YASHIRO?
UH ...
!
Oh!
GOOD JOB!
All right!
YOU WANNA GO CHANGE?
YES ...
I WILL, BUT...
MR. YASHIRO... HAS SOMETHING HAPPENED?
HUH?
WHY?
YOU'VE HAD THIS SERIOUS LOOK ON YOUR FACE SINCE YESTERDAY WHENEVER YOU LOOK AT ME...
Why?
...SO I WAS WONDERING IF YOU WANTED TO TELL ME SOMETHING ...
UH ...

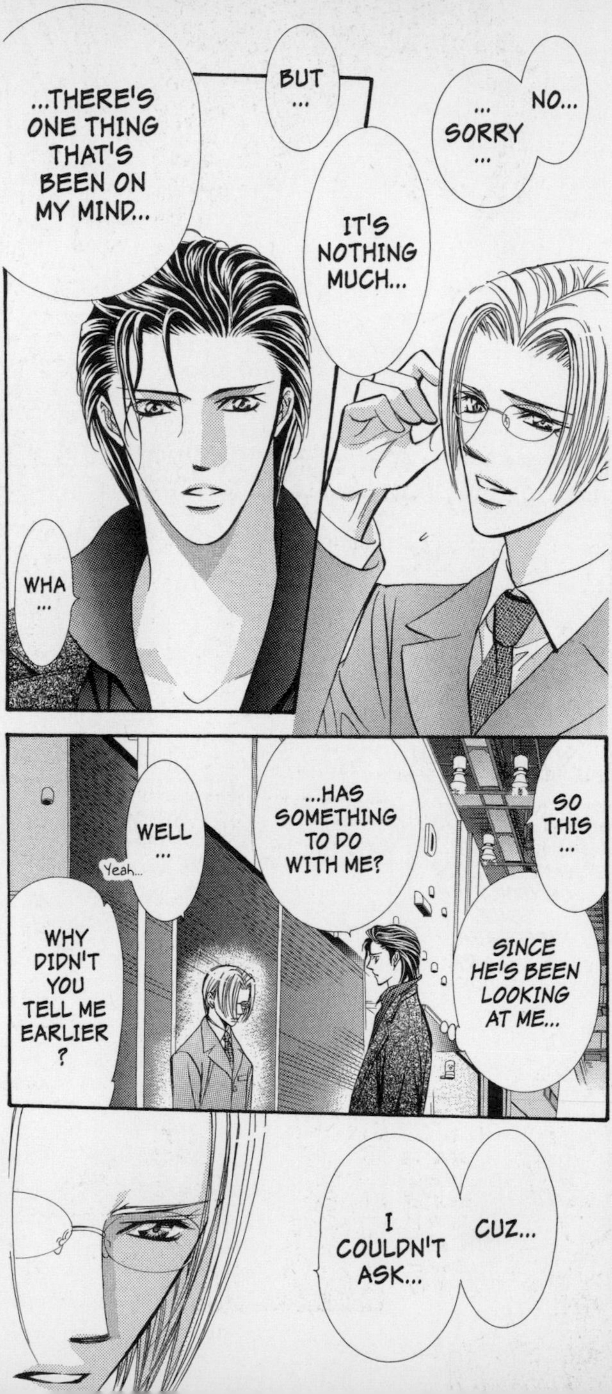
NO... ...SORRY...
IT'S NOTHING MUCH...
BUT...
...THERE'S ONE THING THAT'S BEEN ON MY MIND...
WHA...
SO THIS...
SINCE HE'S BEEN LOOKING AT ME...
...HAS SOMETHING TO DO WITH ME?
WELL...
Yeah...
WHY DIDN'T YOU TELL ME EARLIER?
CUZ...
I COULDN'T ASK...

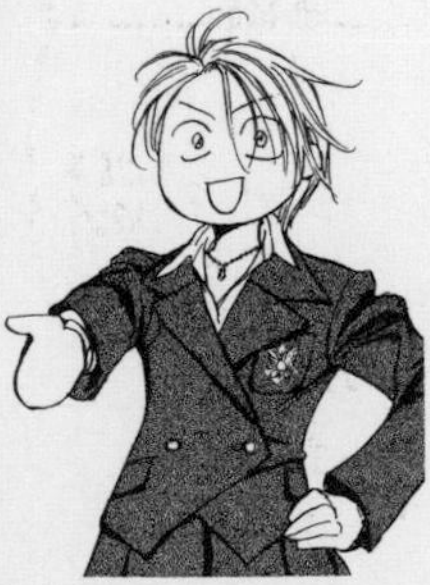

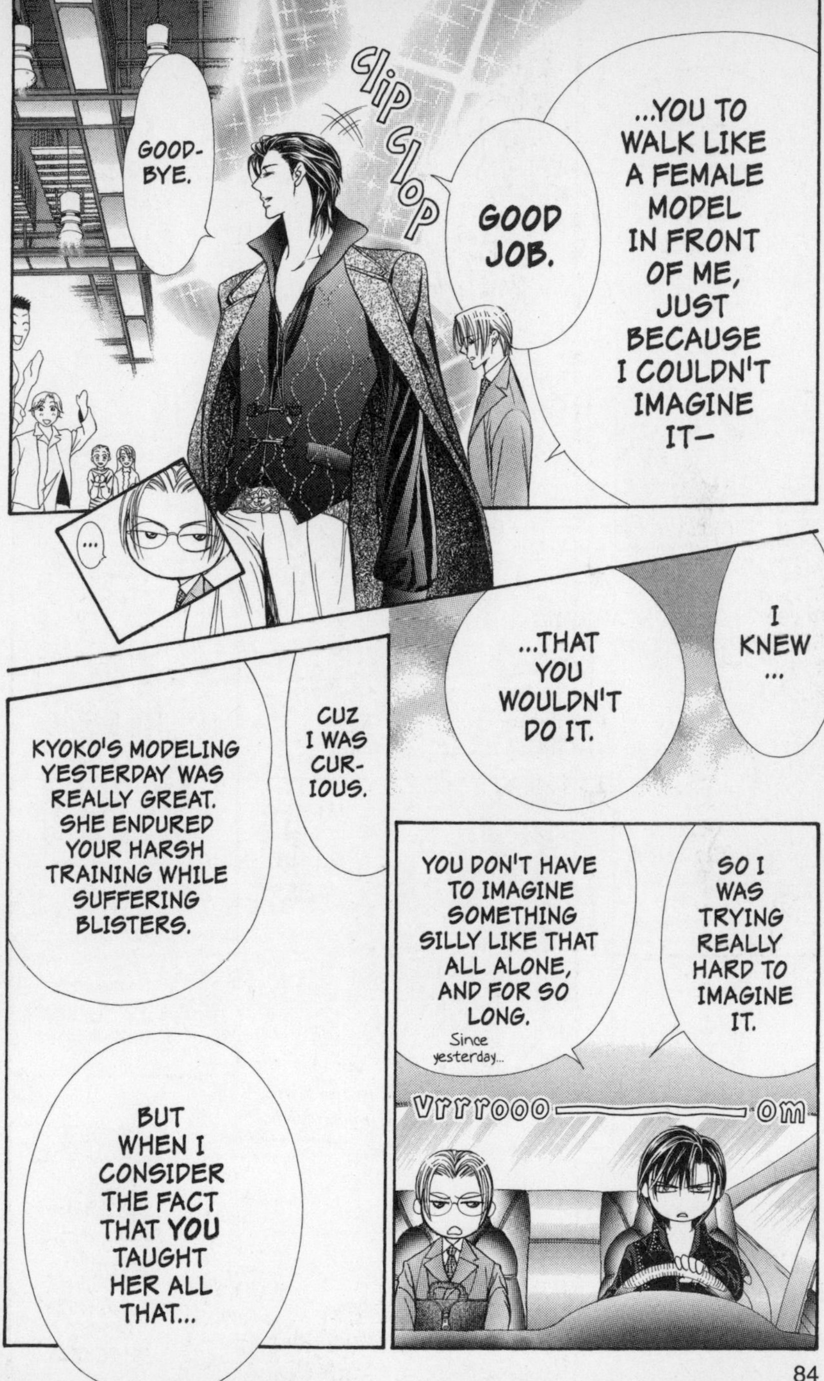
...YOU TO WALK LIKE A FEMALE MODEL IN FRONT OF ME, JUST BECAUSE I COULDN'T IMAGINE IT—
GOOD JOB.
CLIP CLOP
GOOD-BYE.
...
I KNEW...
...THAT YOU WOULDN'T DO IT.
SO I WAS TRYING REALLY HARD TO IMAGINE IT.
YOU DON'T HAVE TO IMAGINE SOMETHING SILLY LIKE THAT ALL ALONE, AND FOR SO LONG.
Since yesterday...
VRRROOO————OM
CUZ I WAS CURIOUS.
KYOKO'S MODELING YESTERDAY WAS REALLY GREAT. SHE ENDURED YOUR HARSH TRAINING WHILE SUFFERING BLISTERS.
BUT WHEN I CONSIDER THE FACT THAT YOU TAUGHT HER ALL THAT...

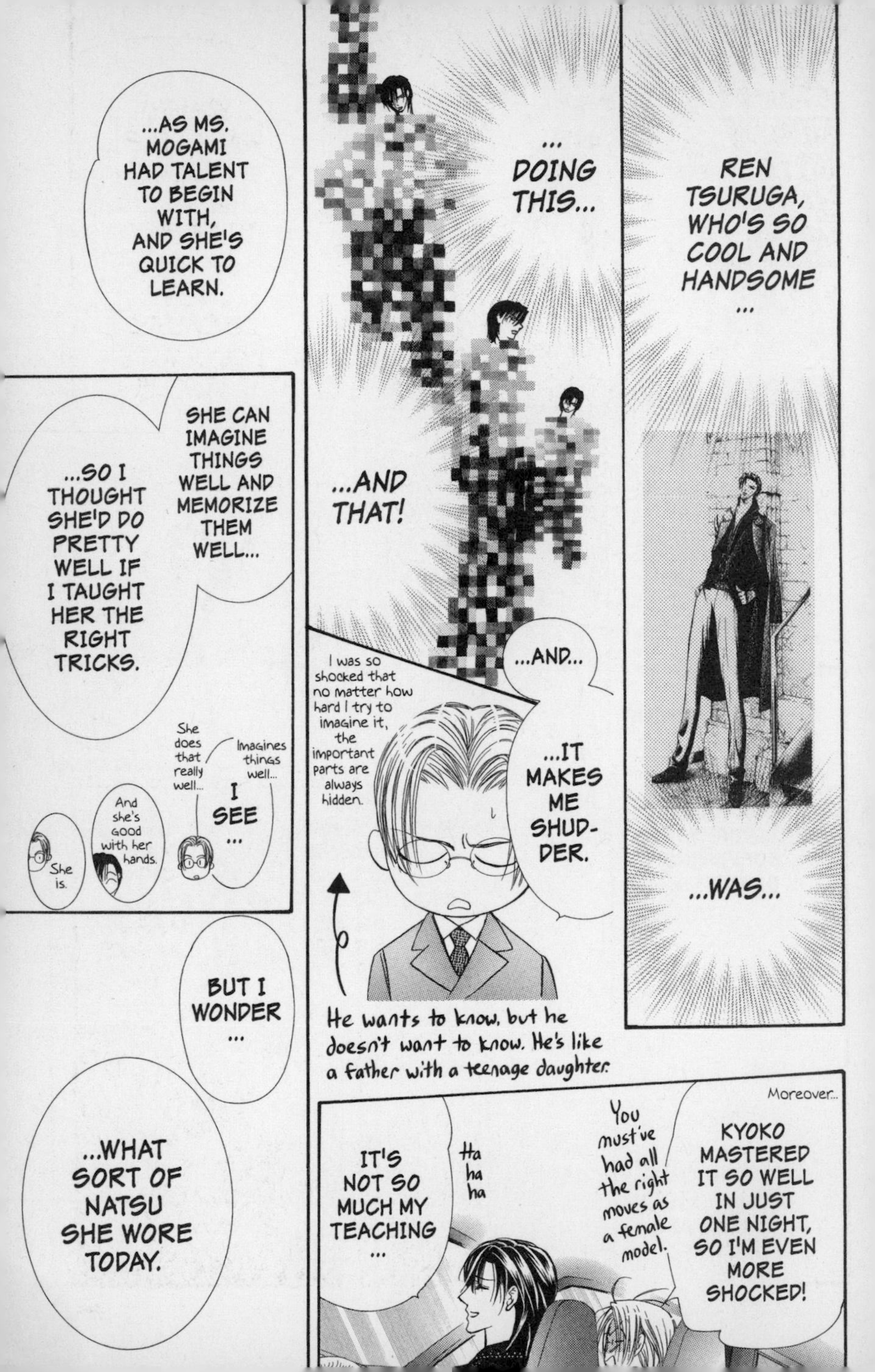
REN TSURUGA, WHO'S SO COOL AND HANDSOME ...
...WAS...
... DOING THIS...
...AND THAT!
...AND...
...IT MAKES ME SHUD-DER.
I was so shocked that no matter how hard I try to imagine it, the important parts are always hidden.
He wants to know, but he doesn't want to know. He's like a father with a teenage daughter.
Moreover...
KYOKO MASTERED IT SO WELL IN JUST ONE NIGHT, SO I'M EVEN MORE SHOCKED!
You must've had all the right moves as a female model.
Ha ha ha
IT'S NOT SO MUCH MY TEACHING ...
...AS MS. MOGAMI HAD TALENT TO BEGIN WITH, AND SHE'S QUICK TO LEARN.
SHE CAN IMAGINE THINGS WELL AND MEMORIZE THEM WELL...
...SO I THOUGHT SHE'D DO PRETTY WELL IF I TAUGHT HER THE RIGHT TRICKS.
I SEE ...
Imagines things well...
She does that really well...
And she's good with her hands.
She is.
BUT I WONDER ...
...WHAT SORT OF NATSU SHE WORE TODAY.

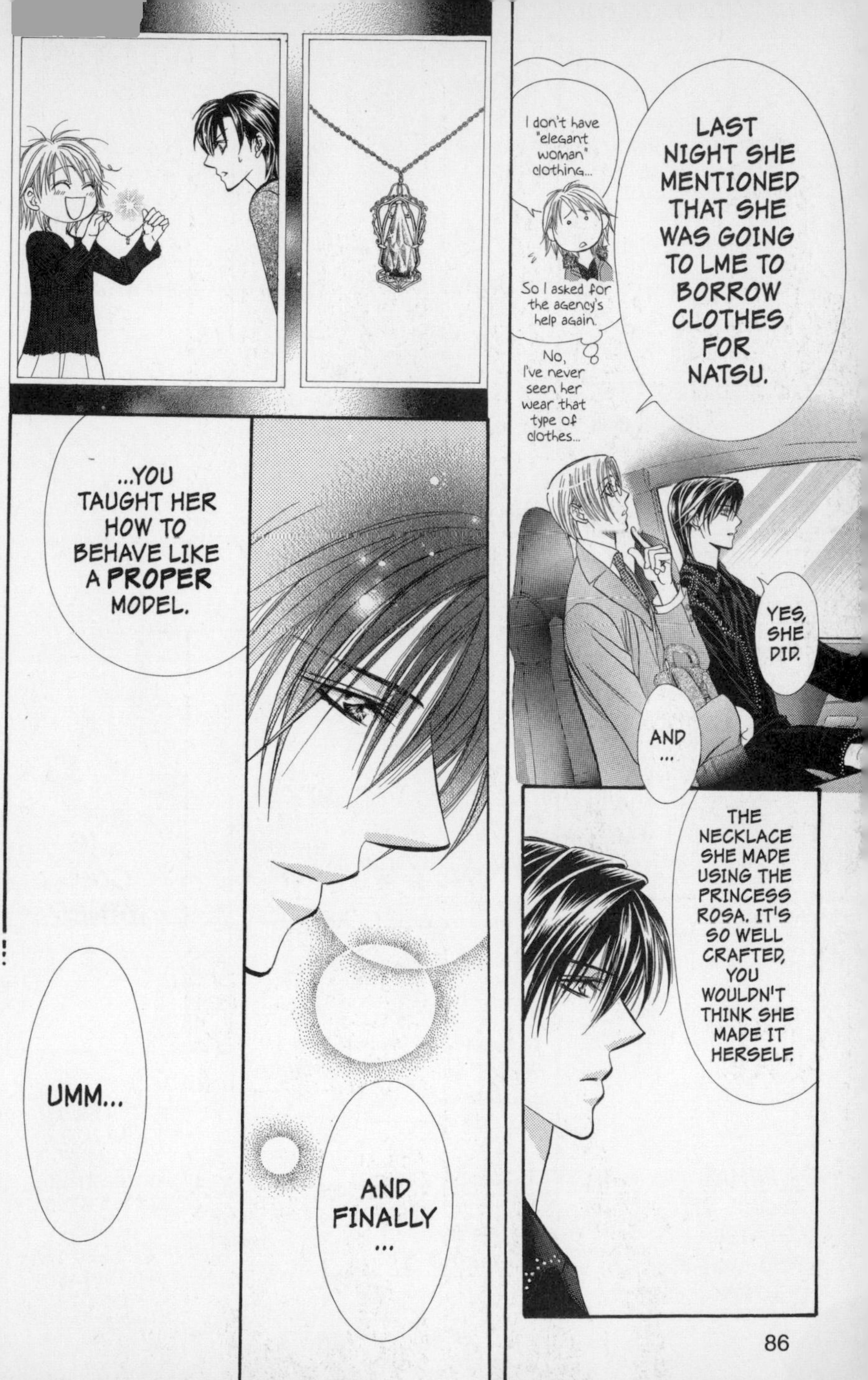
LAST NIGHT SHE MENTIONED THAT SHE WAS GOING TO LME TO BORROW CLOTHES FOR NATSU.
I don't have "elegant woman" clothing...
So I asked for the agency's help again.
No, I've never seen her wear that type of clothes...
YES, SHE DID.
AND ...
THE NECKLACE SHE MADE USING THE PRINCESS ROSA. IT'S SO WELL CRAFTED, YOU WOULDN'T THINK SHE MADE IT HERSELF.
...YOU TAUGHT HER HOW TO BEHAVE LIKE A PROPER MODEL.
AND FINALLY ...
UMM...

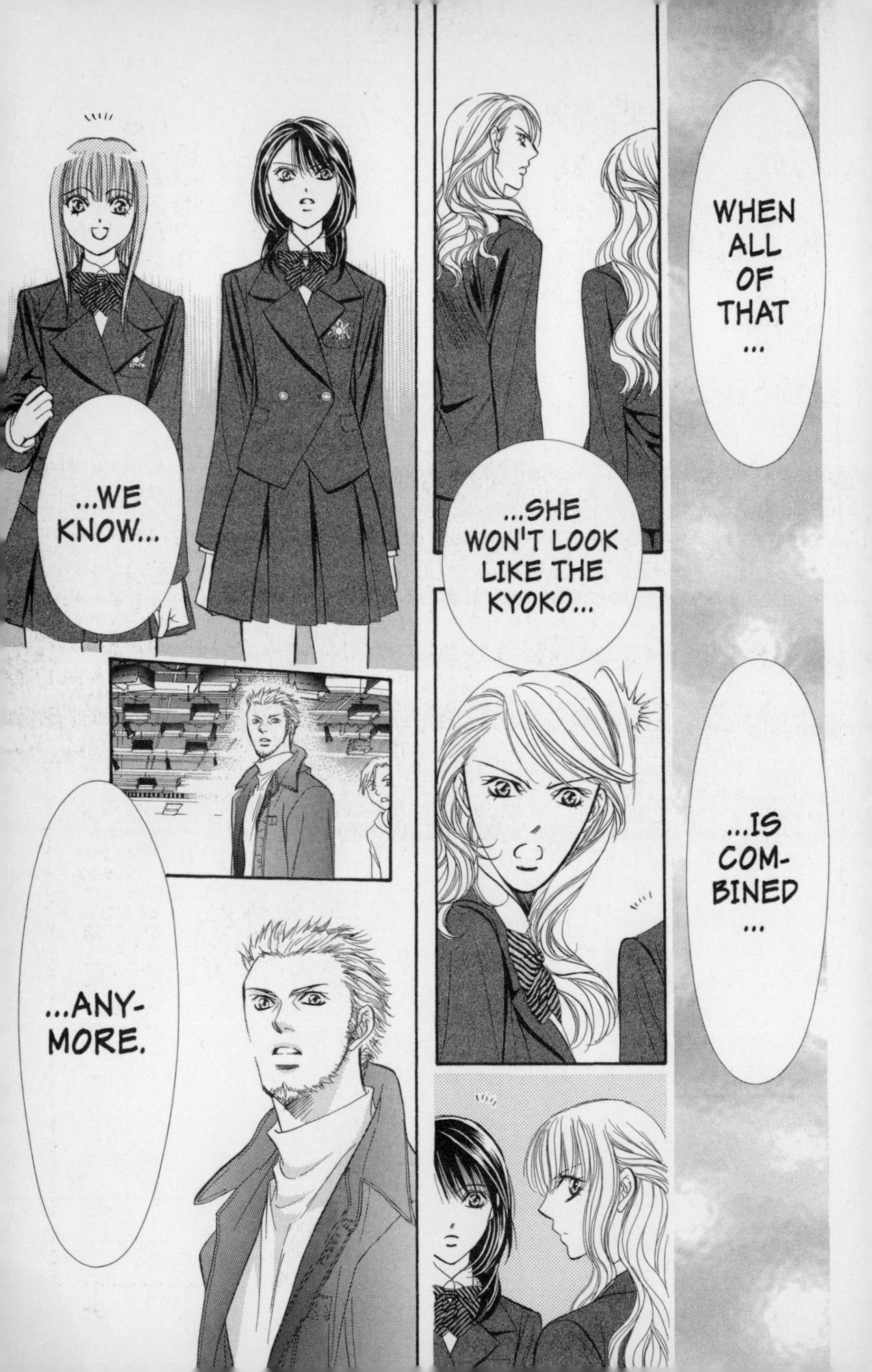
WHEN ALL OF THAT ...
...IS COM-BINED ...
...SHE WON'T LOOK LIKE THE KYOKO...
...WE KNOW...
...ANY-MORE.

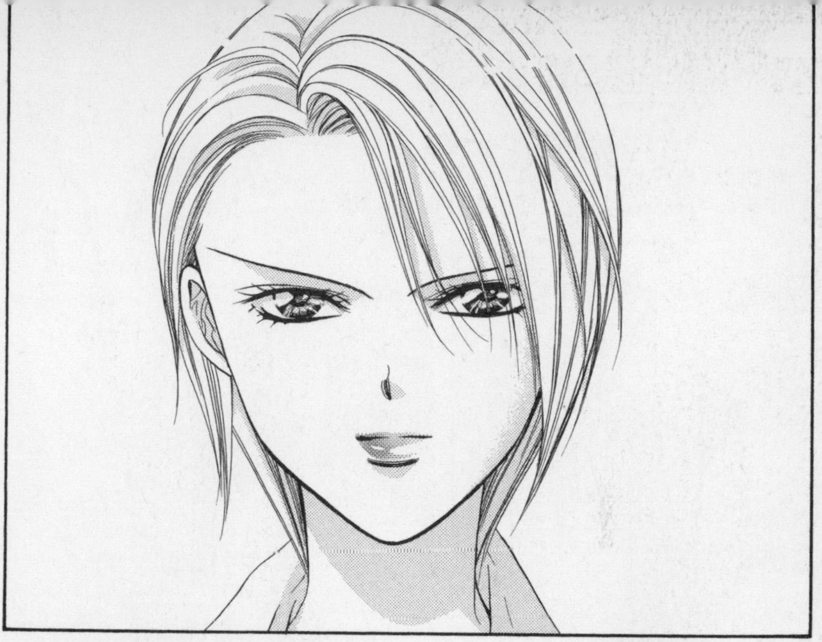
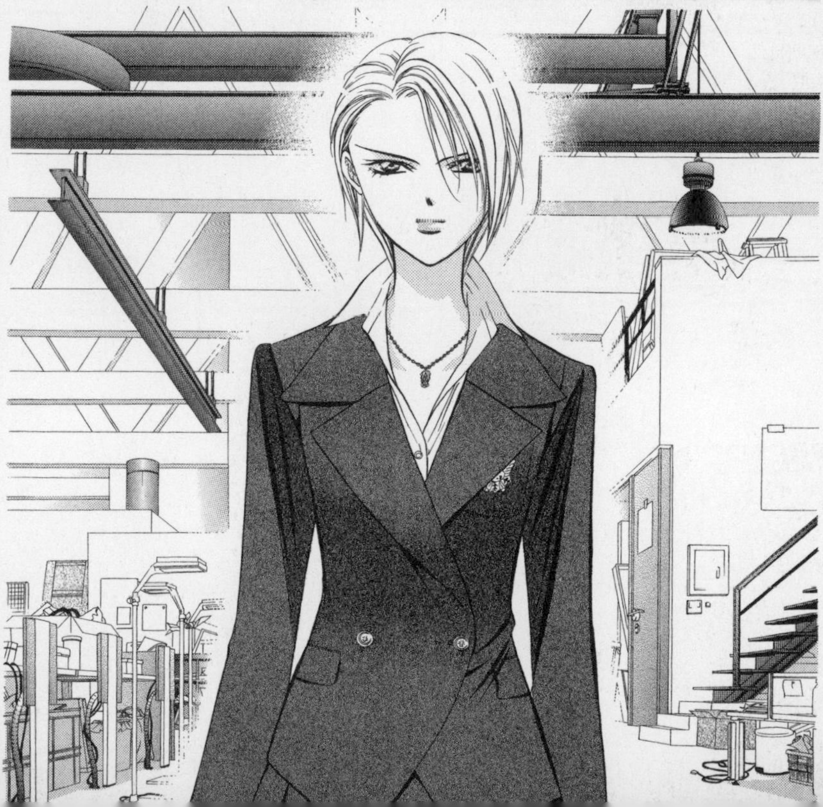

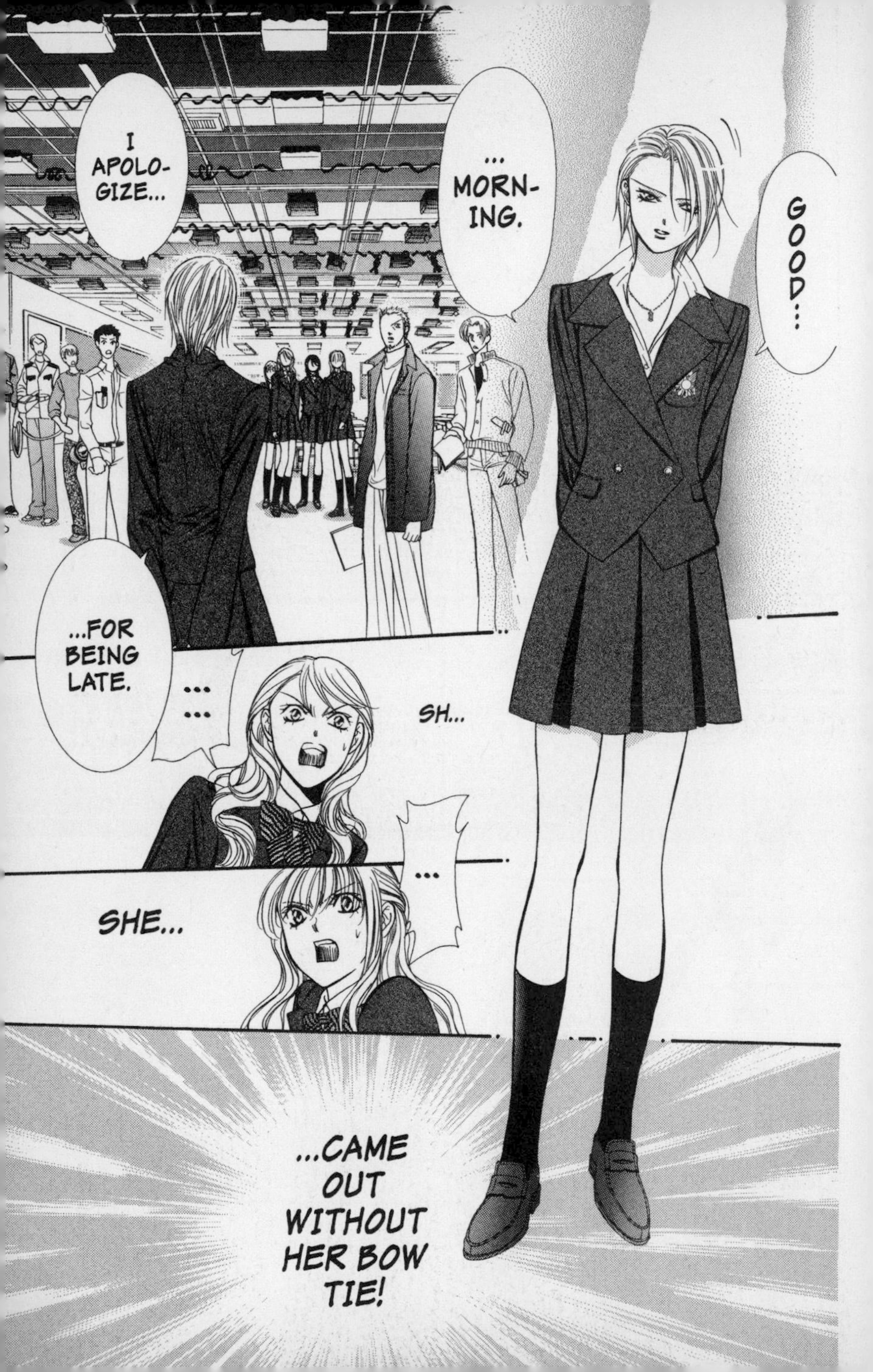
GOOD...
...MORNING.
I APOLOGIZE...
...FOR BEING LATE.
SH...
......
...
SHE...
...CAME OUT WITHOUT HER BOW TIE!

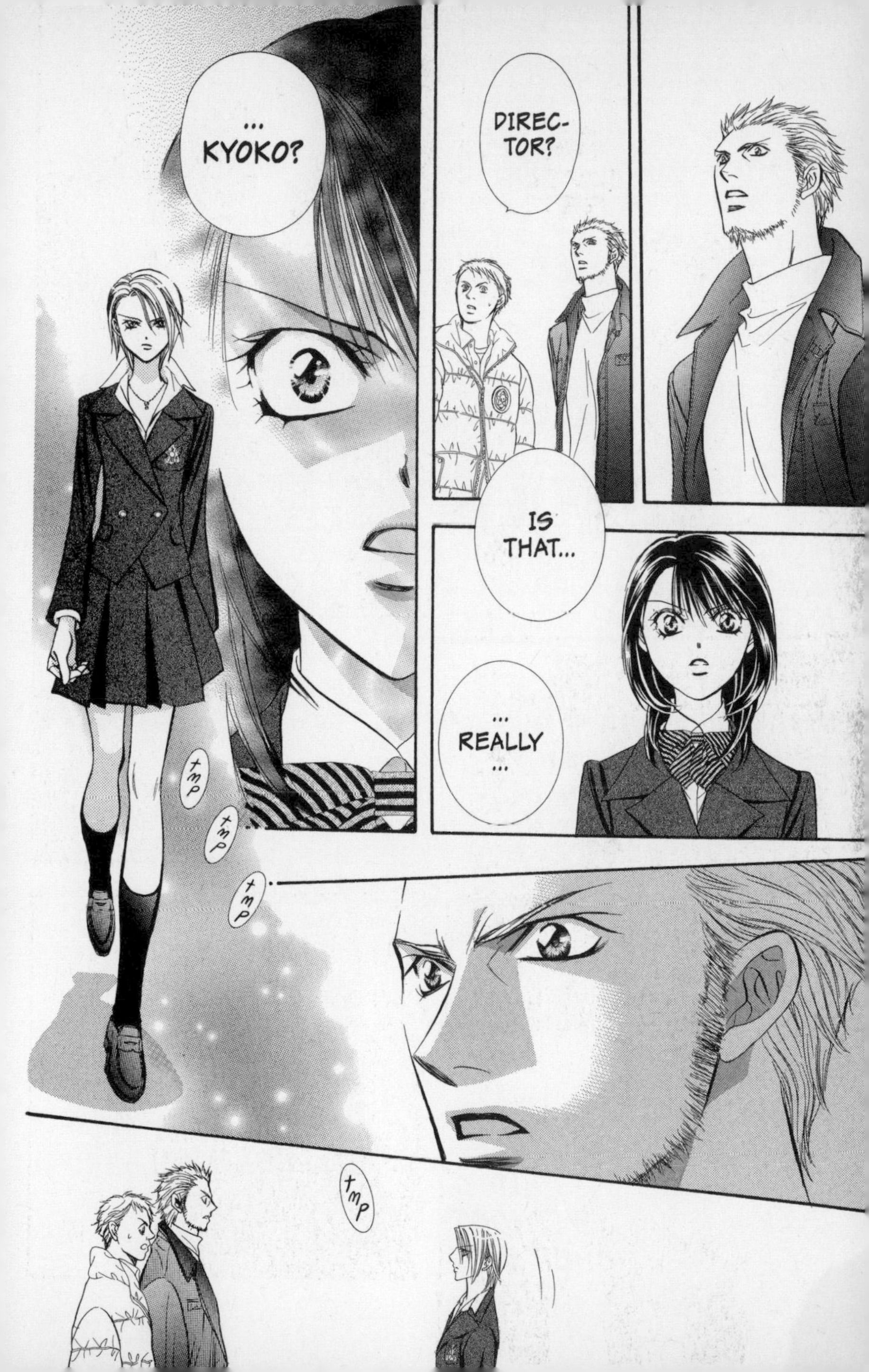
DIREC-
TOR?
IS THAT...
...REALLY...
...KYOKO?
tmp
tmp
tmp
tmp

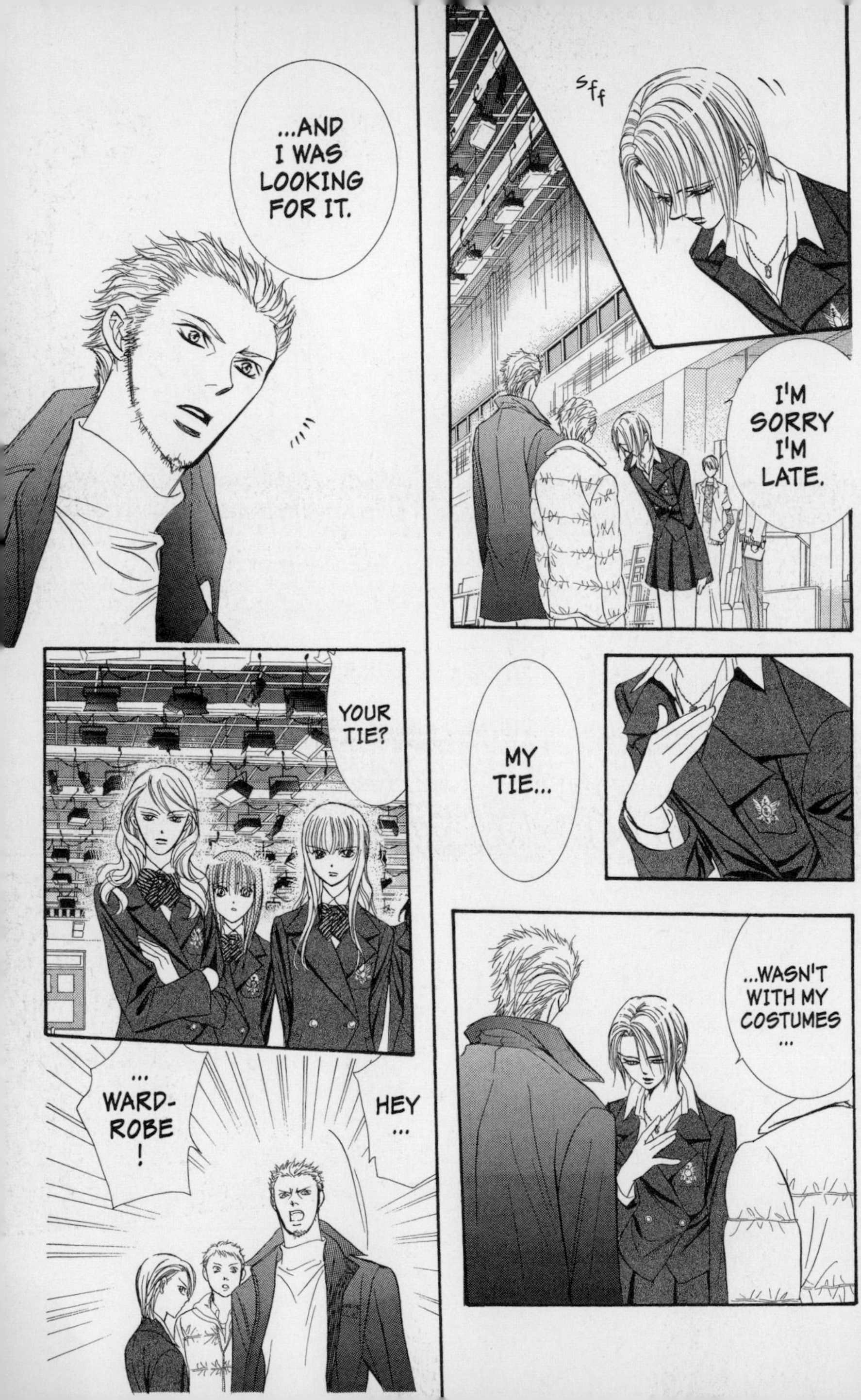
sff
I'M SORRY I'M LATE.
MY TIE...
...WASN'T WITH MY COSTUMES ...
...AND I WAS LOOKING FOR IT.
YOUR TIE?
HEY ...
... WARD-ROBE !

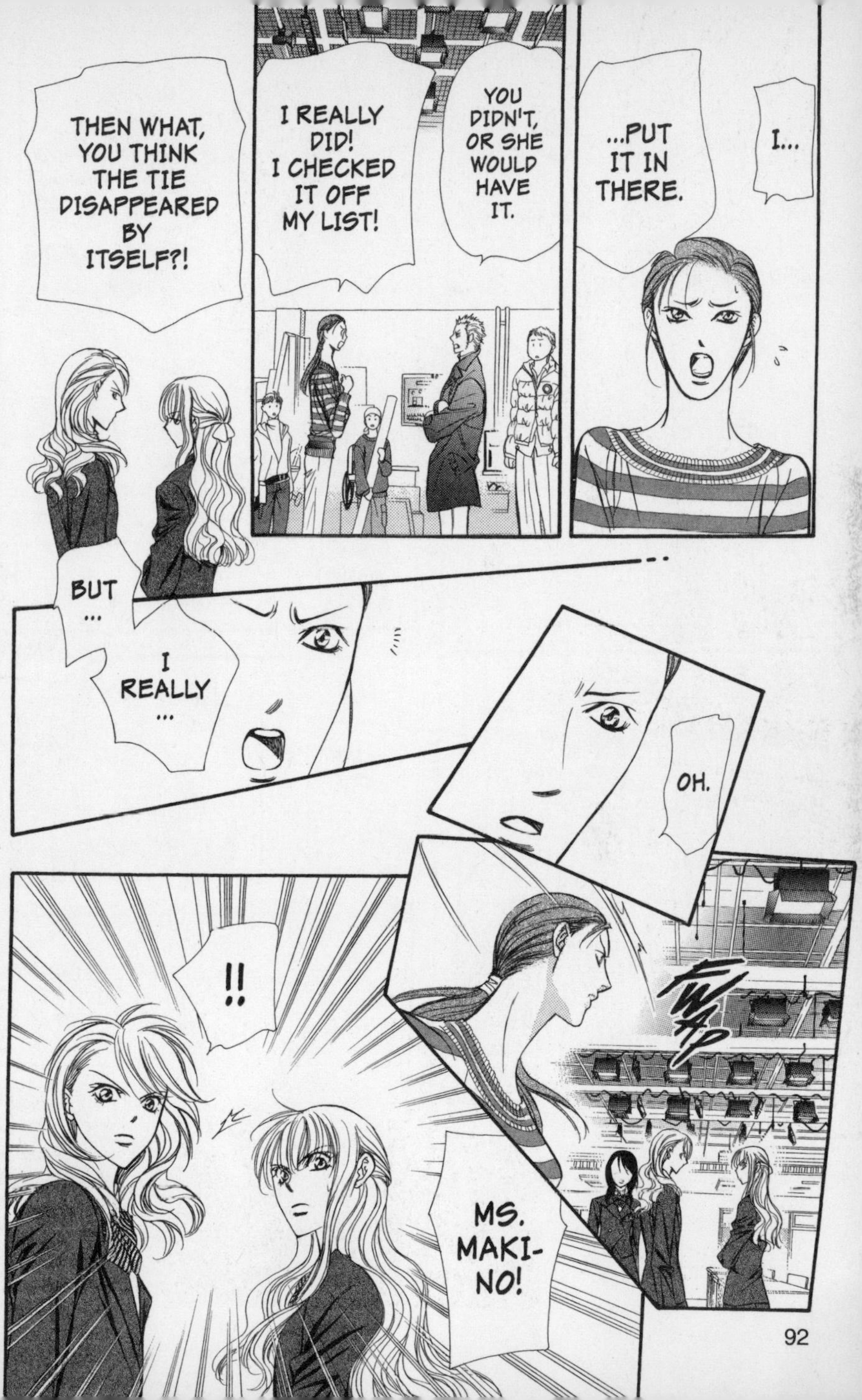
I...
...PUT IT IN THERE.
YOU DIDN'T, OR SHE WOULD HAVE IT.
I REALLY DID! I CHECKED IT OFF MY LIST!
THEN WHAT, YOU THINK THE TIE DISAPPEARED BY ITSELF?!
BUT ...
I REALLY ...
OH.
FWAP
MS. MAKI-NO!
!!

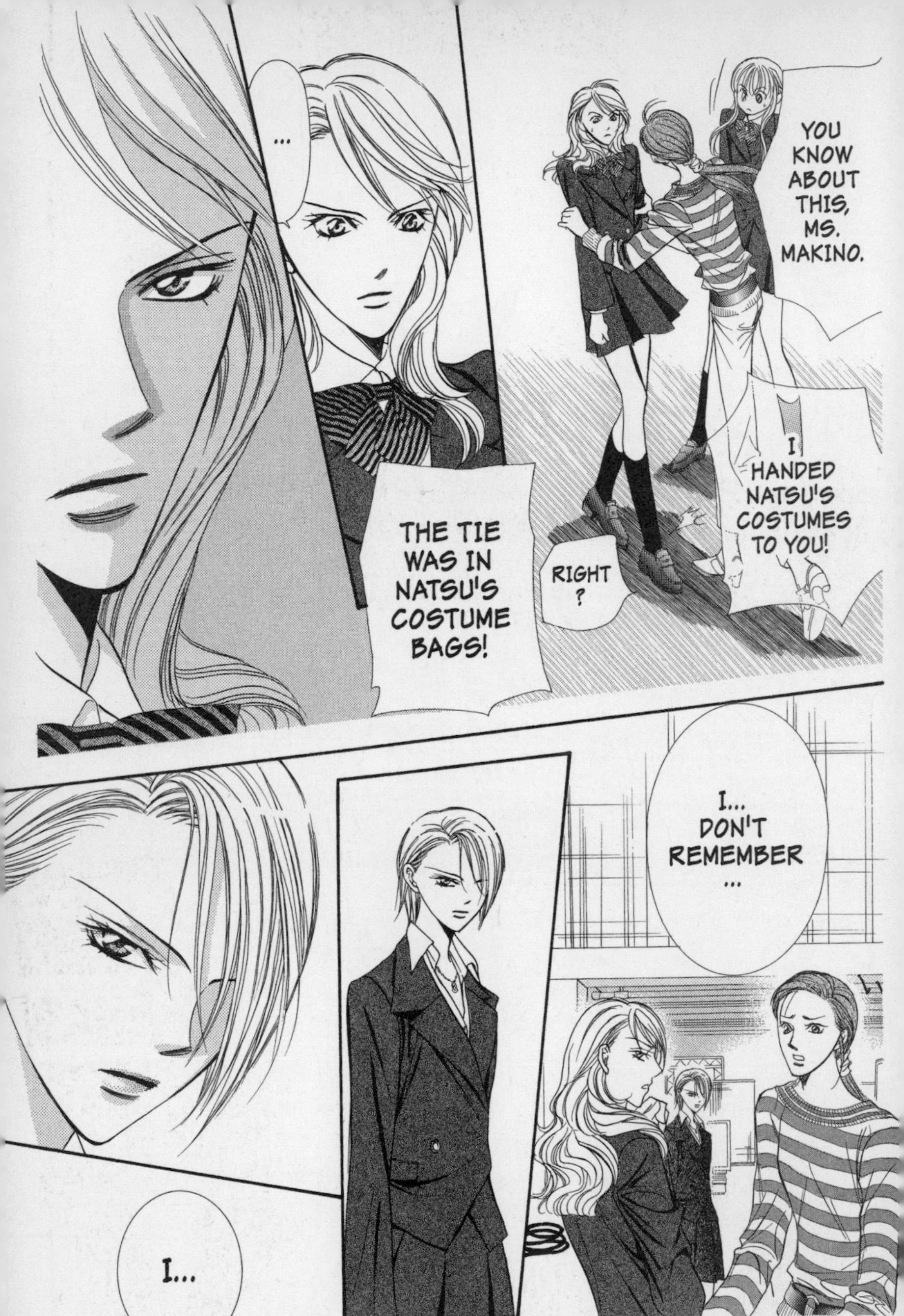

YOU KNOW ABOUT THIS, MS. MAKINO.
I HANDED NATSU'S COSTUMES TO YOU!
RIGHT?
THE TIE WAS IN NATSU'S COSTUME BAGS!
...
I... DON'T REMEMBER ...
I...

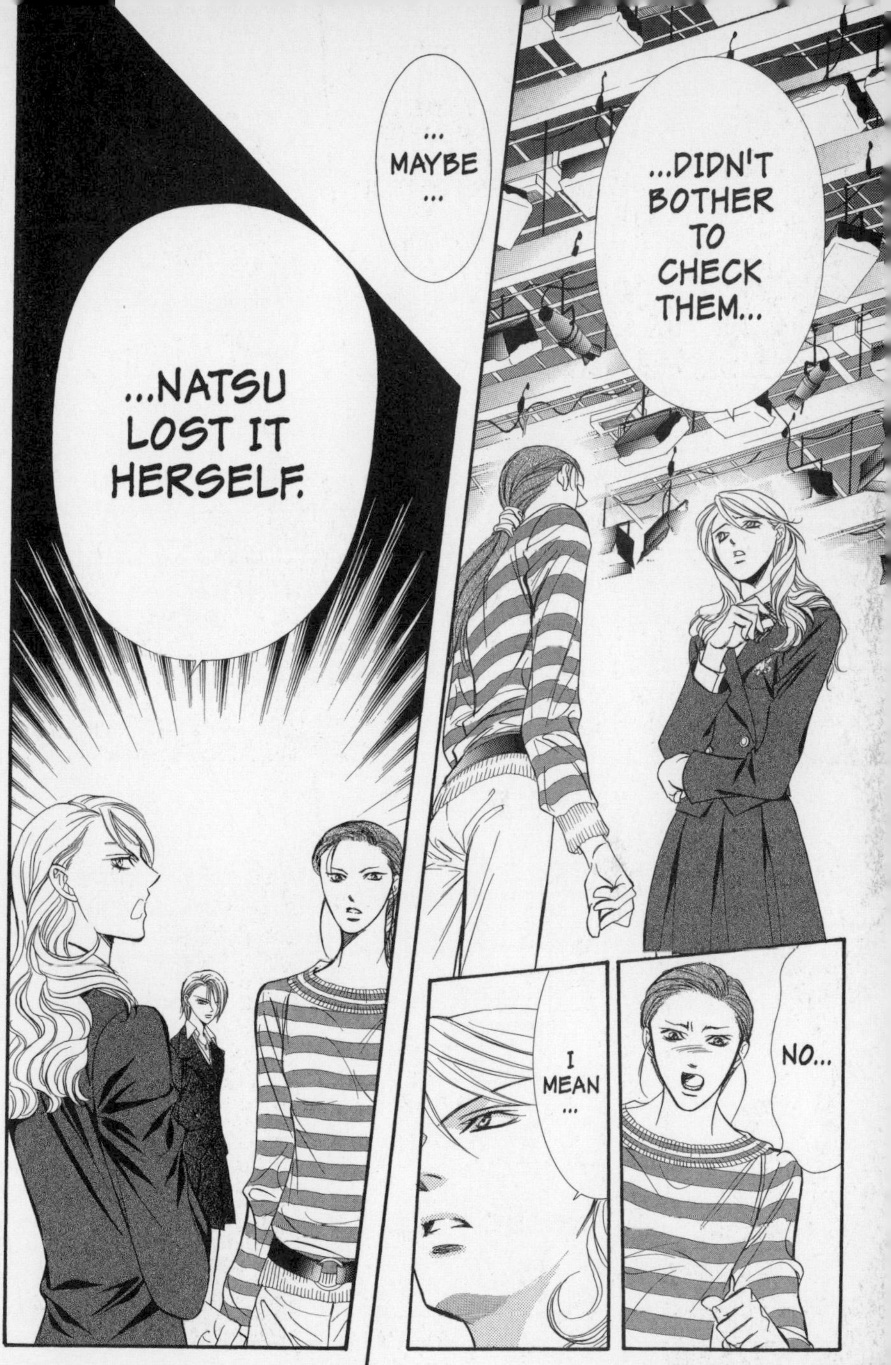
...DIDN'T BOTHER TO CHECK THEM...
NO...
I MEAN ...
... MAYBE ...
...NATSU LOST IT HERSELF.

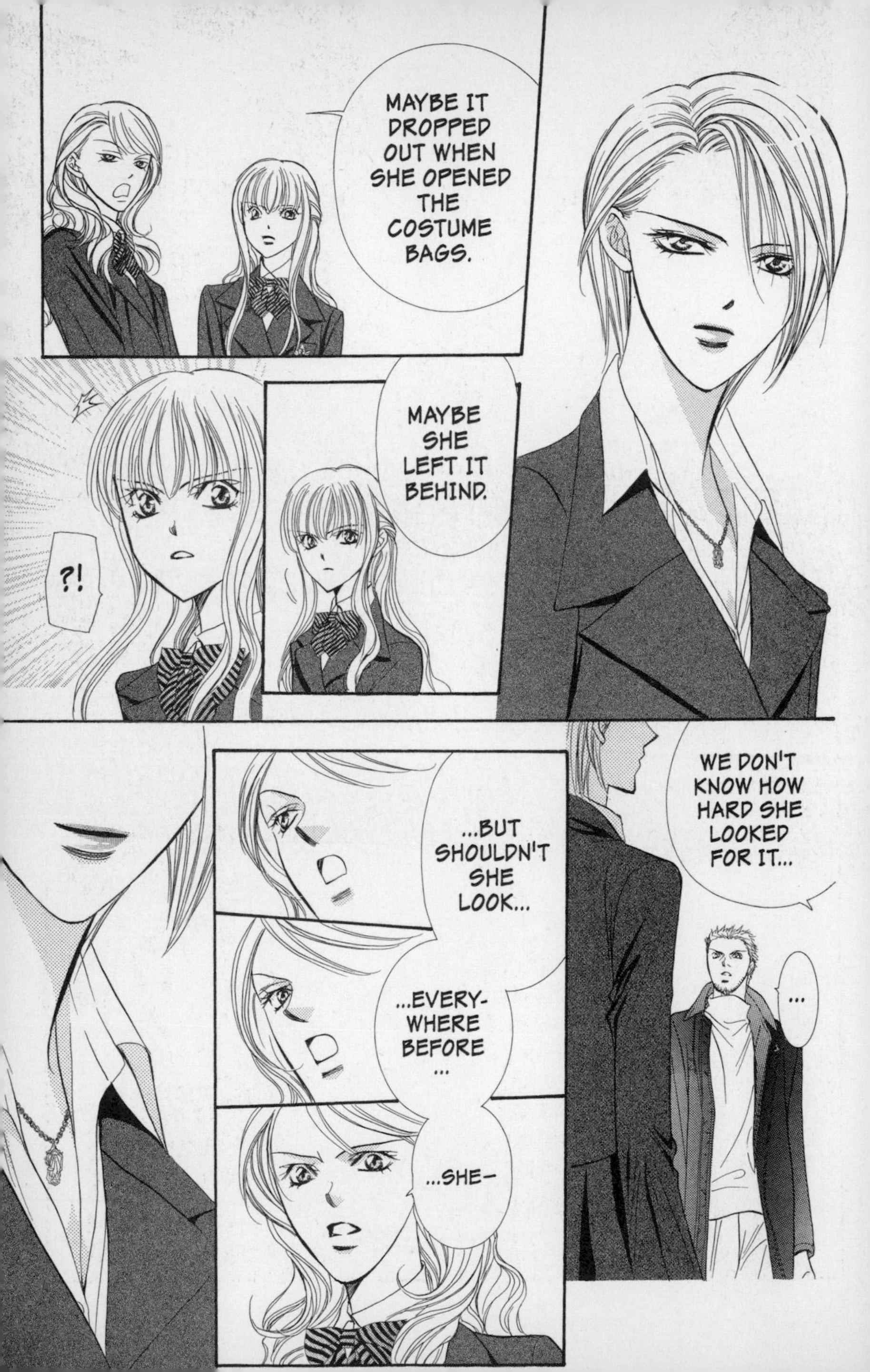
MAYBE IT DROPPED OUT WHEN SHE OPENED THE COSTUME BAGS.
MAYBE SHE LEFT IT BEHIND.
?!
WE DON'T KNOW HOW HARD SHE LOOKED FOR IT...
...
...BUT SHOULDN'T SHE LOOK...
...EVERY-WHERE BEFORE ...
...SHE-

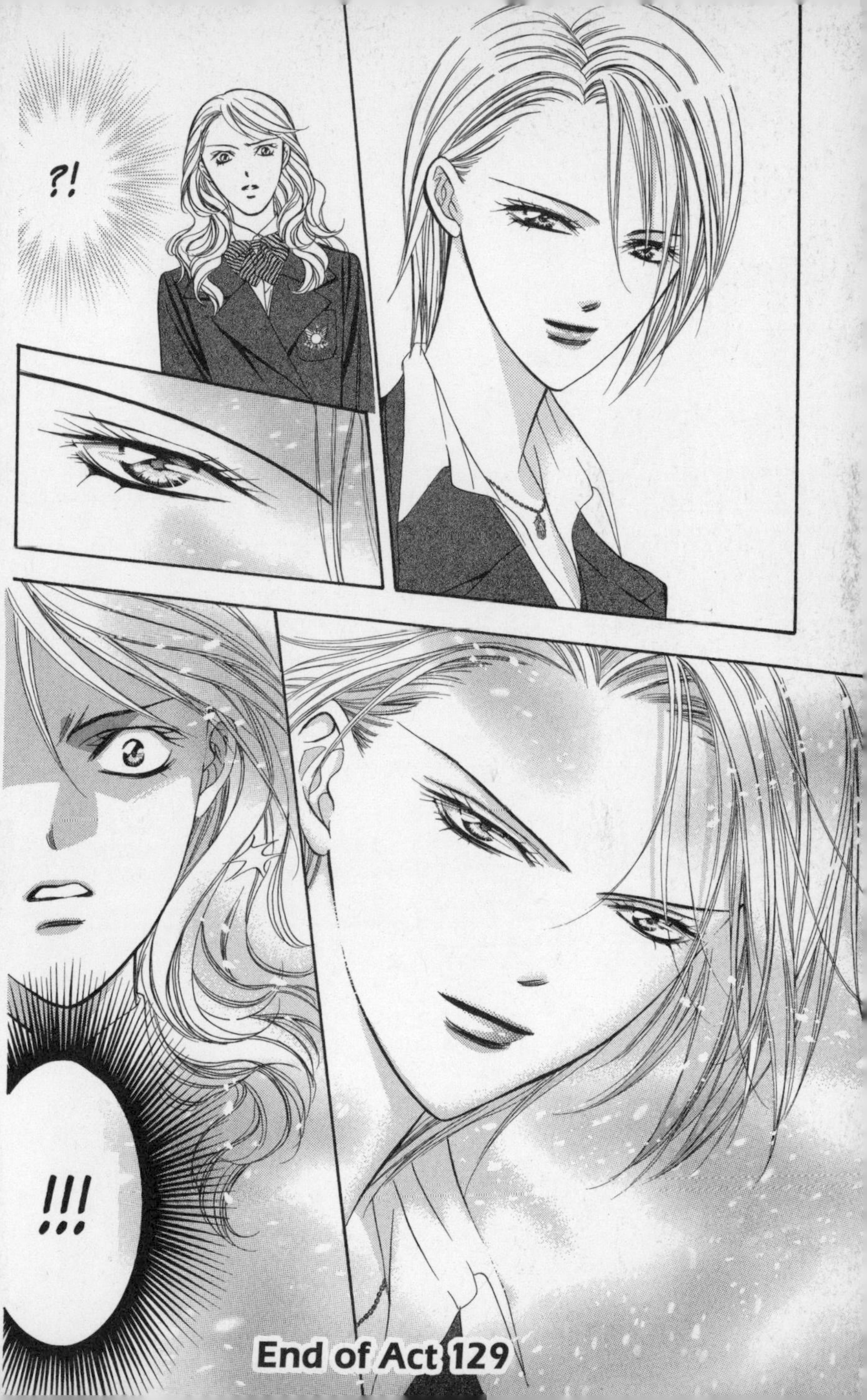
?!
!!!
End of Act 129

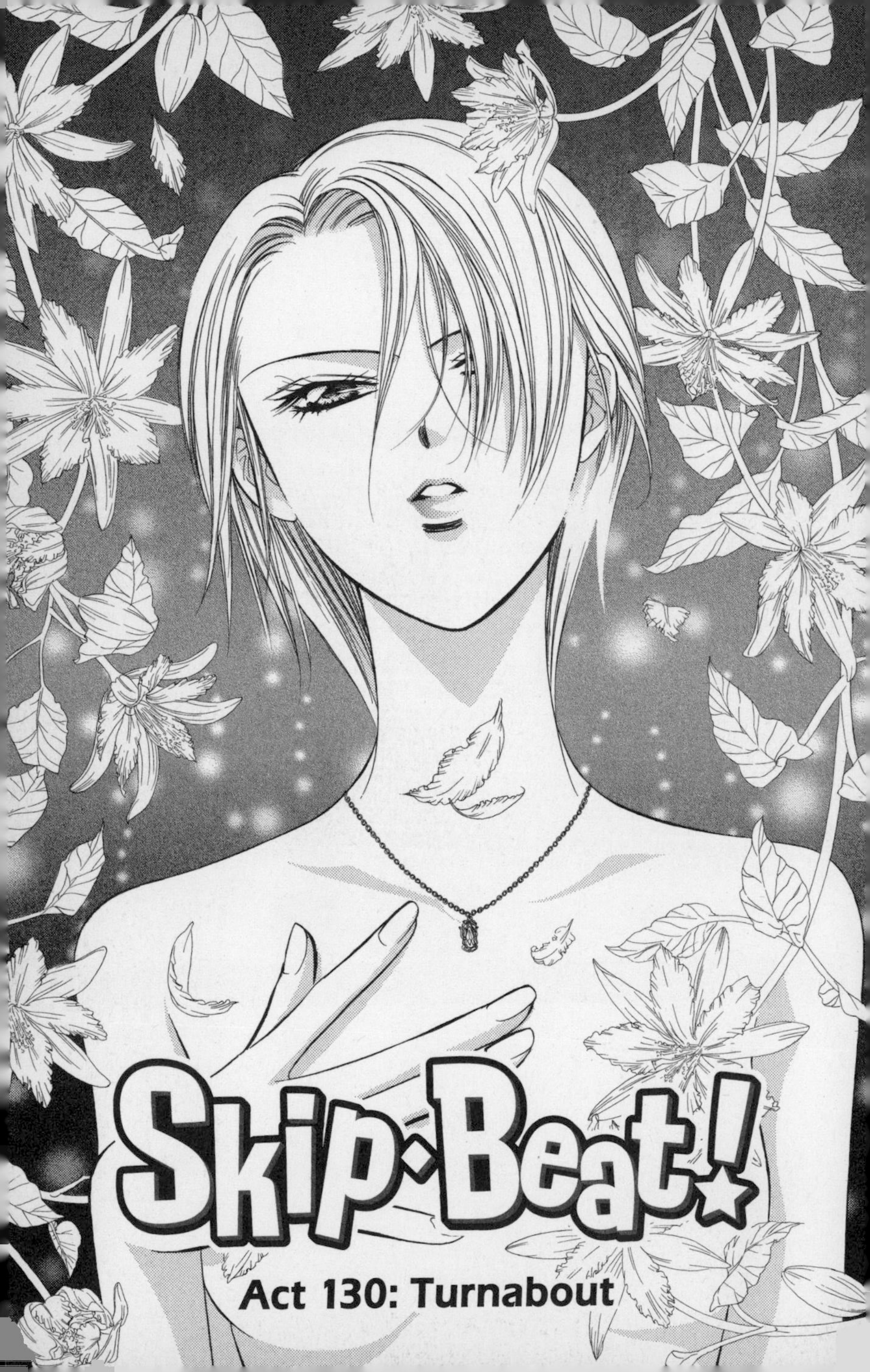
Skip·Beat!
Act 130: Turnabout

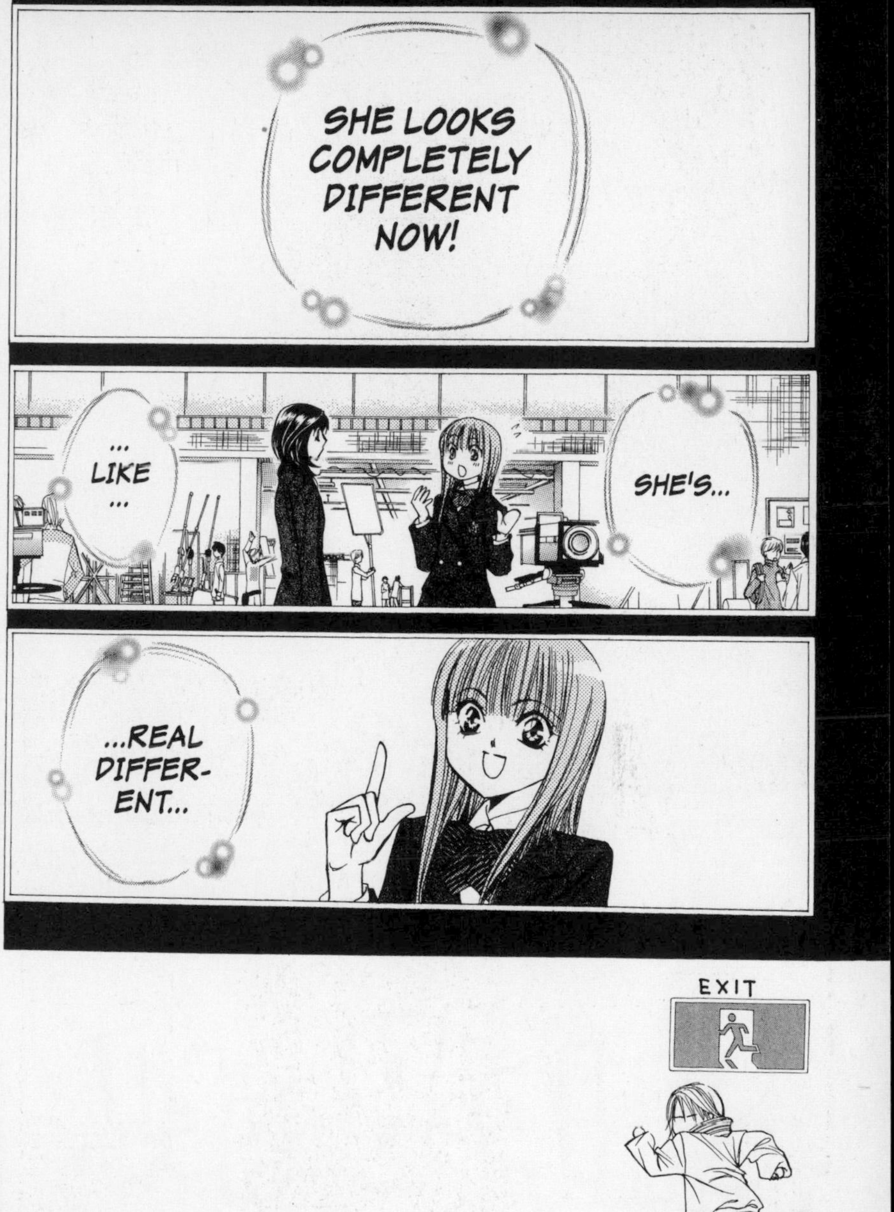
SHE LOOKS COMPLETELY DIFFERENT NOW!
SHE'S...
...LIKE...
...REAL DIFFER-ENT...
EXIT

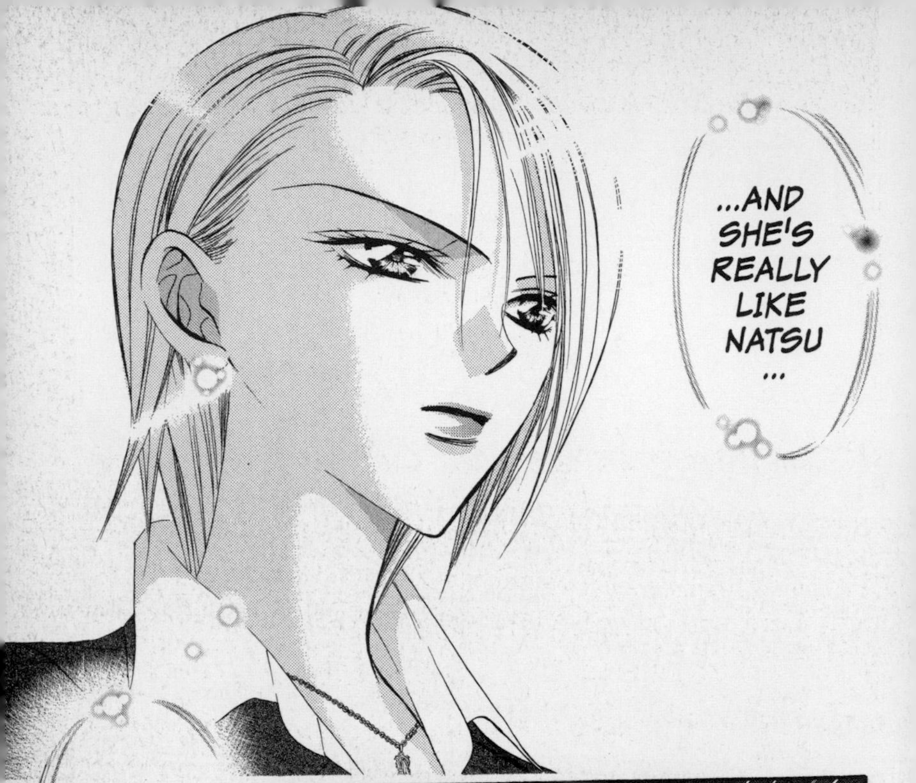
...AND SHE'S REALLY LIKE NATSU ...

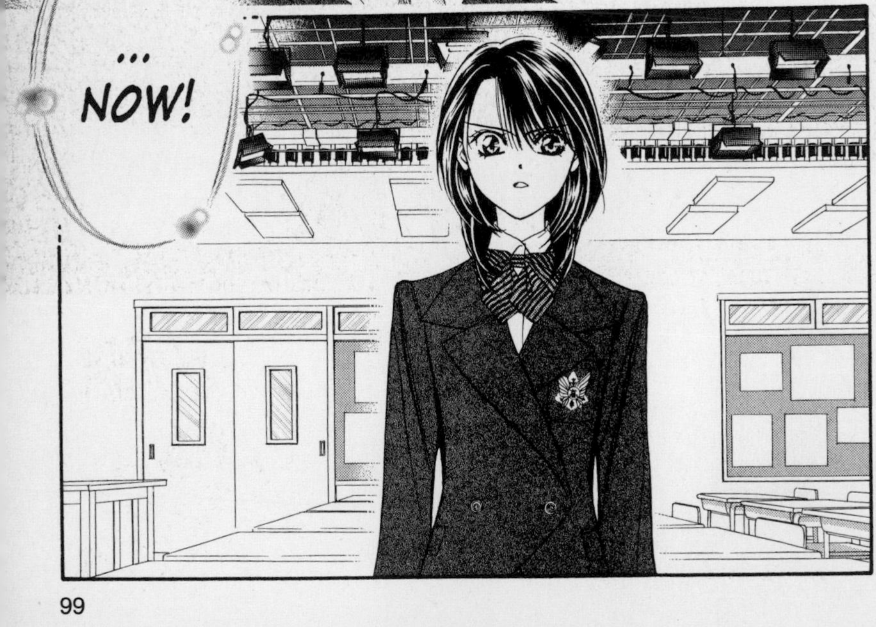
... NOW!

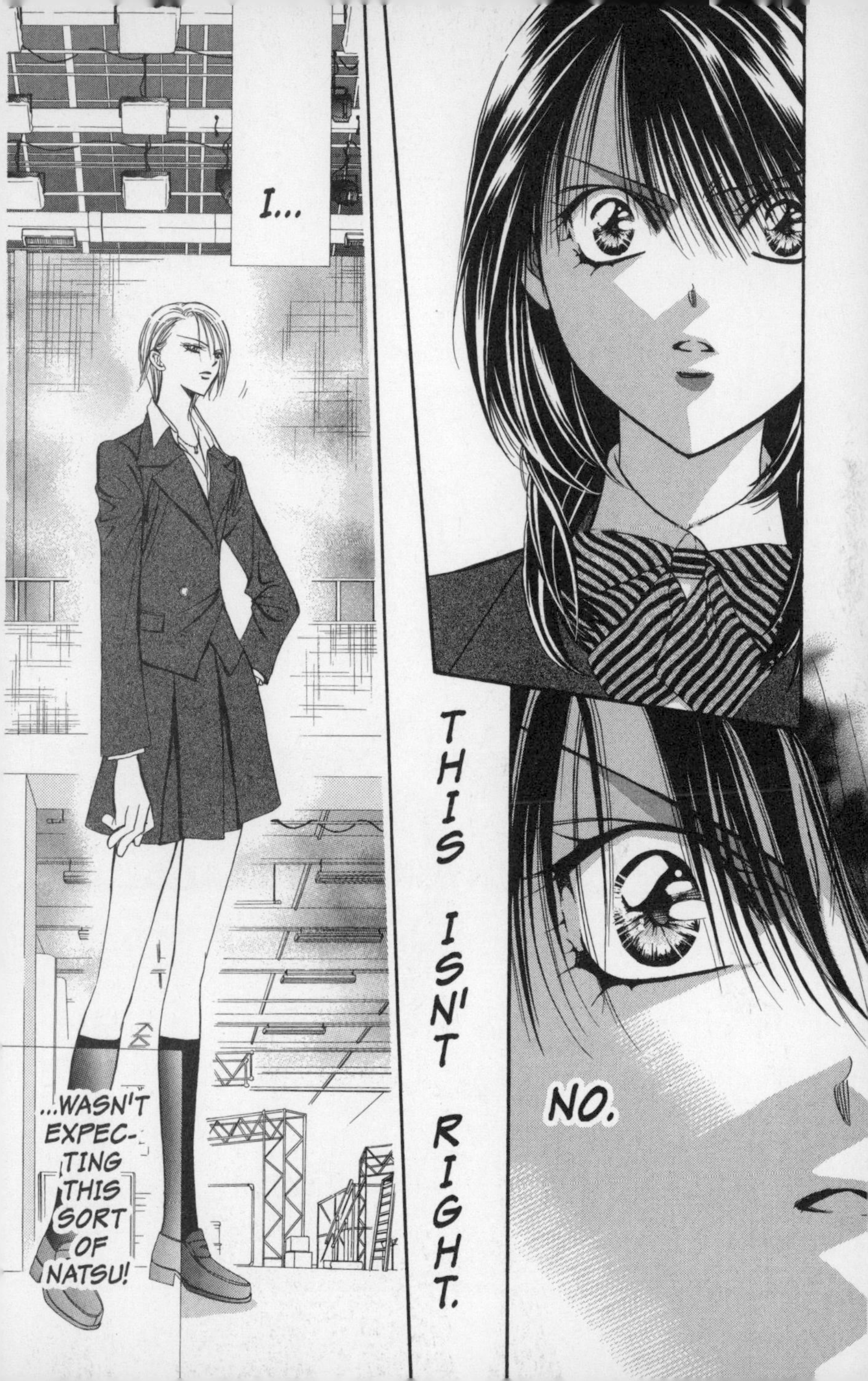
THIS ISN'T RIGHT.
NO.
I...
...WASN'T EXPEC-TING THIS SORT OF NATSU!

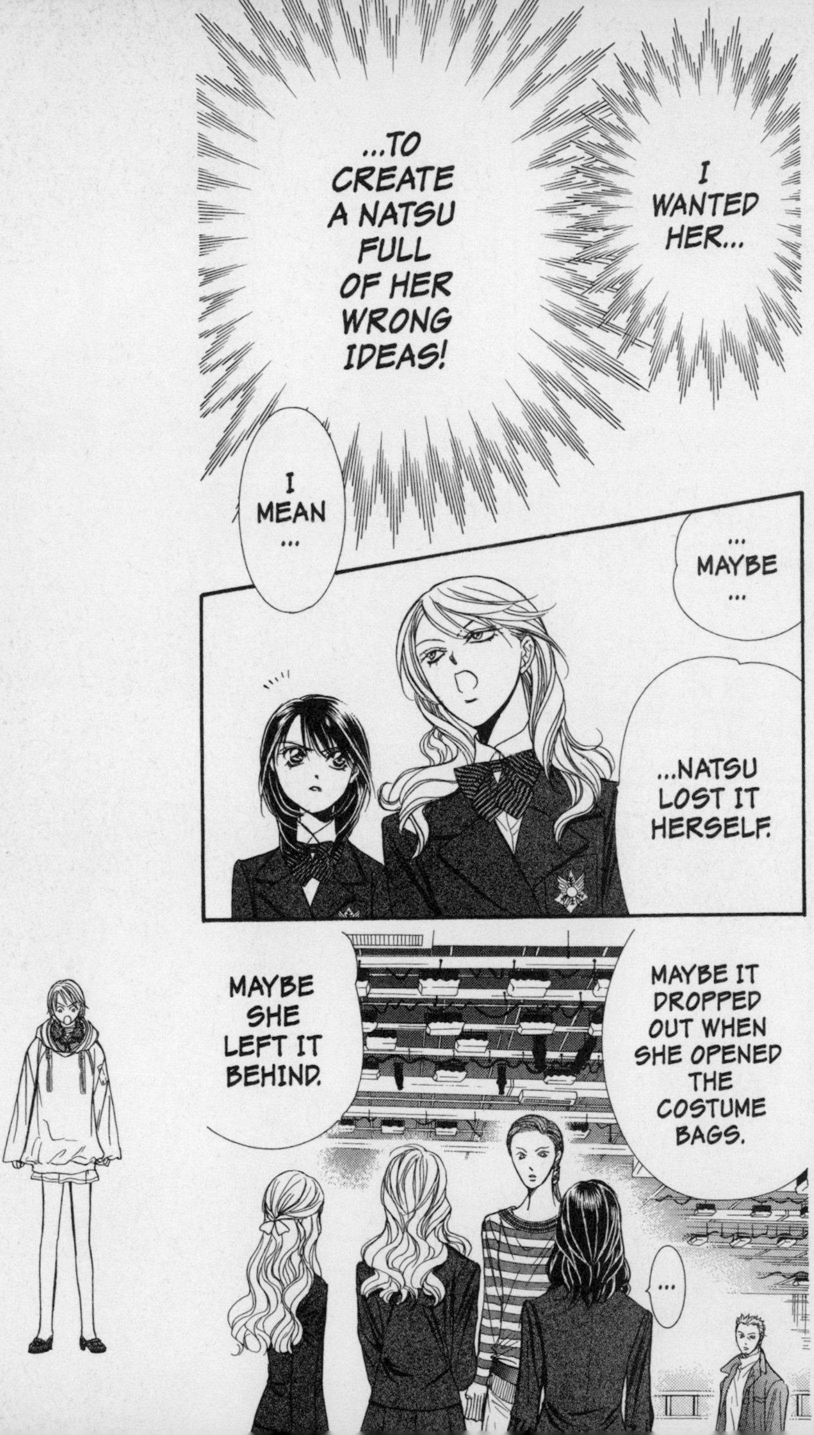
I WANTED HER...
...TO CREATE A NATSU FULL OF HER WRONG IDEAS!
I MEAN...
...MAYBE...
...NATSU LOST IT HERSELF.
MAYBE IT DROPPED OUT WHEN SHE OPENED THE COSTUME BAGS.
MAYBE SHE LEFT IT BEHIND.
...

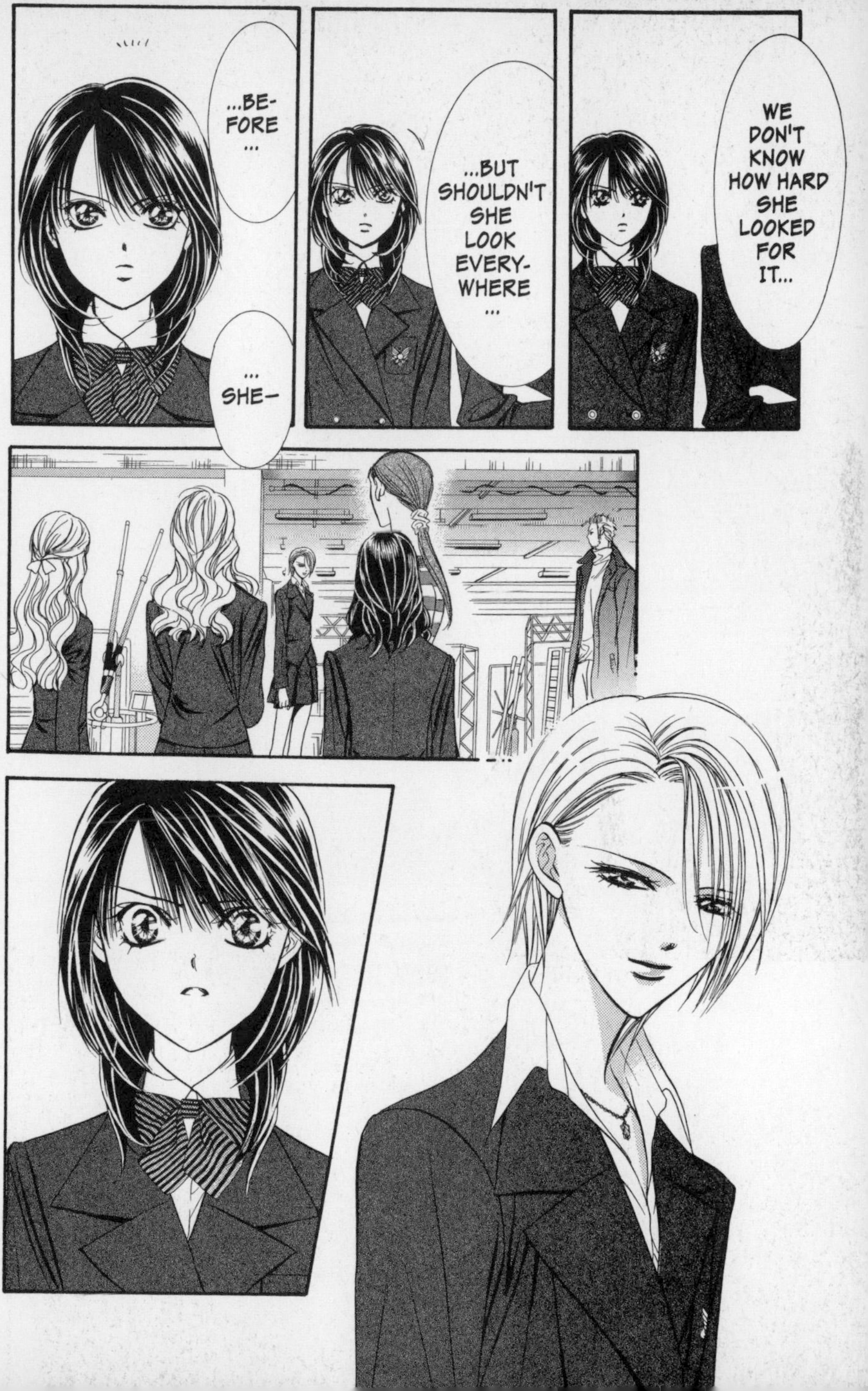
WE DON'T KNOW HOW HARD SHE LOOKED FOR IT...
...BUT SHOULDN'T SHE LOOK EVERY-WHERE ...
...BE-FORE ...
... SHE–

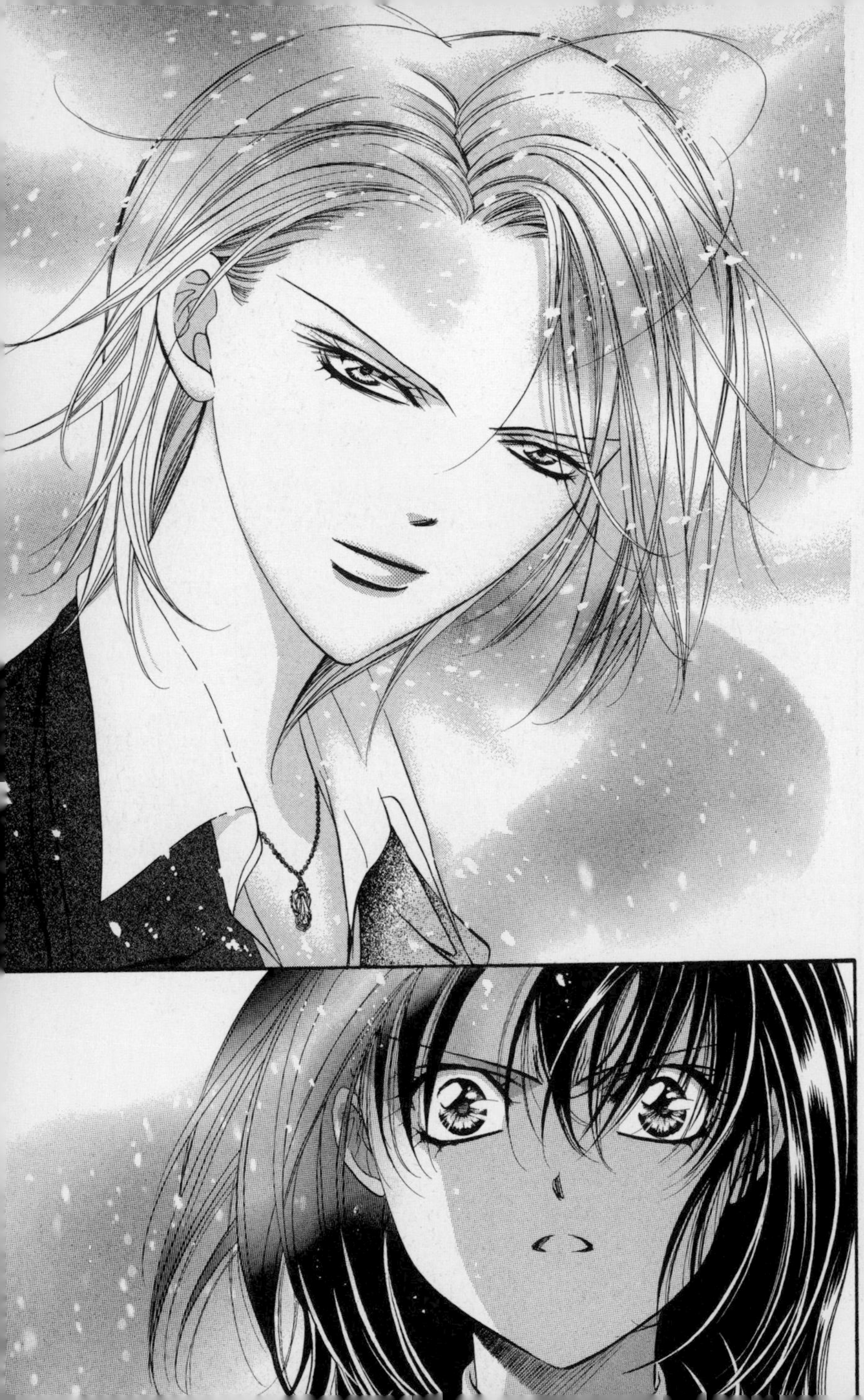

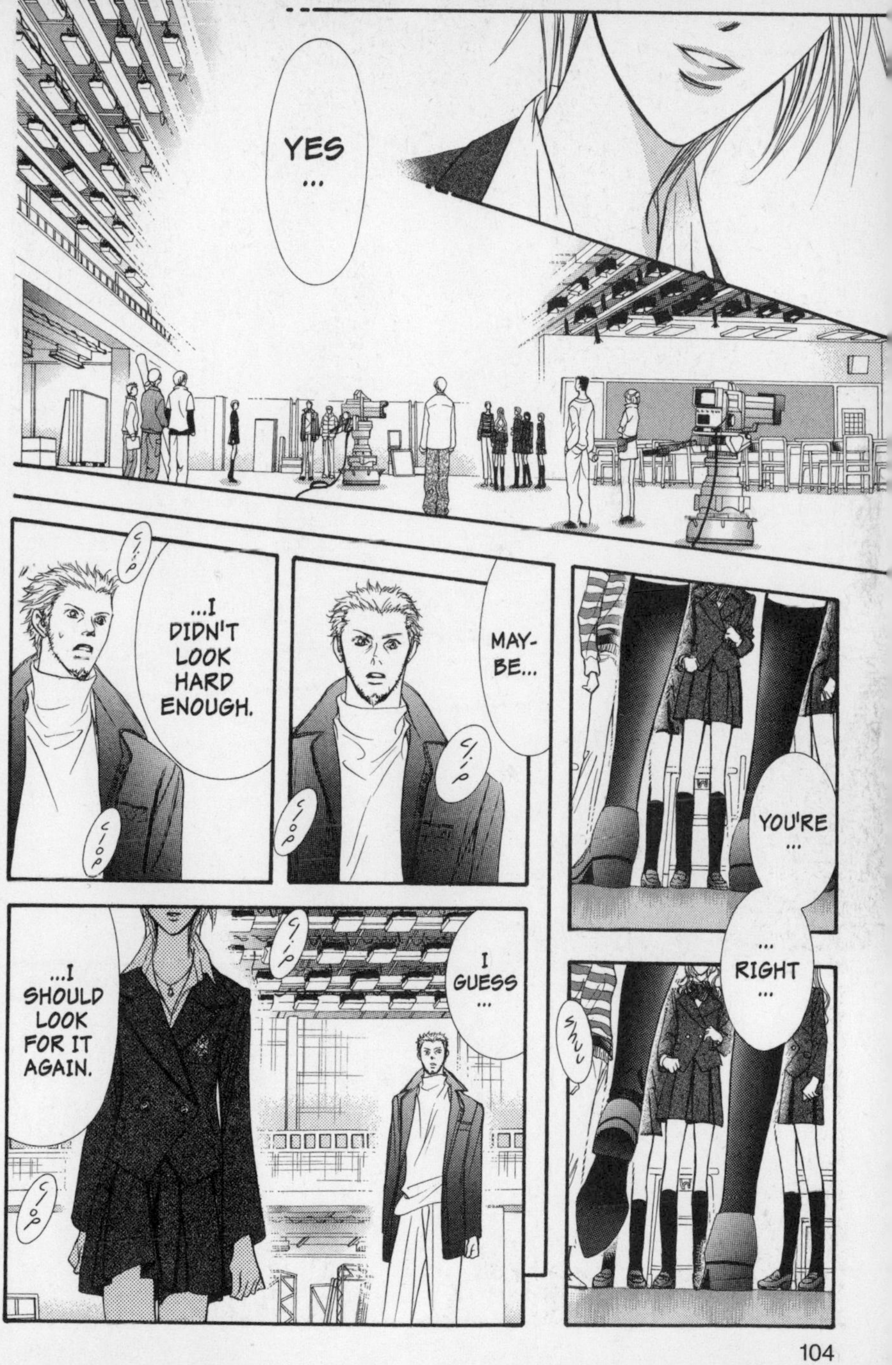
YES ...
YOU'RE ...
... RIGHT ...
MAY-BE...
clip
clop
...I DIDN'T LOOK HARD ENOUGH.
clip
clop
shuu
clip
I GUESS ...
...I SHOULD LOOK FOR IT AGAIN.
clop

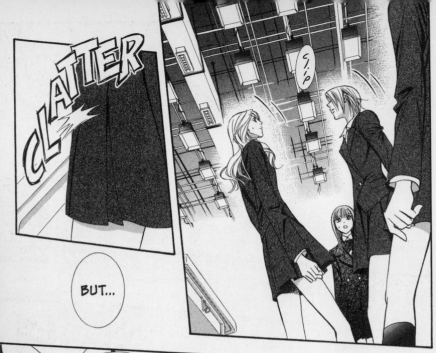

CLATTER

...♭♪♪

BUT...

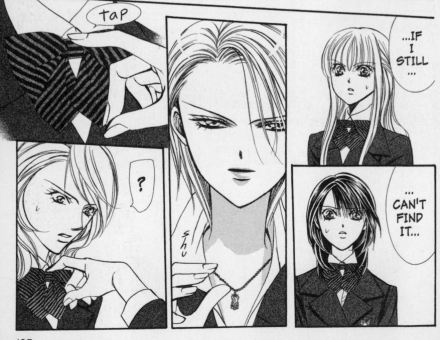

TAP

...IF
I
STILL
...

?

SHU

...CAN'T
FIND
IT...

105

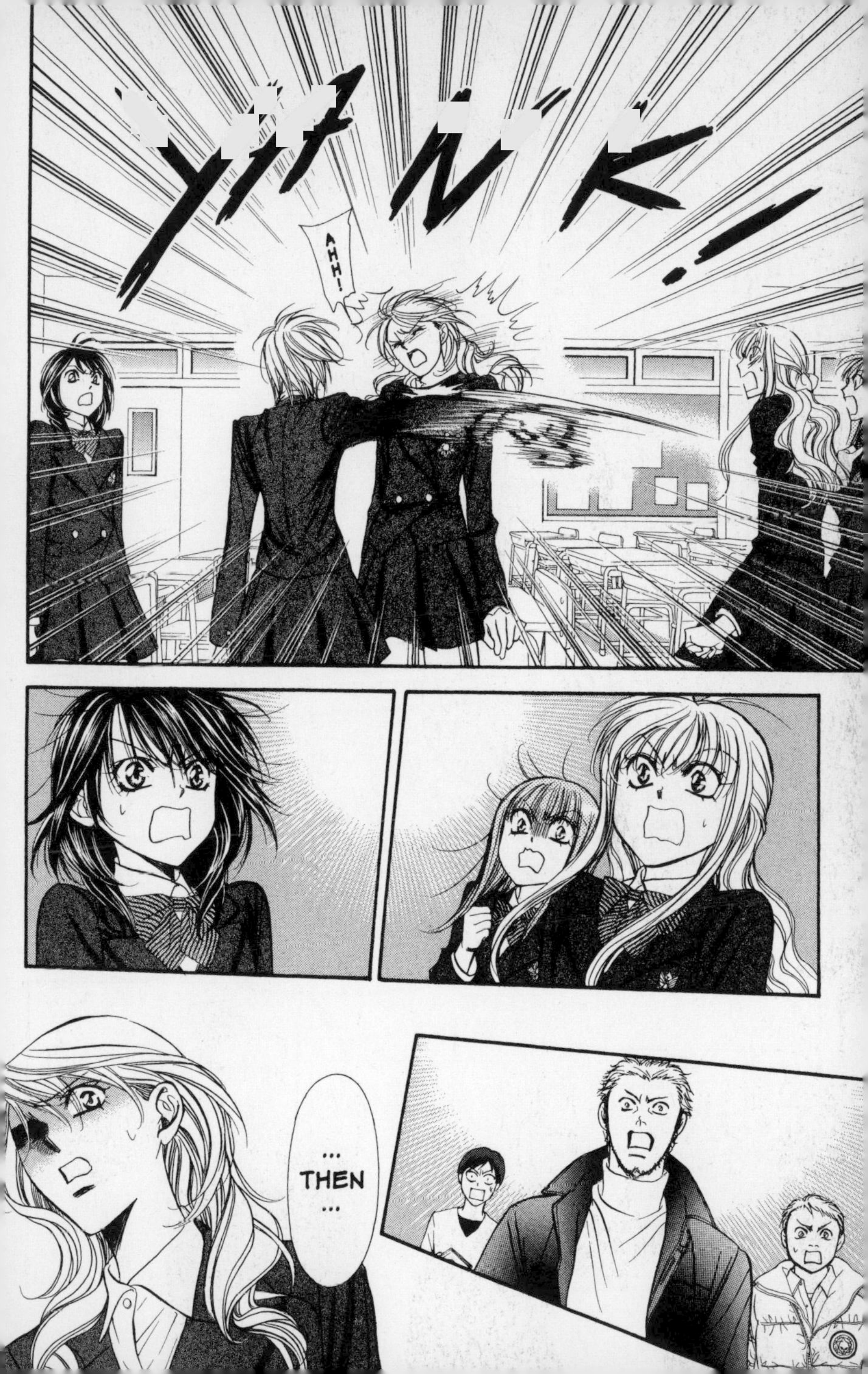
AHH!
... THEN ...

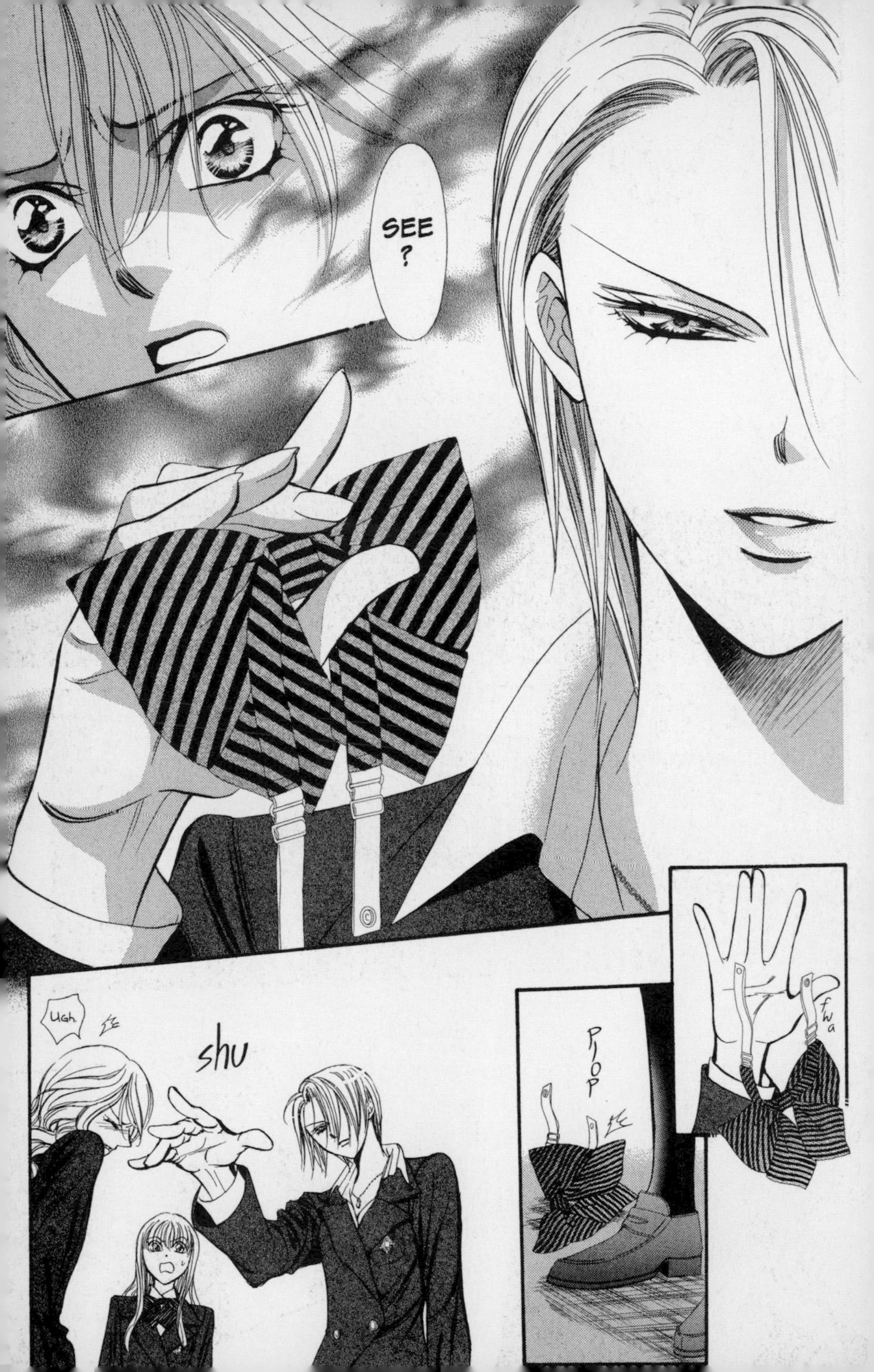
SEE ?
fwa
PLOP
Ugh.
shu

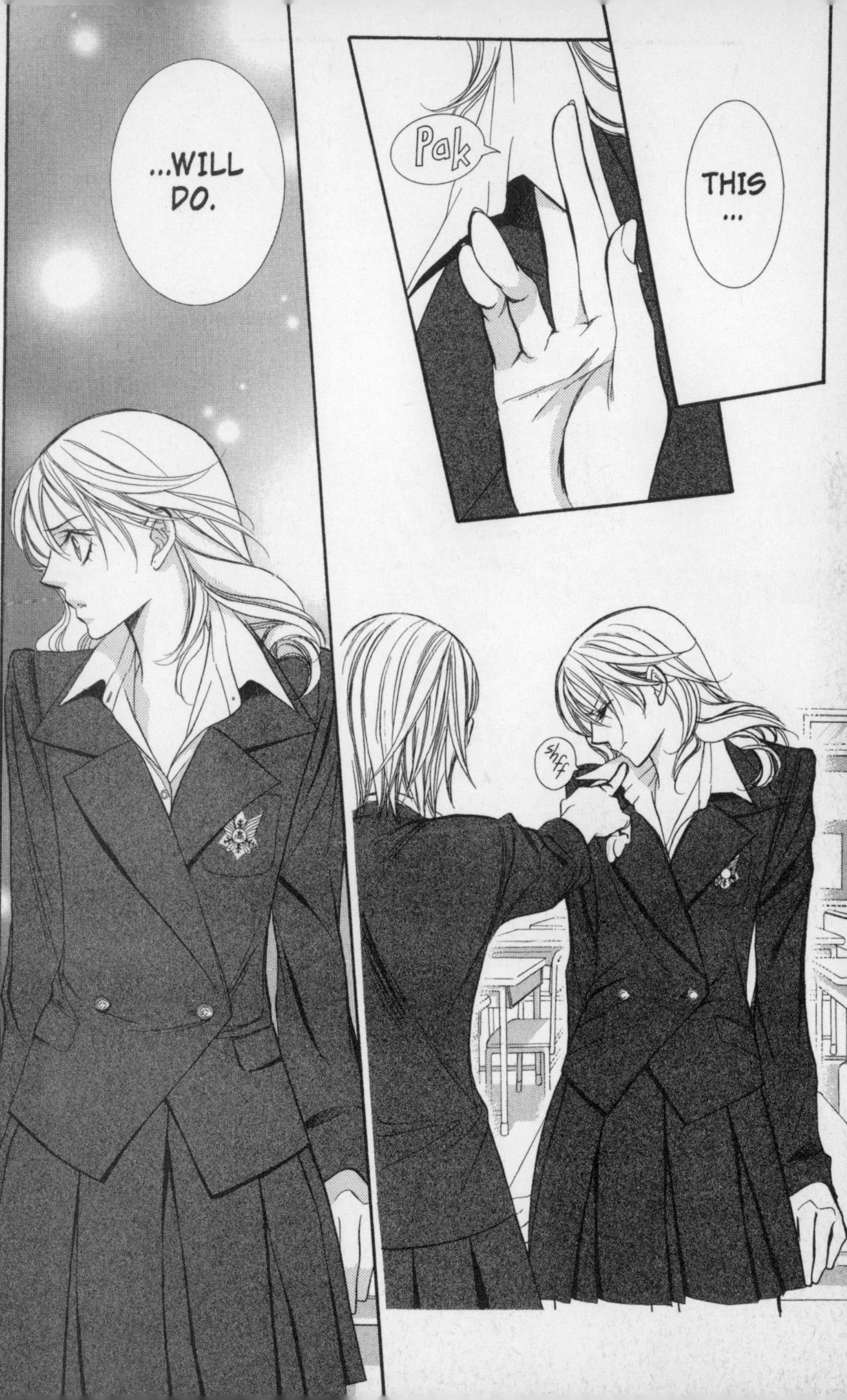
THIS ...
Pak
shff
...WILL DO.

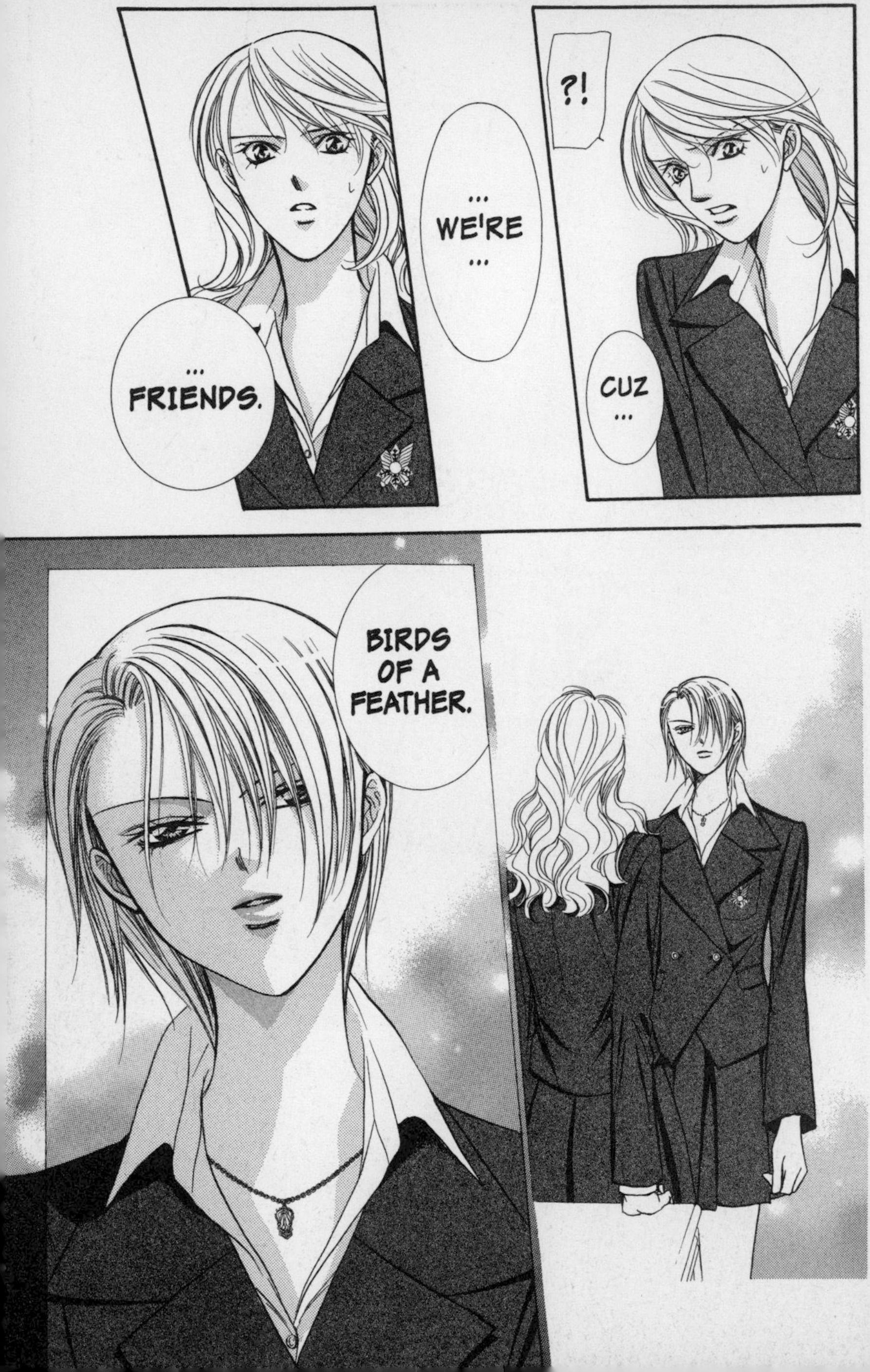
?!
CUZ ...
... WE'RE ...
... FRIENDS.
BIRDS OF A FEATHER.

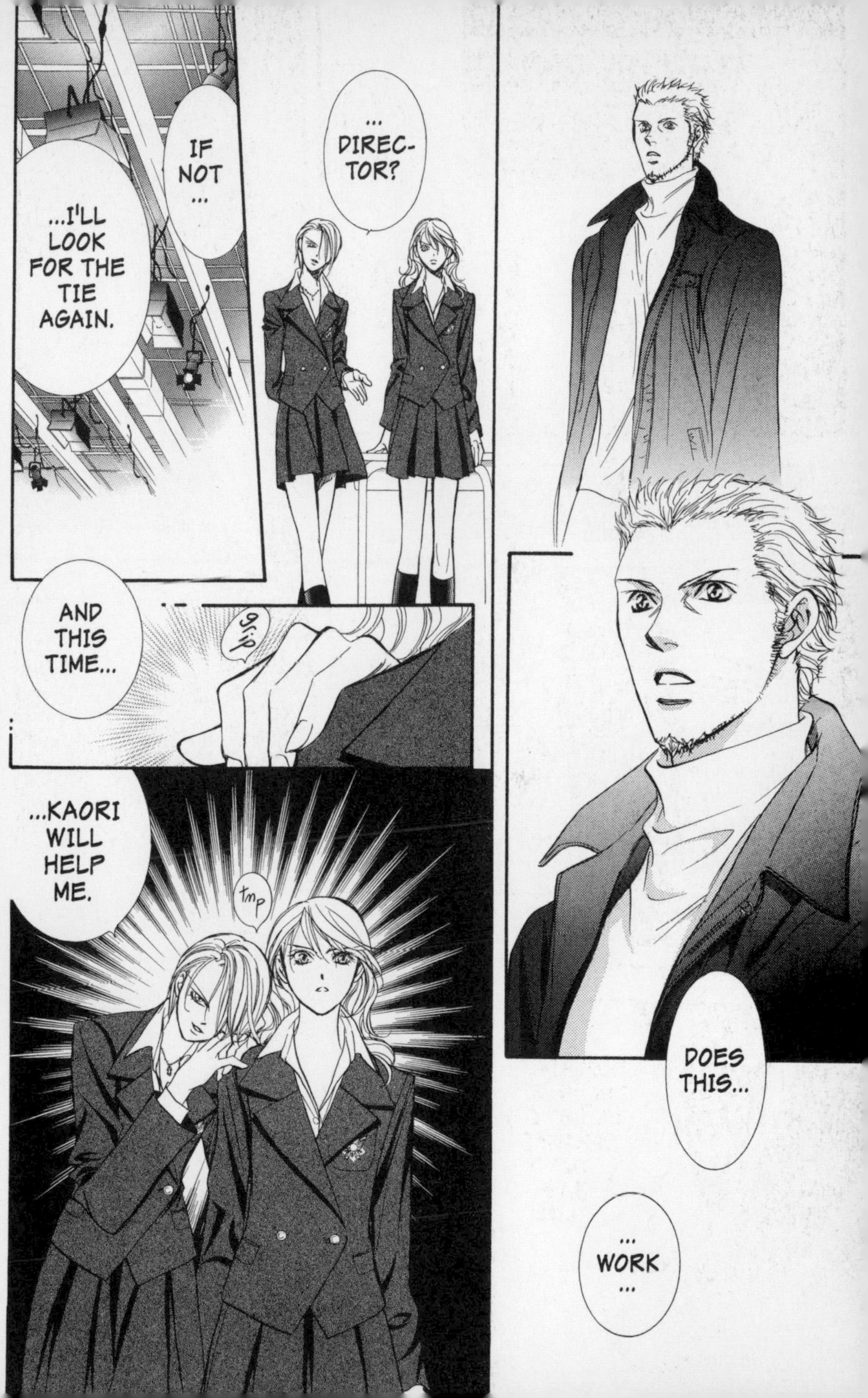
DOES THIS...
...WORK...
...DIRECTOR?
IF NOT...
...I'LL LOOK FOR THE TIE AGAIN.
AND THIS TIME...
grip
...KAORI WILL HELP ME.
tmp

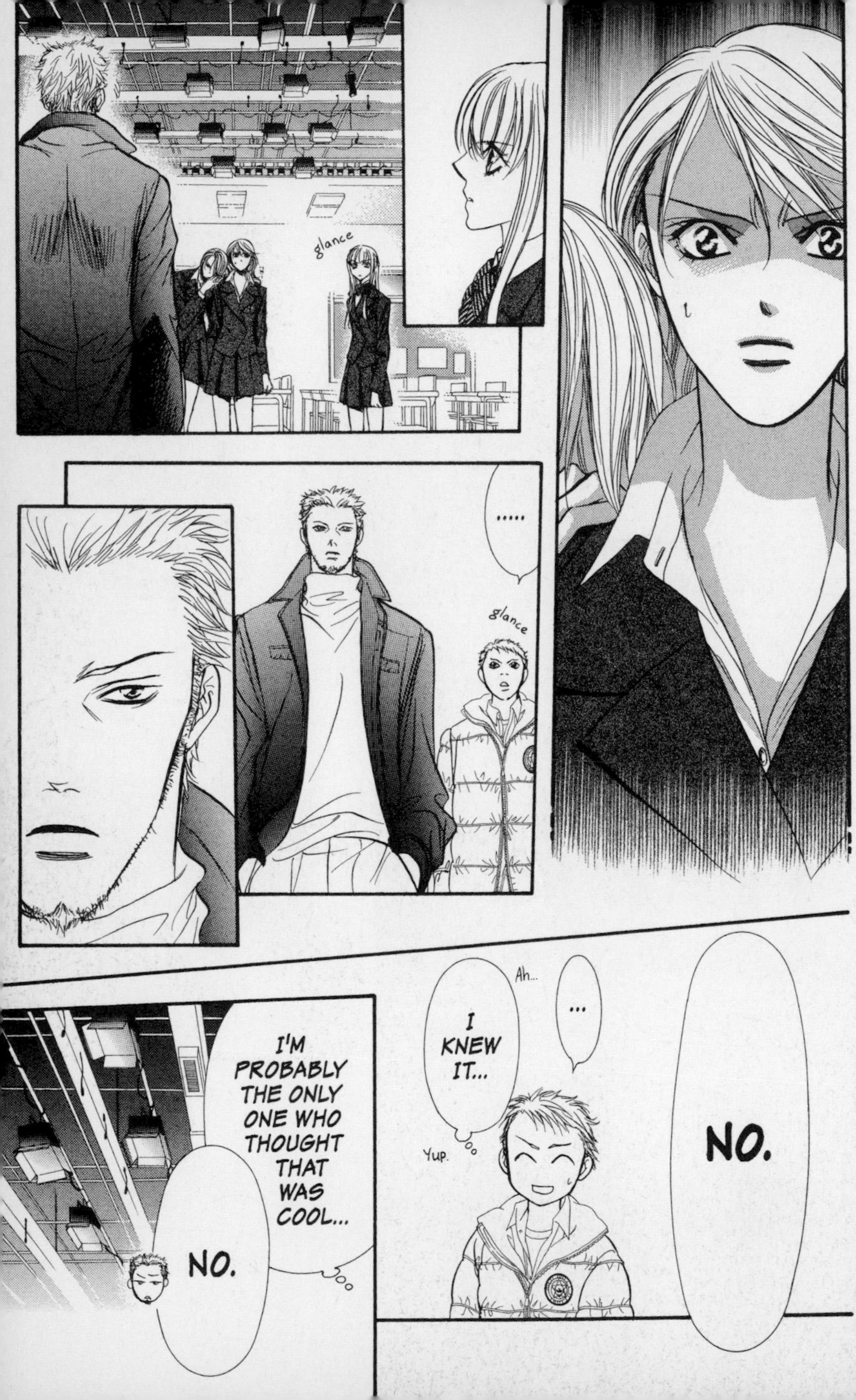
glance
.....
glance
NO.
...
Ah...
I KNEW IT...
Yup.
I'M PROBABLY THE ONLY ONE WHO THOUGHT THAT WAS COOL...
NO.

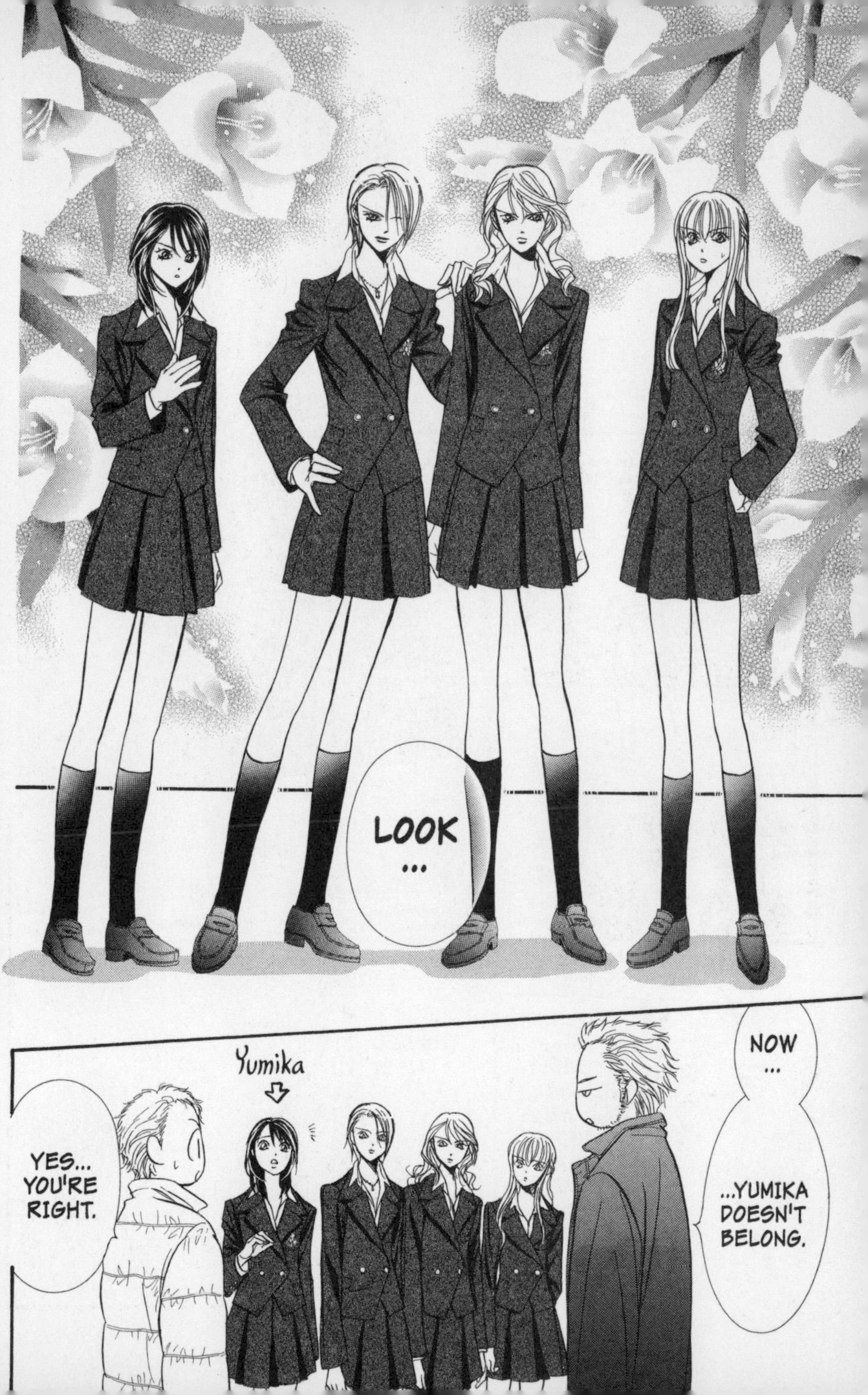
LOOK ...
NOW ...
...YUMIKA DOESN'T BELONG.
Yumika
YES... YOU'RE RIGHT.

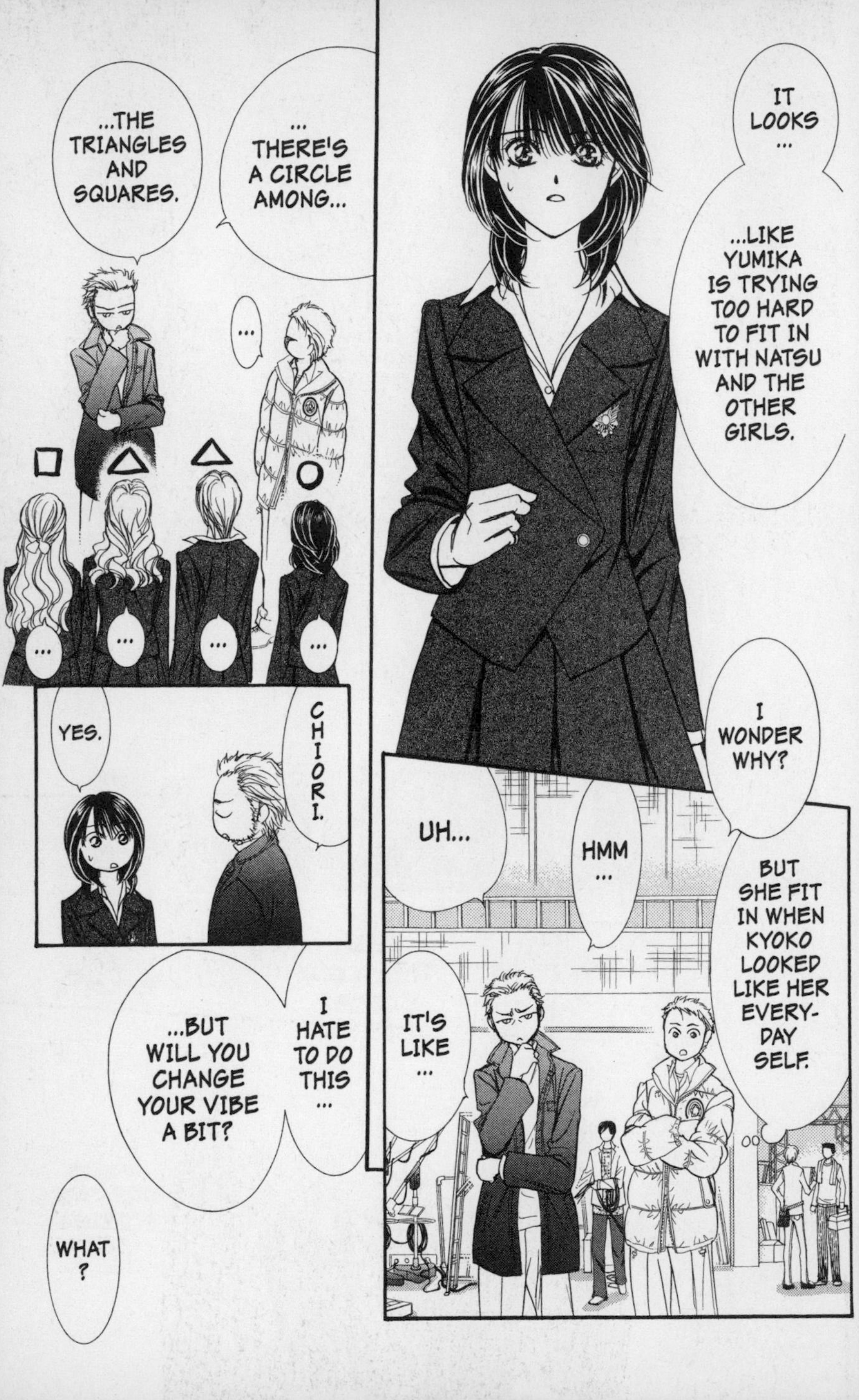
IT LOOKS ...
...LIKE YUMIKA IS TRYING TOO HARD TO FIT IN WITH NATSU AND THE OTHER GIRLS.
I WONDER WHY?
BUT SHE FIT IN WHEN KYOKO LOOKED LIKE HER EVERY-DAY SELF.
HMM ...
UH...
IT'S LIKE ...
... THERE'S A CIRCLE AMONG...
...THE TRIANGLES AND SQUARES.
...
...
...
...
...
CHIORI.
YES.
I HATE TO DO THIS ...
...BUT WILL YOU CHANGE YOUR VIBE A BIT?
WHAT ?

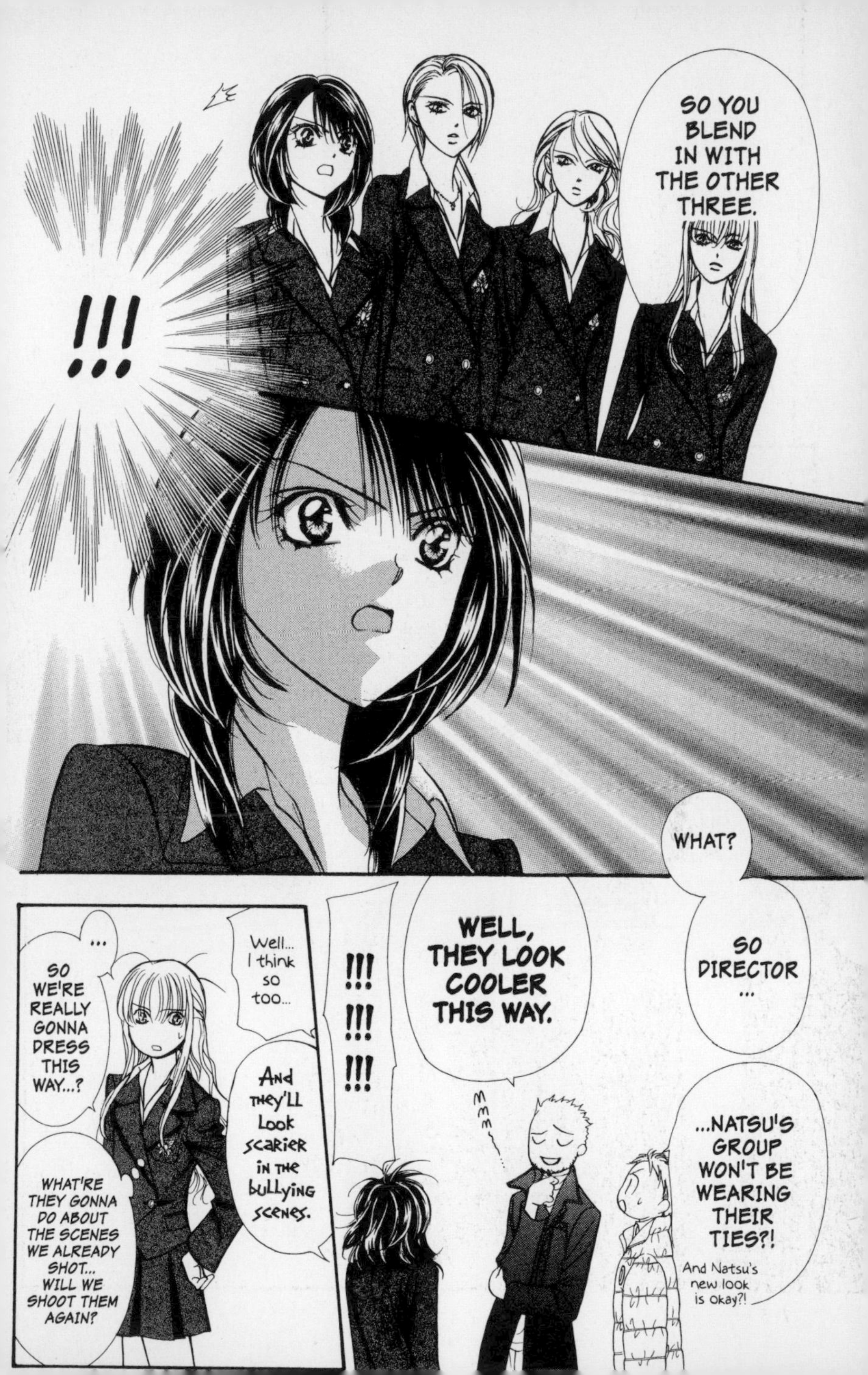
SO YOU BLEND IN WITH THE OTHER THREE.
!!!
WHAT?
SO DIRECTOR ...
...NATSU'S GROUP WON'T BE WEARING THEIR TIES?!
And Natsu's new look is okay?!
WELL, THEY LOOK COOLER THIS WAY.
!!! !!! !!!
Well... I think so too...
And they'll look scarier in the bullying scenes.
...
SO WE'RE REALLY GONNA DRESS THIS WAY...?
WHAT'RE THEY GONNA DO ABOUT THE SCENES WE ALREADY SHOT... WILL WE SHOOT THEM AGAIN?

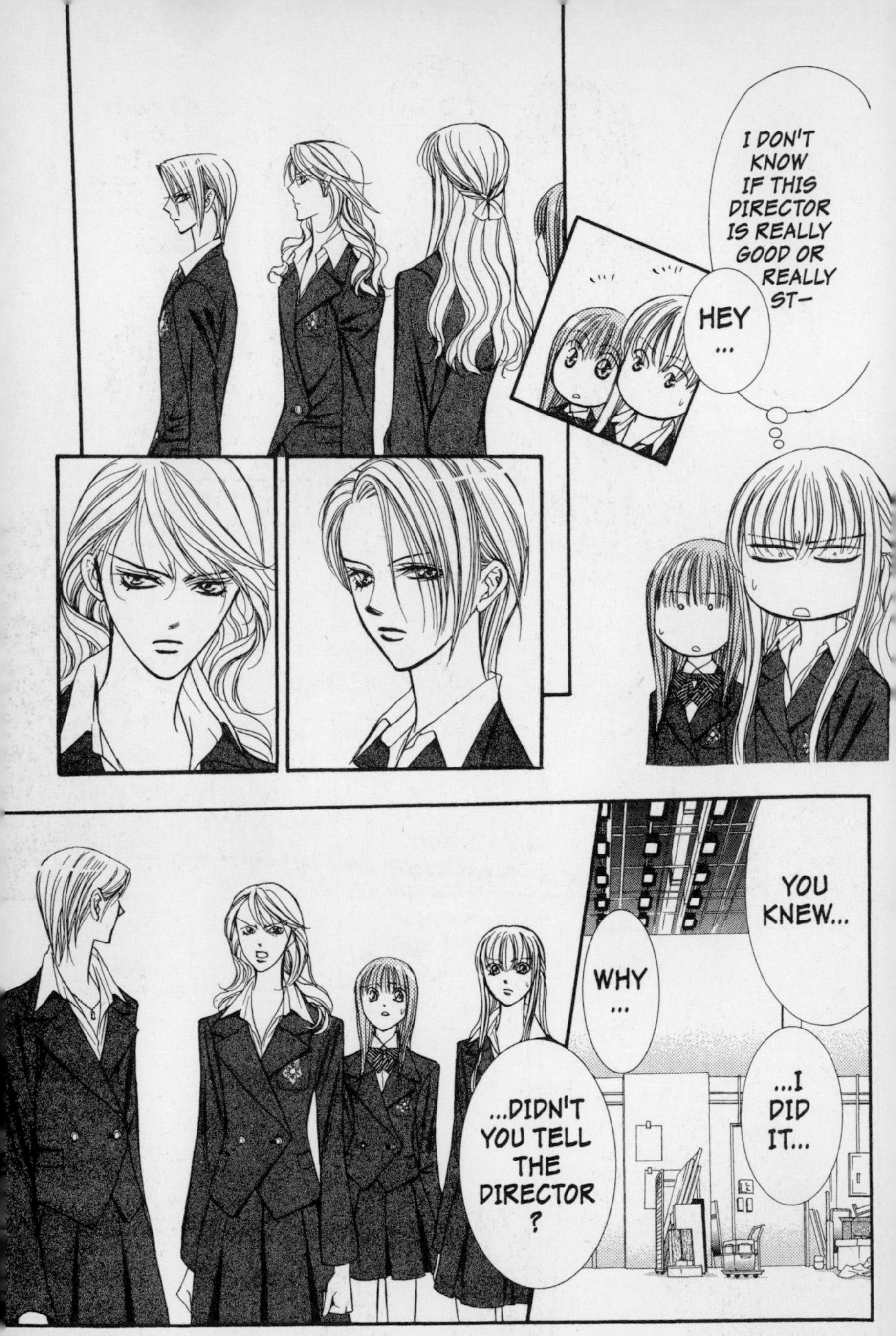
I DON'T KNOW IF THIS DIRECTOR IS REALLY GOOD OR REALLY ST—
HEY ...
YOU KNEW...
...I DID IT...
WHY ...
...DIDN'T YOU TELL THE DIRECTOR ?

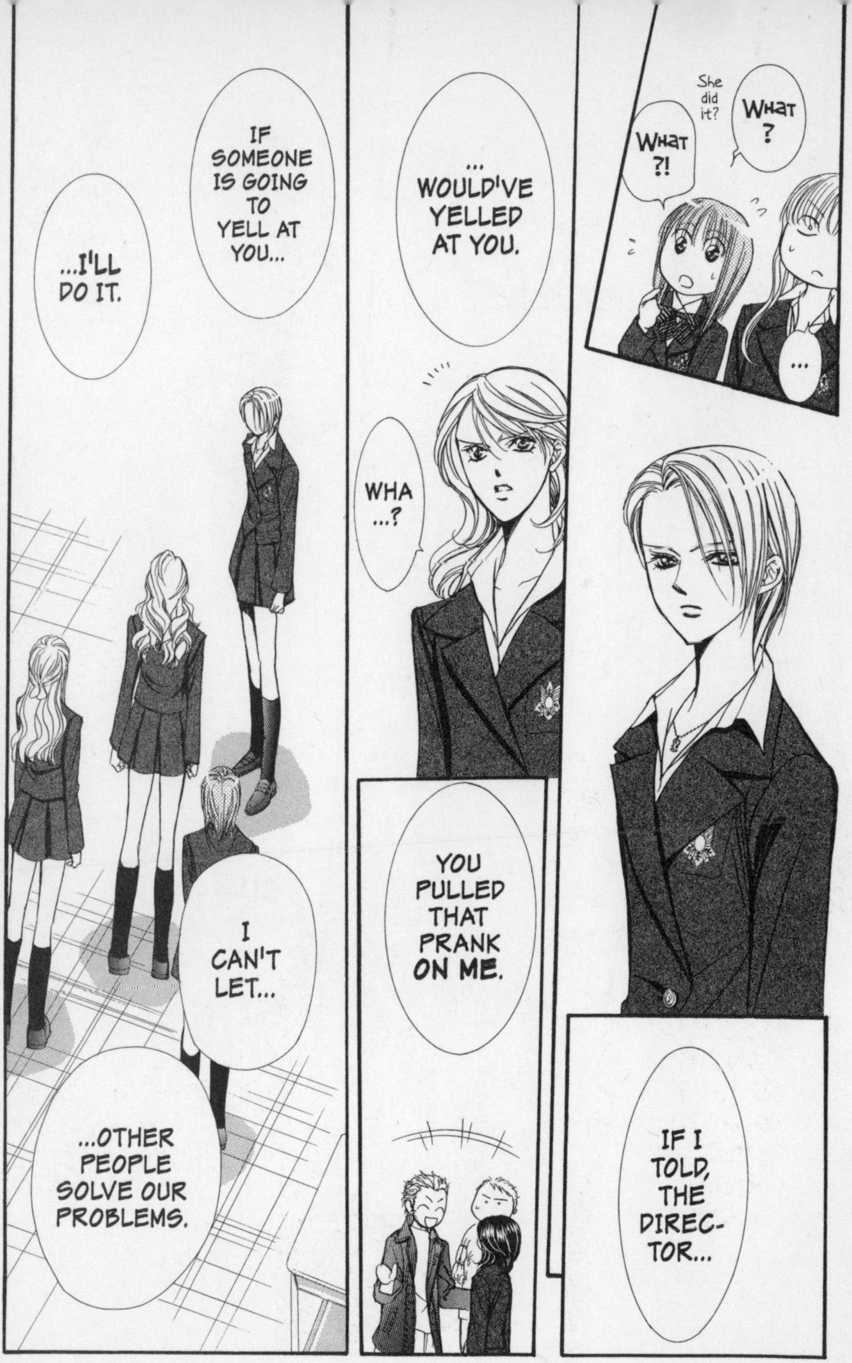
WHAT ?
She did it?
WHAT ?!
...
IF I TOLD, THE DIRECTOR...
... WOULD'VE YELLED AT YOU.
WHA ...?
YOU PULLED THAT PRANK ON ME.
IF SOMEONE IS GOING TO YELL AT YOU...
...I'LL DO IT.
I CAN'T LET...
...OTHER PEOPLE SOLVE OUR PROBLEMS.

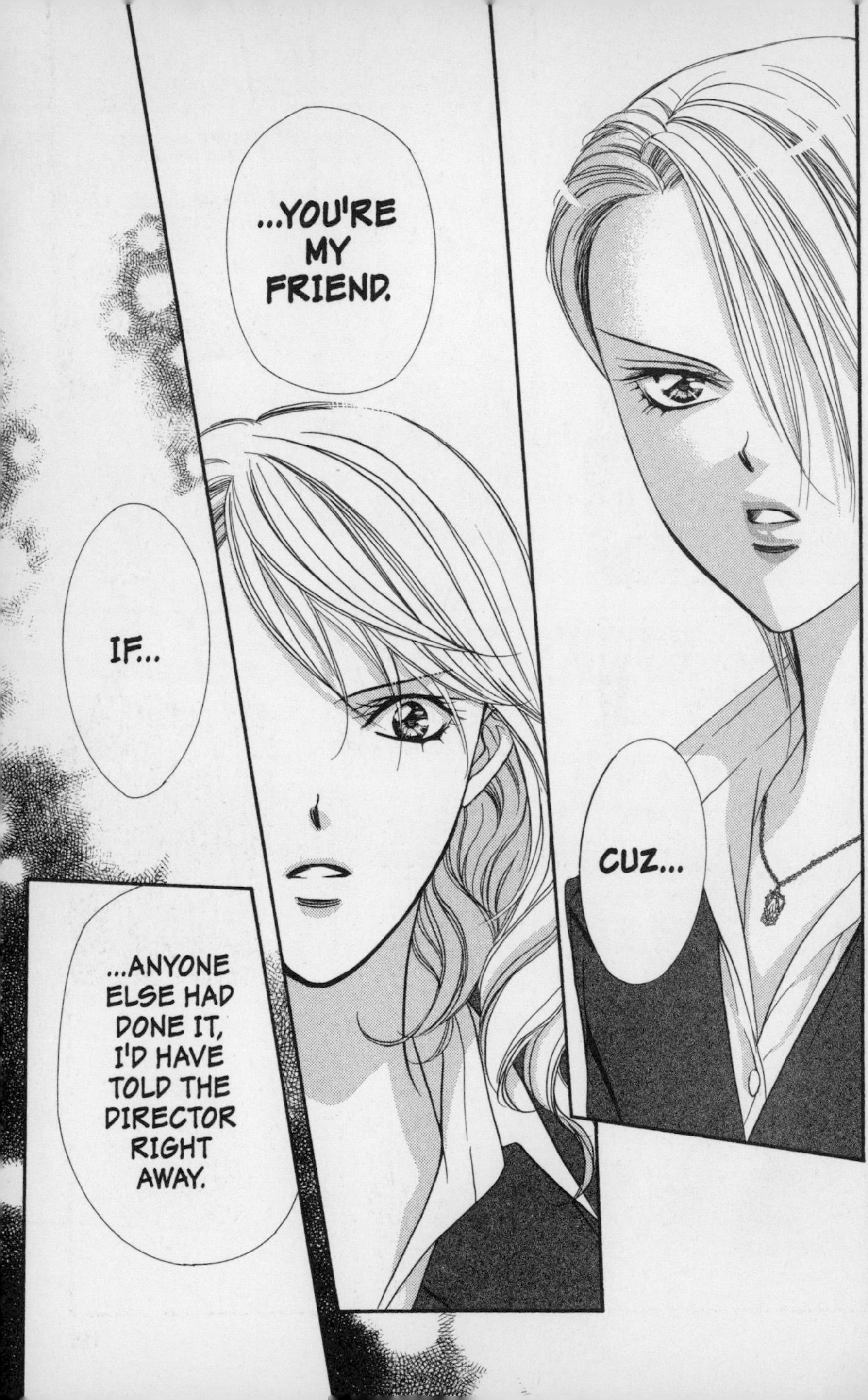
CUZ...
...YOU'RE MY FRIEND.
IF...
...ANYONE ELSE HAD DONE IT, I'D HAVE TOLD THE DIRECTOR RIGHT AWAY.

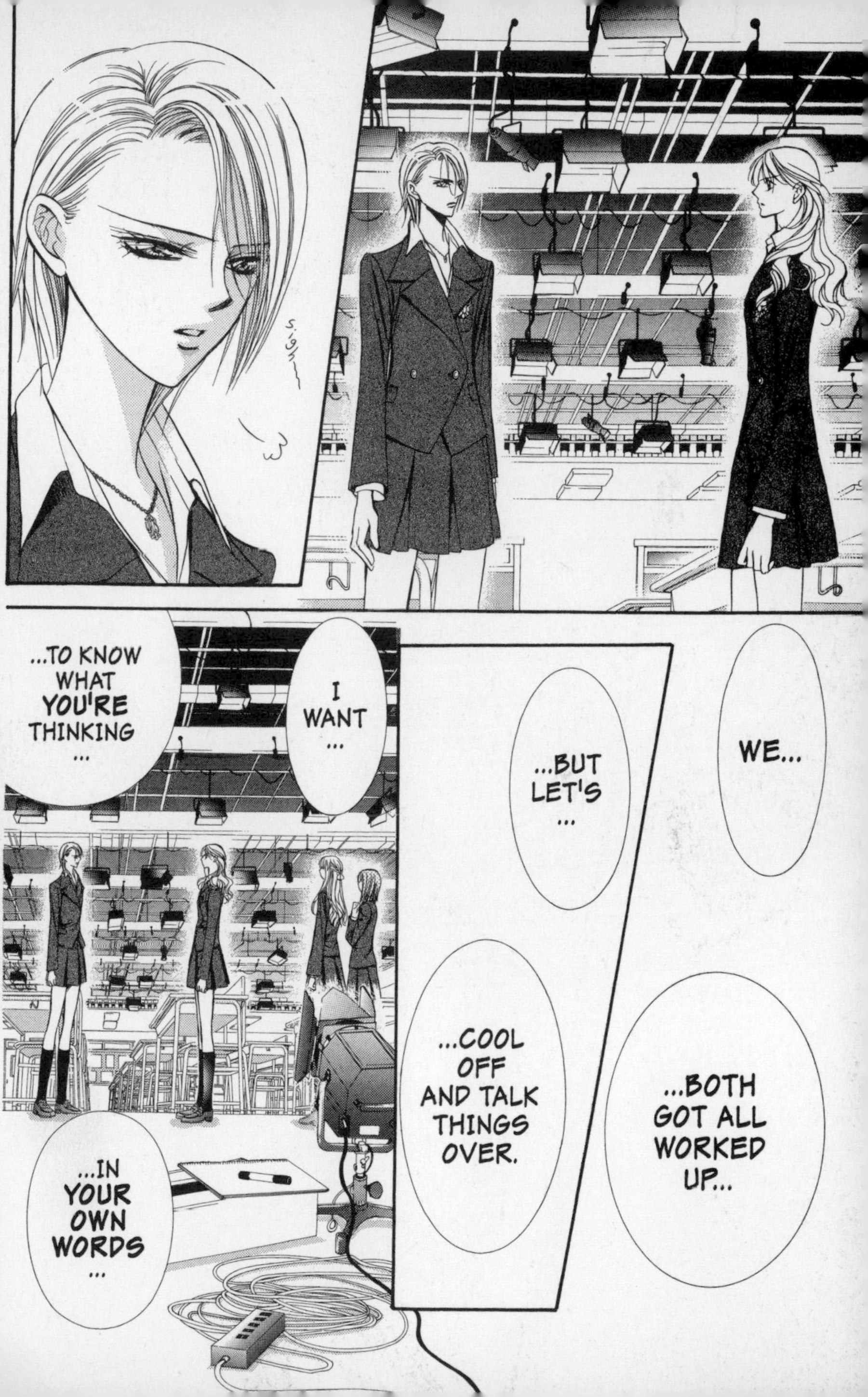
sigh
WE...
...BOTH GOT ALL WORKED UP...
...BUT LET'S...
...COOL OFF AND TALK THINGS OVER.
I WANT...
...TO KNOW WHAT YOU'RE THINKING...
...IN YOUR OWN WORDS...

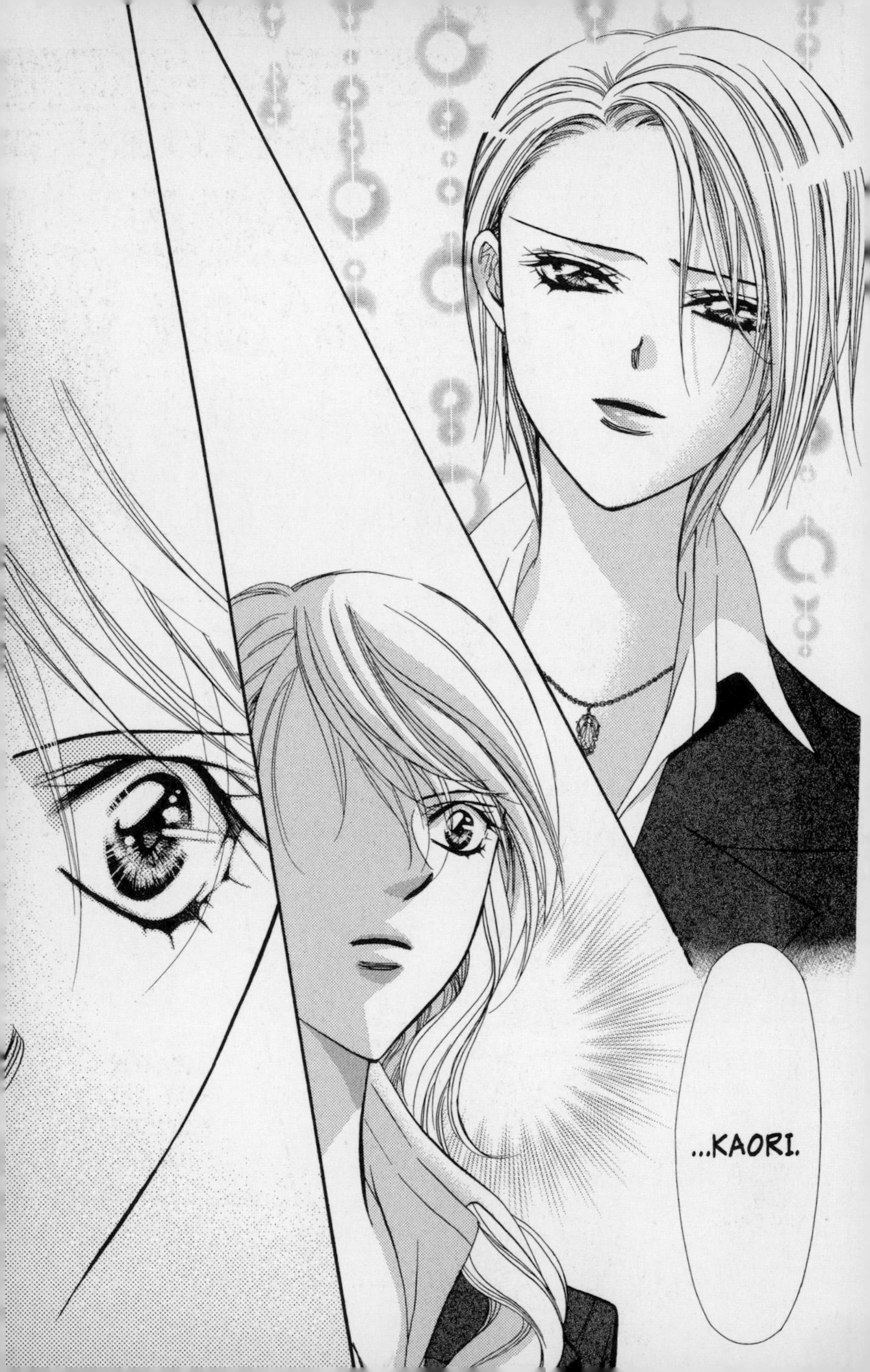
...KAORI.

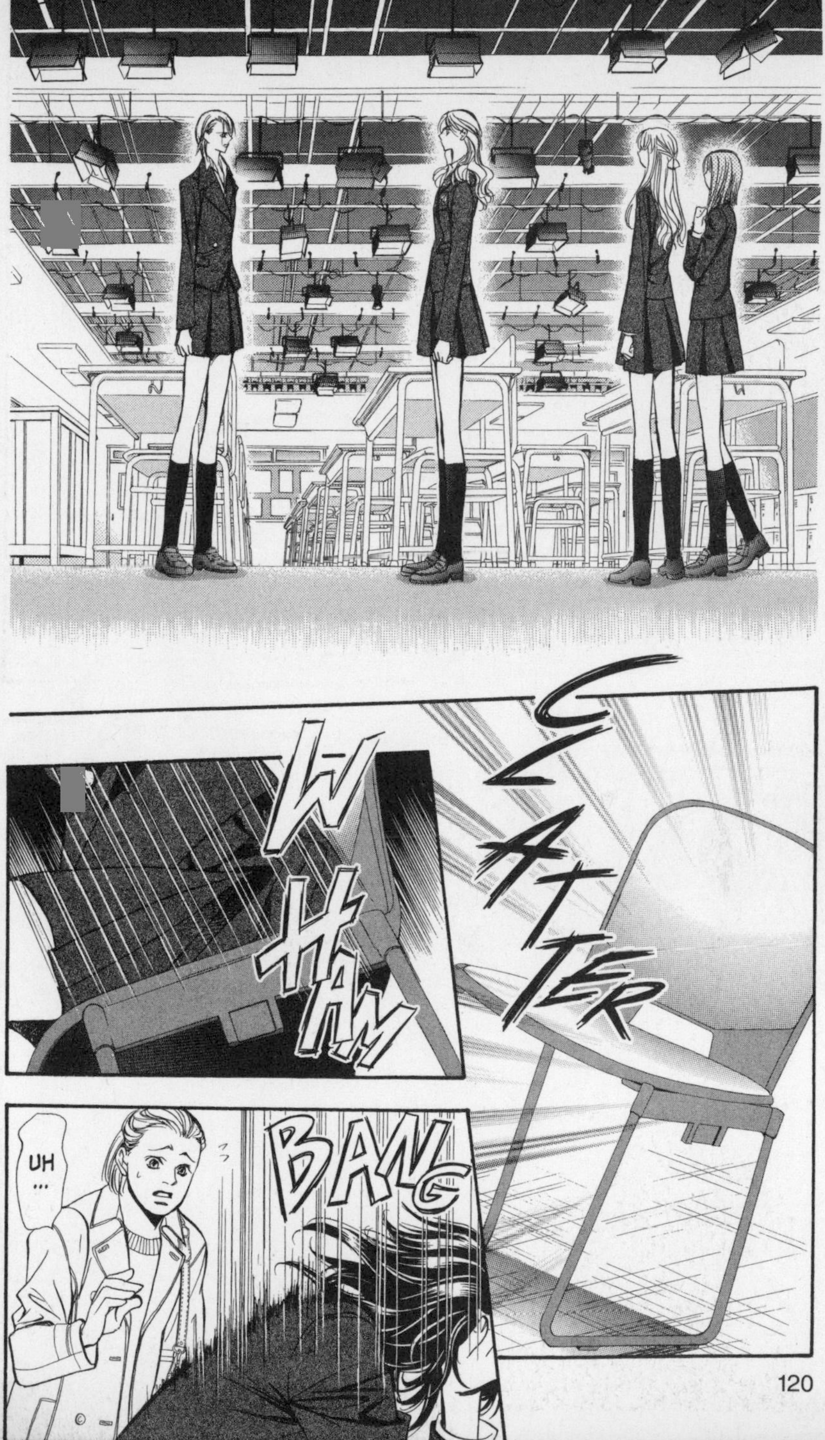
CLATTER
WHAM
BANG
UH ...

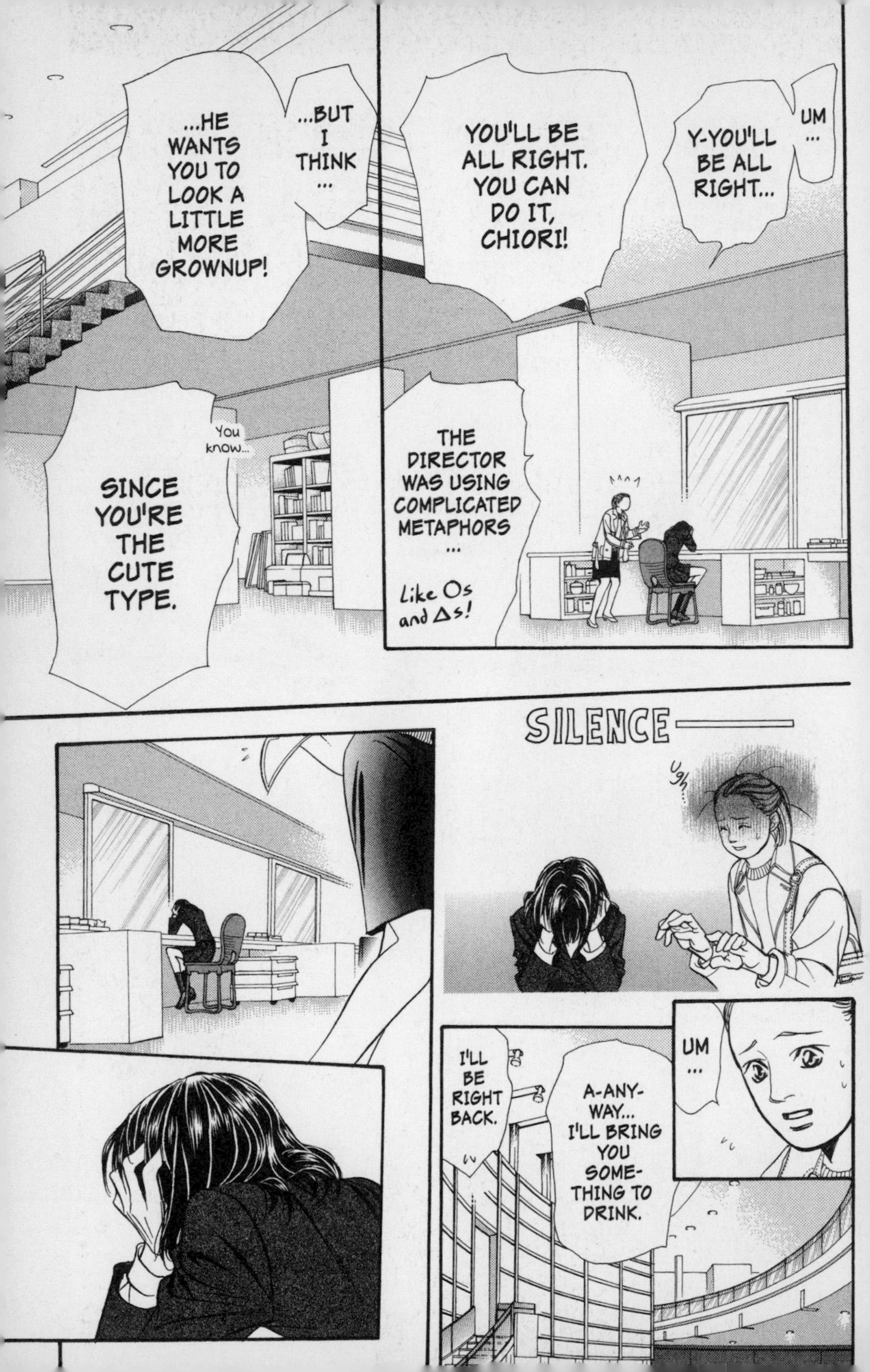
UM ...
Y-YOU'LL BE ALL RIGHT...
YOU'LL BE ALL RIGHT. YOU CAN DO IT, CHIORI!
THE DIRECTOR WAS USING COMPLICATED METAPHORS ...
Like Os and Δs!
...BUT I THINK ...
...HE WANTS YOU TO LOOK A LITTLE MORE GROWNUP!
You know...
SINCE YOU'RE THE CUTE TYPE.
SILENCE—
ugh...
UM ...
A-ANY-WAY... I'LL BRING YOU SOME-THING TO DRINK.
I'LL BE RIGHT BACK.

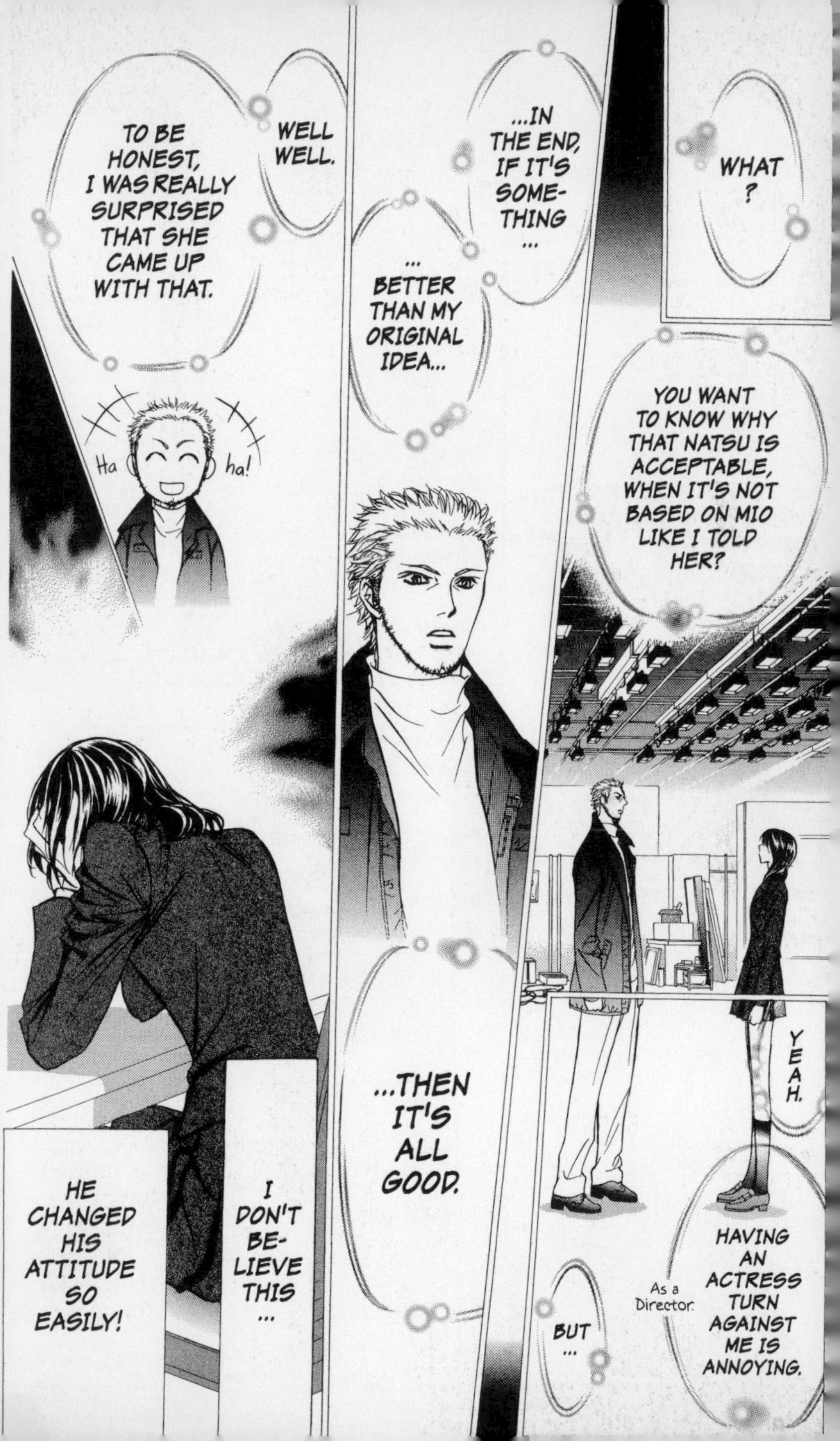
WHAT?
YOU WANT TO KNOW WHY THAT NATSU IS ACCEPTABLE, WHEN IT'S NOT BASED ON MIO LIKE I TOLD HER?
YEAH.
HAVING AN ACTRESS TURN AGAINST ME IS ANNOYING.
As a Director.
BUT...
...IN THE END, IF IT'S SOMETHING...
...BETTER THAN MY ORIGINAL IDEA...
...THEN IT'S ALL GOOD.
WELL WELL.
TO BE HONEST, I WAS REALLY SURPRISED THAT SHE CAME UP WITH THAT.
Ha ha!
I DON'T BELIEVE THIS...
HE CHANGED HIS ATTITUDE SO EASILY!

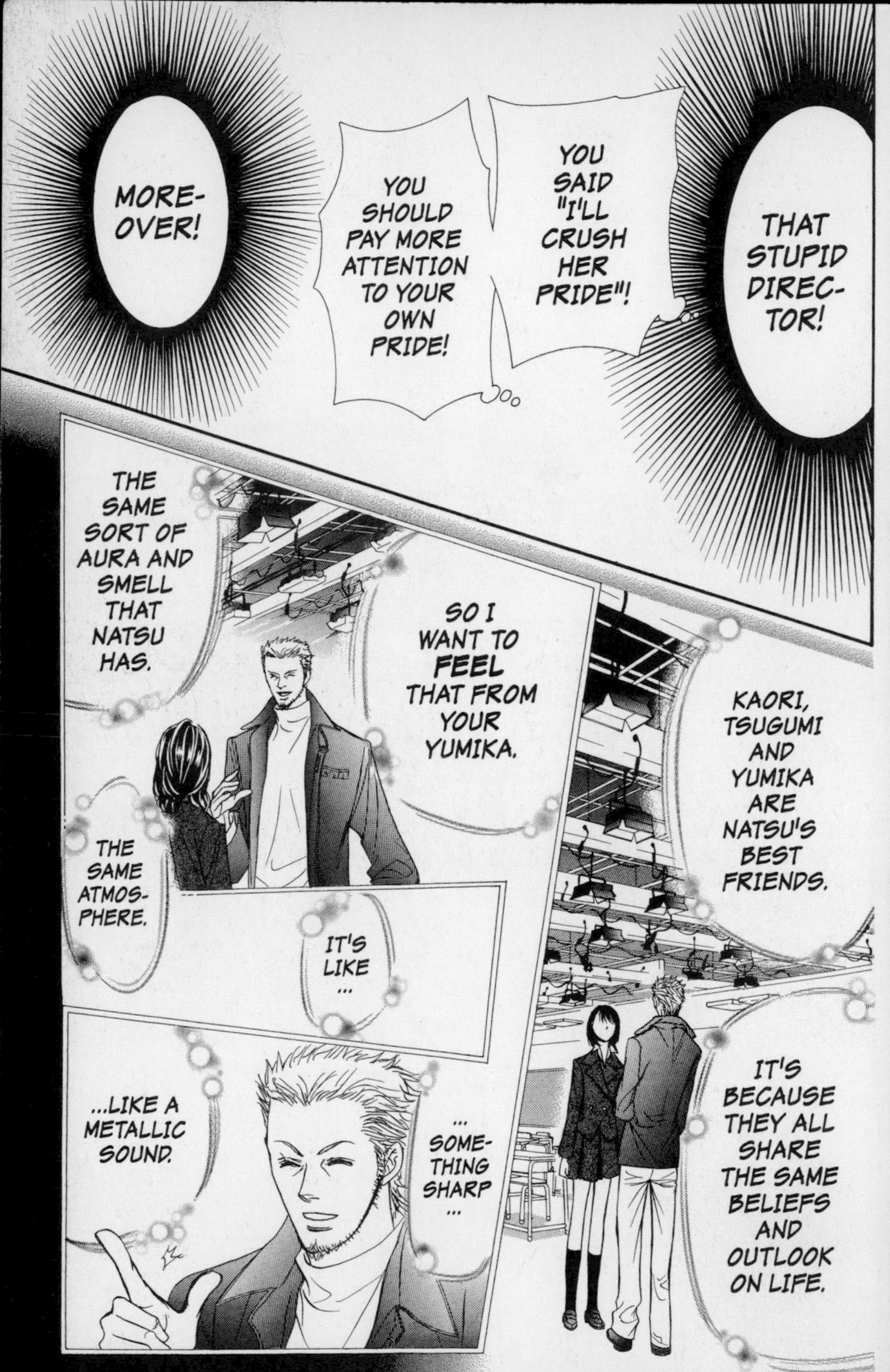
THAT STUPID DIREC-TOR!
YOU SAID "I'LL CRUSH HER PRIDE"!
YOU SHOULD PAY MORE ATTENTION TO YOUR OWN PRIDE!
MORE-OVER!
KAORI, TSUGUMI AND YUMIKA ARE NATSU'S BEST FRIENDS.
IT'S BECAUSE THEY ALL SHARE THE SAME BELIEFS AND OUTLOOK ON LIFE.
SO I WANT TO FEEL THAT FROM YOUR YUMIKA.
THE SAME SORT OF AURA AND SMELL THAT NATSU HAS.
THE SAME ATMOS-PHERE.
IT'S LIKE ...
... SOME-THING SHARP ...
...LIKE A METALLIC SOUND.

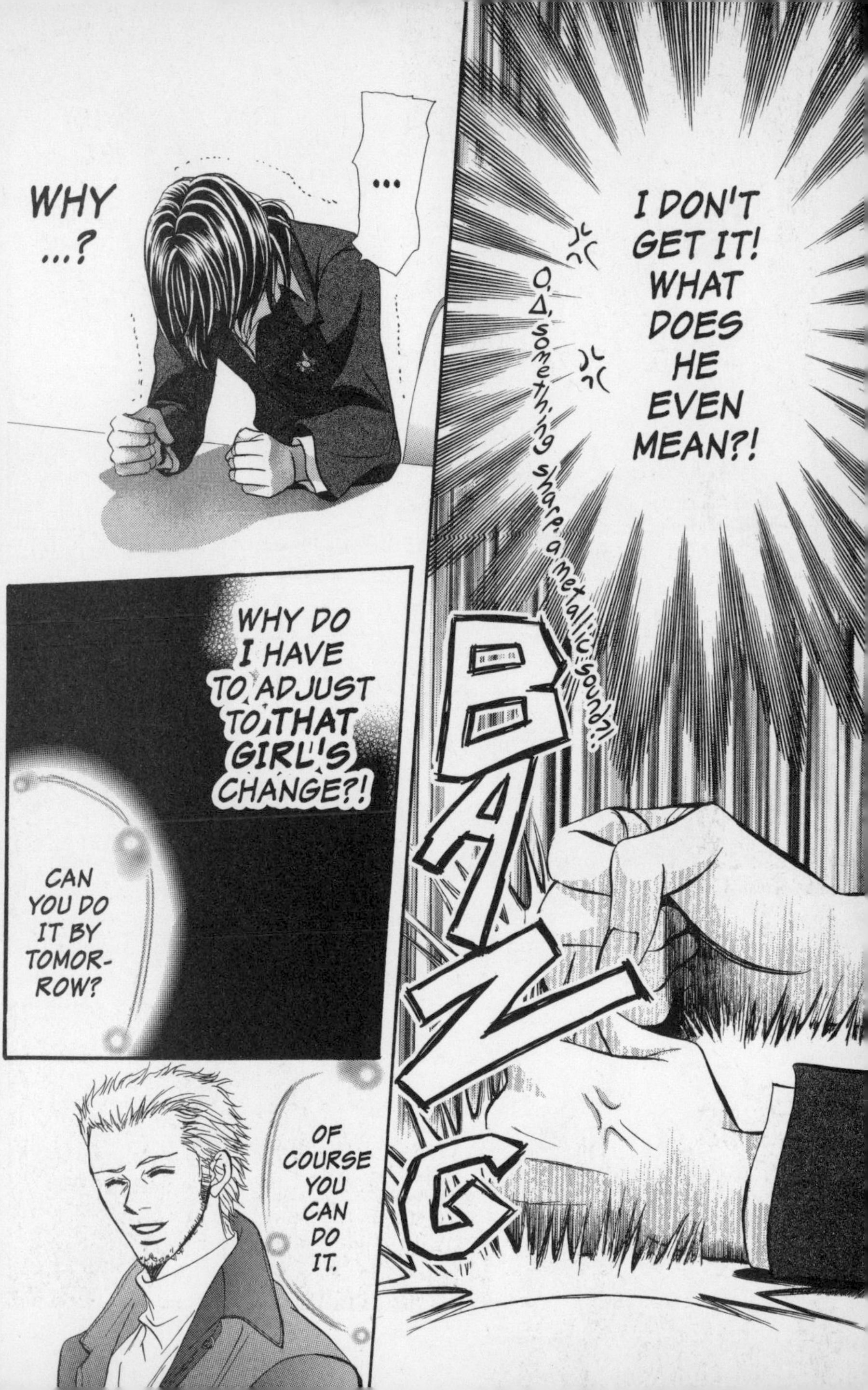
I DON'T GET IT! WHAT DOES HE EVEN MEAN?!
O, Δ, something sharp, a metallic sound?!
BANG
...
WHY ...?
WHY DO I HAVE TO ADJUST TO THAT GIRL'S CHANGE?!
CAN YOU DO IT BY TOMOR-ROW?
OF COURSE YOU CAN DO IT.

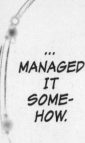

EVEN THE NEW-COMER TALENTO KYOKO...

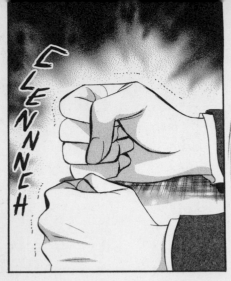

CLENNNCH

...MANAGED IT SOME-HOW.

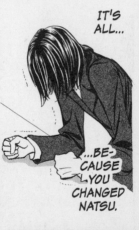

IT'S ALL...

...BE-CAUSE YOU CHANGED NATSU.

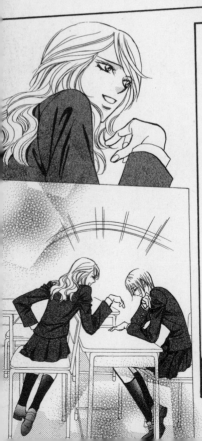

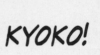

KYOKO!

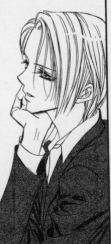

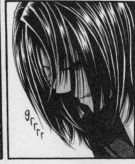

grrrr

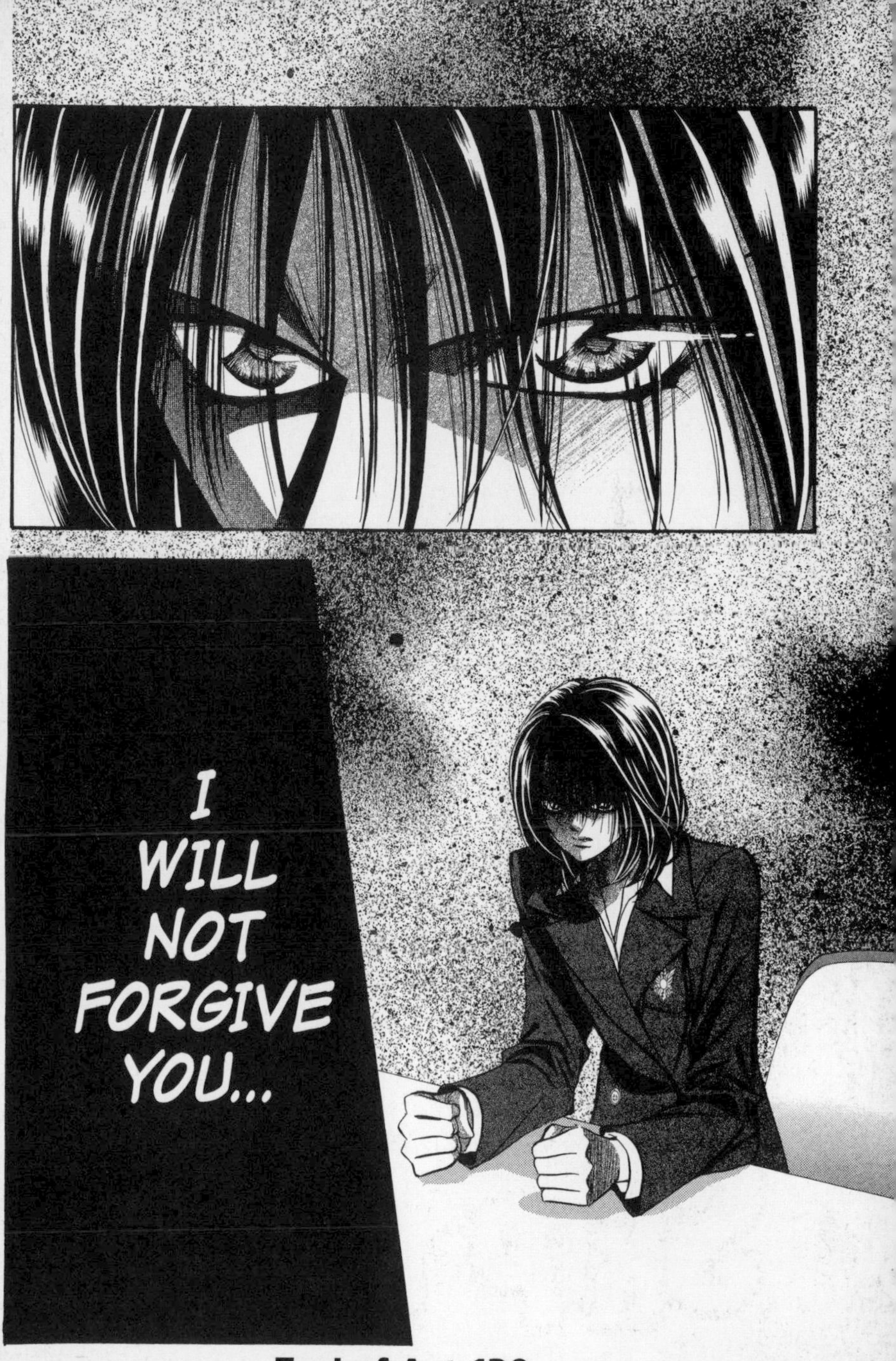
I WILL NOT FORGIVE YOU...

End of Act 130

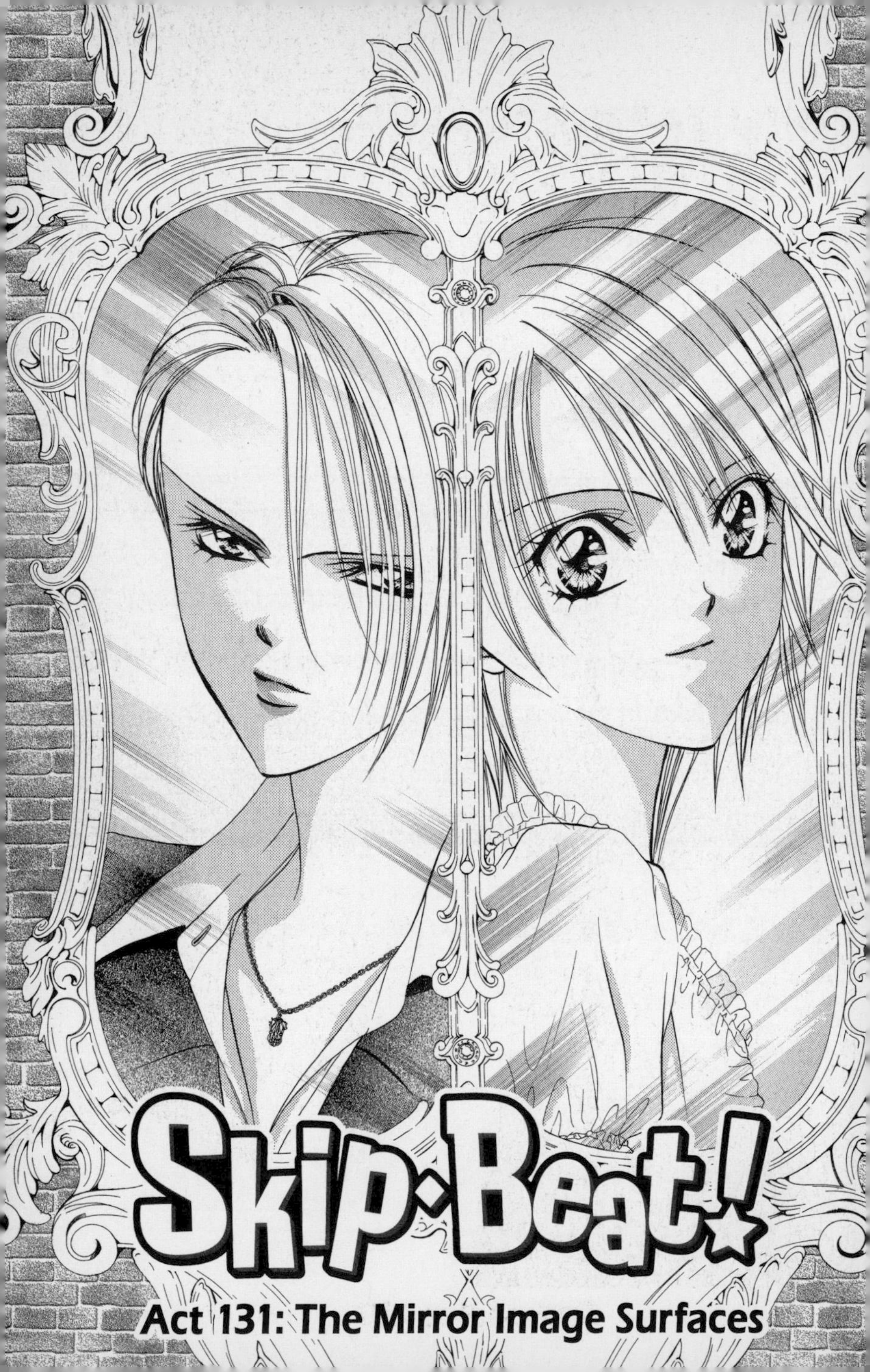
Skip·Beat!
Act 131: The Mirror Image Surfaces

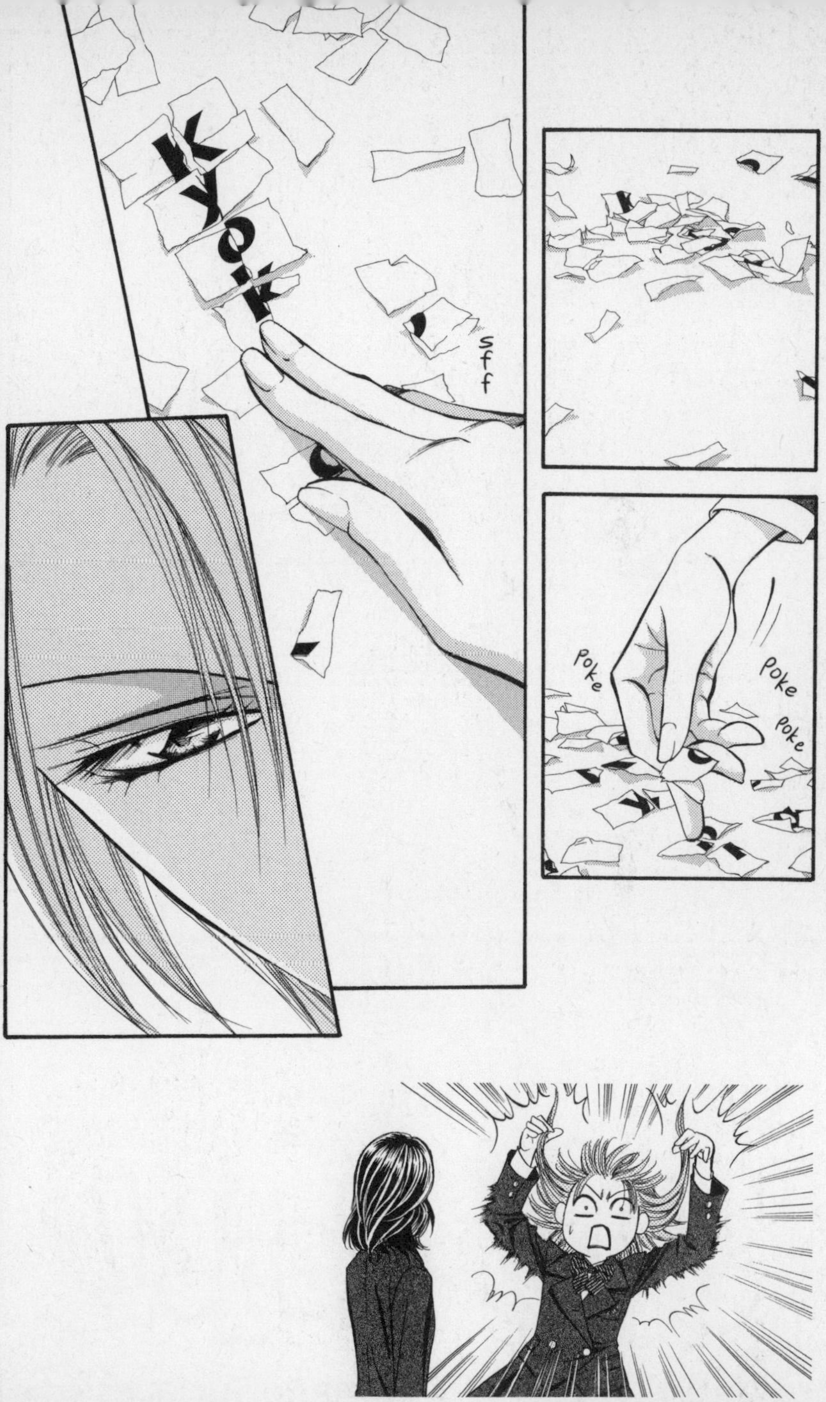
Poke
Poke
Poke
Kyok
sff

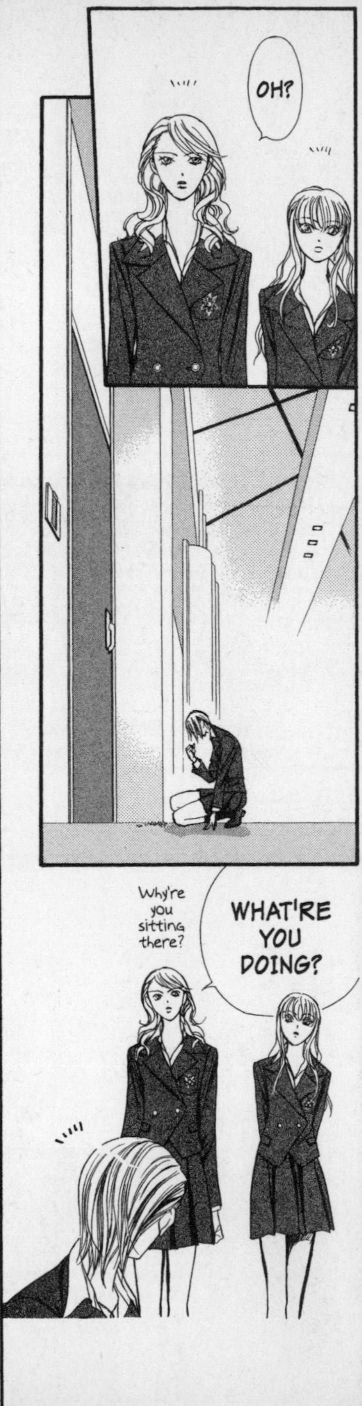
OH?
WHAT'RE YOU DOING?
Why're you sitting there?
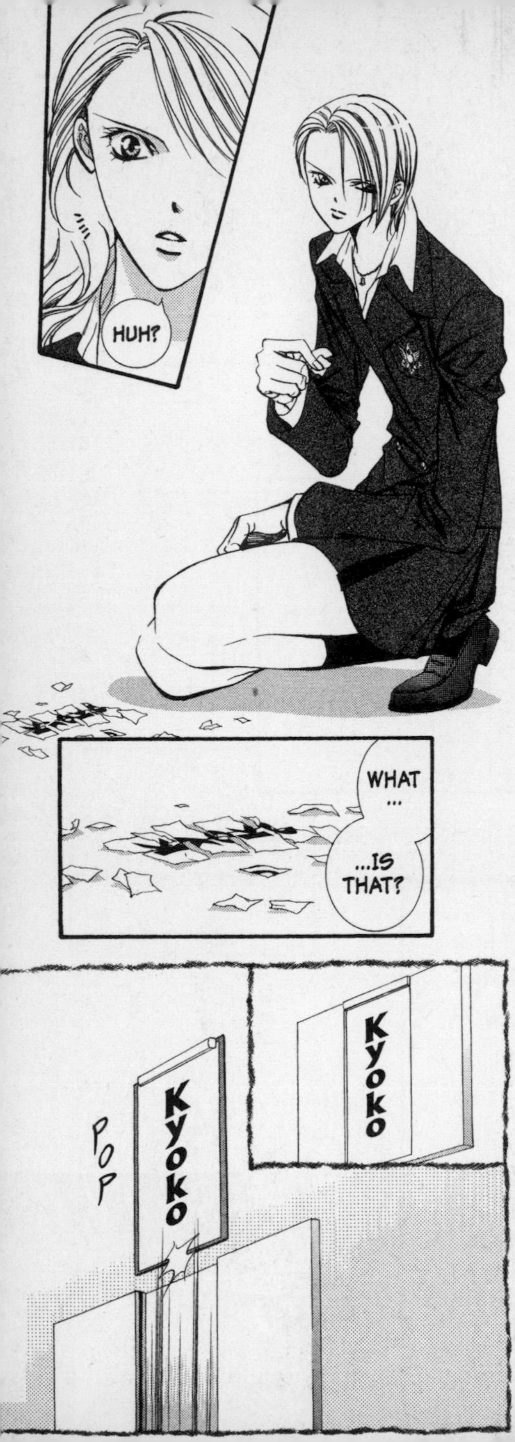
HUH?
WHAT ...
...IS THAT?
KYOKO
POP
KYOKO

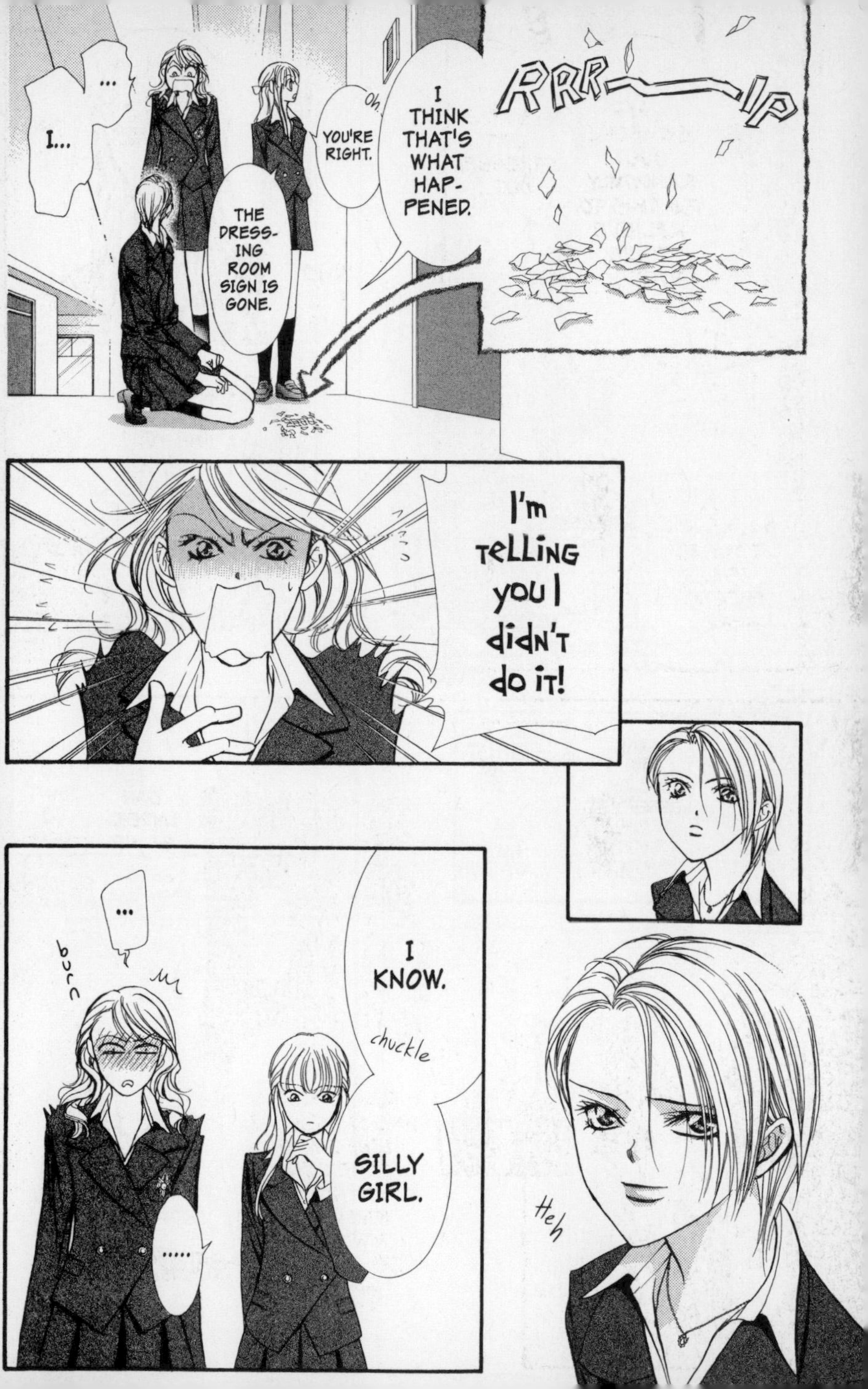
RRR—IP
I THINK THAT'S WHAT HAP-PENED.
Oh, YOU'RE RIGHT.
THE DRESS-ING ROOM SIGN IS GONE.
...
I...
I'm telling you I didn't do it!
Heh
I KNOW.
chuckle
SILLY GIRL.
...
burn
......

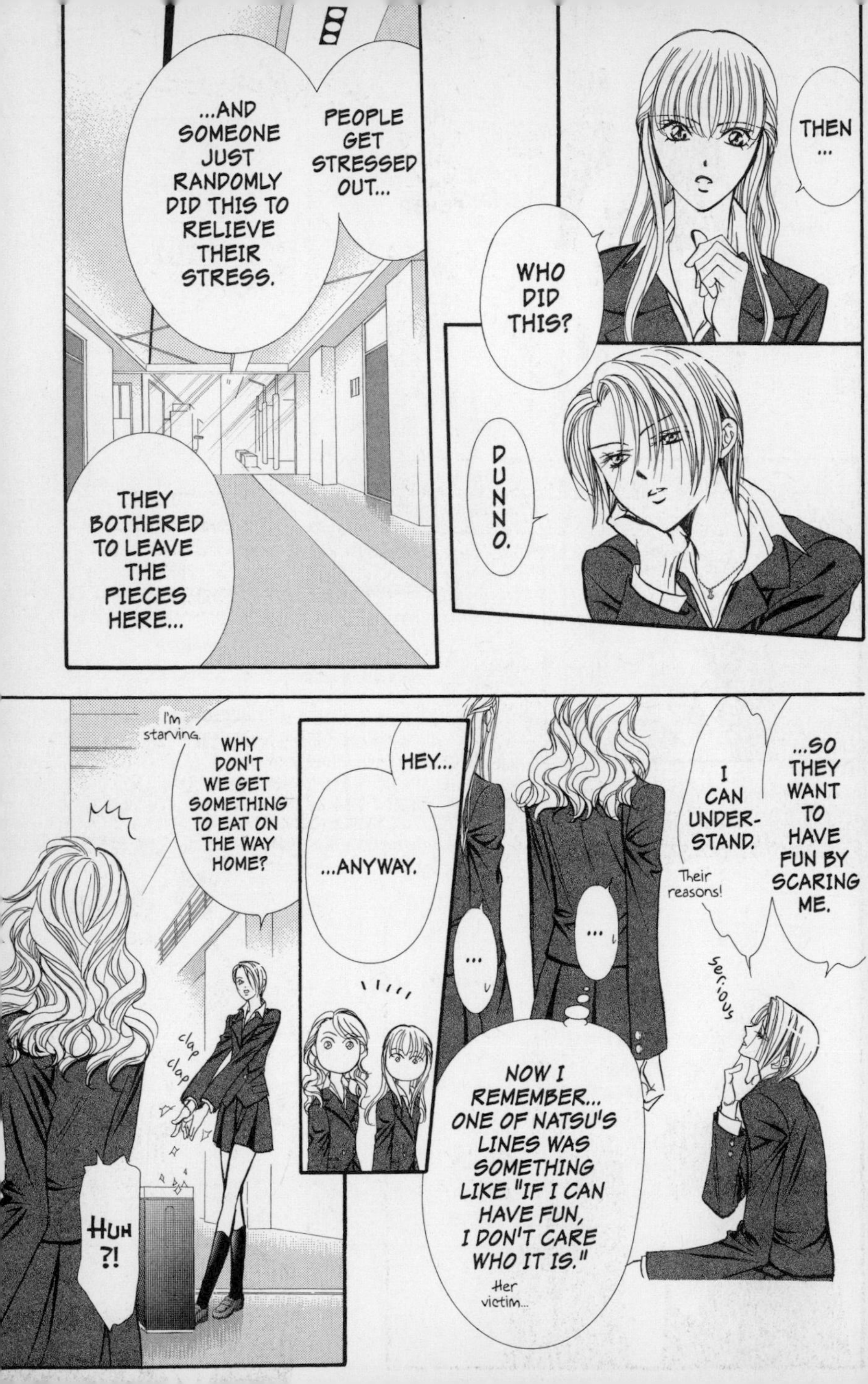
THEN ...
WHO DID THIS?
DUNNO.
PEOPLE GET STRESSED OUT...
...AND SOMEONE JUST RANDOMLY DID THIS TO RELIEVE THEIR STRESS.
THEY BOTHERED TO LEAVE THE PIECES HERE...
...SO THEY WANT TO HAVE FUN BY SCARING ME.
I CAN UNDER-STAND.
Their reasons!
serious
...
...
NOW I REMEMBER... ONE OF NATSU'S LINES WAS SOMETHING LIKE "IF I CAN HAVE FUN, I DON'T CARE WHO IT IS."
Her victim...
HEY...
...ANYWAY.
I'm starving.
WHY DON'T WE GET SOMETHING TO EAT ON THE WAY HOME?
clap clap
HUH ?!

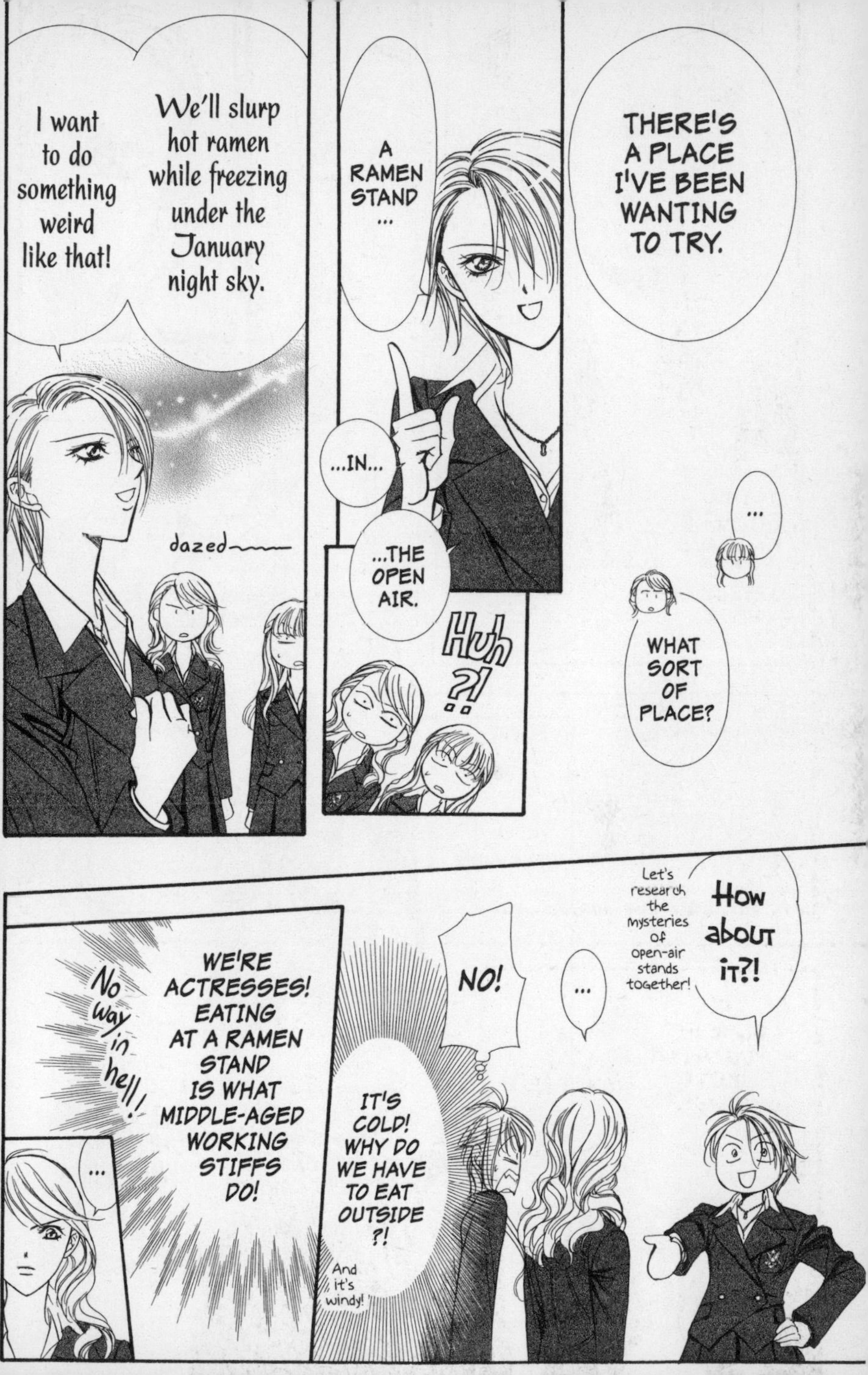
THERE'S A PLACE I'VE BEEN WANTING TO TRY.
...
WHAT SORT OF PLACE?
A RAMEN STAND ...
...IN...
...THE OPEN AIR.
Huh ?!
We'll slurp hot ramen while freezing under the January night sky.
I want to do something weird like that!
dazed
How about it?!
Let's research the mysteries of open-air stands together!
...
NO!
IT'S COLD! WHY DO WE HAVE TO EAT OUTSIDE ?!
And it's windy!
WE'RE ACTRESSES! EATING AT A RAMEN STAND IS WHAT MIDDLE-AGED WORKING STIFFS DO!
No way in hell!
...

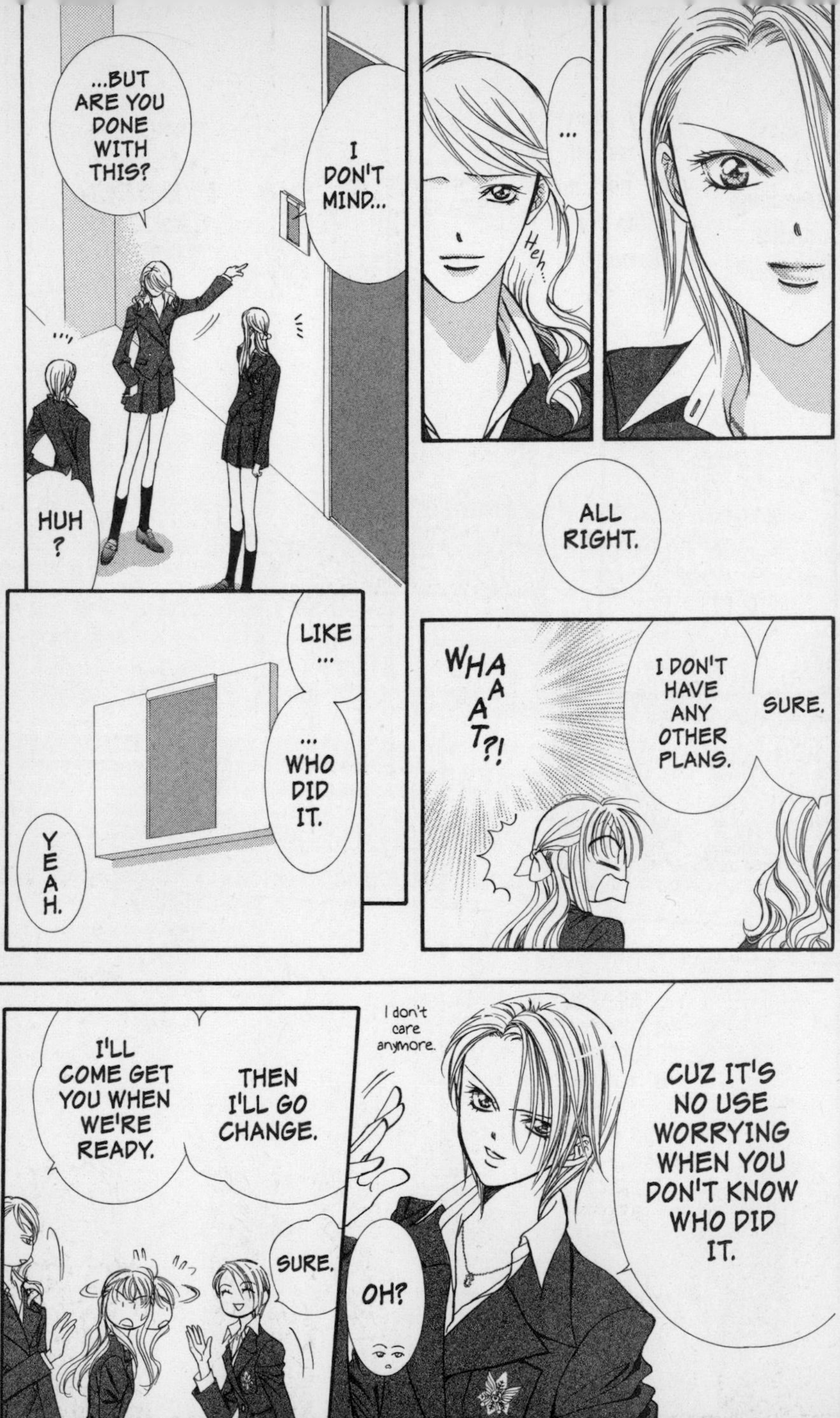
...
Heh...
ALL RIGHT.
I DON'T MIND...
...BUT ARE YOU DONE WITH THIS?
HUH?
SURE.
I DON'T HAVE ANY OTHER PLANS.
WHAAAT?!
LIKE...
...WHO DID IT.
YEAH.
CUZ IT'S NO USE WORRYING WHEN YOU DON'T KNOW WHO DID IT.
I don't care anymore.
OH?
THEN I'LL GO CHANGE.
I'LL COME GET YOU WHEN WE'RE READY.
SURE.

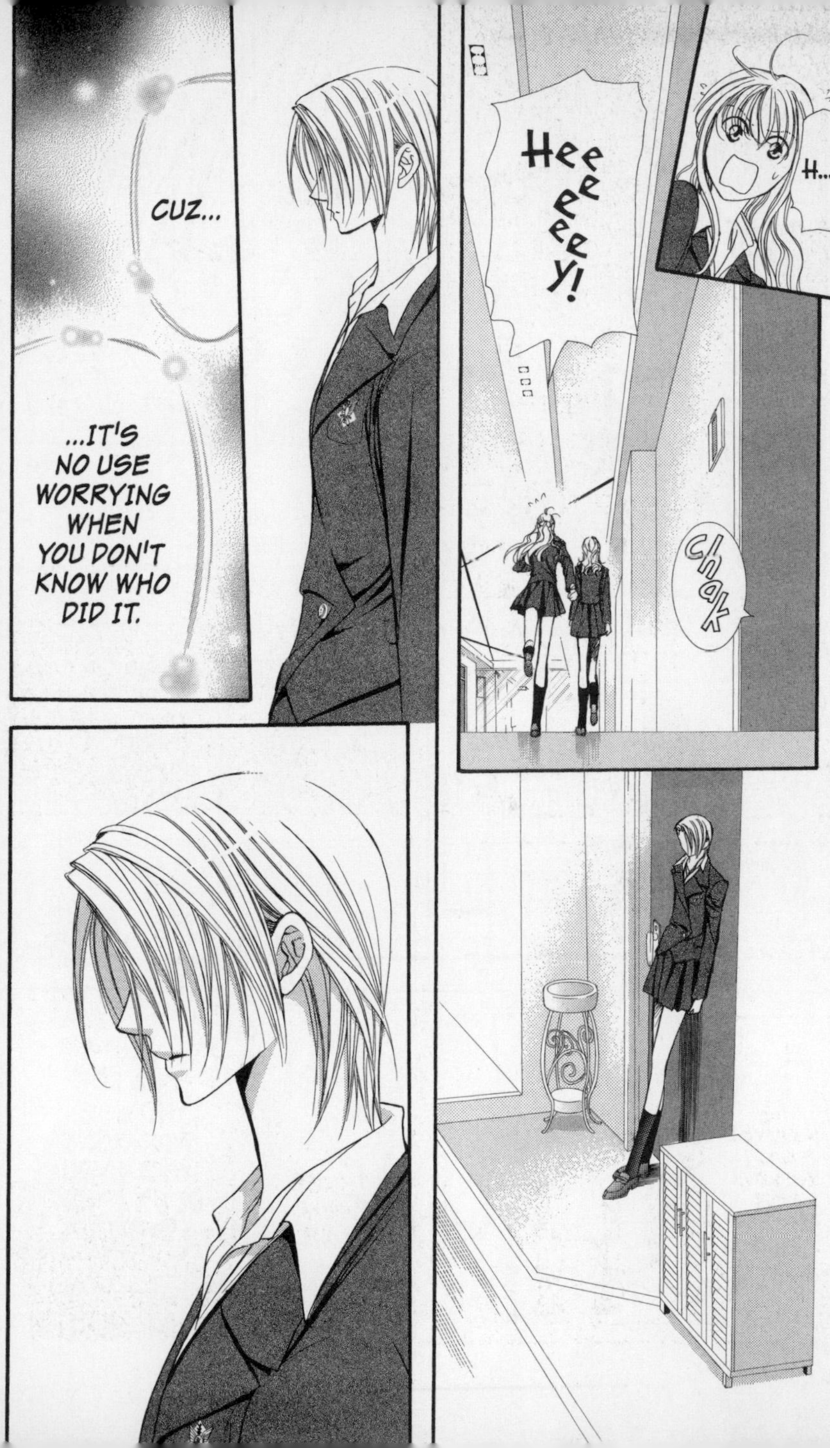
H...
Heeeeeey!
Chak
CUZ...
...IT'S NO USE WORRYING WHEN YOU DON'T KNOW WHO DID IT.

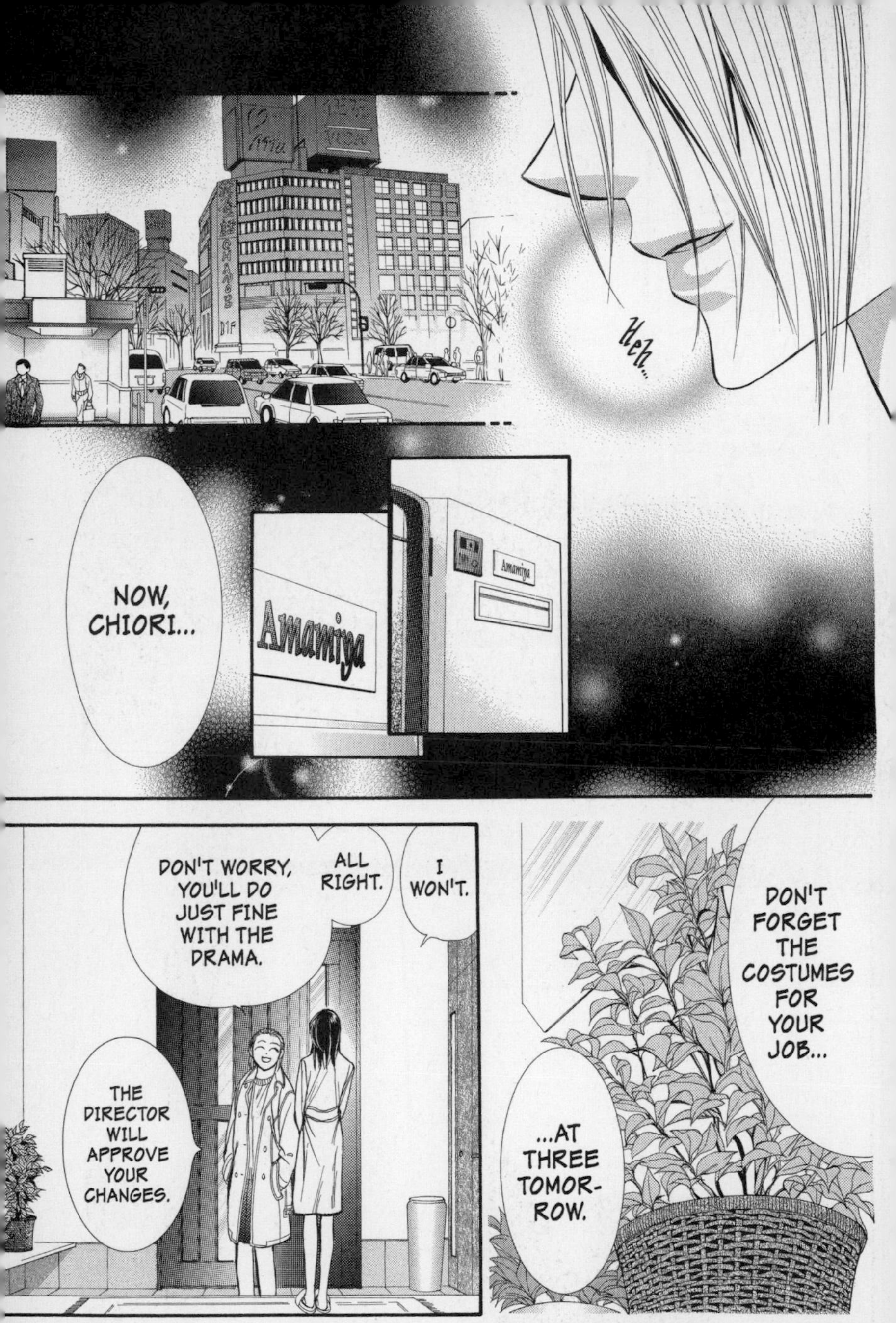
Heh...
NOW, CHIORI...
Amamiya
Amamiya
DON'T FORGET THE COSTUMES FOR YOUR JOB...
...AT THREE TOMOR-ROW.
I WON'T.
ALL RIGHT.
DON'T WORRY, YOU'LL DO JUST FINE WITH THE DRAMA.
THE DIRECTOR WILL APPROVE YOUR CHANGES.

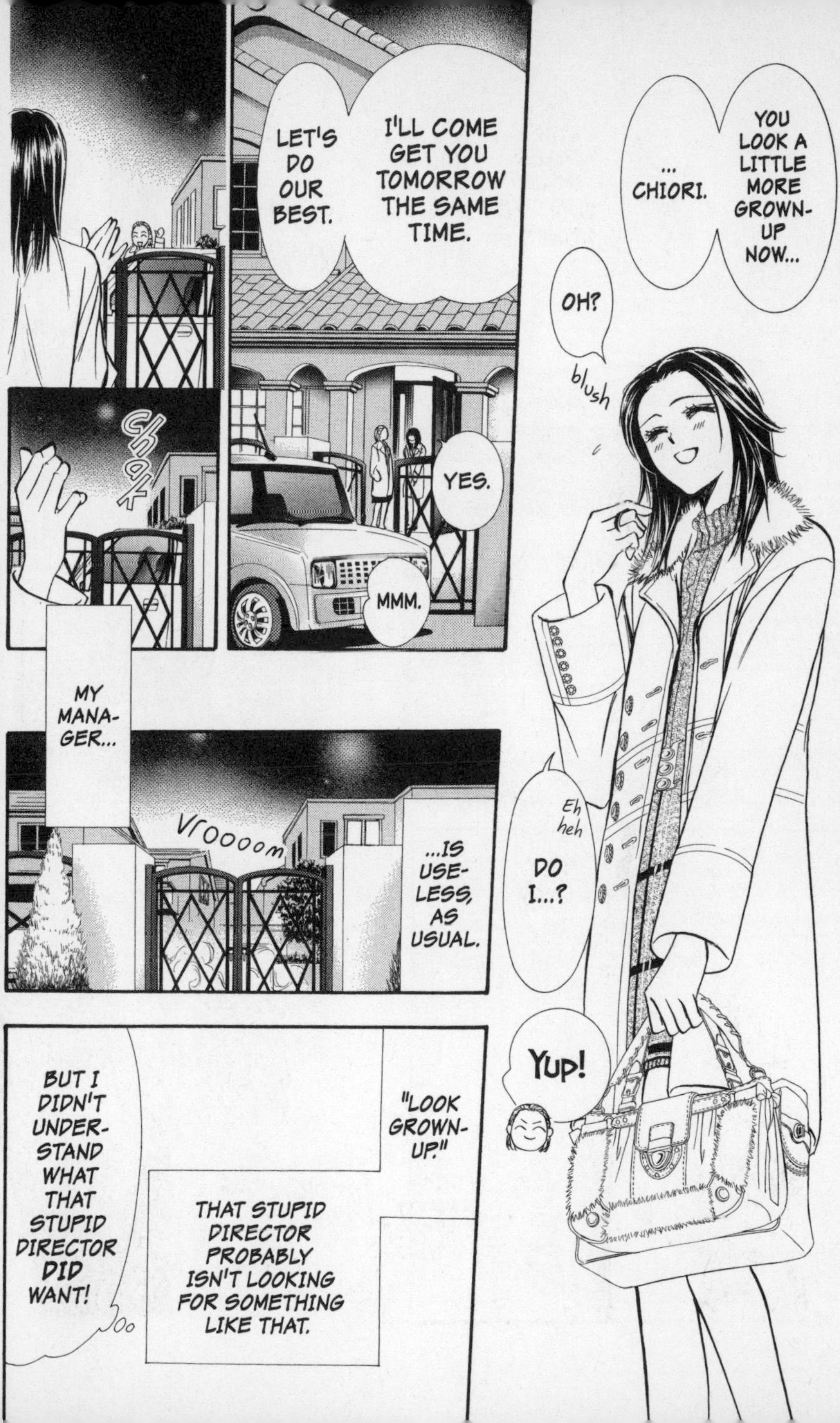
YOU LOOK A LITTLE MORE GROWN-UP NOW...
... CHIORI.
OH?
blush
Eh heh
DO I...?
YUP!
I'LL COME GET YOU TOMORROW THE SAME TIME.
LET'S DO OUR BEST.
YES.
MMM.
Chak
MY MANAGER...
...IS USELESS, AS USUAL.
Vroooom
"LOOK GROWN-UP."
THAT STUPID DIRECTOR PROBABLY ISN'T LOOKING FOR SOMETHING LIKE THAT.
BUT I DIDN'T UNDERSTAND WHAT THAT STUPID DIRECTOR DID WANT!

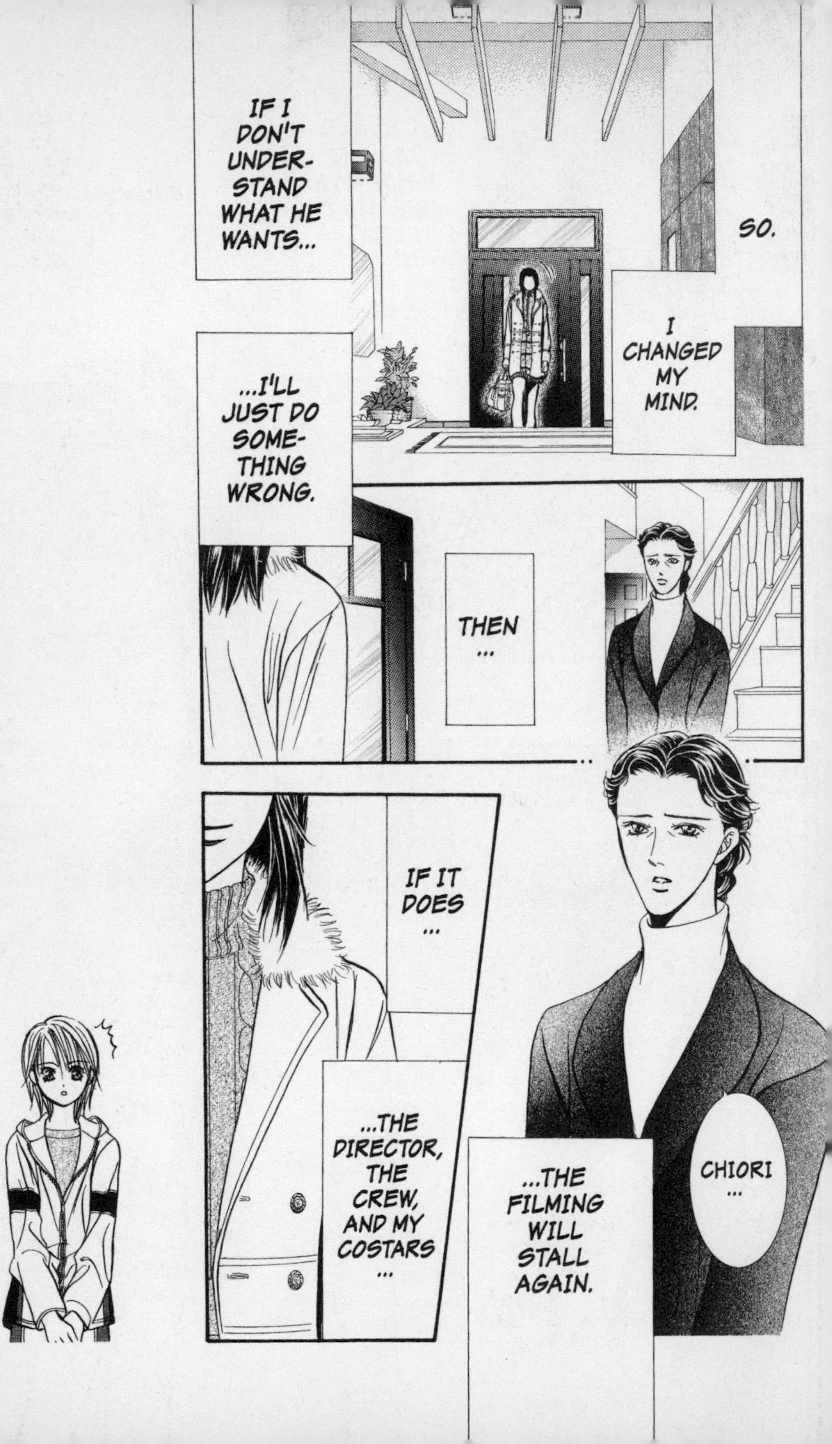
SO.
I CHANGED MY MIND.
IF I DON'T UNDER-STAND WHAT HE WANTS...
...I'LL JUST DO SOME-THING WRONG.
THEN ...
......
CHIORI ...
...THE FILMING WILL STALL AGAIN.
IF IT DOES ...
...THE DIRECTOR, THE CREW, AND MY COSTARS ...

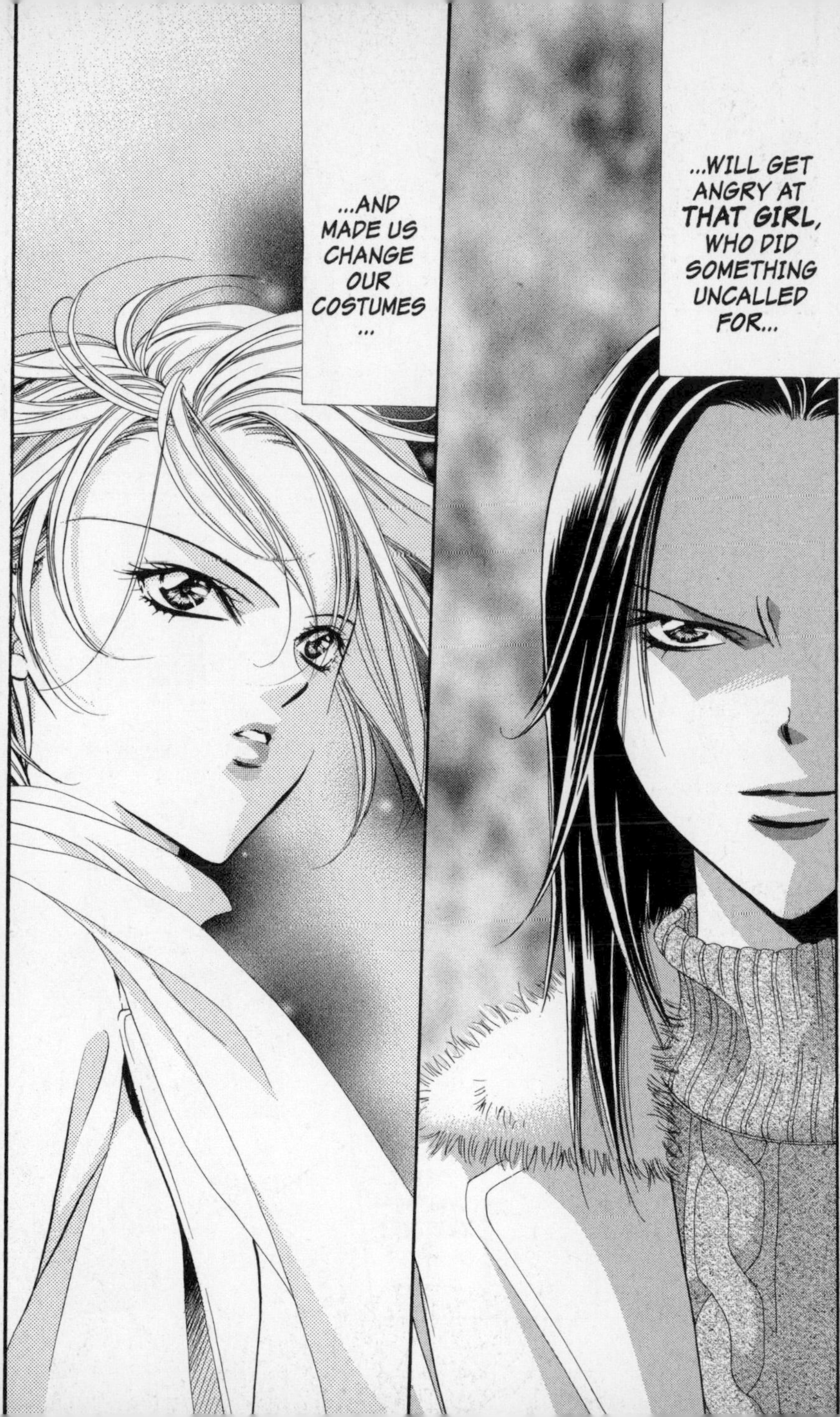
...WILL GET ANGRY AT THAT GIRL, WHO DID SOMETHING UNCALLED FOR...
...AND MADE US CHANGE OUR COSTUMES ...

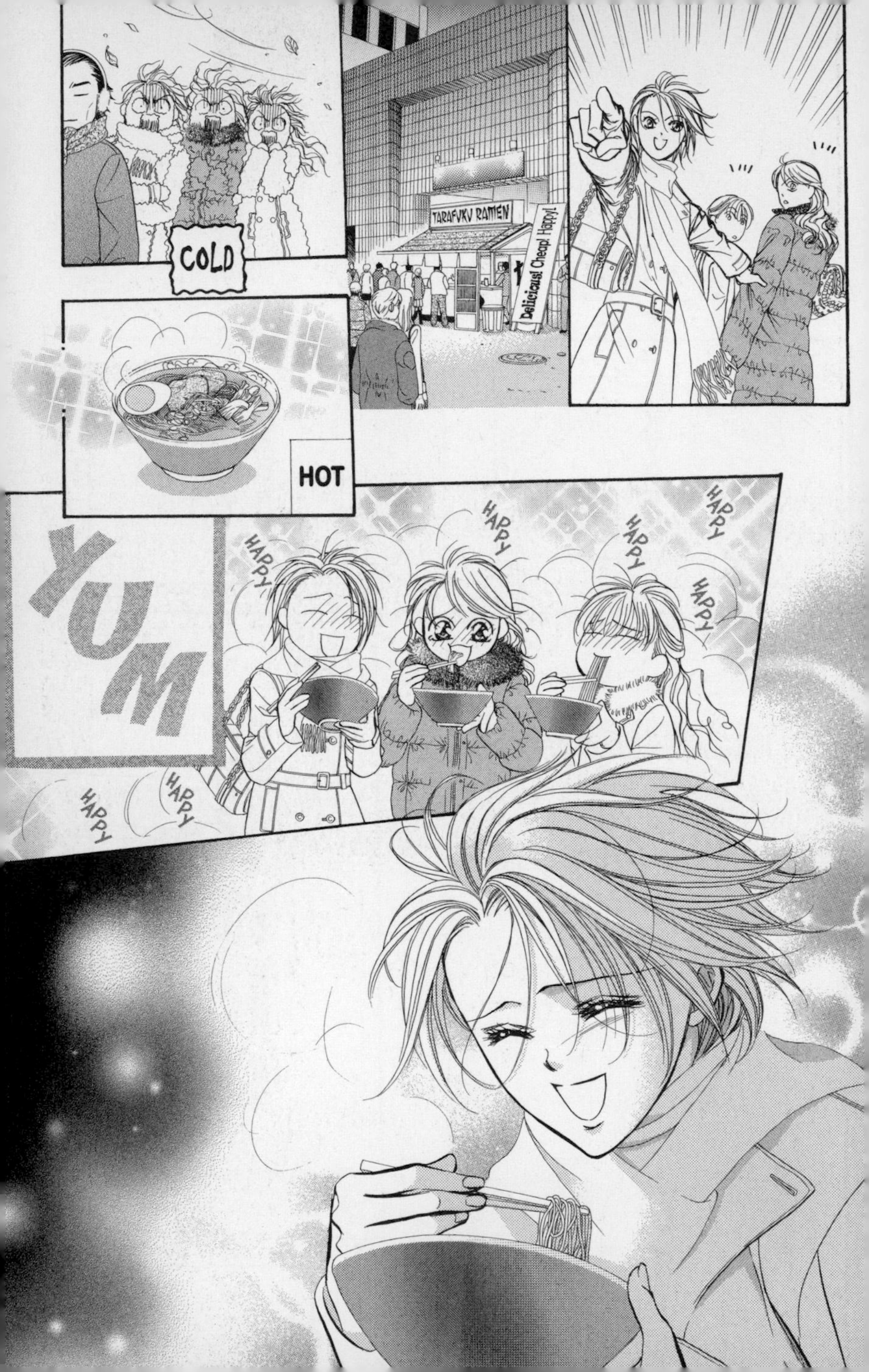
TARAFUKU RAMEN
Delicious! Cheap! Happy!
COLD
HOT
HAPPY
HAPPY
HAPPY
HAPPY
HAPPY
HAPPY
HAPPY
YUM

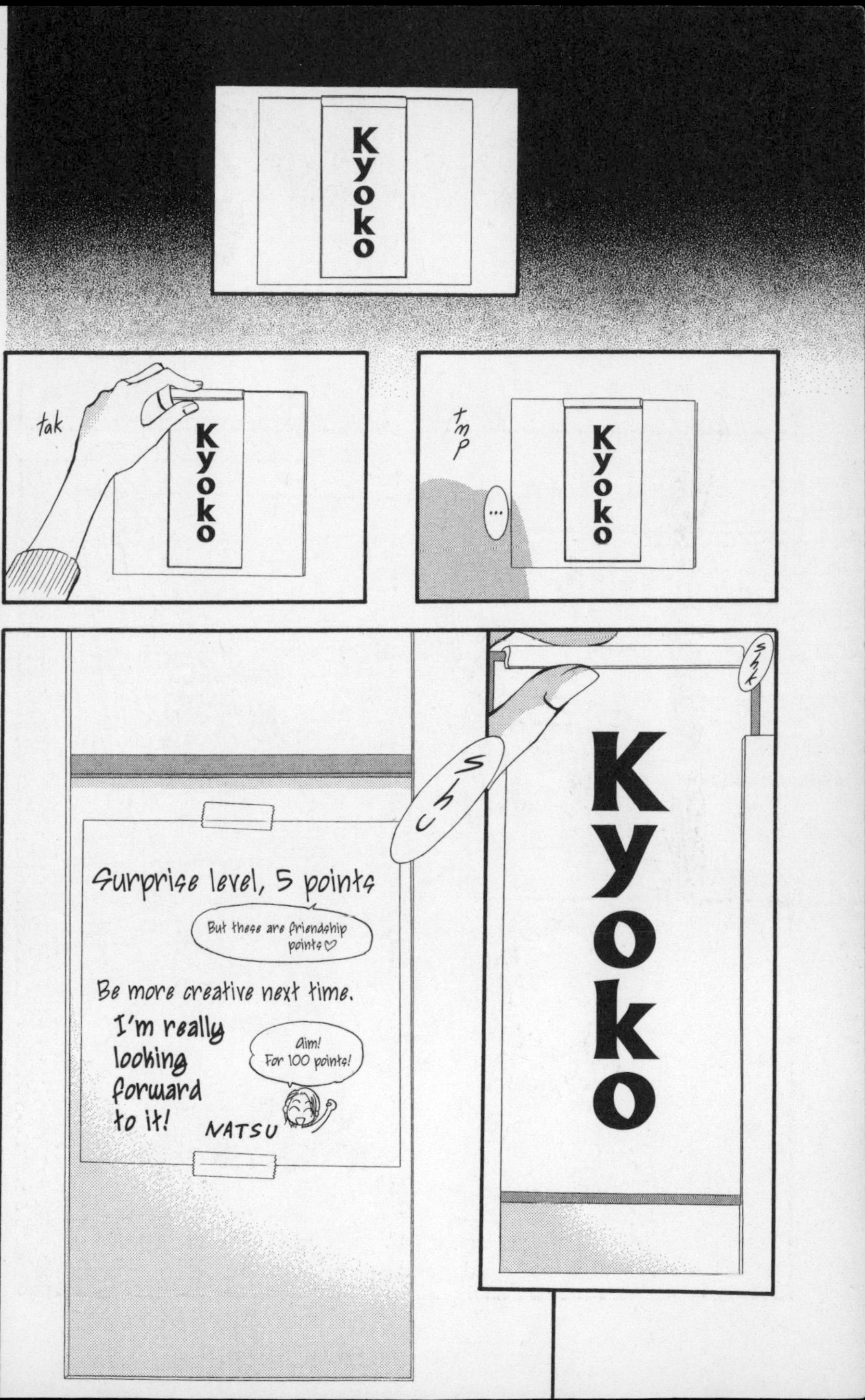
Kyoko
tmp
...
Kyoko
tak
Kyoko
shk
Kyoko
shu
Surprise level, 5 points
But these are friendship points♡
Be more creative next time.
I'm really looking forward to it!
Aim! For 100 points!
NATSU

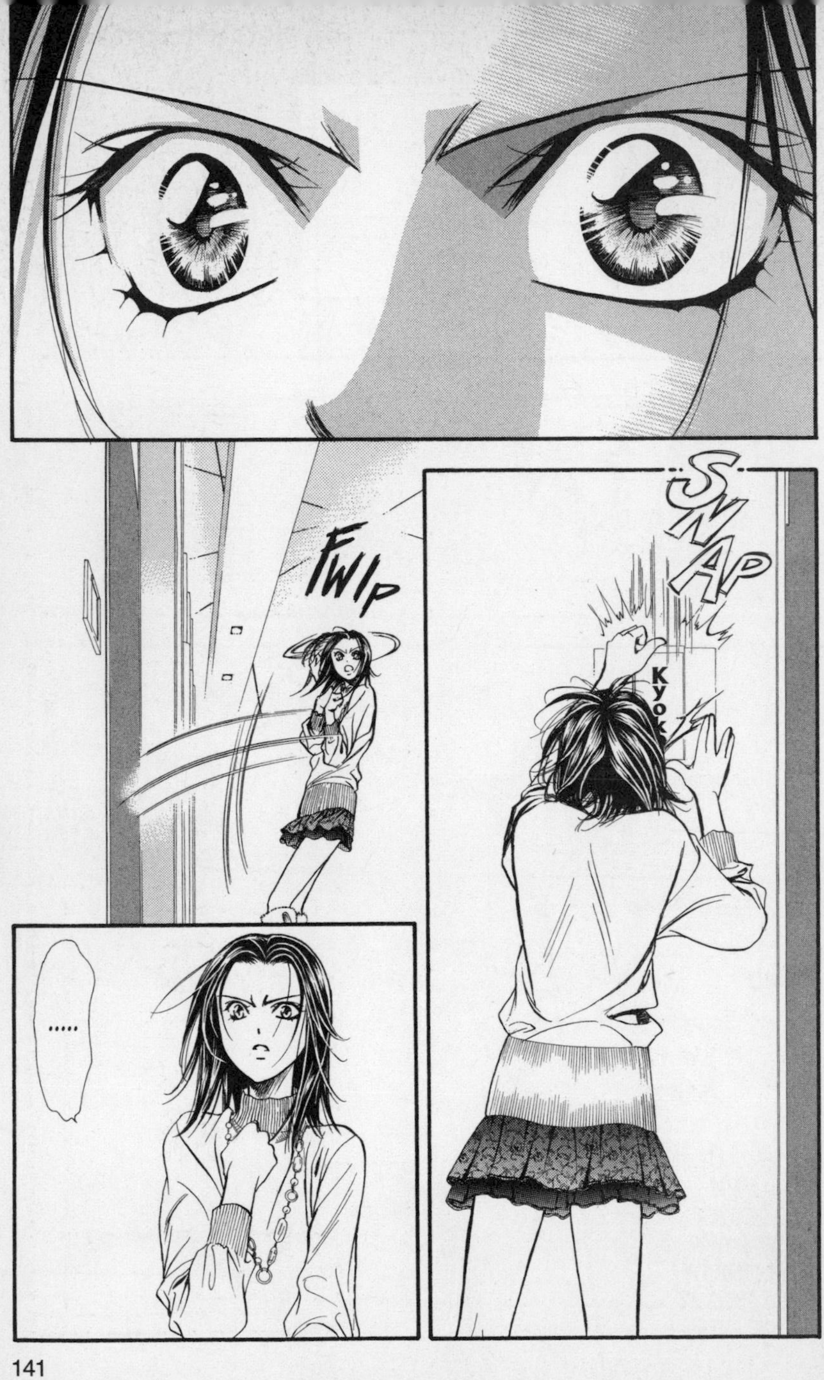
SNAP
Kyok
FWIP
......

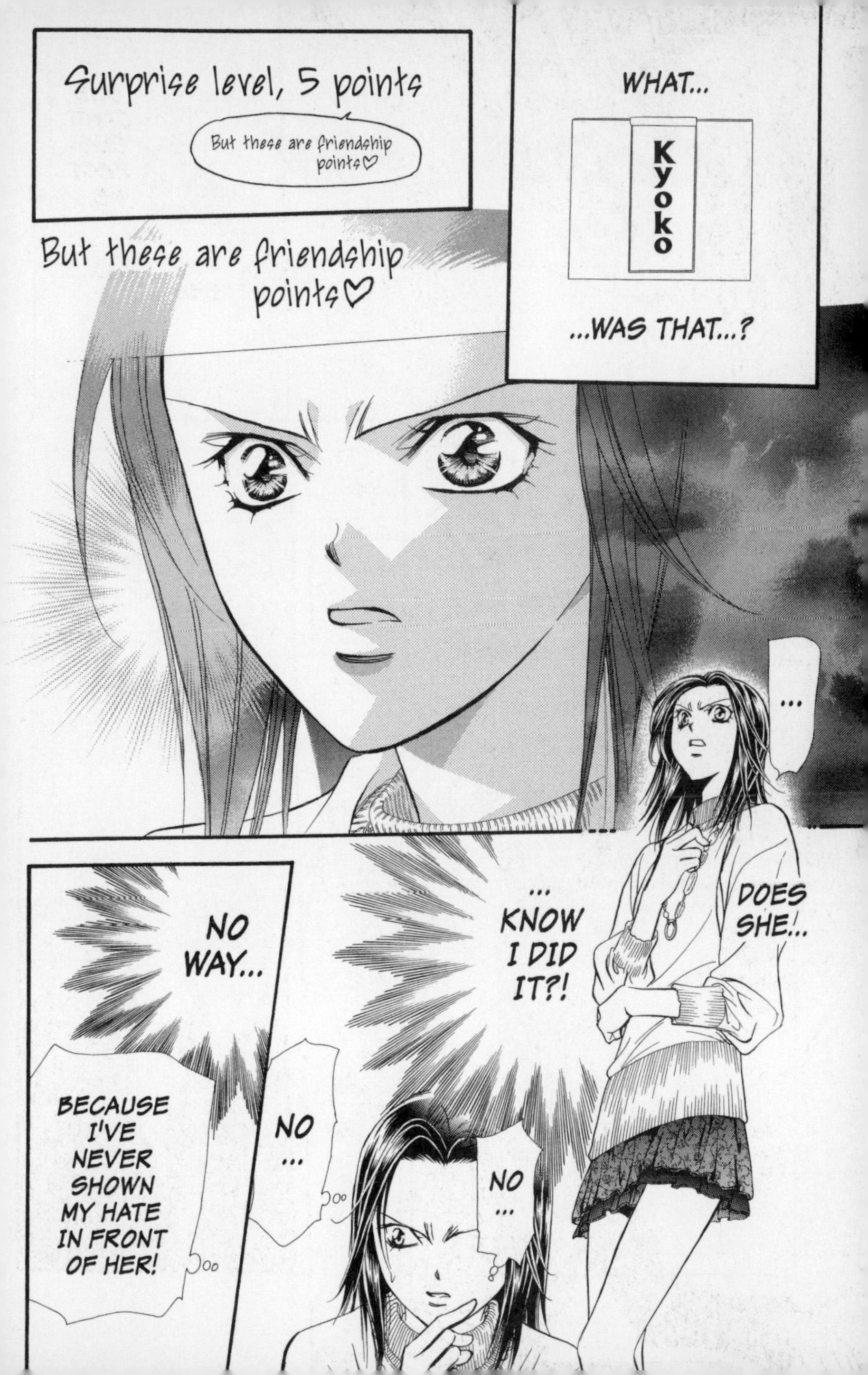
WHAT...
Kyoko
...WAS THAT...?
Surprise level, 5 points
But these are friendship points♡
But these are friendship points♡
...
DOES SHE...
...KNOW I DID IT?!
NO WAY...
NO...
NO...
BECAUSE I'VE NEVER SHOWN MY HATE IN FRONT OF HER!

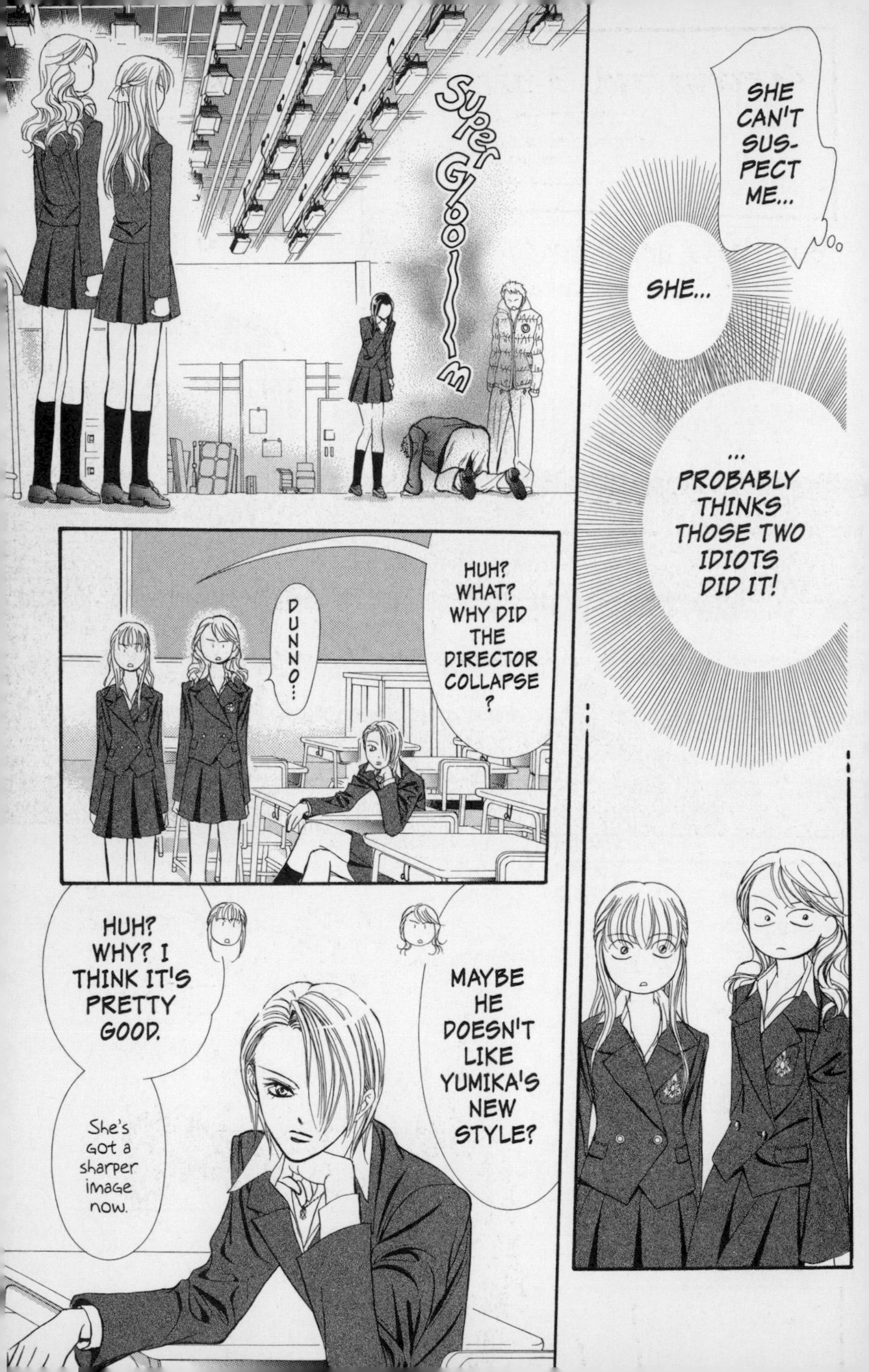
SHE CAN'T SUS-PECT ME...
SHE...
... PROBABLY THINKS THOSE TWO IDIOTS DID IT!
Super Gloom
HUH? WHAT? WHY DID THE DIRECTOR COLLAPSE?
DUNNO...
MAYBE HE DOESN'T LIKE YUMIKA'S NEW STYLE?
HUH? WHY? I THINK IT'S PRETTY GOOD.
She's got a sharper image now.

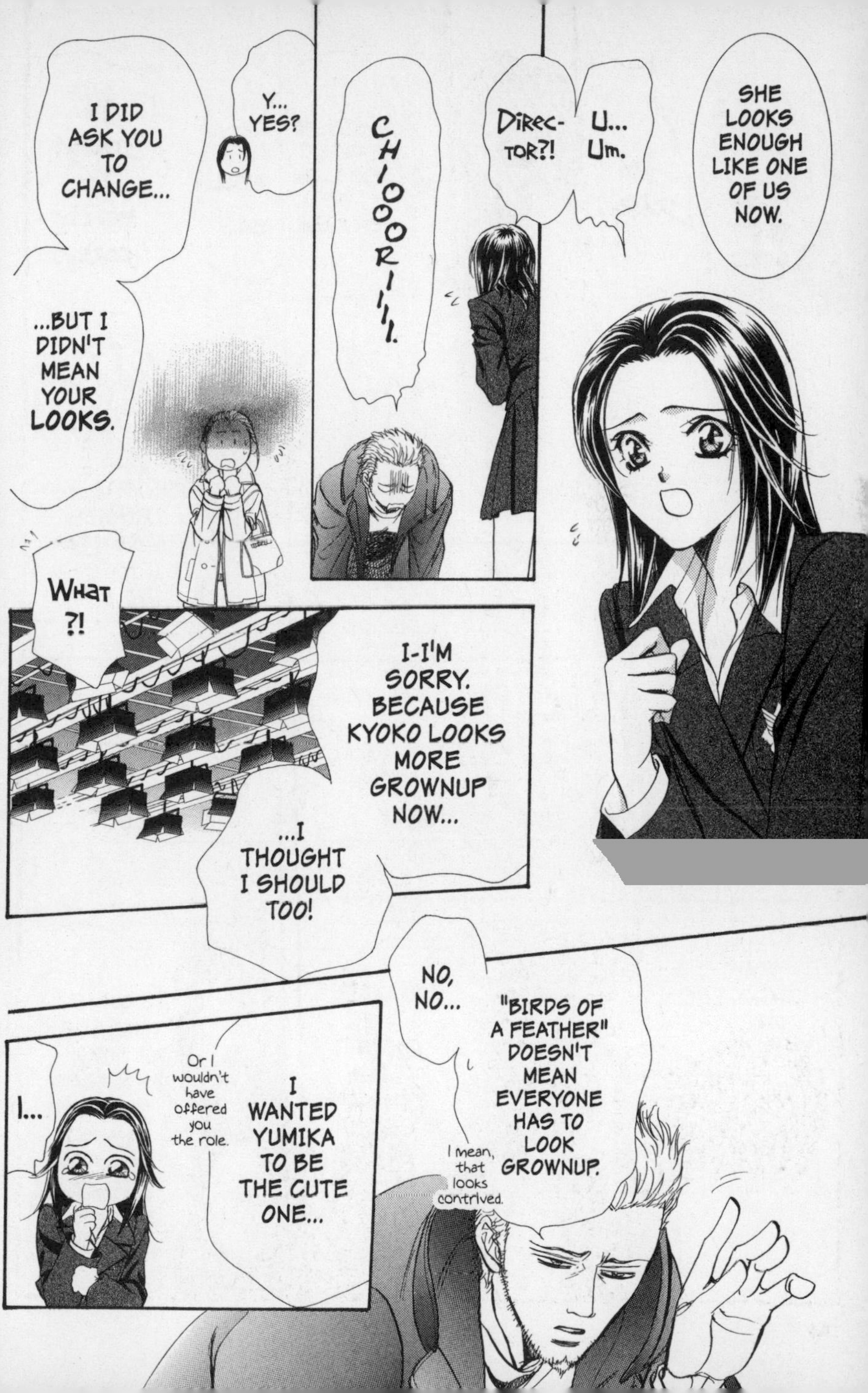
SHE LOOKS ENOUGH LIKE ONE OF US NOW.
U... Um.
Direc-tor?!
CHIOOORIIII.
Y... YES?
I DID ASK YOU TO CHANGE...
...BUT I DIDN'T MEAN YOUR LOOKS.
What?!
I-I'M SORRY. BECAUSE KYOKO LOOKS MORE GROWNUP NOW...
...I THOUGHT I SHOULD TOO!
NO, NO...
"BIRDS OF A FEATHER" DOESN'T MEAN EVERYONE HAS TO LOOK GROWNUP.
I mean, that looks contrived.
I WANTED YUMIKA TO BE THE CUTE ONE...
Or I wouldn't have offered you the role.
I...

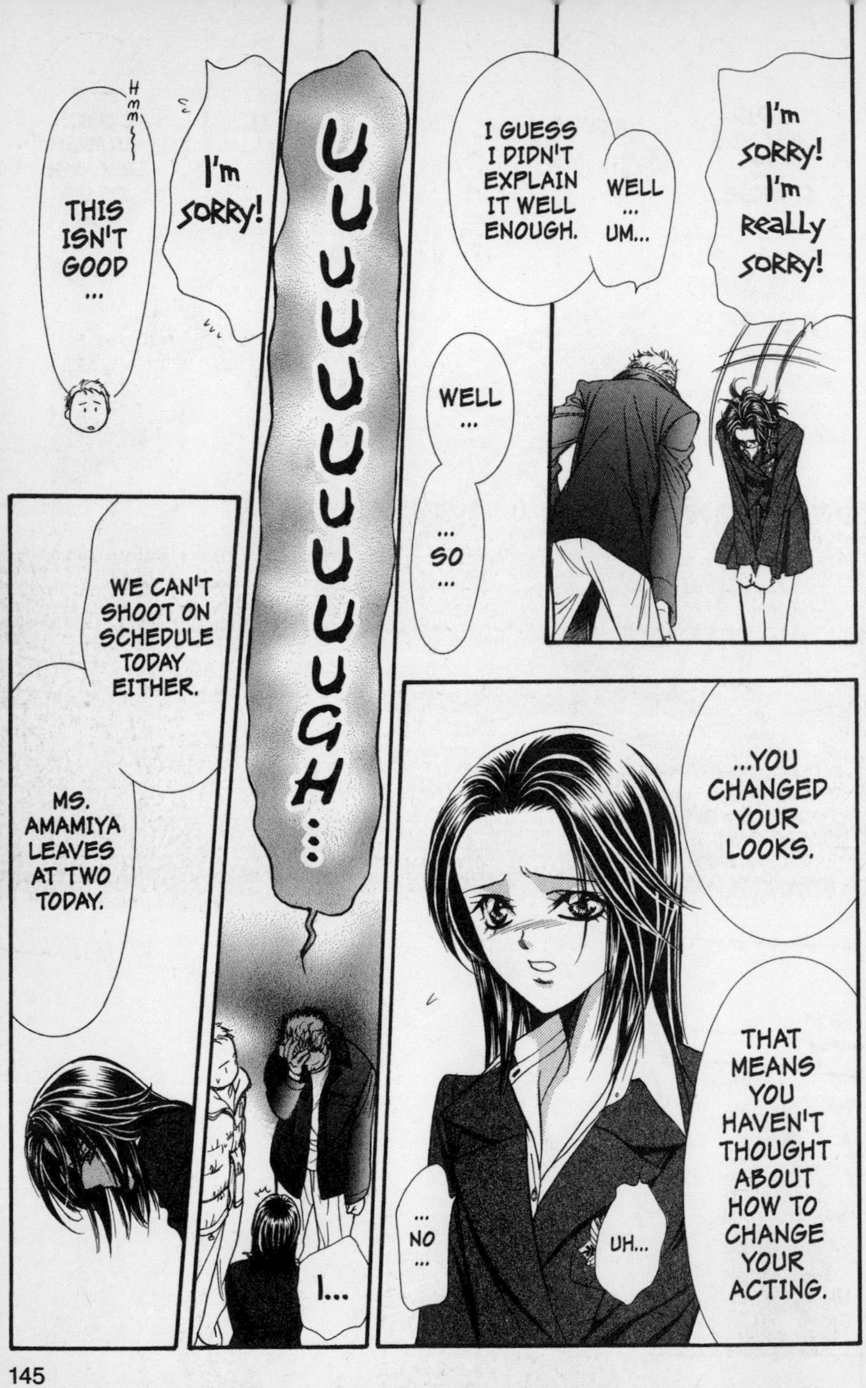
I'm SORRY! I'm ReaLLy SORRY!
I GUESS I DIDN'T EXPLAIN IT WELL ENOUGH.
WELL ... UM...
WELL ... ... SO ...
...YOU CHANGED YOUR LOOKS.
THAT MEANS YOU HAVEN'T THOUGHT ABOUT HOW TO CHANGE YOUR ACTING.
UH...
... NO ...
UUUUUUUUUUGH...
I'm SORRY!
I...
HMM~
THIS ISN'T GOOD ...
WE CAN'T SHOOT ON SCHEDULE TODAY EITHER.
MS. AMAMIYA LEAVES AT TWO TODAY.

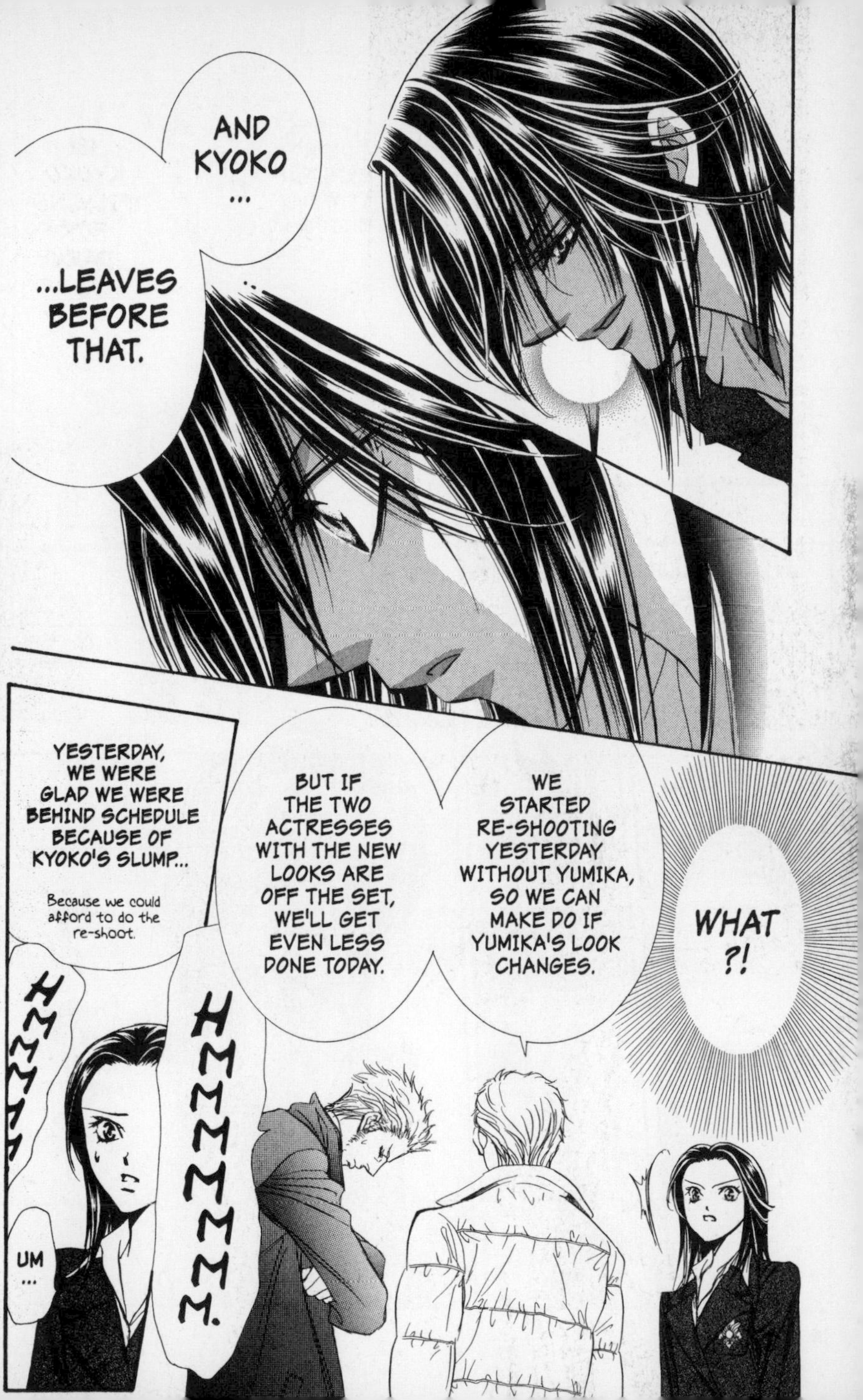
AND KYOKO ...
...LEAVES BEFORE THAT.
WHAT ?!
WE STARTED RE-SHOOTING YESTERDAY WITHOUT YUMIKA, SO WE CAN MAKE DO IF YUMIKA'S LOOK CHANGES.
BUT IF THE TWO ACTRESSES WITH THE NEW LOOKS ARE OFF THE SET, WE'LL GET EVEN LESS DONE TODAY.
YESTERDAY, WE WERE GLAD WE WERE BEHIND SCHEDULE BECAUSE OF KYOKO'S SLUMP...
Because we could afford to do the re-shoot.
HMMMMMMM.
UM ...

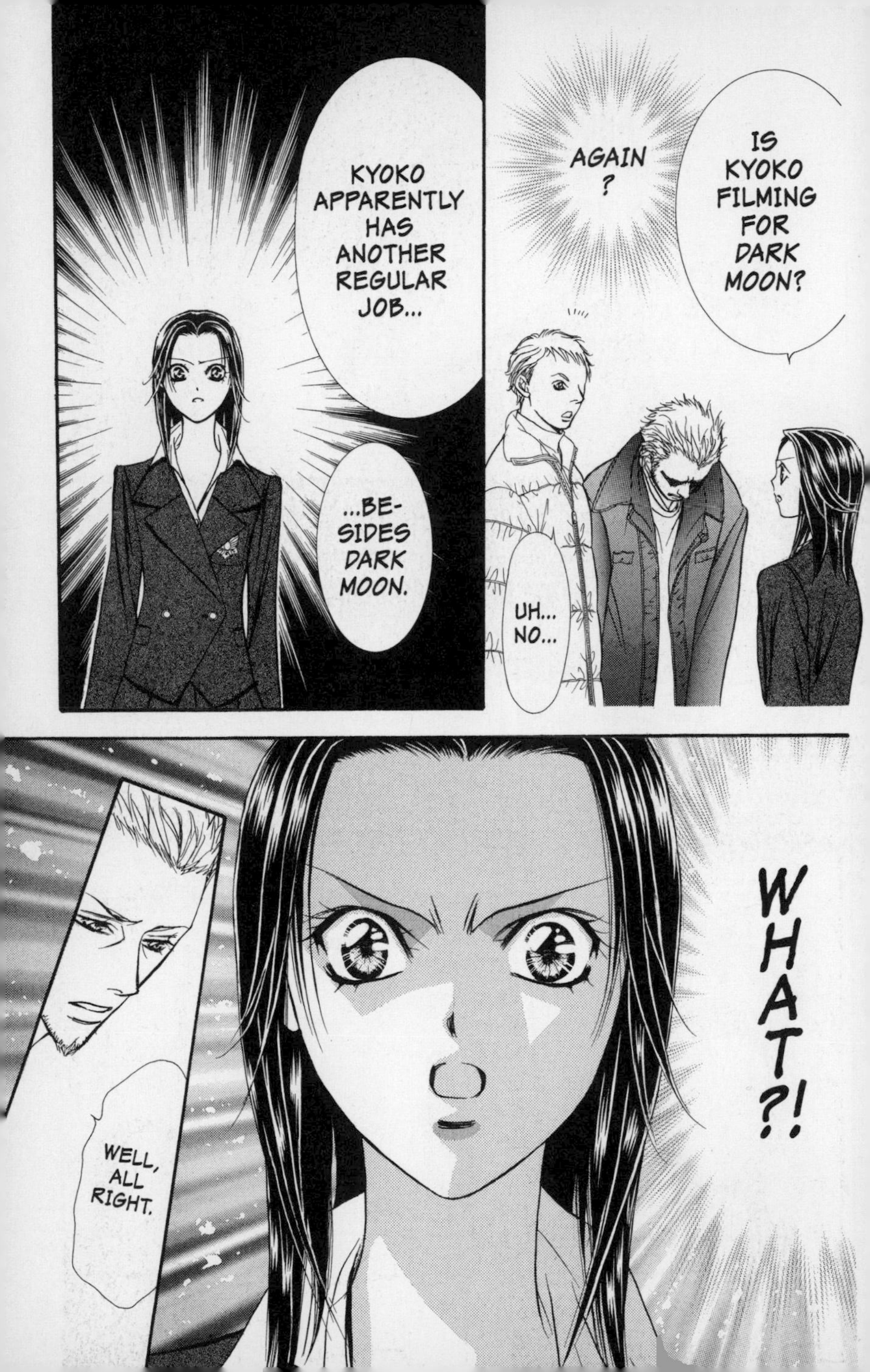
IS KYOKO FILMING FOR DARK MOON?
AGAIN ?
UH... NO...
KYOKO APPARENTLY HAS ANOTHER REGULAR JOB...
...BE-SIDES DARK MOON.
WHAT?!
WELL, ALL RIGHT.

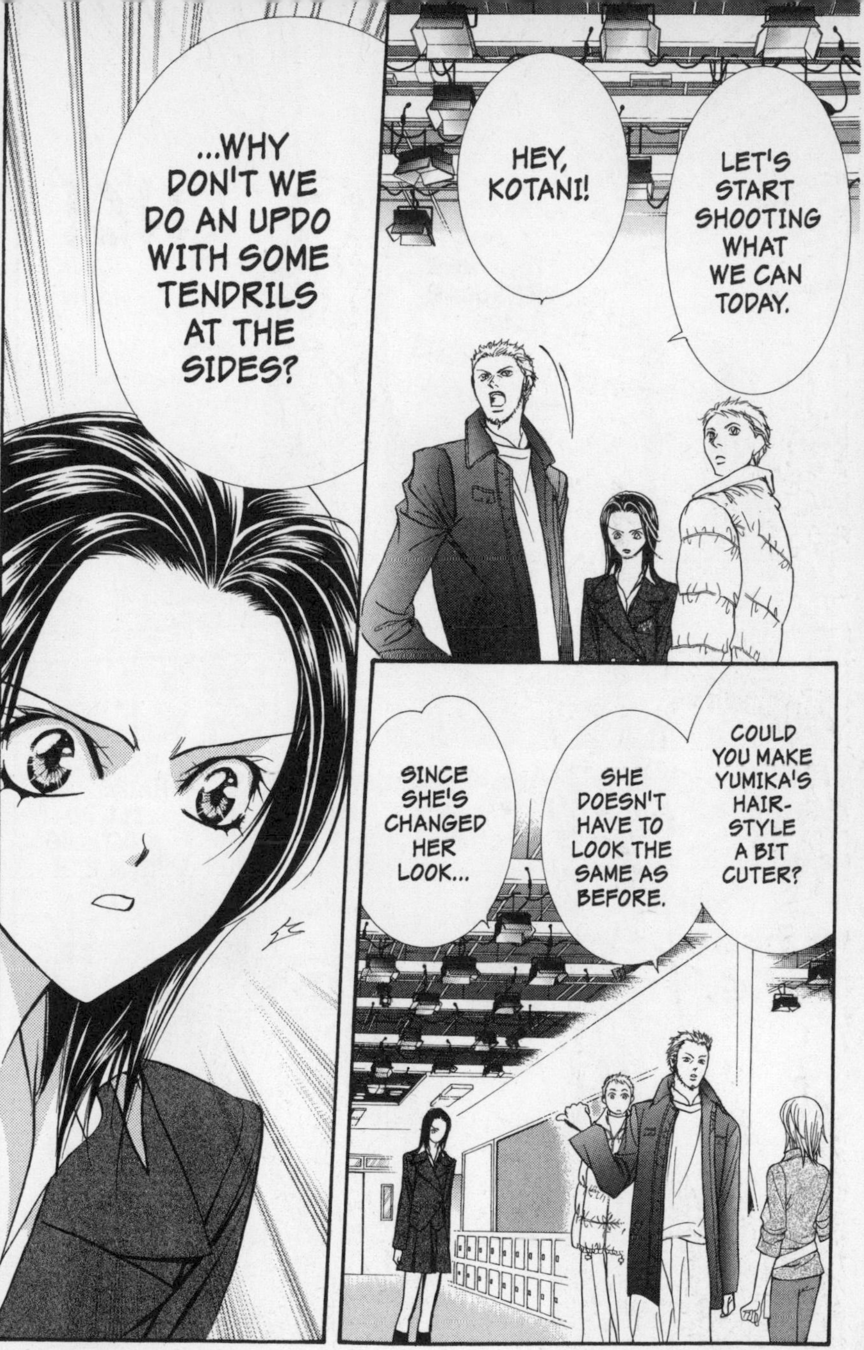
LET'S START SHOOTING WHAT WE CAN TODAY.
HEY, KOTANI!
COULD YOU MAKE YUMIKA'S HAIR-STYLE A BIT CUTER?
SHE DOESN'T HAVE TO LOOK THE SAME AS BEFORE.
SINCE SHE'S CHANGED HER LOOK...
...WHY DON'T WE DO AN UPDO WITH SOME TENDRILS AT THE SIDES?

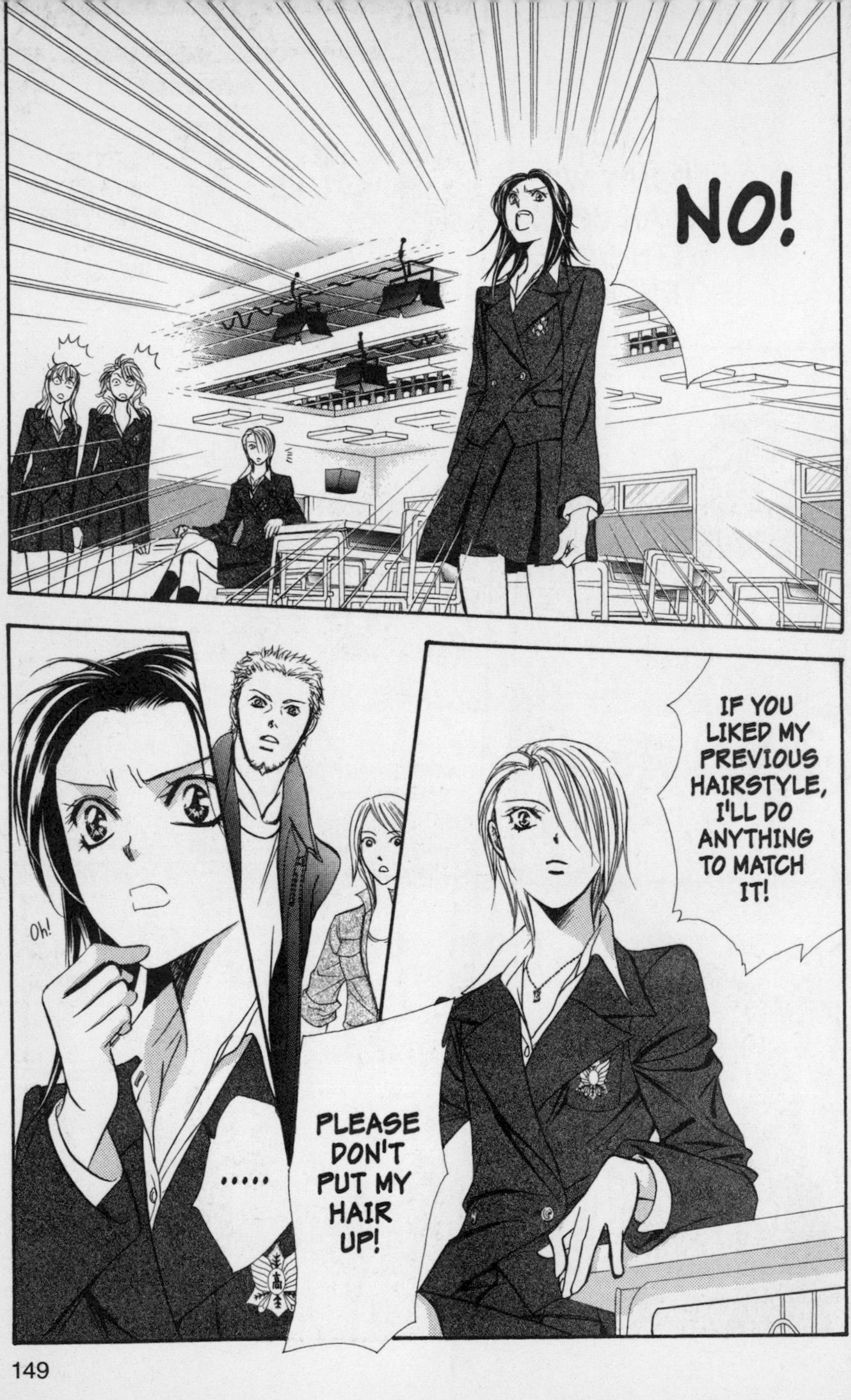
NO!
IF YOU LIKED MY PREVIOUS HAIRSTYLE, I'LL DO ANYTHING TO MATCH IT!
PLEASE DON'T PUT MY HAIR UP!
Oh!
.....

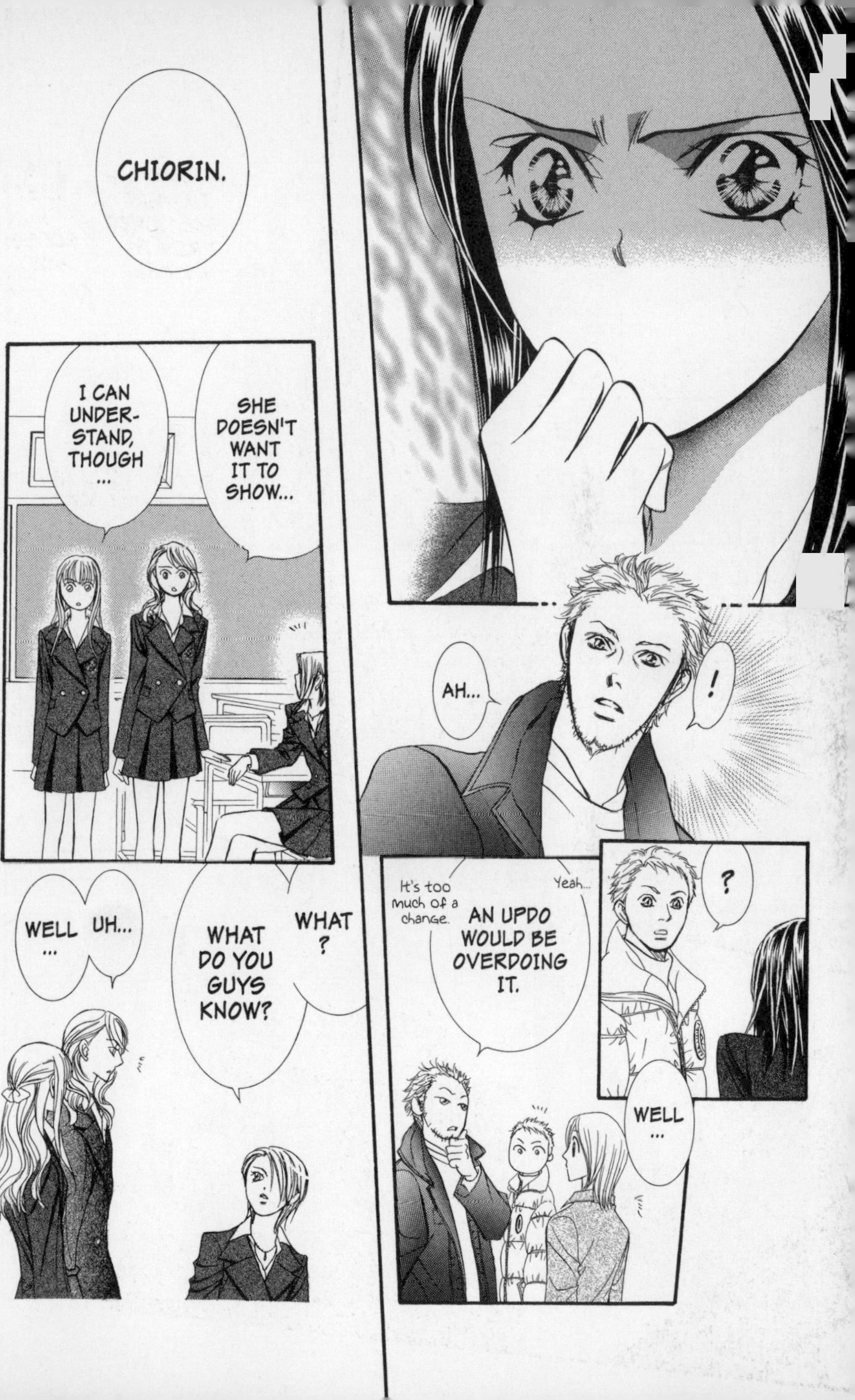
!
AH...
?
WELL ...
Yeah...
AN UPDO WOULD BE OVERDOING IT.
It's too much of a change.
CHIORIN.
SHE DOESN'T WANT IT TO SHOW...
I CAN UNDERSTAND, THOUGH ...
WHAT ?
WHAT DO YOU GUYS KNOW?
UH...
WELL ...

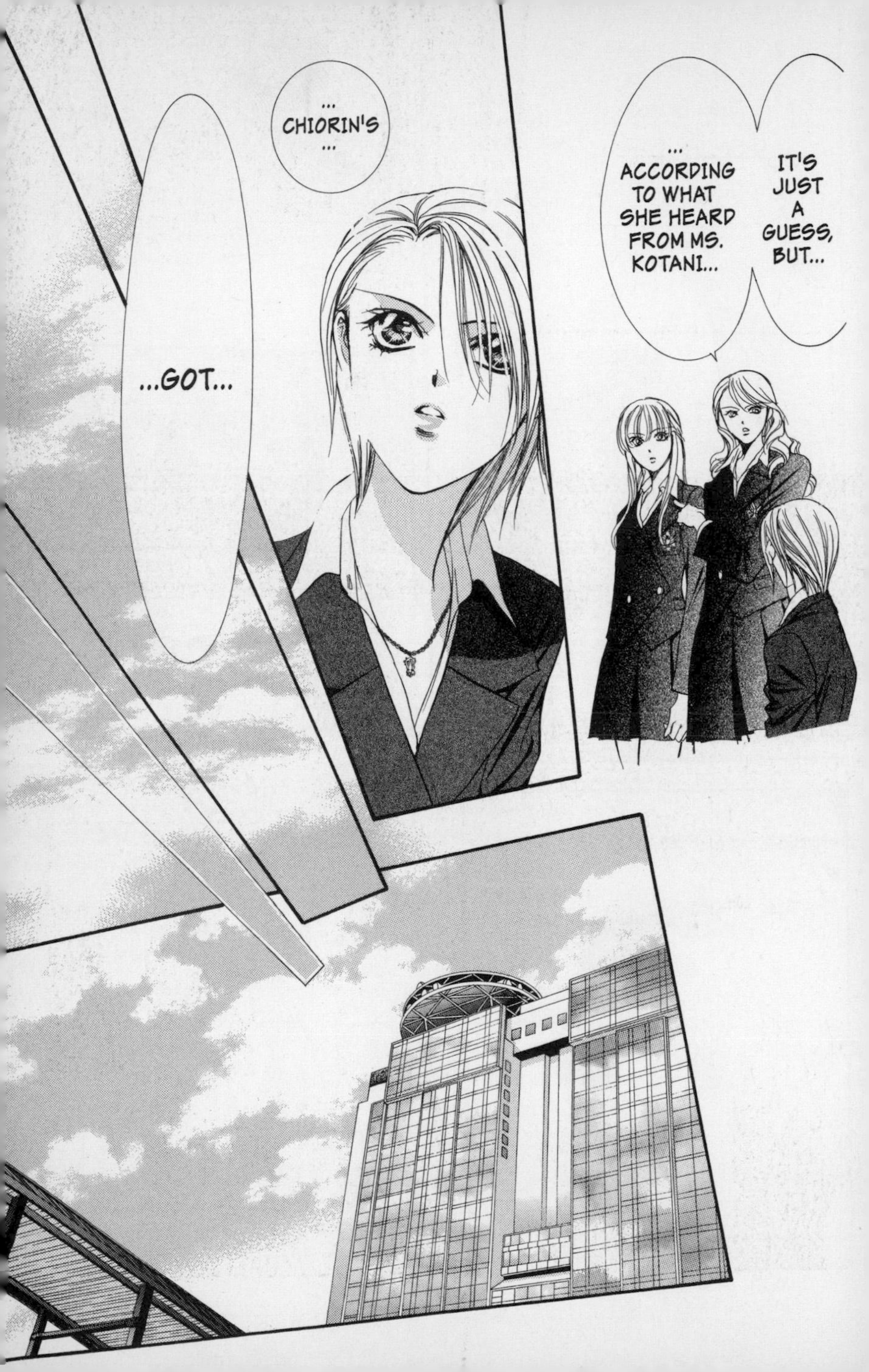
IT'S JUST A GUESS, BUT...
...ACCORDING TO WHAT SHE HEARD FROM MS. KOTANI...
...CHIORIN'S...
...GOT...

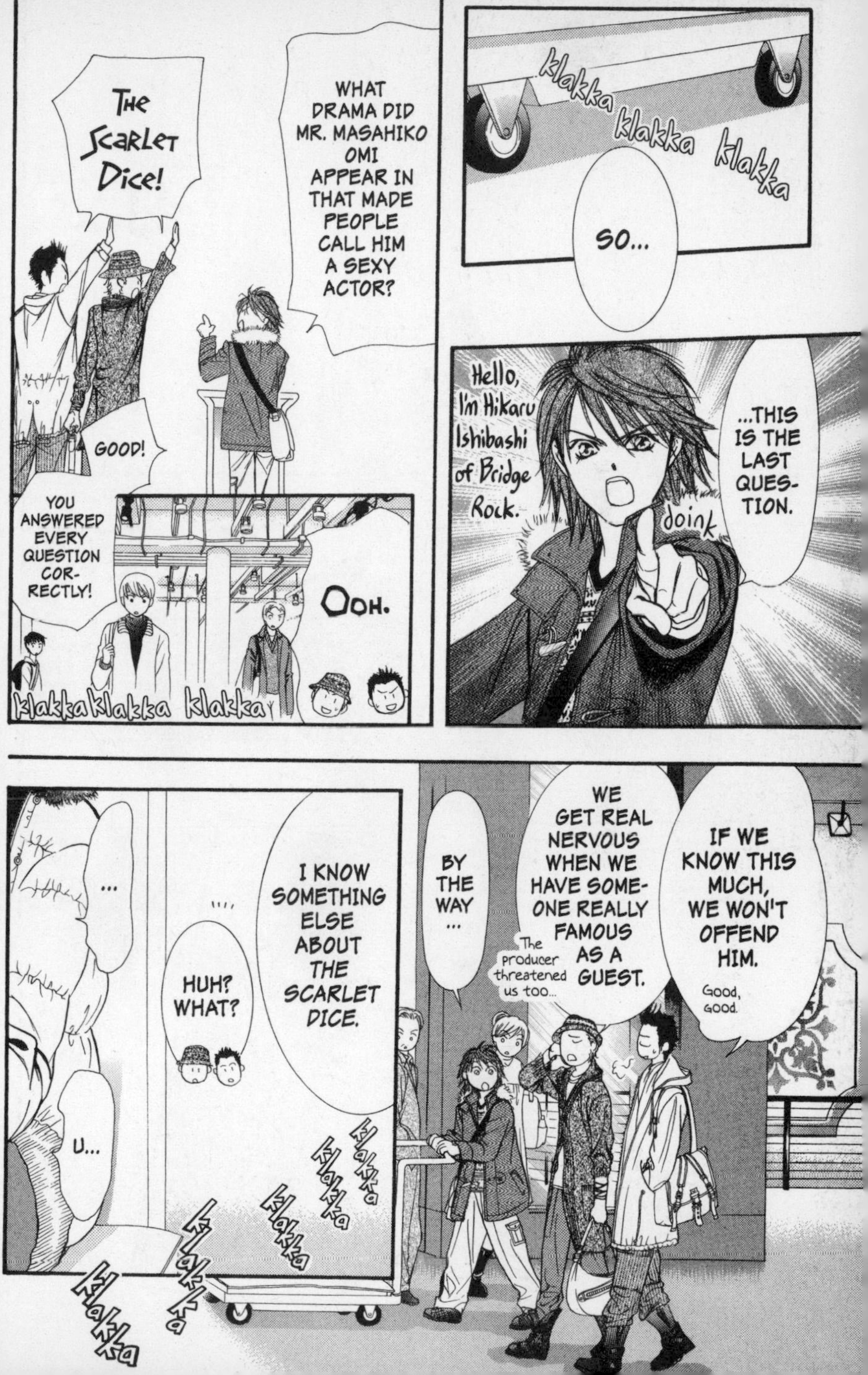

klakka klakka klakka klakka
SO...
...THIS IS THE LAST QUES-TION.
Hello, I'm Hikaru Ishibashi of Bridge Rock.
doink
WHAT DRAMA DID MR. MASAHIKO OMI APPEAR IN THAT MADE PEOPLE CALL HIM A SEXY ACTOR?
The Scarlet Dice!
GOOD!
YOU ANSWERED EVERY QUESTION COR-RECTLY!
OOH.
klakka klakka klakka
IF WE KNOW THIS MUCH, WE WON'T OFFEND HIM.
Good, good.
WE GET REAL NERVOUS WHEN WE HAVE SOME-ONE REALLY FAMOUS AS A GUEST.
The producer threatened us too...
BY THE WAY...
klakka klakka klakka klakka klakka
I KNOW SOMETHING ELSE ABOUT THE SCARLET DICE.
HUH? WHAT?
...
U...

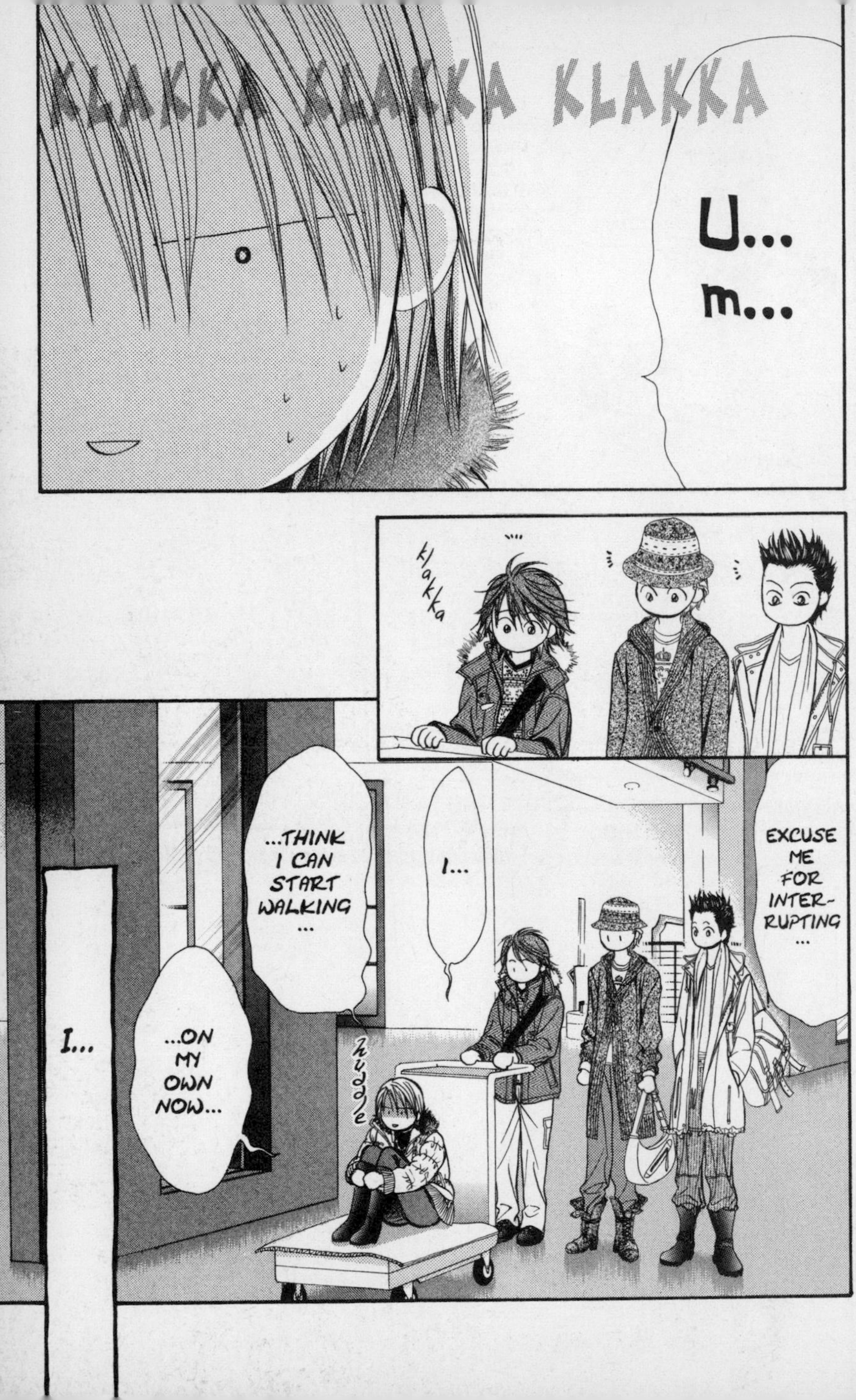
KLAKKA KLAKKA KLAKKA
U... m...
klakka
EXCUSE ME FOR INTER-RUPTING...
I...
...THINK I CAN START WALKING...
huddle
...ON MY OWN NOW...
I...

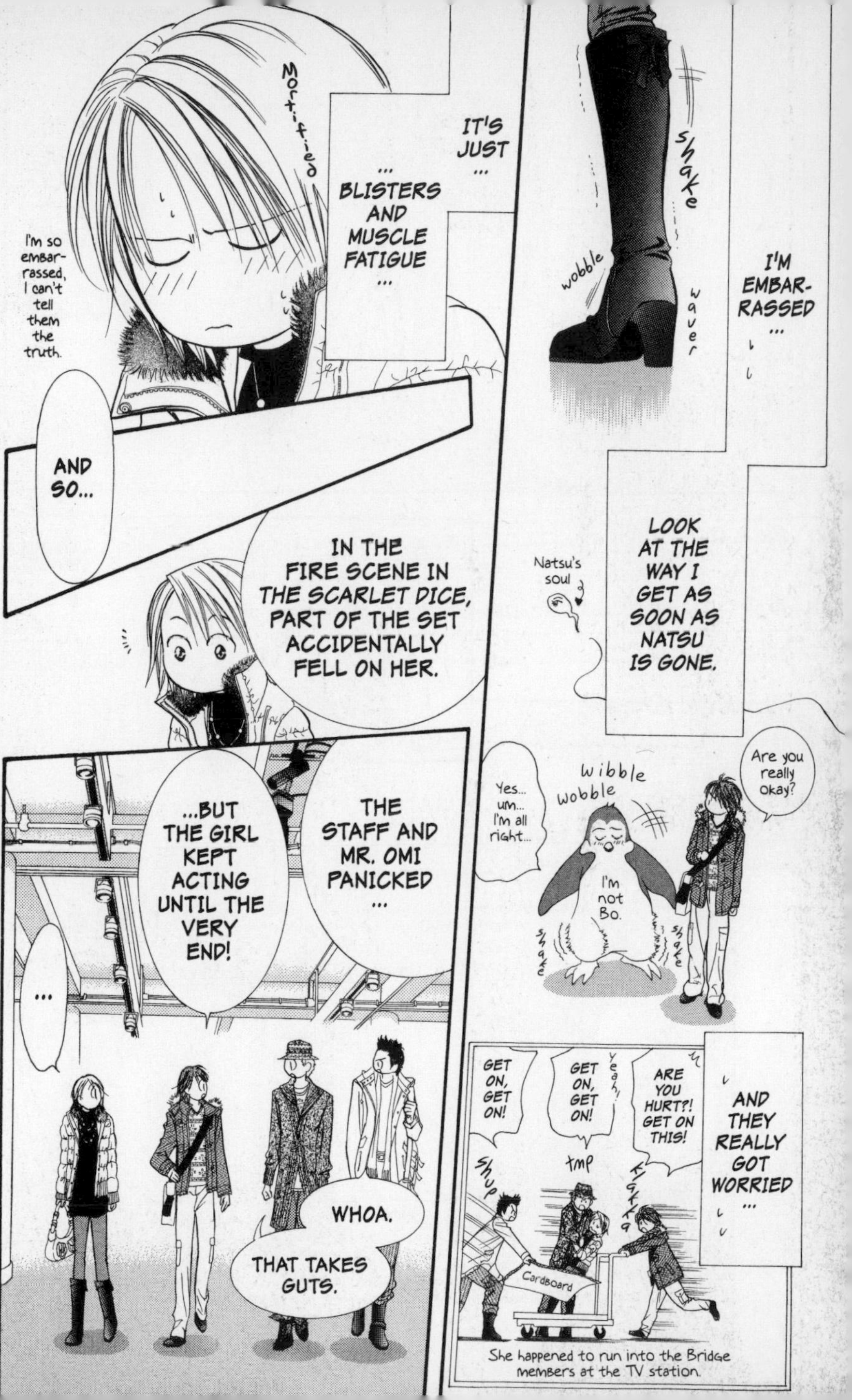
shake
wobble
waver
I'M EMBARRASSED...
LOOK AT THE WAY I GET AS SOON AS NATSU IS GONE.
Natsu's soul
Are you really okay?
Yes... um... I'm all right...
wibble wobble
I'm not Bo.
shake
shake
AND THEY REALLY GOT WORRIED...
ARE YOU HURT?! GET ON THIS!
GET ON, GET ON!
yeah!
GET ON, GET ON!
kick kick
tmp
shup
Cardboard
She happened to run into the Bridge members at the TV station.
IT'S JUST...
...BLISTERS AND MUSCLE FATIGUE...
Mortified
I'm so embarrassed, I can't tell them the truth.
AND SO...
IN THE FIRE SCENE IN THE SCARLET DICE, PART OF THE SET ACCIDENTALLY FELL ON HER.
THE STAFF AND MR. OMI PANICKED...
...BUT THE GIRL KEPT ACTING UNTIL THE VERY END!
...
WHOA.
THAT TAKES GUTS.

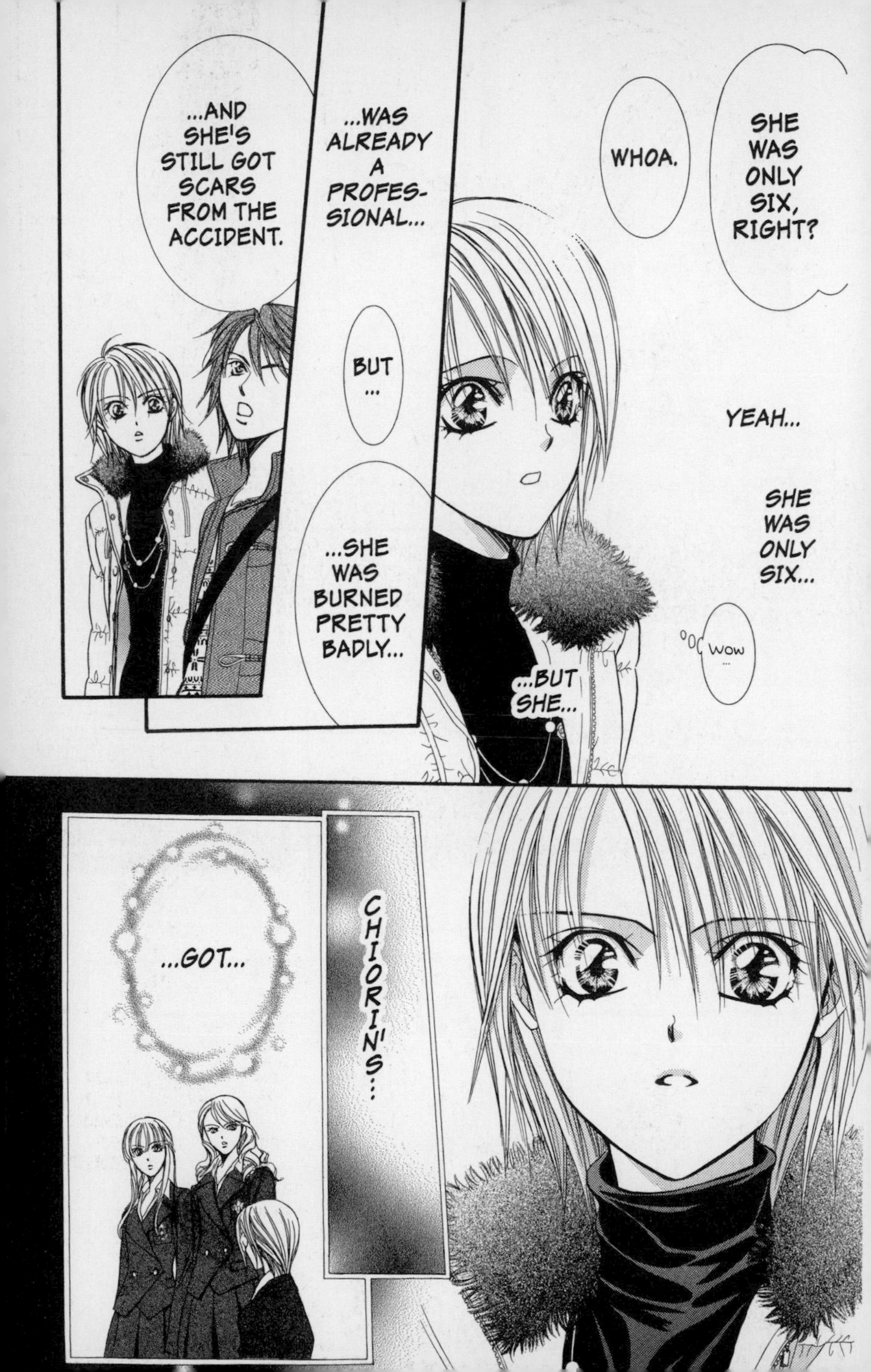
SHE WAS ONLY SIX, RIGHT?
WHOA.
YEAH...
SHE WAS ONLY SIX...
WOW...
...BUT SHE...
...WAS ALREADY A PROFESSIONAL...
BUT...
...SHE WAS BURNED PRETTY BADLY...
...AND SHE'S STILL GOT SCARS FROM THE ACCIDENT.
CHIORIN'S...
...GOT...

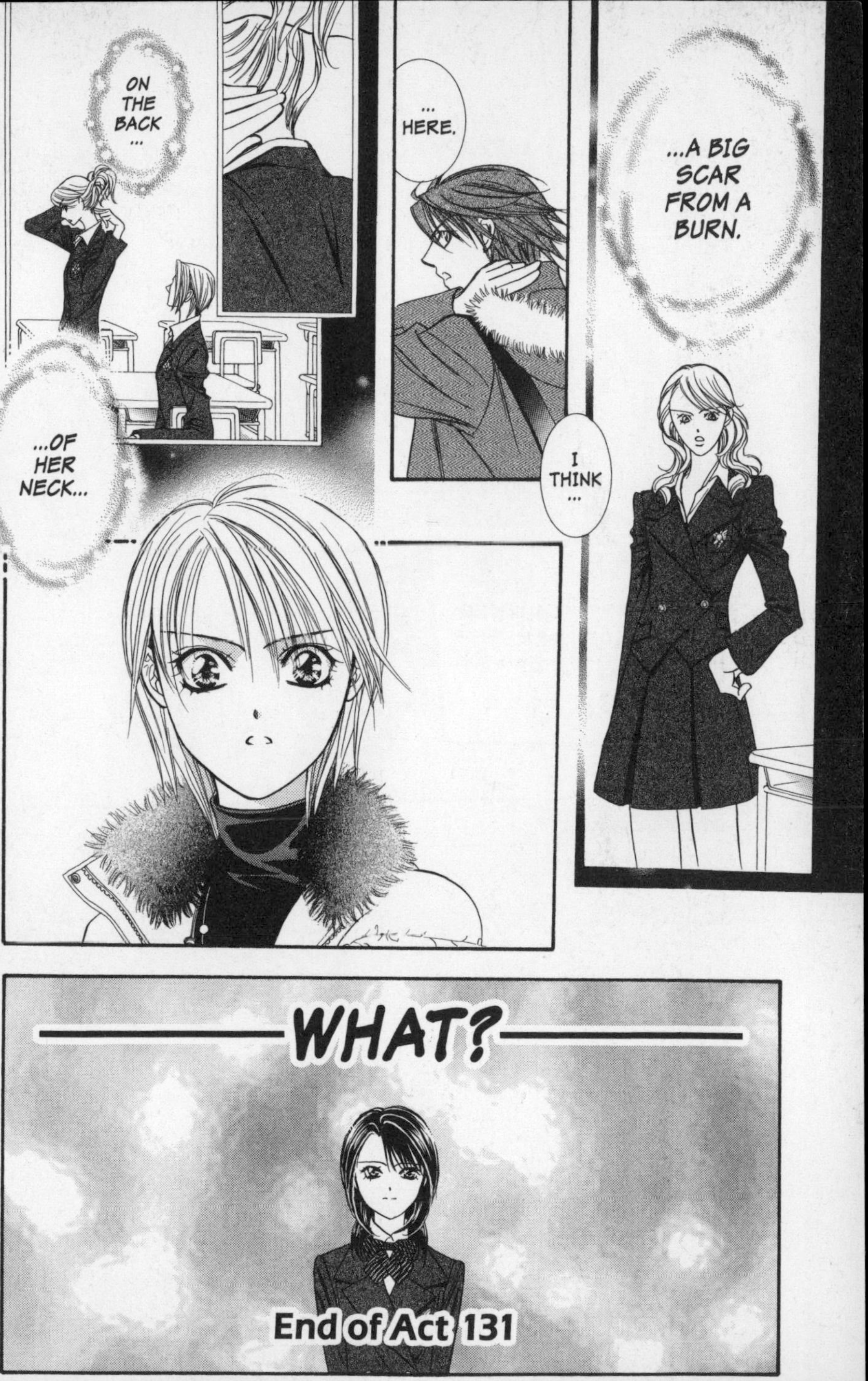
I THINK...
ON THE BACK...
...OF HER NECK...
...HERE.
...A BIG SCAR FROM A BURN.
WHAT?
End of Act 131

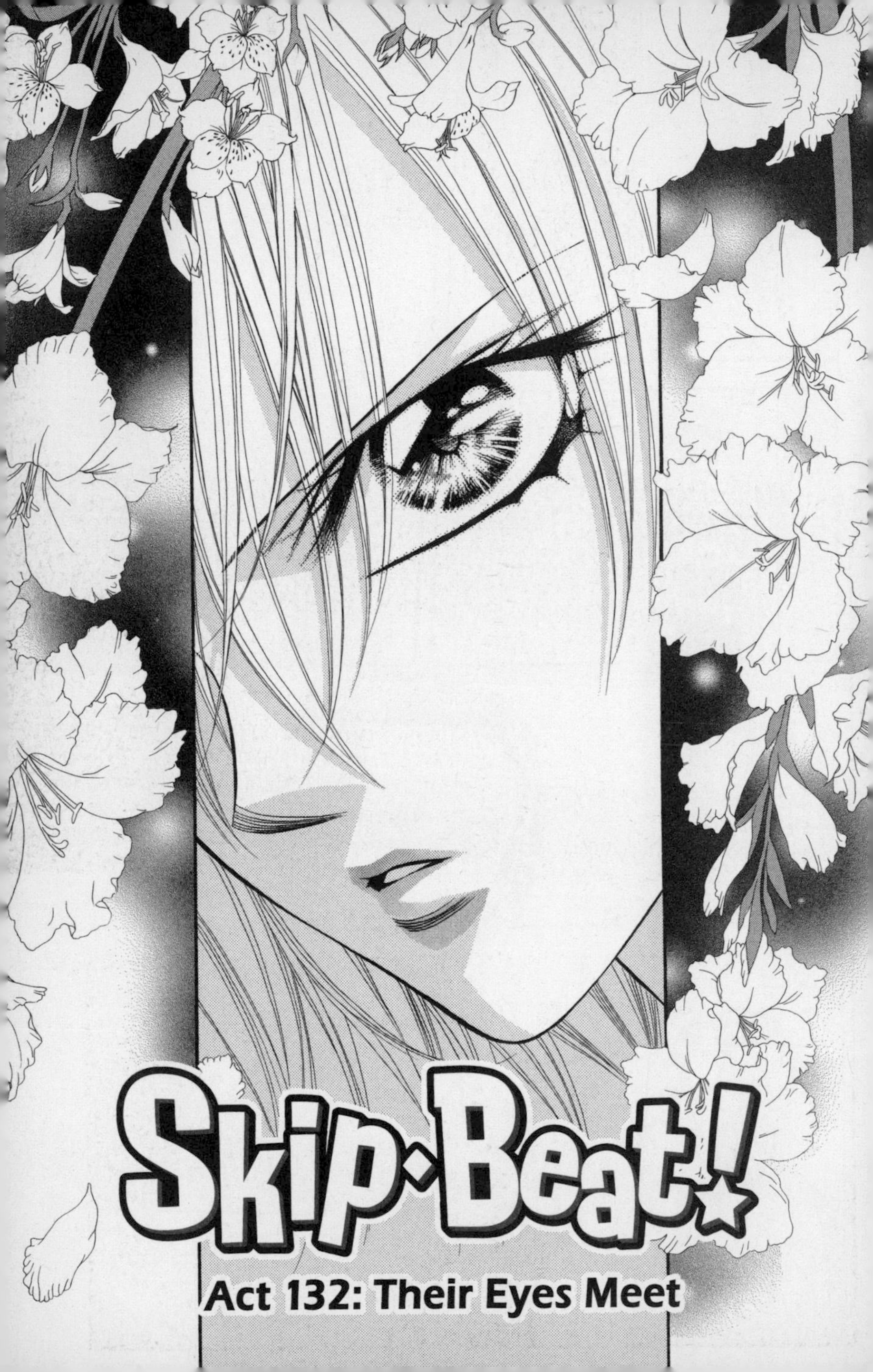
Skip·Beat!
Act 132: Their Eyes Meet

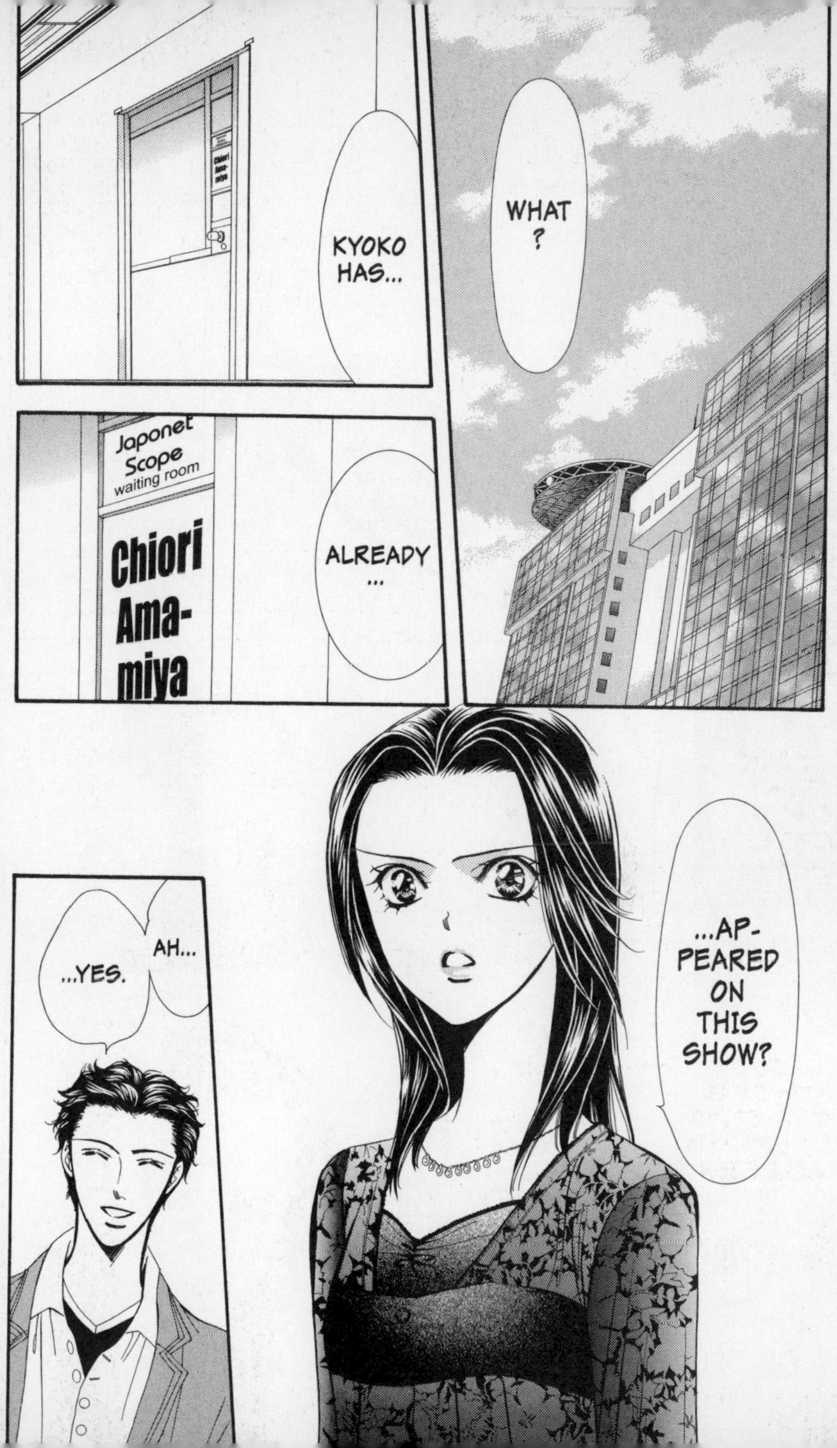
WHAT?
KYOKO HAS...
ALREADY...
Japonet Scope waiting room
Chiori Ama-miya
...AP-PEARED ON THIS SHOW?
AH...
...YES.

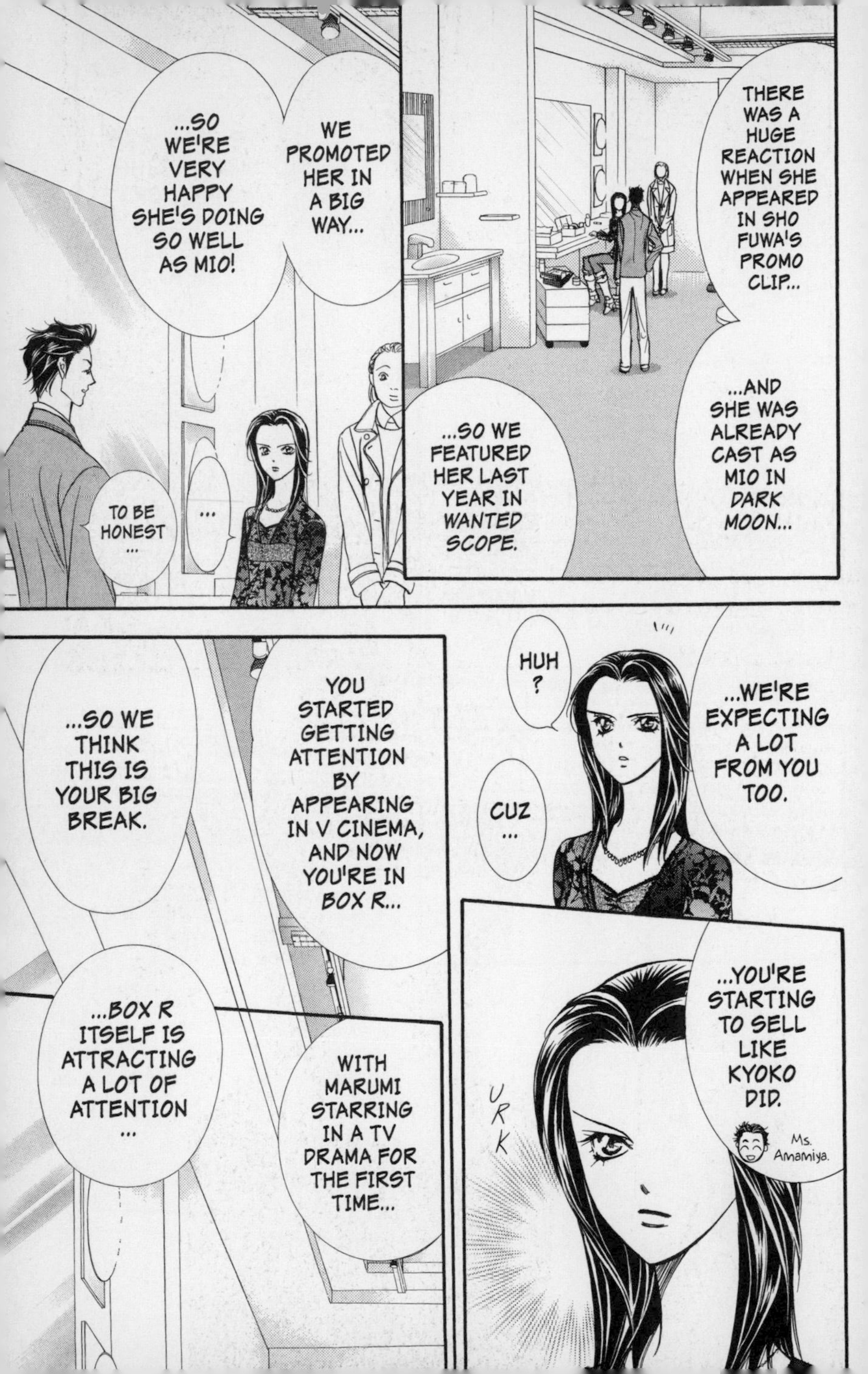
THERE WAS A HUGE REACTION WHEN SHE APPEARED IN SHO FUWA'S PROMO CLIP...
...AND SHE WAS ALREADY CAST AS MIO IN DARK MOON...
...SO WE FEATURED HER LAST YEAR IN WANTED SCOPE.
WE PROMOTED HER IN A BIG WAY...
...SO WE'RE VERY HAPPY SHE'S DOING SO WELL AS MIO!
TO BE HONEST...
...
WITH MARUMI STARRING IN A TV DRAMA FOR THE FIRST TIME...
...BOX R ITSELF IS ATTRACTING A LOT OF ATTENTION...
YOU STARTED GETTING ATTENTION BY APPEARING IN V CINEMA, AND NOW YOU'RE IN BOX R...
...SO WE THINK THIS IS YOUR BIG BREAK.
...WE'RE EXPECTING A LOT FROM YOU TOO.
HUH?
CUZ...
...YOU'RE STARTING TO SELL LIKE KYOKO DID.
Ms. Amamiya.
URK

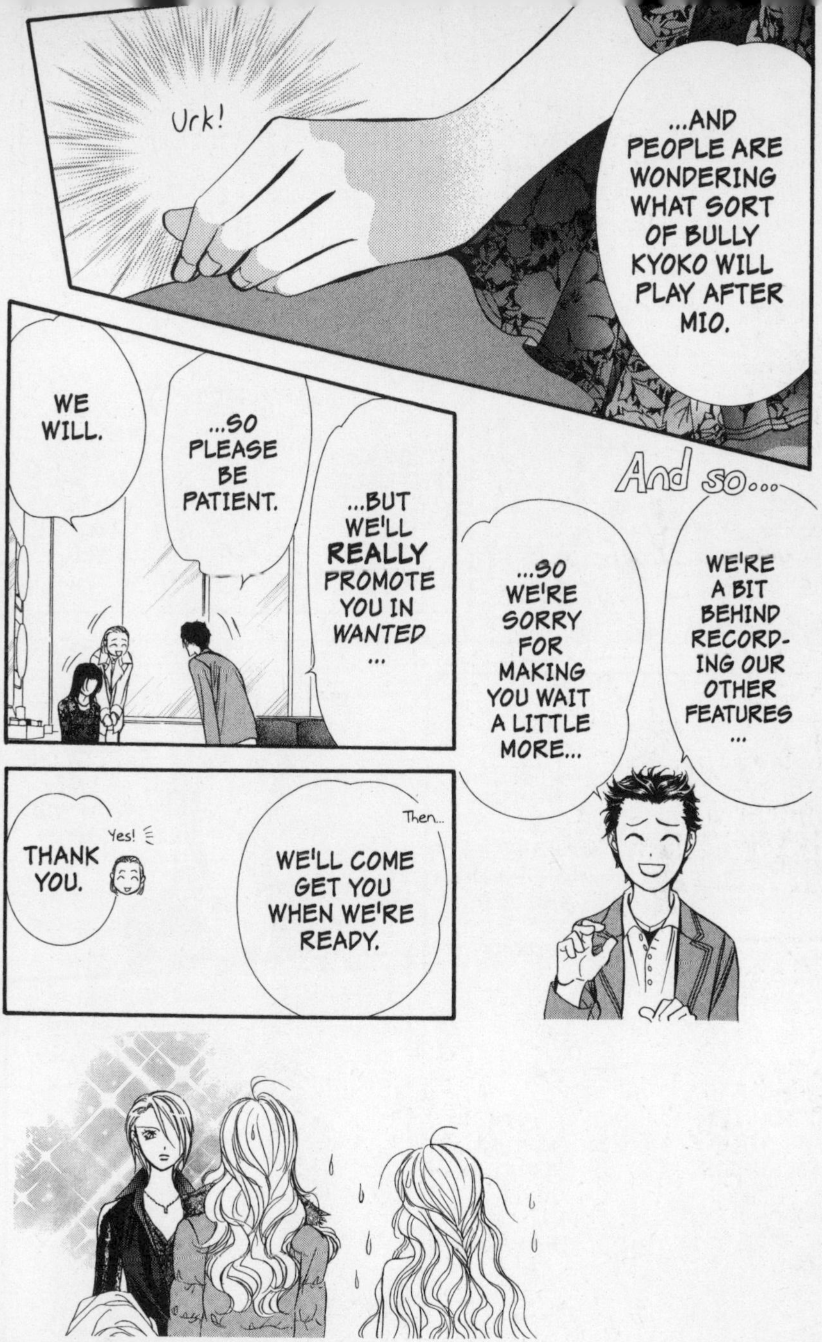
...AND PEOPLE ARE WONDERING WHAT SORT OF BULLY KYOKO WILL PLAY AFTER MIO.
Urk!
And so...
WE'RE A BIT BEHIND RECORDING OUR OTHER FEATURES ...
...SO WE'RE SORRY FOR MAKING YOU WAIT A LITTLE MORE...
...BUT WE'LL REALLY PROMOTE YOU IN WANTED ...
...SO PLEASE BE PATIENT.
WE WILL.
Then...
WE'LL COME GET YOU WHEN WE'RE READY.
Yes!
THANK YOU.

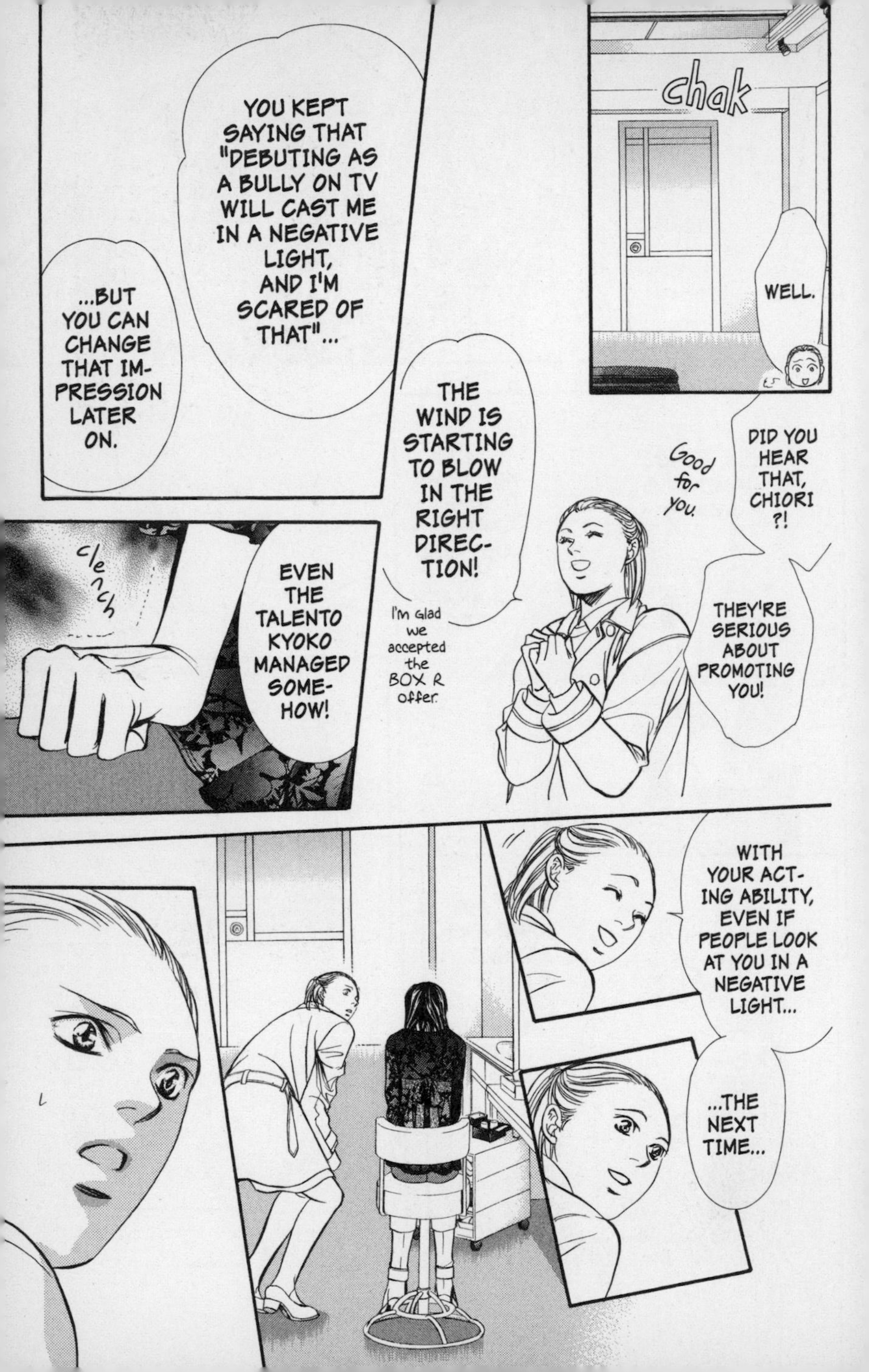
chak
WELL.
YOU KEPT SAYING THAT "DEBUTING AS A BULLY ON TV WILL CAST ME IN A NEGATIVE LIGHT, AND I'M SCARED OF THAT"...
...BUT YOU CAN CHANGE THAT IMPRESSION LATER ON.
DID YOU HEAR THAT, CHIORI?!
Good for you.
THEY'RE SERIOUS ABOUT PROMOTING YOU!
THE WIND IS STARTING TO BLOW IN THE RIGHT DIRECTION!
I'm Glad we accepted the BOX R offer.
EVEN THE TALENTO KYOKO MANAGED SOMEHOW!
clench
WITH YOUR ACTING ABILITY, EVEN IF PEOPLE LOOK AT YOU IN A NEGATIVE LIGHT...
...THE NEXT TIME...

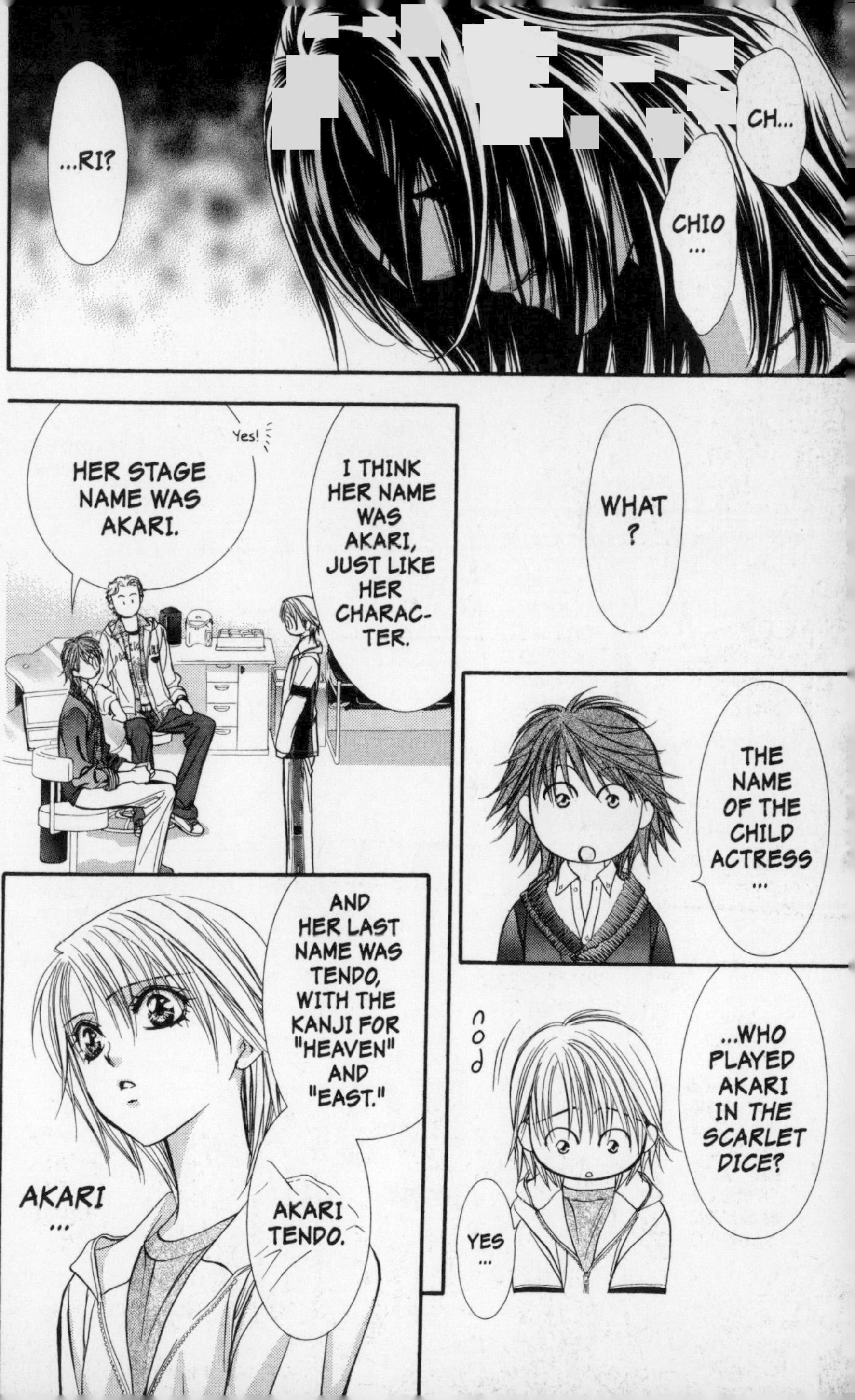
CH...
CHIO ...
...RI?
WHAT ?
I THINK HER NAME WAS AKARI, JUST LIKE HER CHARACTER.
Yes!
HER STAGE NAME WAS AKARI.
THE NAME OF THE CHILD ACTRESS ...
...WHO PLAYED AKARI IN THE SCARLET DICE?
nod
YES ...
AND HER LAST NAME WAS TENDO, WITH THE KANJI FOR "HEAVEN" AND "EAST."
AKARI TENDO.
AKARI ...

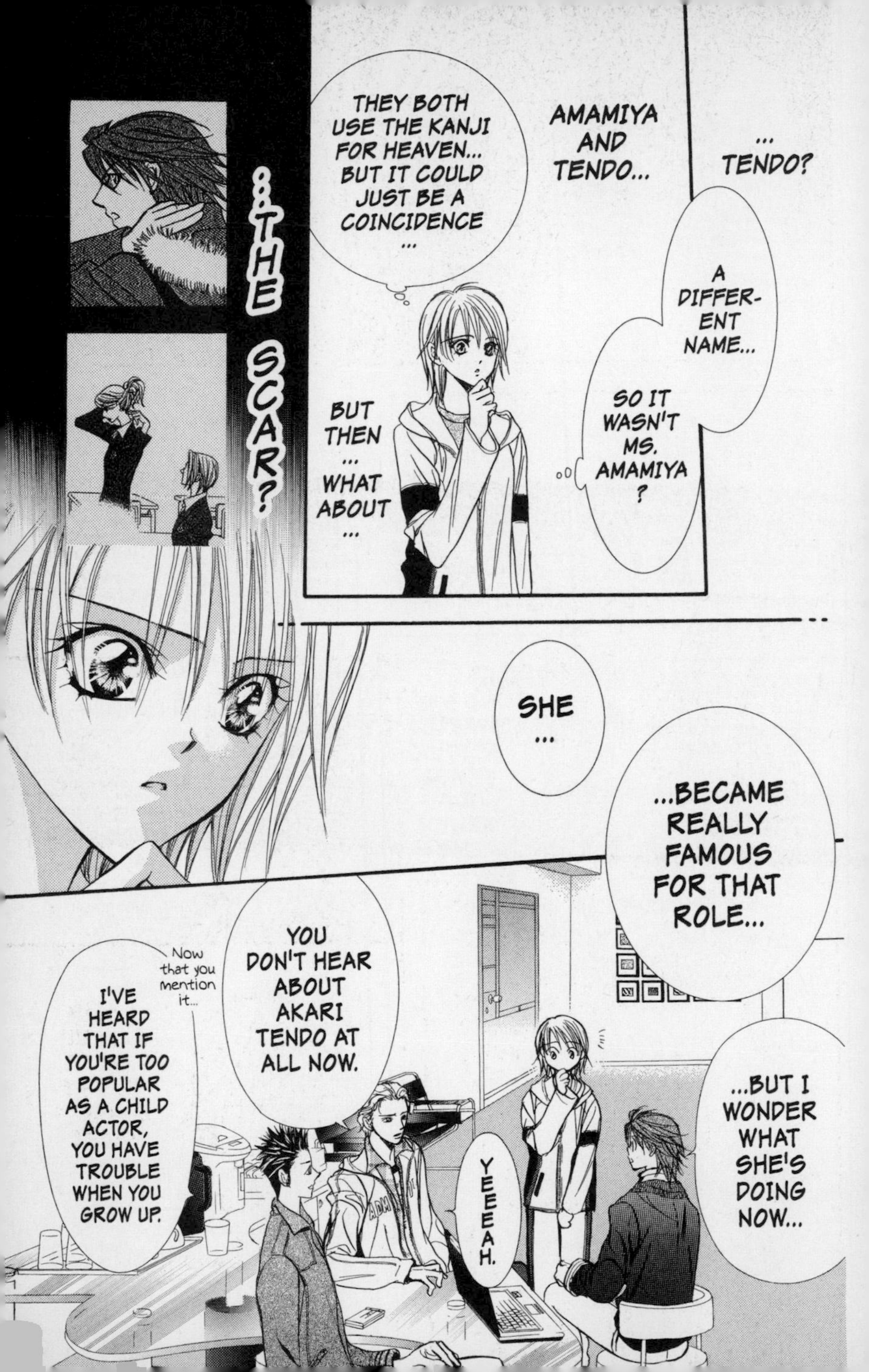
...TENDO?
AMAMIYA AND TENDO...
THEY BOTH USE THE KANJI FOR HEAVEN... BUT IT COULD JUST BE A COINCIDENCE ...
A DIFFERENT NAME...
SO IT WASN'T MS. AMAMIYA?
BUT THEN ... WHAT ABOUT ...
...THE SCAR?
SHE ...
...BECAME REALLY FAMOUS FOR THAT ROLE...
...BUT I WONDER WHAT SHE'S DOING NOW...
YEEEAH.
YOU DON'T HEAR ABOUT AKARI TENDO AT ALL NOW.
Now that you mention it...
I'VE HEARD THAT IF YOU'RE TOO POPULAR AS A CHILD ACTOR, YOU HAVE TROUBLE WHEN YOU GROW UP.

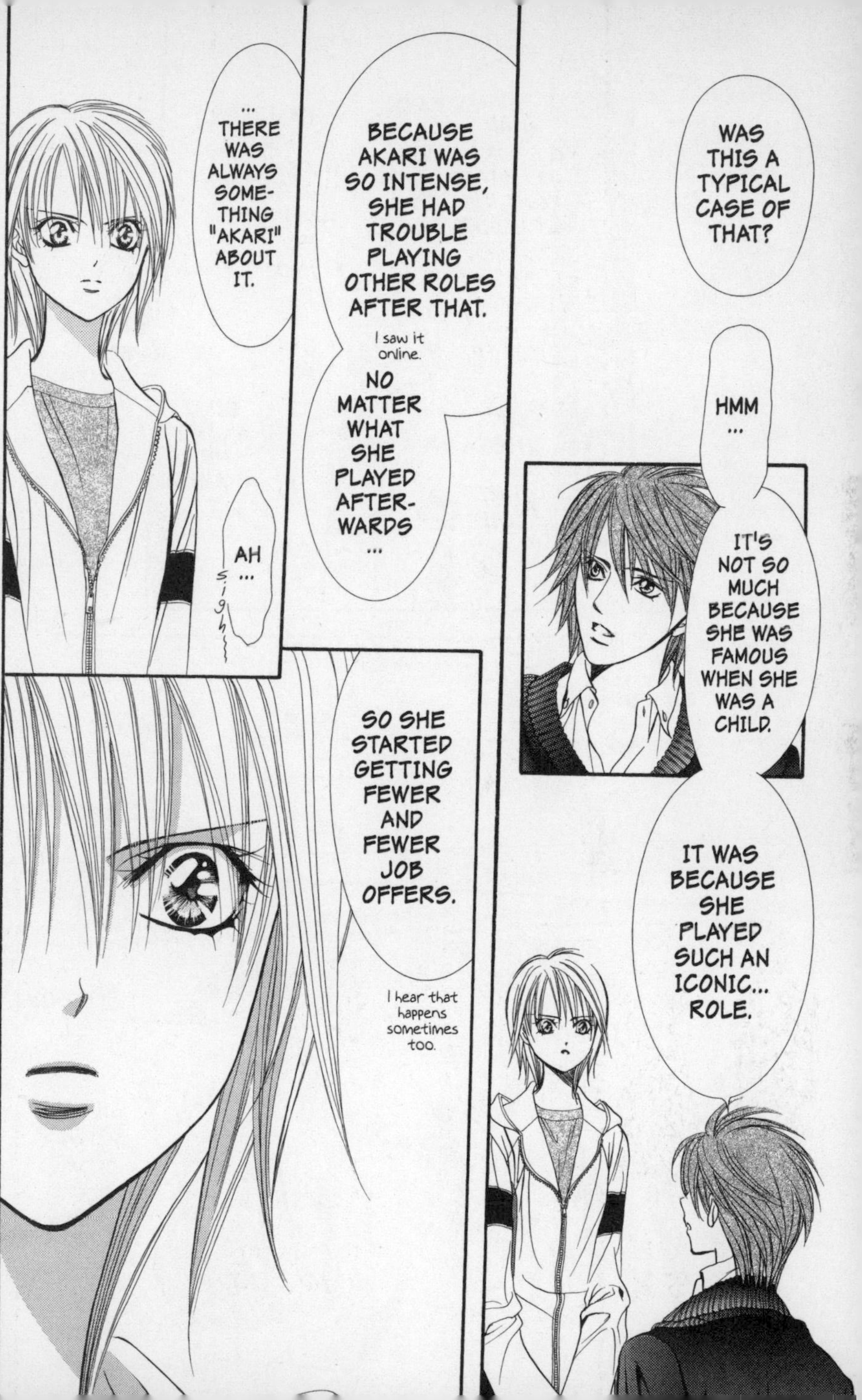
WAS THIS A TYPICAL CASE OF THAT?
HMM ...
IT'S NOT SO MUCH BECAUSE SHE WAS FAMOUS WHEN SHE WAS A CHILD.
IT WAS BECAUSE SHE PLAYED SUCH AN ICONIC... ROLE.
BECAUSE AKARI WAS SO INTENSE, SHE HAD TROUBLE PLAYING OTHER ROLES AFTER THAT.
I saw it online.
NO MATTER WHAT SHE PLAYED AFTER-WARDS ...
... THERE WAS ALWAYS SOME-THING "AKARI" ABOUT IT.
AH ...
sigh~
SO SHE STARTED GETTING FEWER AND FEWER JOB OFFERS.
I hear that happens sometimes too.

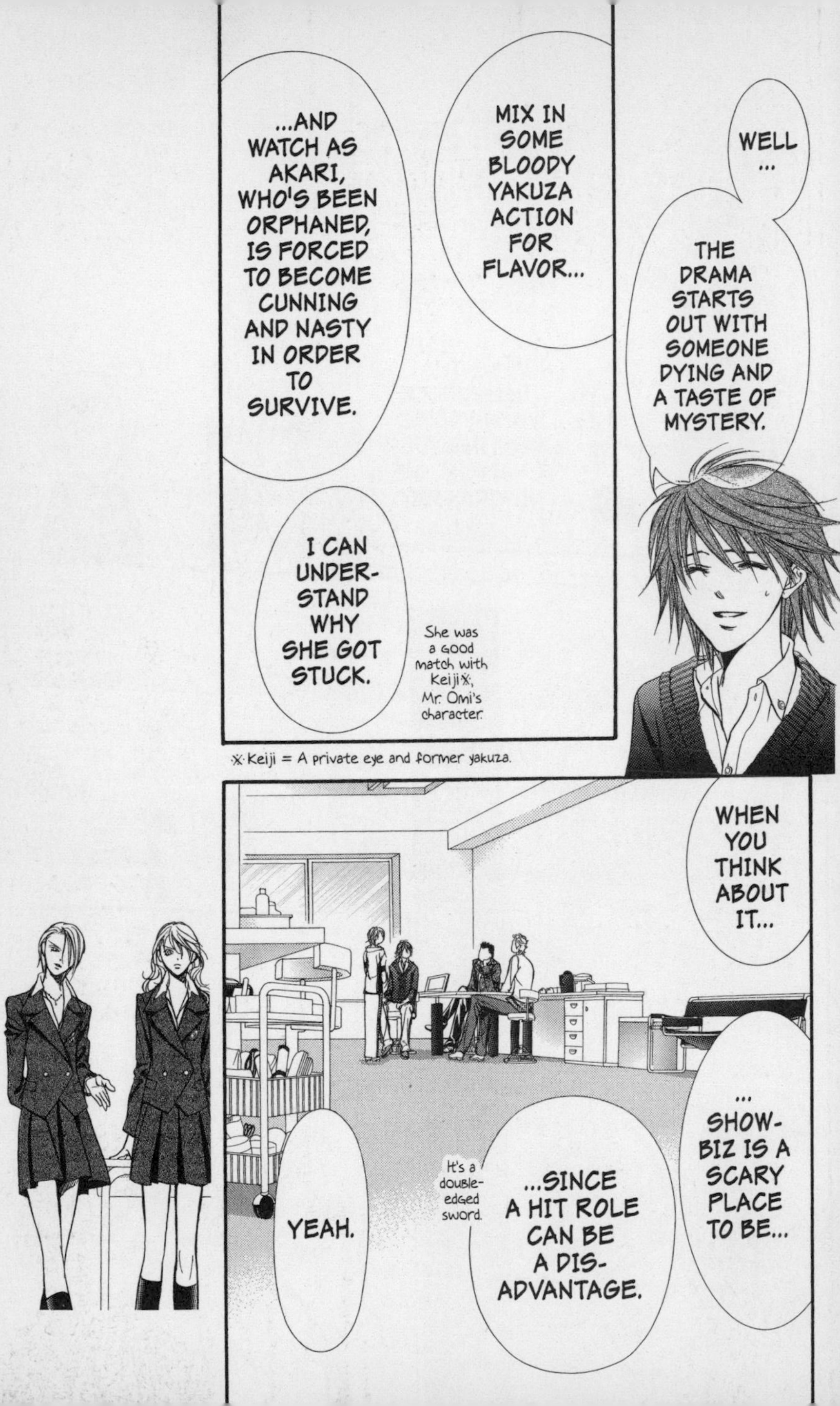
WELL...
THE DRAMA STARTS OUT WITH SOMEONE DYING AND A TASTE OF MYSTERY.
MIX IN SOME BLOODY YAKUZA ACTION FOR FLAVOR...
...AND WATCH AS AKARI, WHO'S BEEN ORPHANED, IS FORCED TO BECOME CUNNING AND NASTY IN ORDER TO SURVIVE.
I CAN UNDER-STAND WHY SHE GOT STUCK.
She was a good match with Keiji※, Mr. Omi's character.
WHEN YOU THINK ABOUT IT...
...SHOW-BIZ IS A SCARY PLACE TO BE...
...SINCE A HIT ROLE CAN BE A DIS-ADVANTAGE.
It's a double-edged sword.
YEAH.

※Keiji = A private eye and former yakuza.

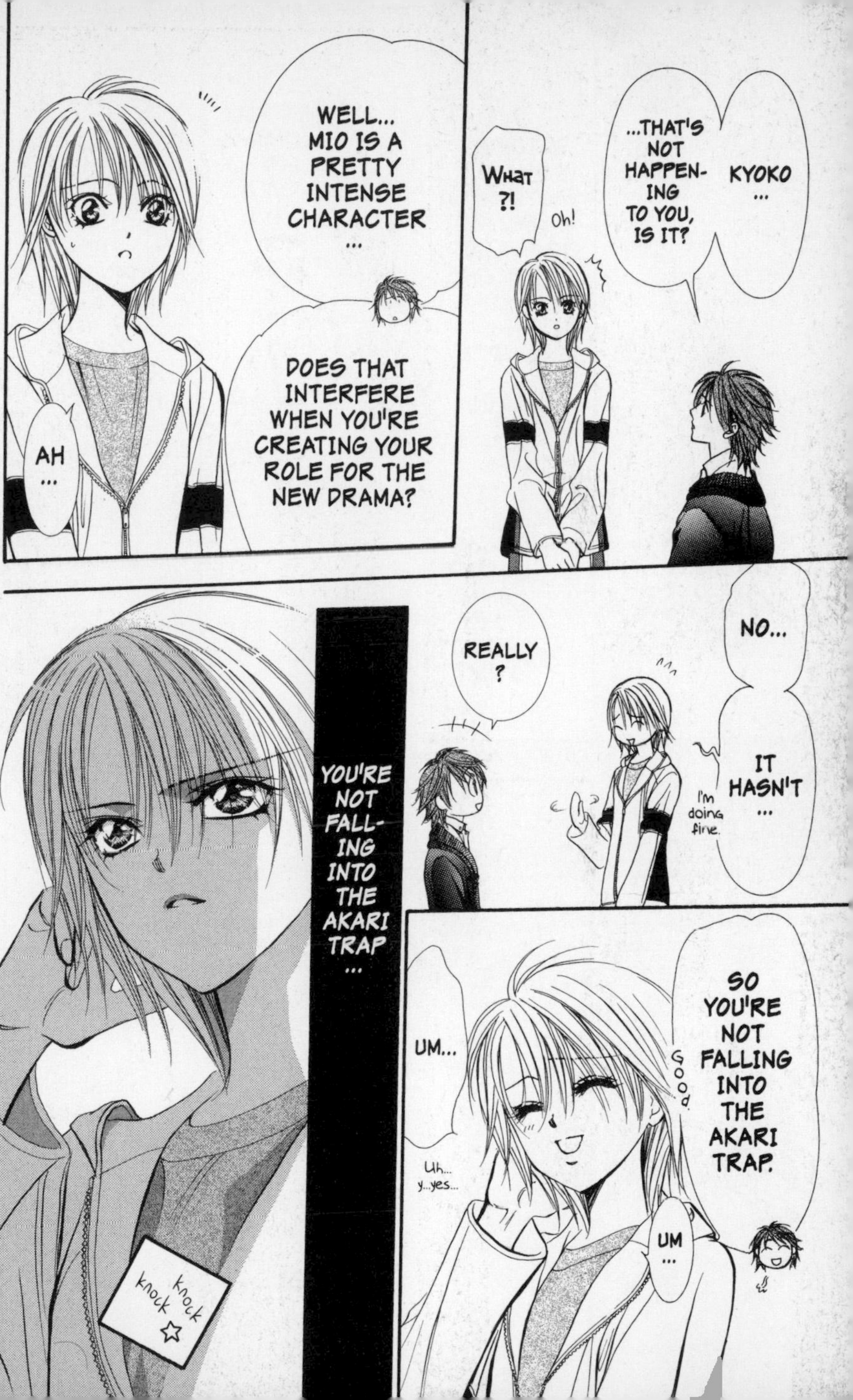
KYOKO ...
...THAT'S NOT HAPPENING TO YOU, IS IT?
WHAT ?!
Oh!
WELL... MIO IS A PRETTY INTENSE CHARACTER ...
DOES THAT INTERFERE WHEN YOU'RE CREATING YOUR ROLE FOR THE NEW DRAMA?
AH ...
NO...
IT HASN'T ...
I'm doing fine.
REALLY ?
SO YOU'RE NOT FALLING INTO THE AKARI TRAP.
Good
UM...
UM ...
Uh... y...yes...
YOU'RE NOT FALLING INTO THE AKARI TRAP ...
knock knock

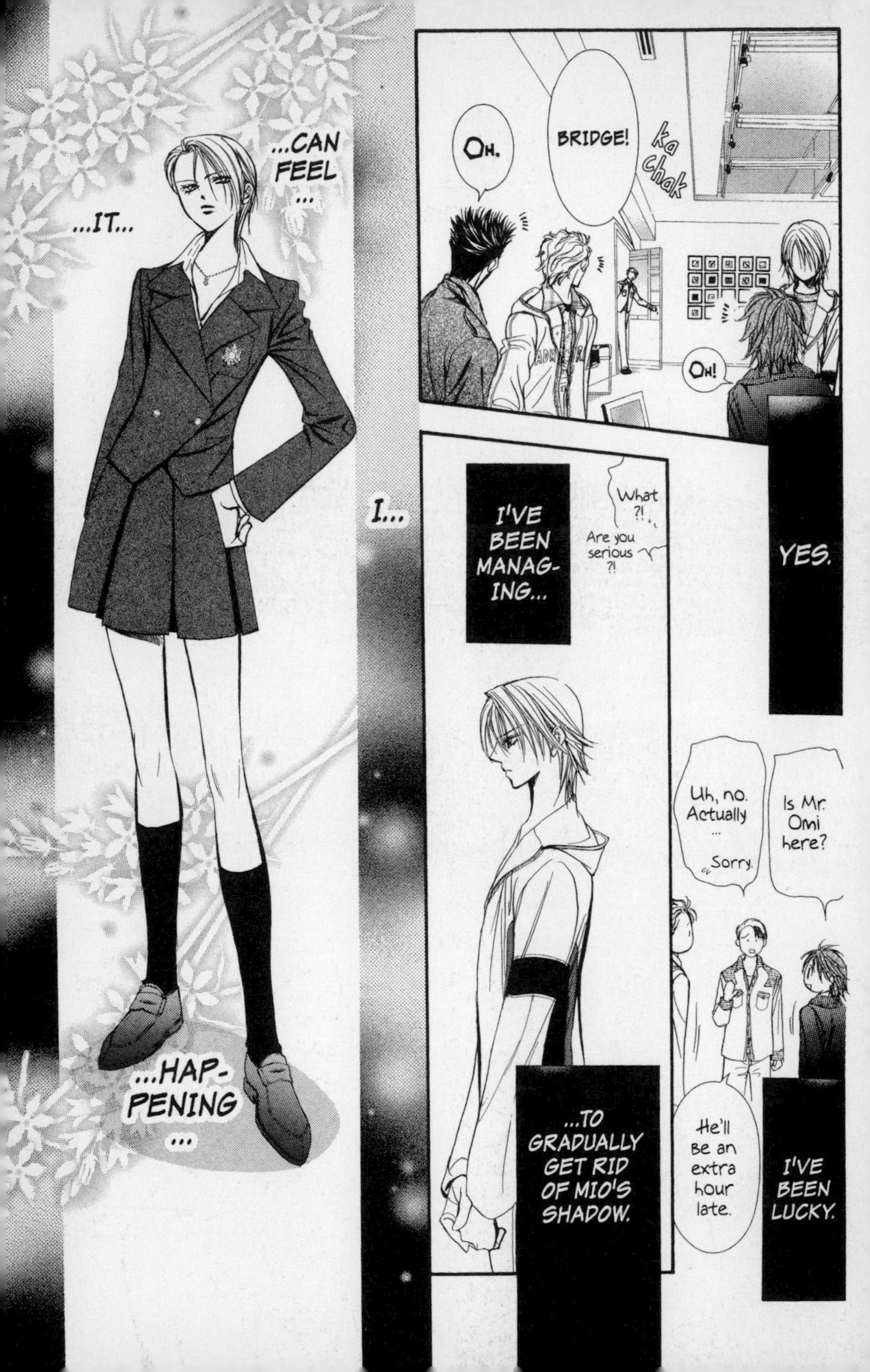
ka Chak
BRIDGE!
Oh.
Oh!
YES.
Is Mr. Omi here?
Uh, no. Actually ... Sorry.
I'VE BEEN LUCKY.
He'll be an extra hour late.
I'VE BEEN MANAGING...
What?!
Are you serious?!
...TO GRADUALLY GET RID OF MIO'S SHADOW.
I...
...CAN FEEL ...
...IT...
...HAPPENING ...

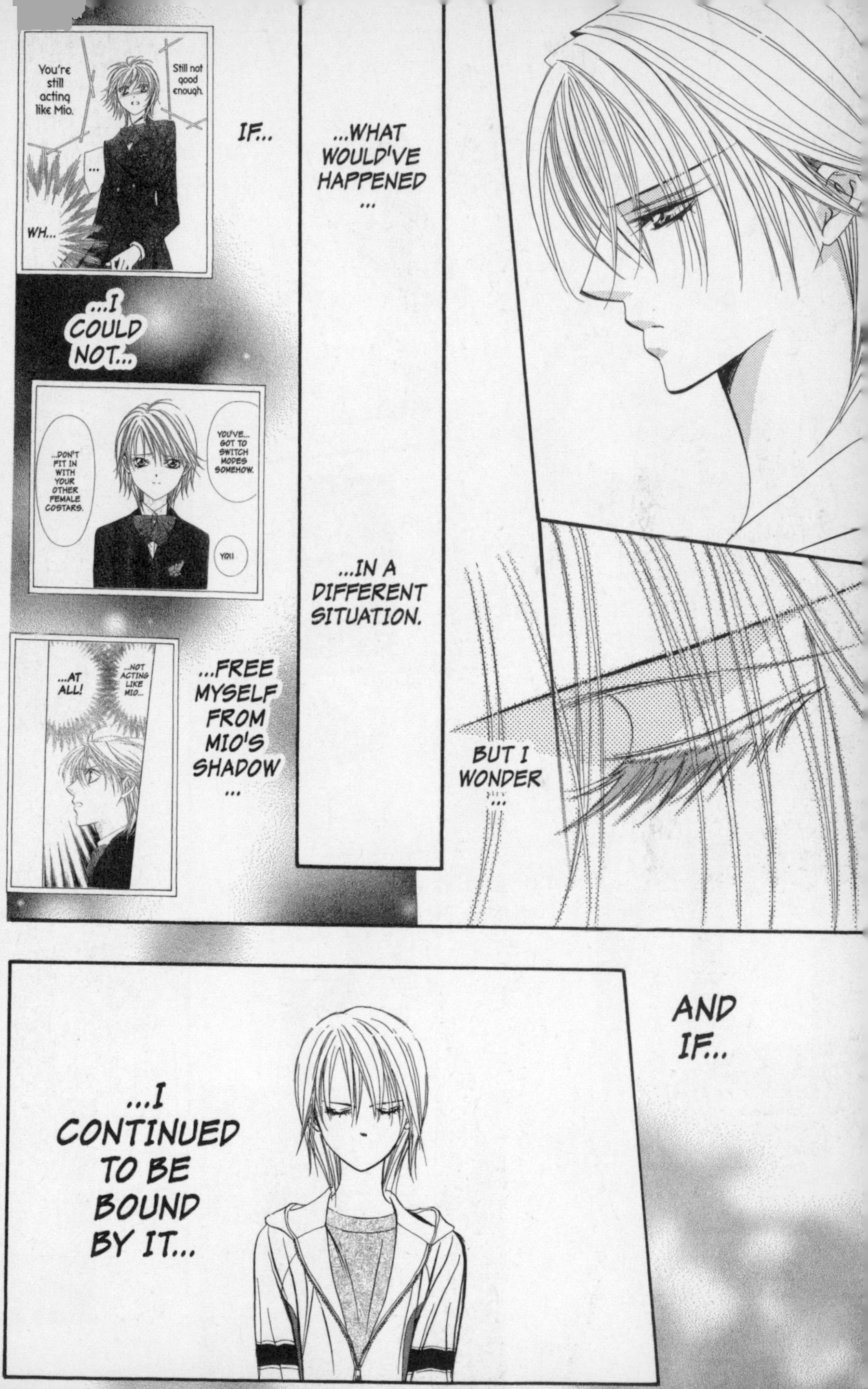
BUT I WONDER...
IF...
You're still acting like Mio.
Still not good enough.
...
WH...
...I COULD NOT...
YOU'VE... GOT TO SWITCH MODES SOMEHOW.
...DON'T FIT IN WITH YOUR OTHER FEMALE COSTARS.
YO!!
...NOT ACTING LIKE MIO...
...AT ALL!
...FREE MYSELF FROM MIO'S SHADOW...
...WHAT WOULD'VE HAPPENED...
...IN A DIFFERENT SITUATION.
AND IF...
...I CONTINUED TO BE BOUND BY IT...

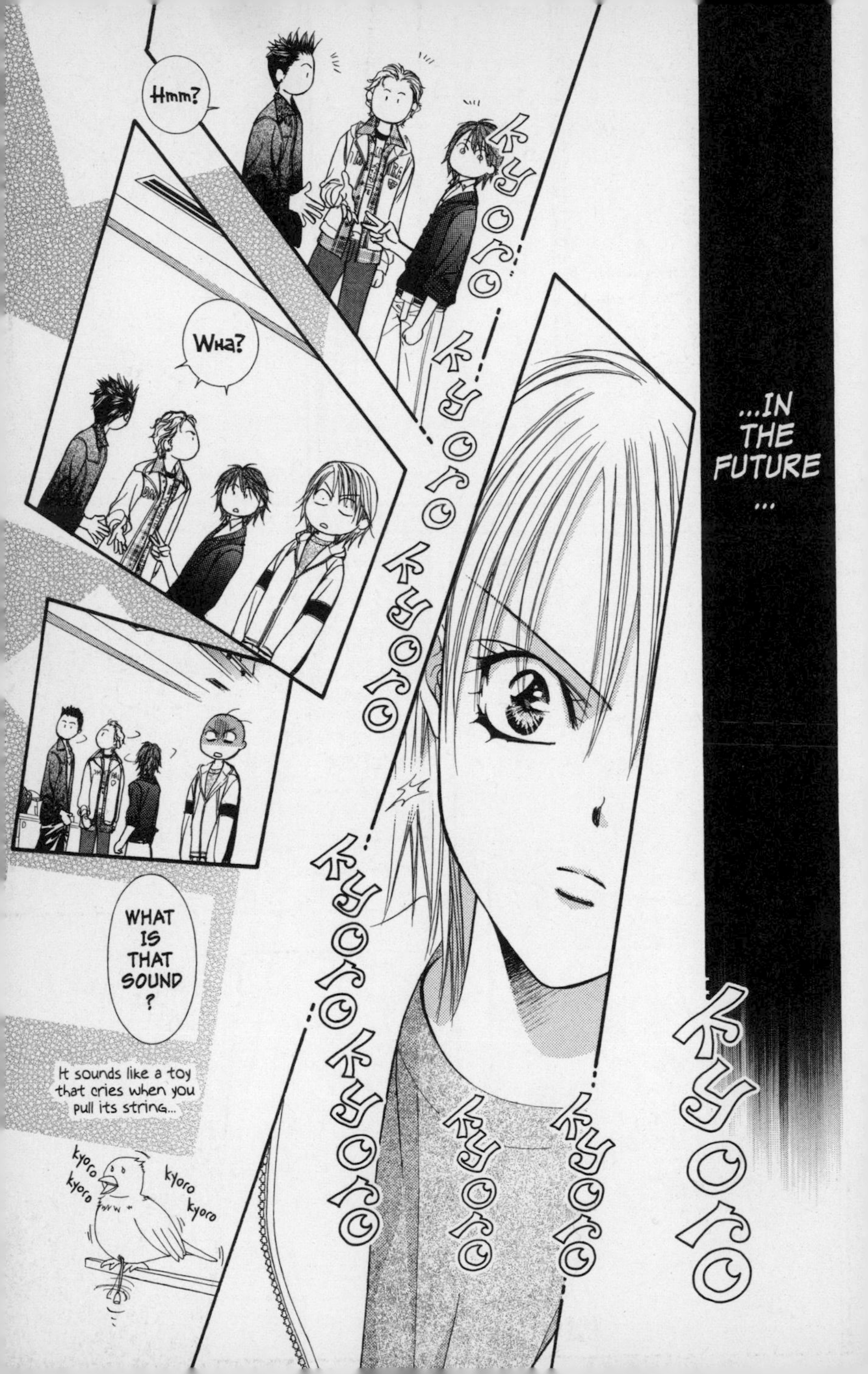
...IN THE FUTURE ...
kyoro
kyoro kyoro
kyoro kyoro kyoro kyoro kyoro
Hmm?
Wha?
WHAT IS THAT SOUND?
It sounds like a toy that cries when you pull its string...
kyoro kyoro
kyoro kyoro

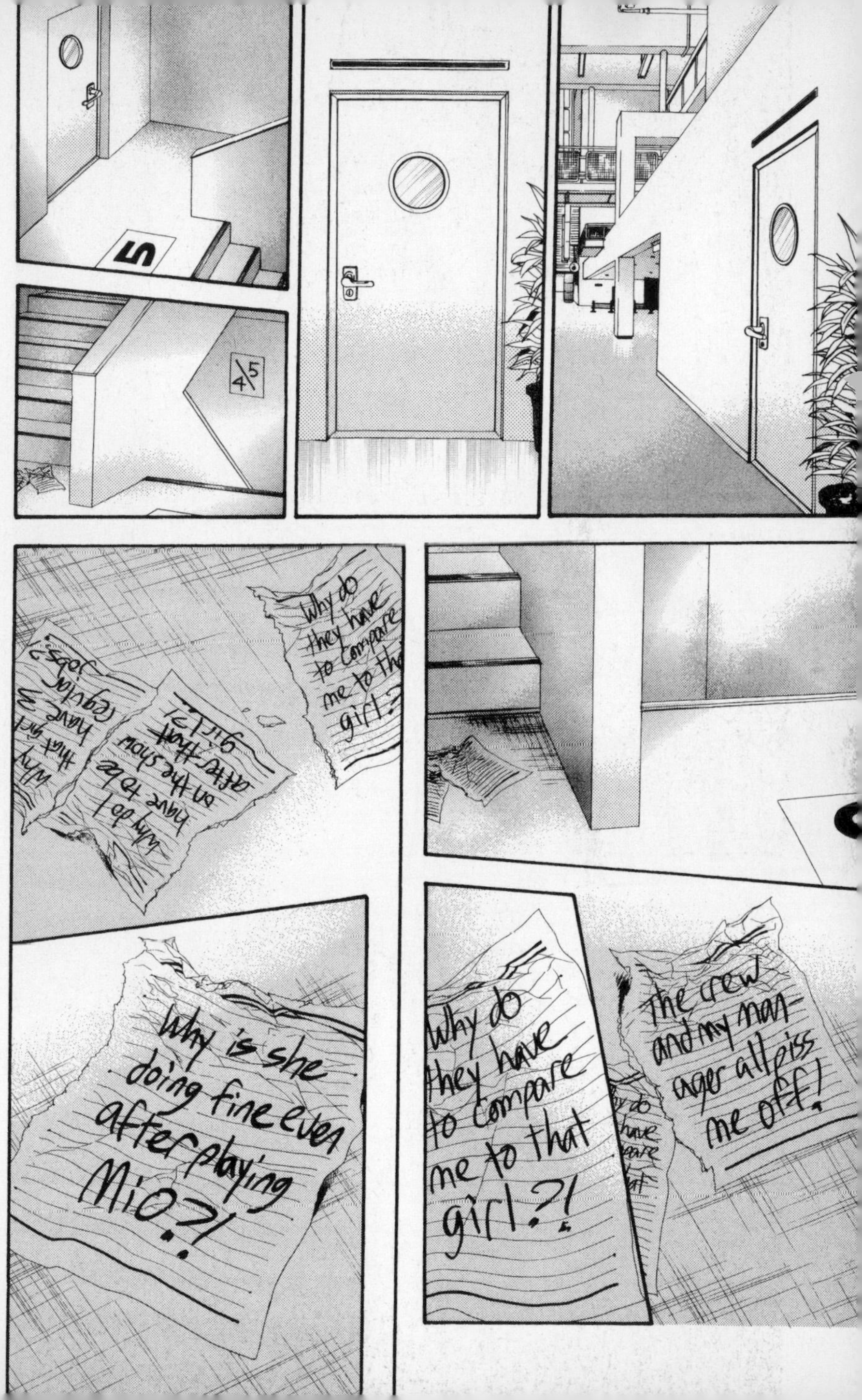
Why do they have to compare me to tha girl?!
Why do I have to be on the show after that girl?!
The crew and my man-ager all piss me off!
Why do they have to compare me to that girl?!
Why is she doing fine even after playing Mio?!

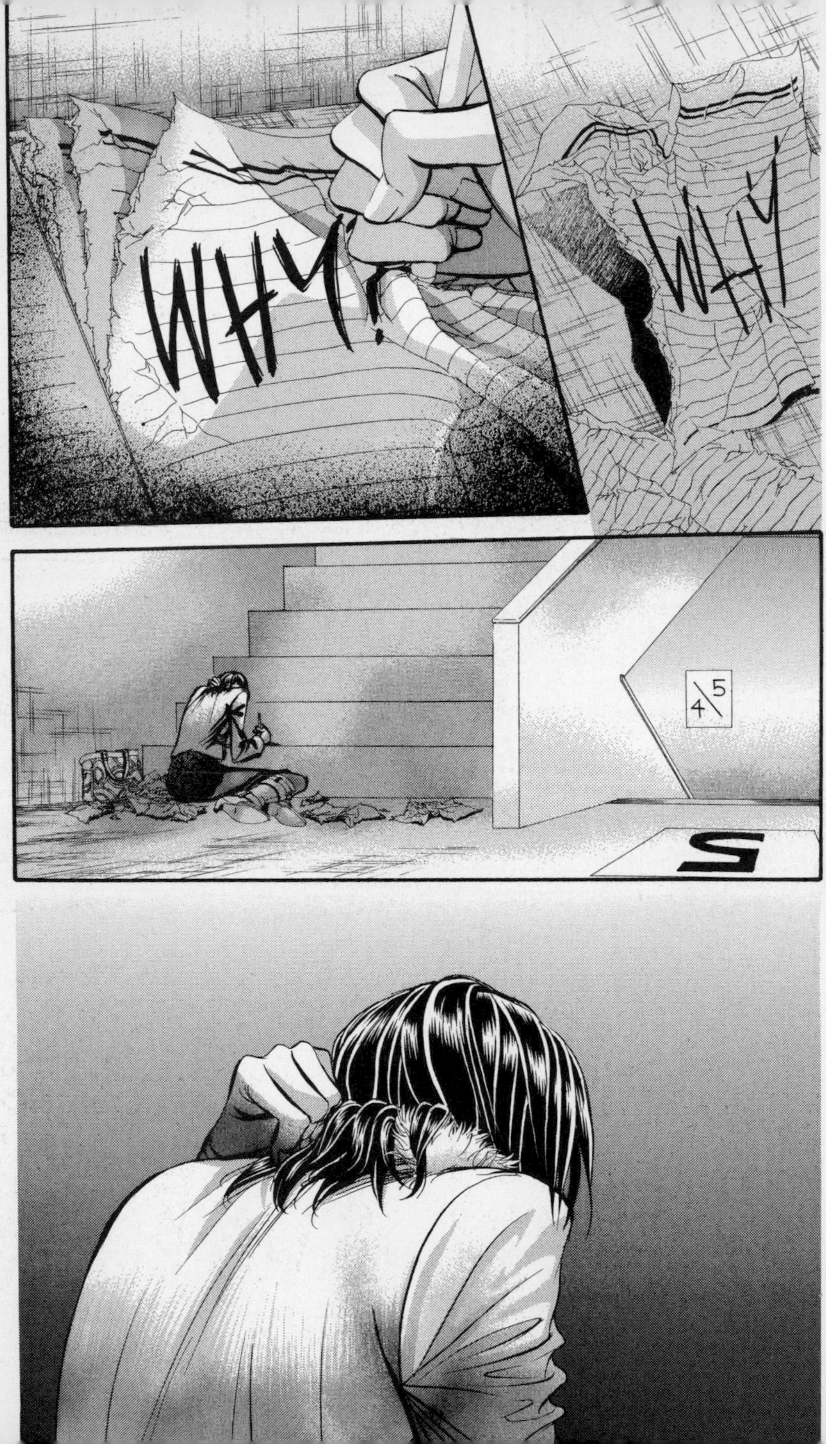
WHY
WHY

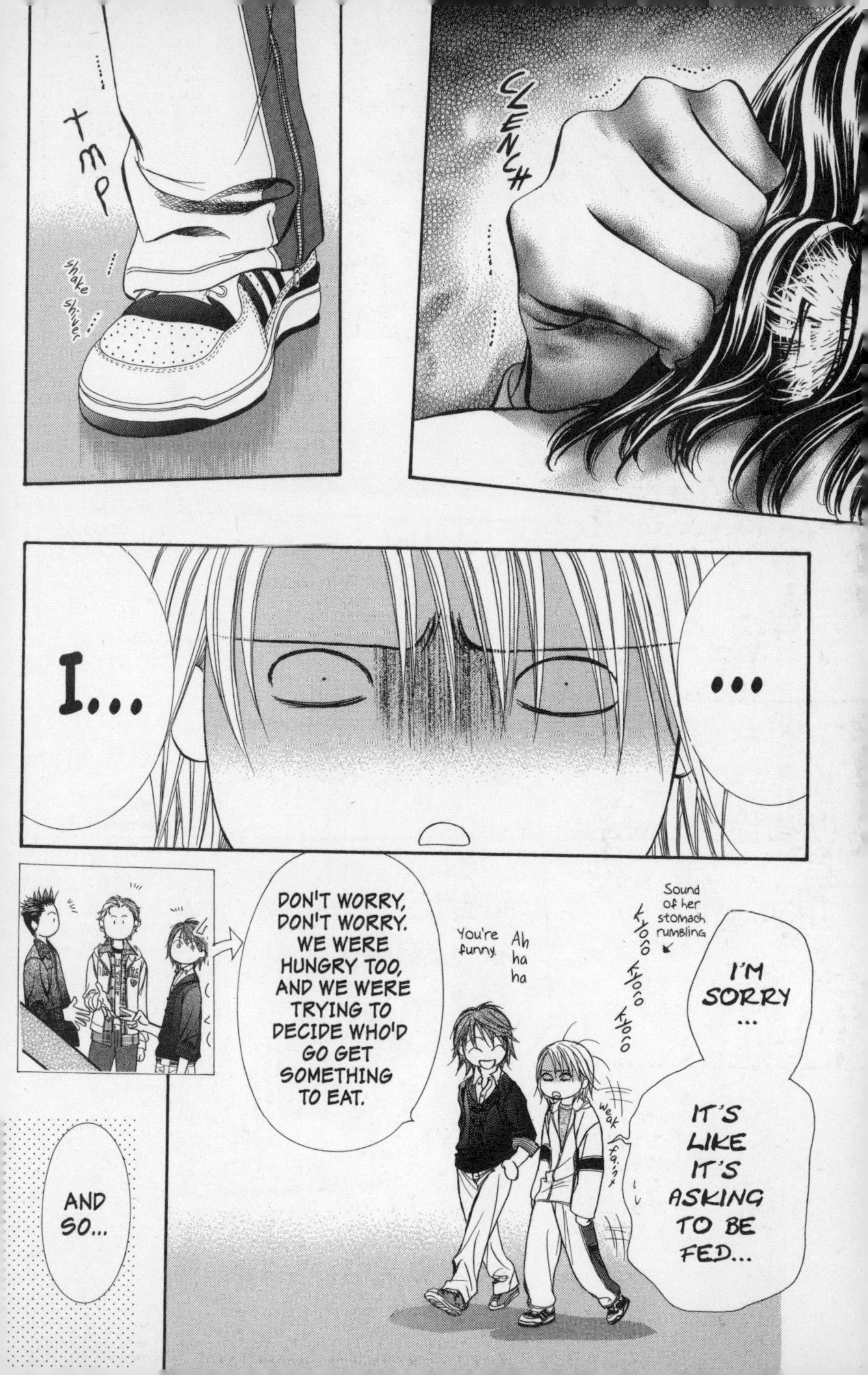

CLENCH
......
......
......
tmp
shake
shiver
...
I...
I'M SORRY ...
IT'S LIKE IT'S ASKING TO BE FED...
Sound of her stomach rumbling
kyoro kyoro kyoro
weak
faint
Ah ha ha
You're funny.
DON'T WORRY, DON'T WORRY. WE WERE HUNGRY TOO, AND WE WERE TRYING TO DECIDE WHO'D GO GET SOMETHING TO EAT.
AND SO...

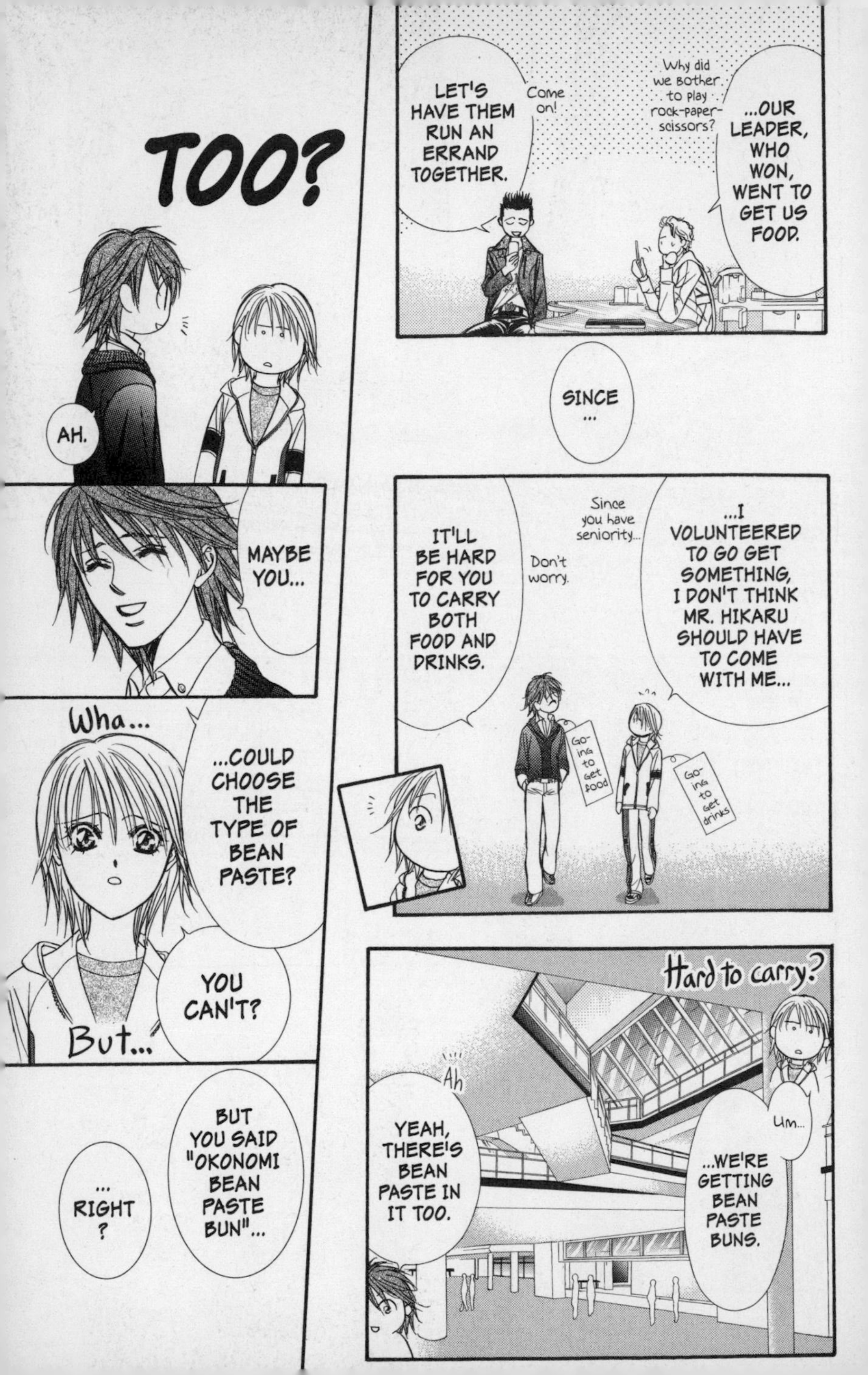
...OUR LEADER, WHO WON, WENT TO GET US FOOD.
Why did we bother to play rock-paper-scissors?
Come on!
LET'S HAVE THEM RUN AN ERRAND TOGETHER.
SINCE ...
...I VOLUNTEERED TO GO GET SOMETHING, I DON'T THINK MR. HIKARU SHOULD HAVE TO COME WITH ME...
Since you have seniority...
Don't worry.
IT'LL BE HARD FOR YOU TO CARRY BOTH FOOD AND DRINKS.
Going to get drinks
Going to get food
Hard to carry?
Um...
...WE'RE GETTING BEAN PASTE BUNS.
Ah
YEAH, THERE'S BEAN PASTE IN IT TOO.
TOO?
AH.
MAYBE YOU...
Wha...
...COULD CHOOSE THE TYPE OF BEAN PASTE?
YOU CAN'T?
But...
BUT YOU SAID "OKONOMI BEAN PASTE BUN"...
... RIGHT?

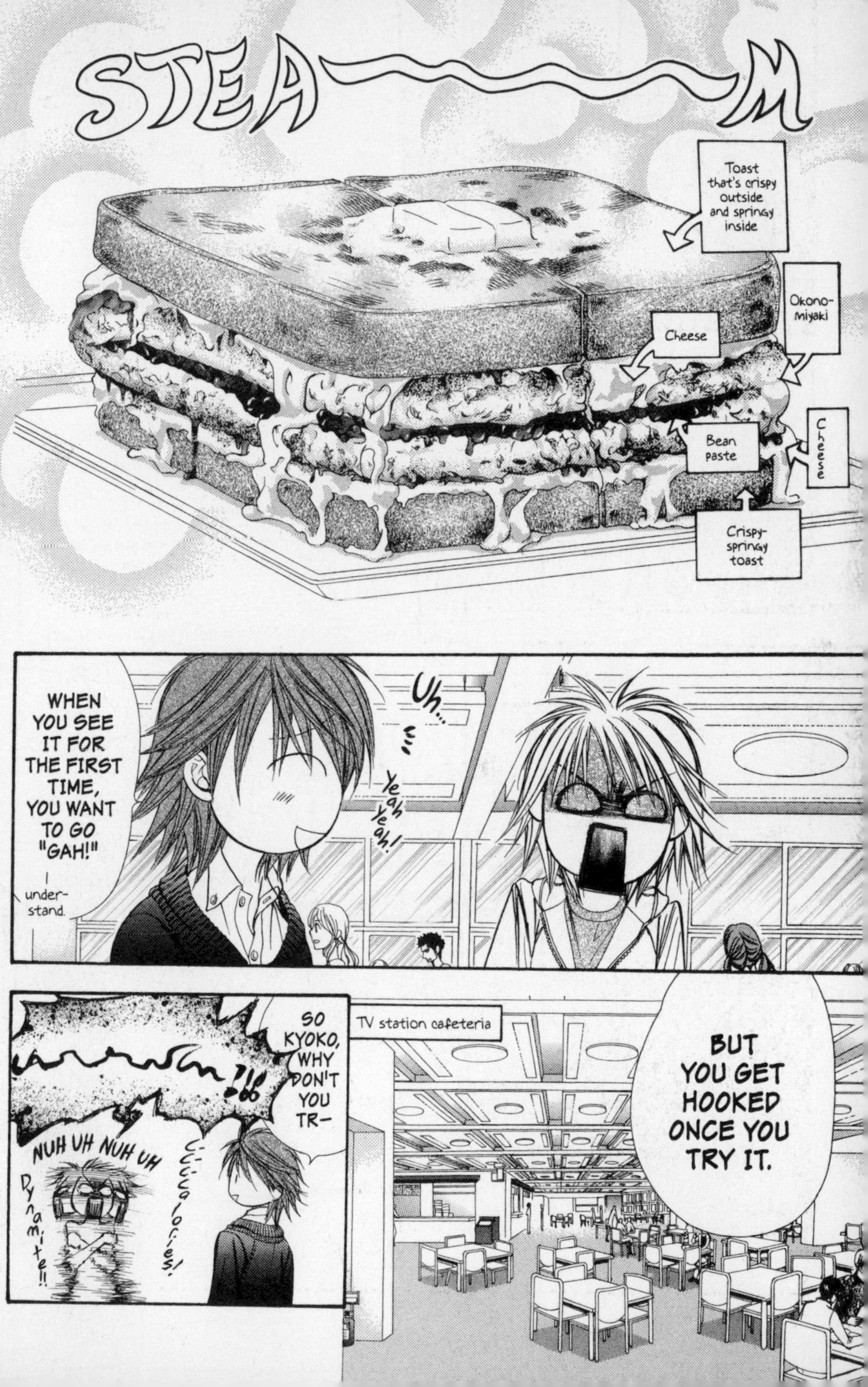
STEA———M
Toast that's crispy outside and springy inside
Okonomiyaki
Cheese
Cheese
Bean paste
Crispy-springy toast
Uh...
Yeah Yeah!
WHEN YOU SEE IT FOR THE FIRST TIME, YOU WANT TO GO "GAH!"
I understand.
BUT YOU GET HOOKED ONCE YOU TRY IT.
TV station cafeteria
SO KYOKO, WHY DON'T YOU TR–
NUH UH NUH UH
Ca-ca-calories!
Dynamite!!

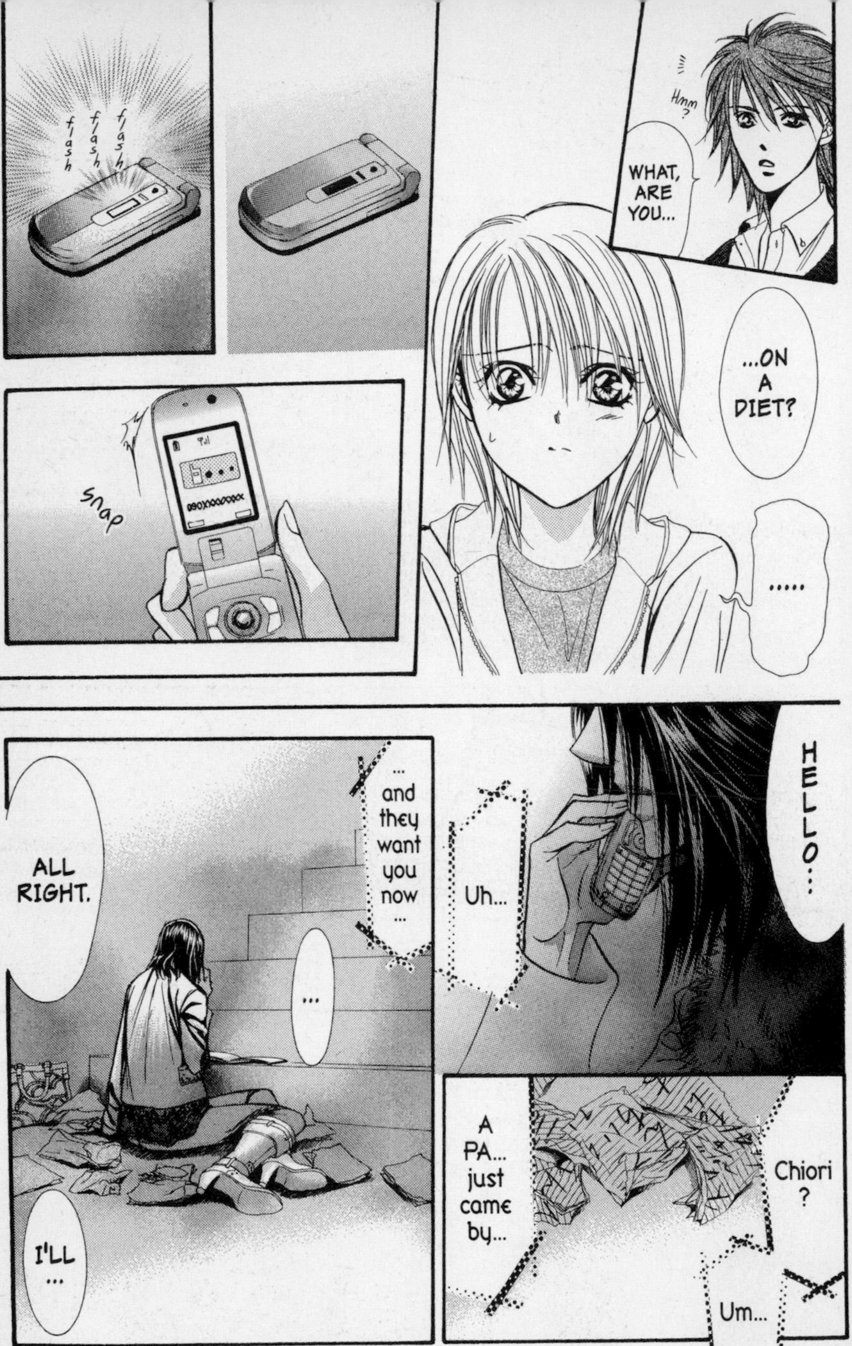
Hmm?
WHAT, ARE YOU...
...ON A DIET?
.....
flash flash flash
snap
HELLO...
Uh...
Chiori?
Um...
A PA... just came by...
... and they want you now ...
...
ALL RIGHT.
I'LL ...

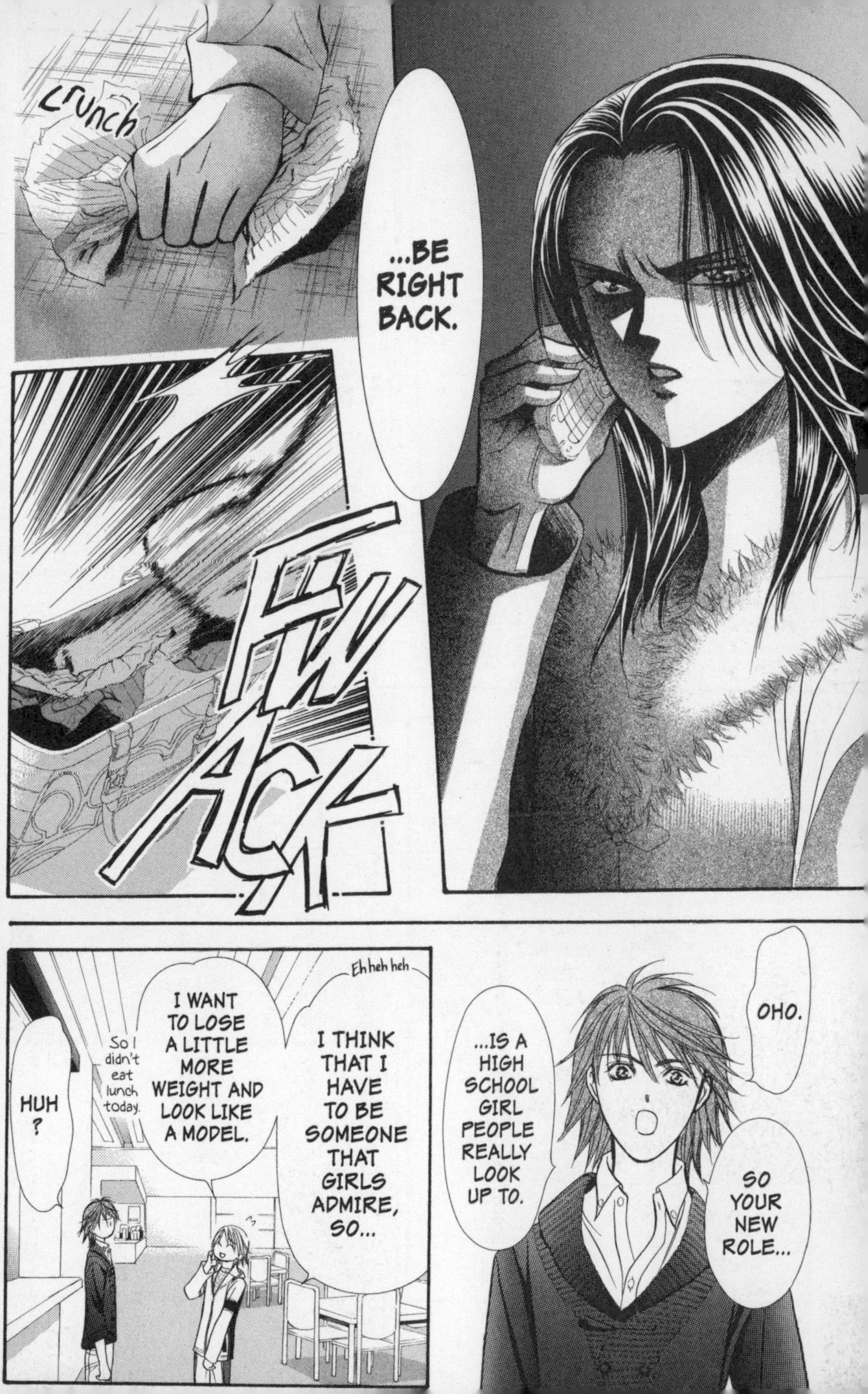
...BE RIGHT BACK.
crunch
FWACK
OHO.
SO YOUR NEW ROLE...
...IS A HIGH SCHOOL GIRL PEOPLE REALLY LOOK UP TO.
Eh heh heh
I THINK THAT I HAVE TO BE SOMEONE THAT GIRLS ADMIRE, SO...
I WANT TO LOSE A LITTLE MORE WEIGHT AND LOOK LIKE A MODEL.
So I didn't eat lunch today.
HUH?

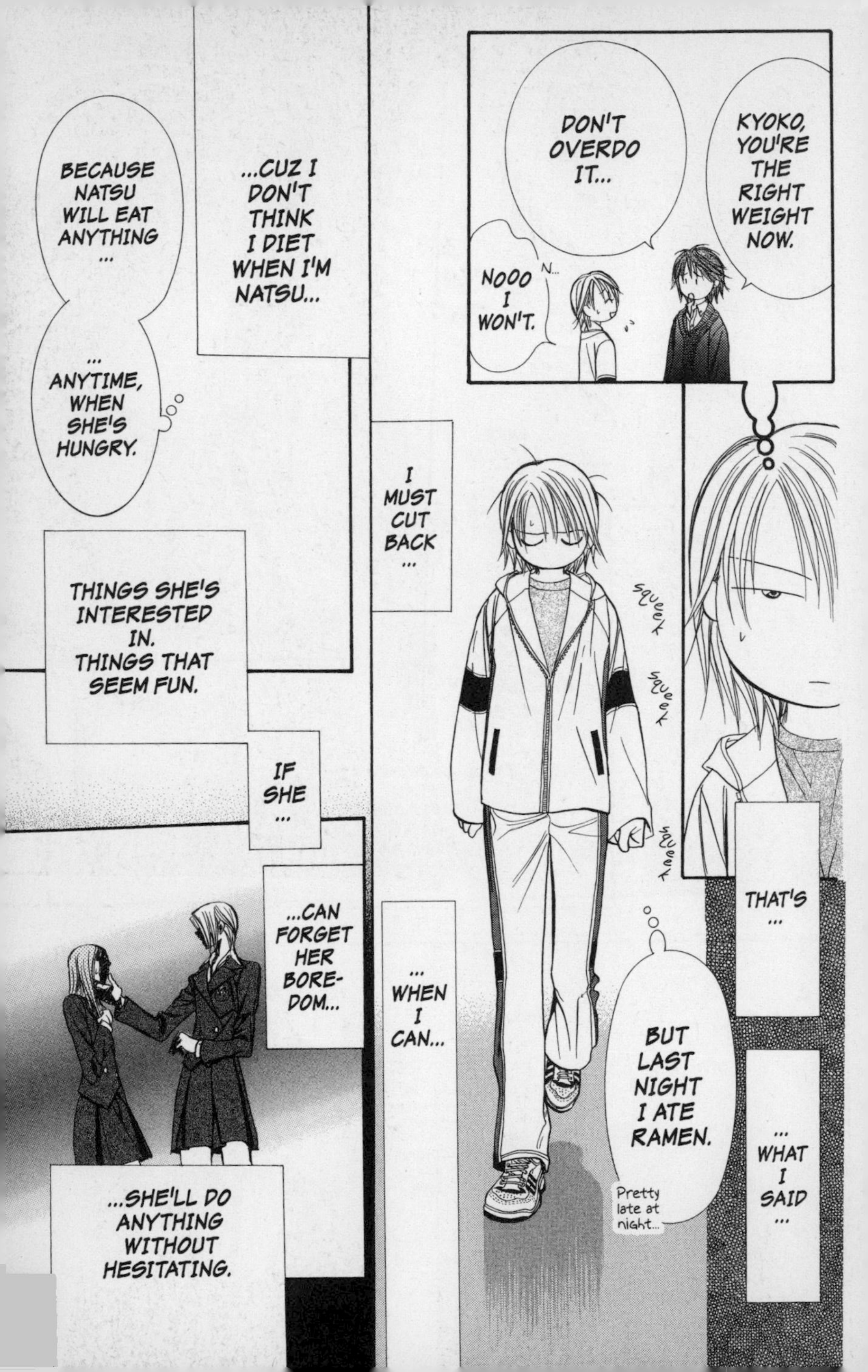
KYOKO, YOU'RE THE RIGHT WEIGHT NOW.
DON'T OVERDO IT...
N...
NOOO I WON'T.
THAT'S ...
... WHAT I SAID ...
I MUST CUT BACK ...
squeak
squeak
squeak
BUT LAST NIGHT I ATE RAMEN.
Pretty late at night...
... WHEN I CAN...
...CUZ I DON'T THINK I DIET WHEN I'M NATSU...
BECAUSE NATSU WILL EAT ANYTHING ...
... ANYTIME, WHEN SHE'S HUNGRY.
THINGS SHE'S INTERESTED IN. THINGS THAT SEEM FUN.
IF SHE ...
...CAN FORGET HER BOREDOM...
...SHE'LL DO ANYTHING WITHOUT HESITATING.

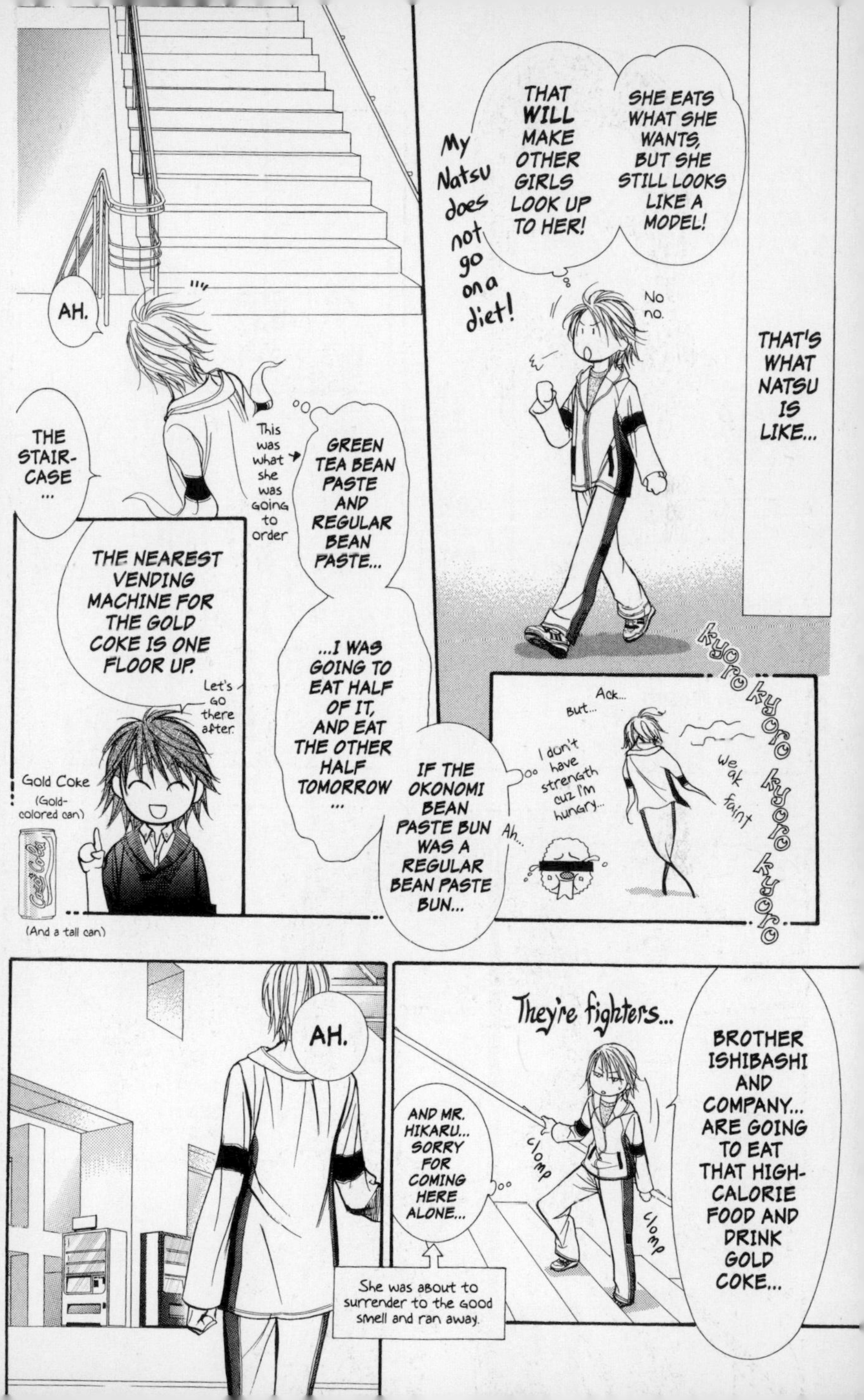
THAT'S WHAT NATSU IS LIKE...
SHE EATS WHAT SHE WANTS, BUT SHE STILL LOOKS LIKE A MODEL!
THAT WILL MAKE OTHER GIRLS LOOK UP TO HER!
My Natsu does not go on a diet!
No no.
AH.
THE STAIR-CASE...
This was what she was going to order
GREEN TEA BEAN PASTE AND REGULAR BEAN PASTE...
...I WAS GOING TO EAT HALF OF IT, AND EAT THE OTHER HALF TOMORROW...
kyoro kyoro kyoro kyoro
Ack...
But...
I don't have strength cuz I'm hungry...
Weak
faint
IF THE OKONOMI BEAN PASTE BUN WAS A REGULAR BEAN PASTE BUN...
Ah...
THE NEAREST VENDING MACHINE FOR THE GOLD COKE IS ONE FLOOR UP.
Let's go there after.
Gold Coke
(Gold-colored can)
(And a tall can)
BROTHER ISHIBASHI AND COMPANY... ARE GOING TO EAT THAT HIGH-CALORIE FOOD AND DRINK GOLD COKE...
They're fighters...
clomp
clomp
AND MR. HIKARU... SORRY FOR COMING HERE ALONE...
She was about to surrender to the good smell and ran away.
AH.

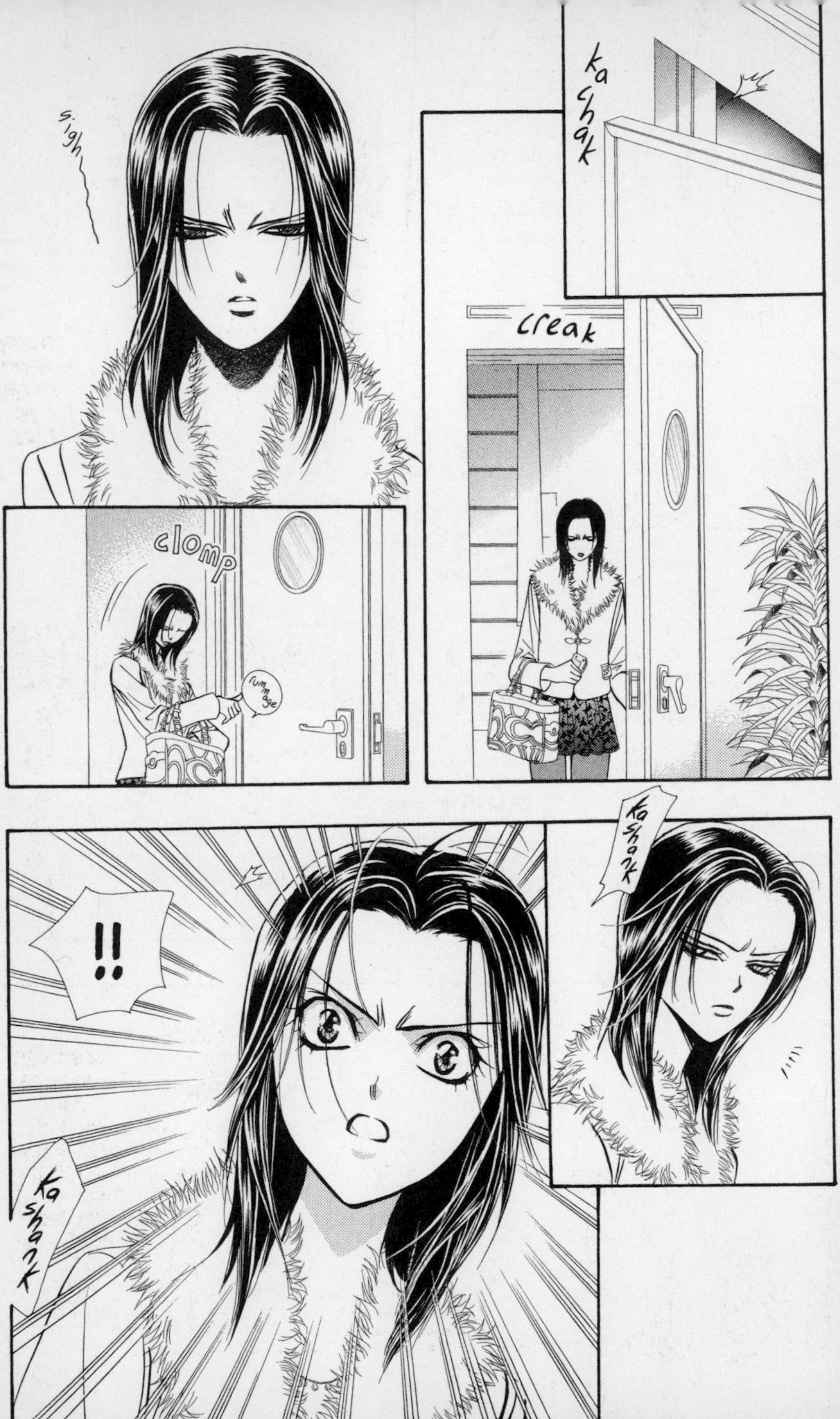
ka chak
creak
sigh
clomp
rummage
ka shank
!!
ka shank

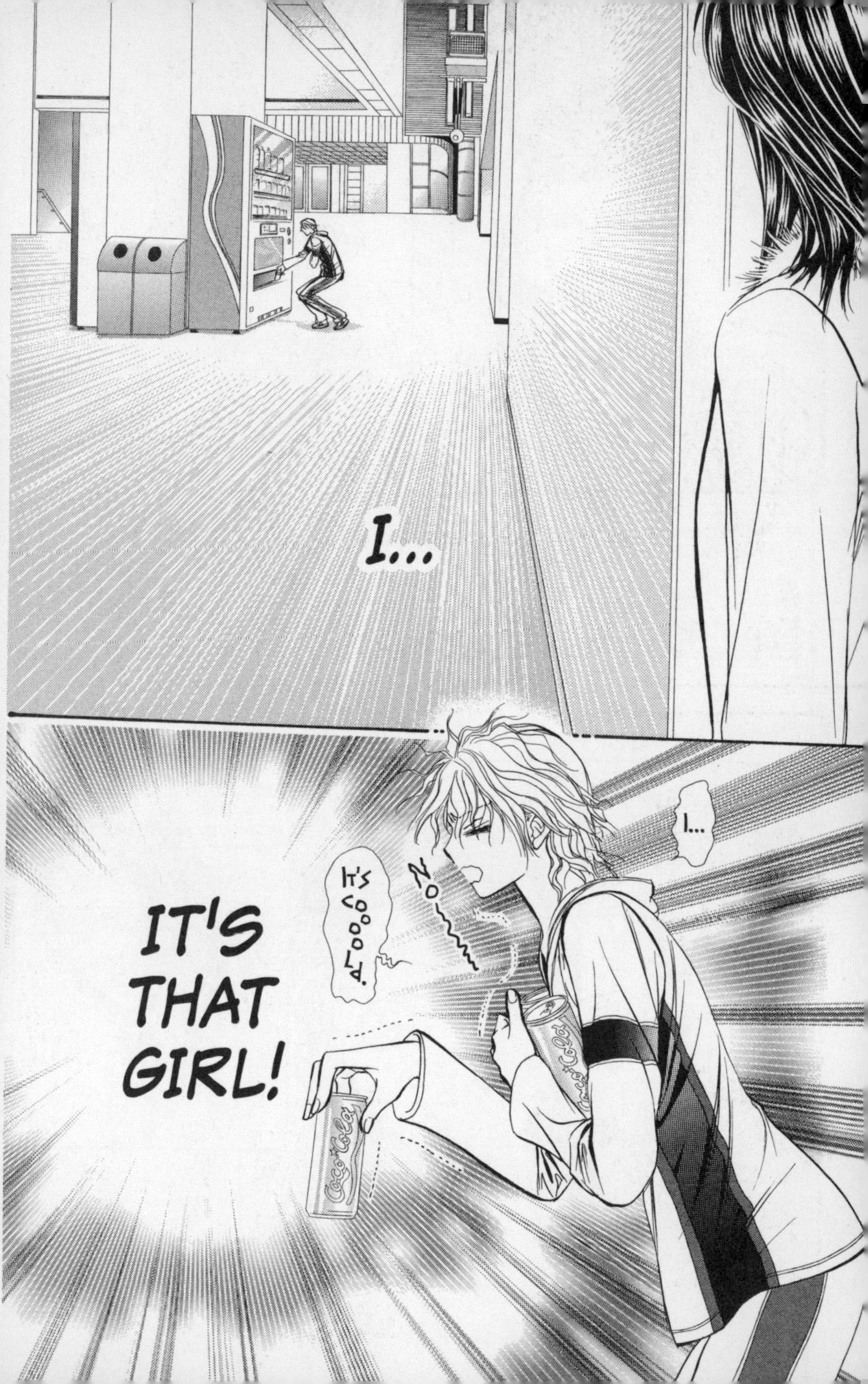
I...
I...
NO~~~
IT'S COOOOOLD.
IT'S THAT GIRL!
Coca-Cola

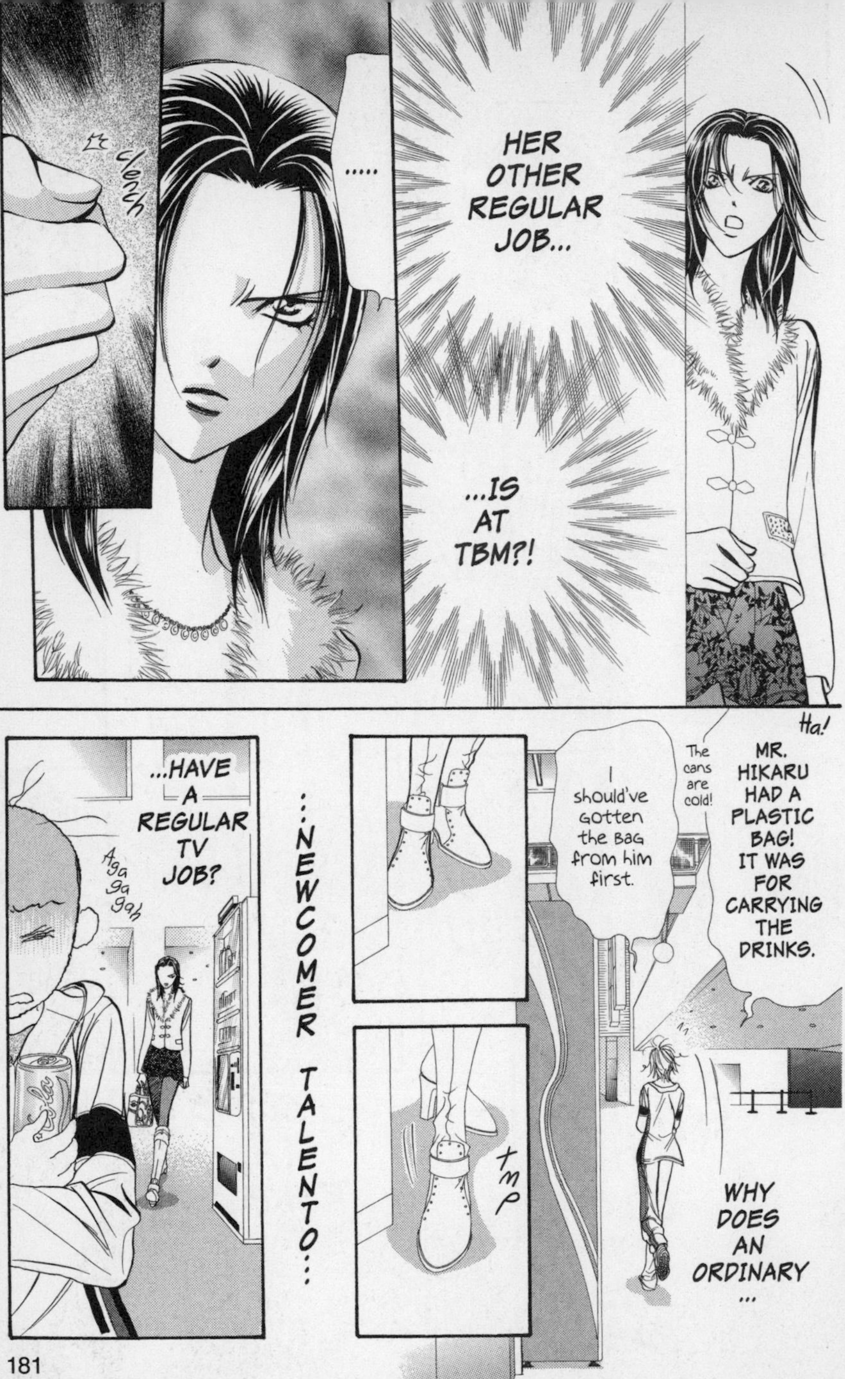
HER OTHER REGULAR JOB...
...IS AT TBM?!
.....
clench
Ha!
MR. HIKARU HAD A PLASTIC BAG! IT WAS FOR CARRYING THE DRINKS.
The cans are cold!
I should've gotten the bag from him first.
WHY DOES AN ORDINARY ...
tmp
...NEWCOMER TALENTO...
...HAVE A REGULAR TV JOB?
Aga ga gah

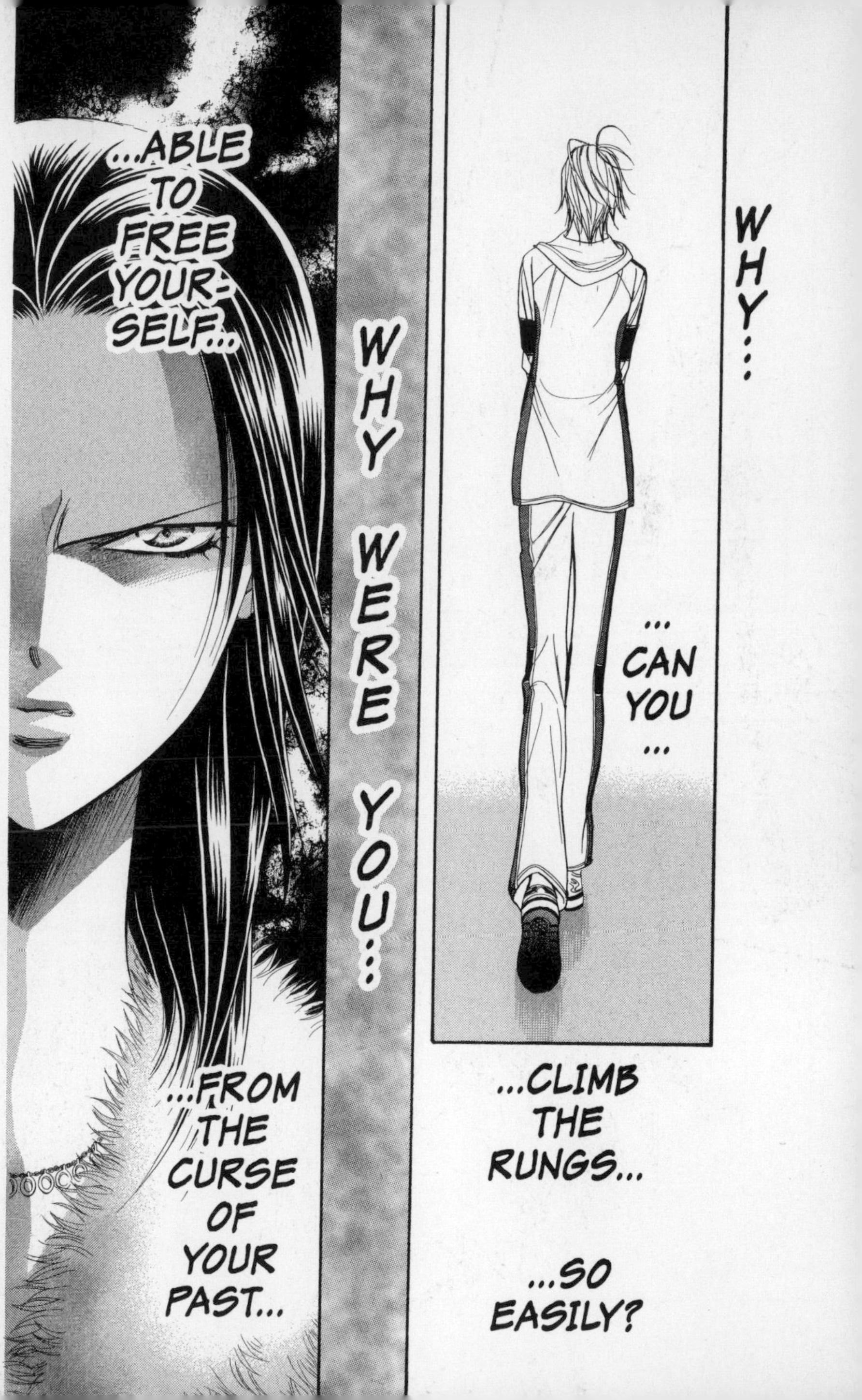
WHY...
...CAN YOU...
...CLIMB THE RUNGS...
...SO EASILY?
WHY WERE YOU...
...ABLE TO FREE YOURSELF...
...FROM THE CURSE OF YOUR PAST...

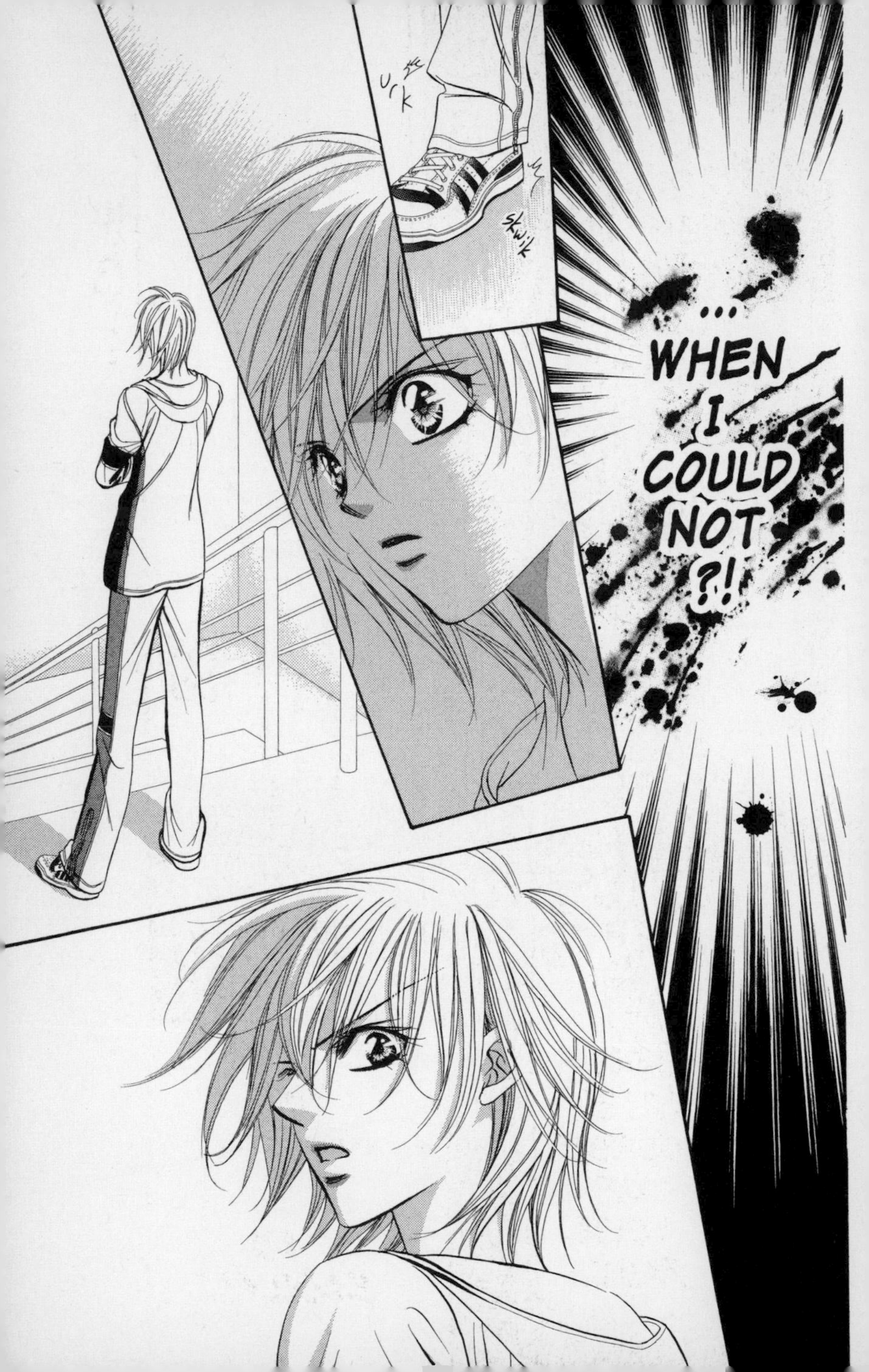
URK
SKWIK
...WHEN I COULD NOT?!

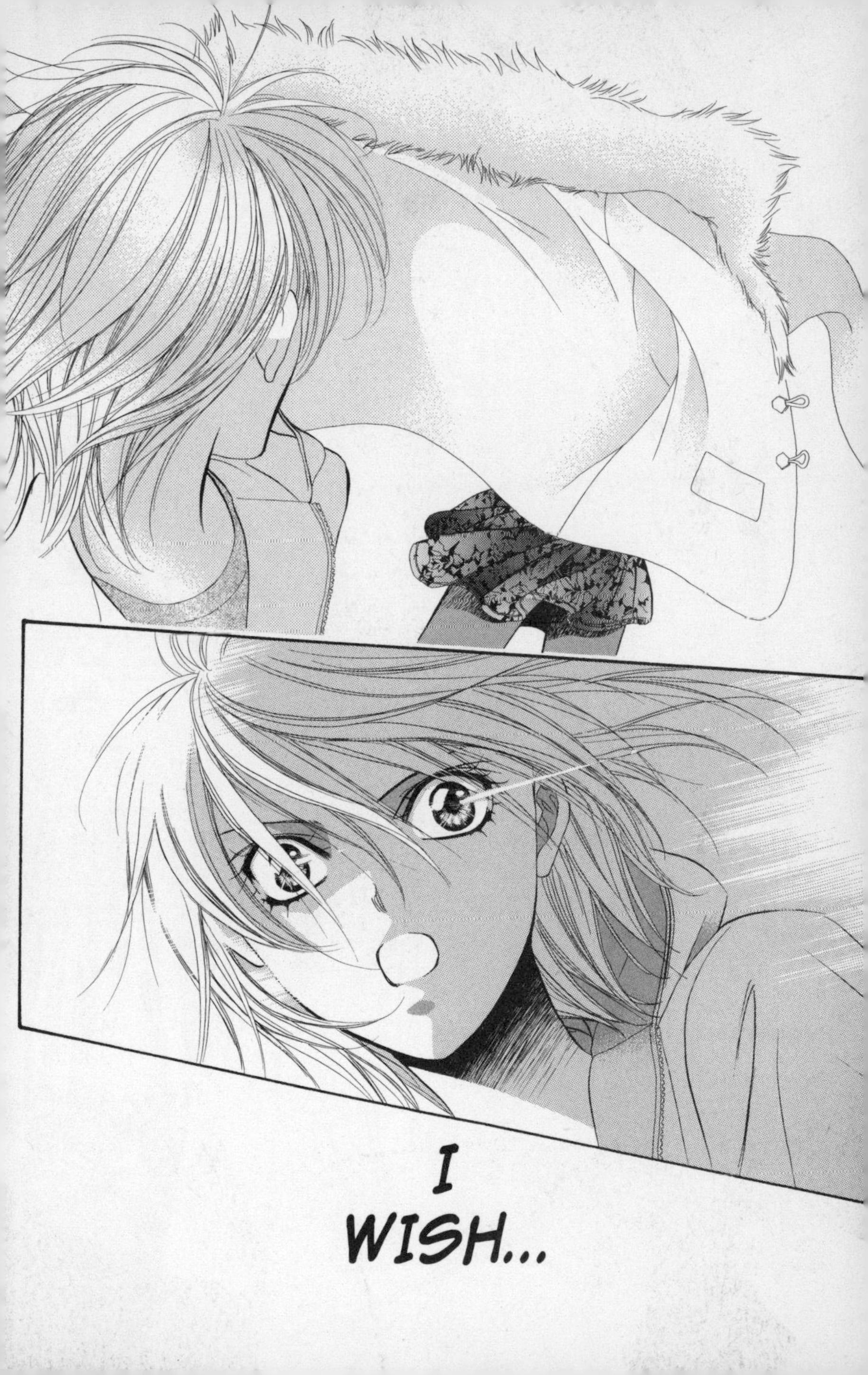
I WISH...

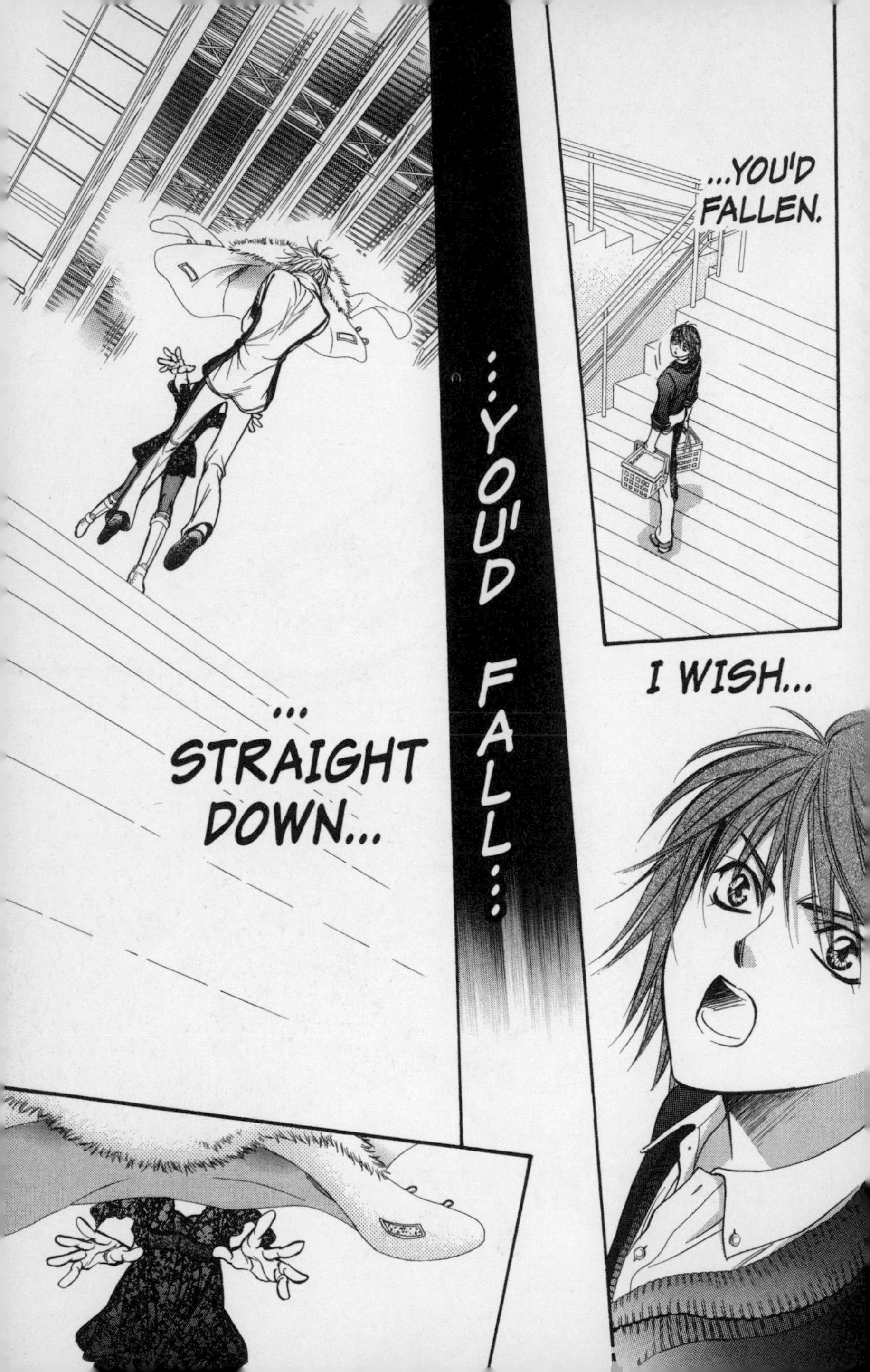
...YOU'D FALLEN.
I WISH...
...YOU'D FALL...
... STRAIGHT DOWN...

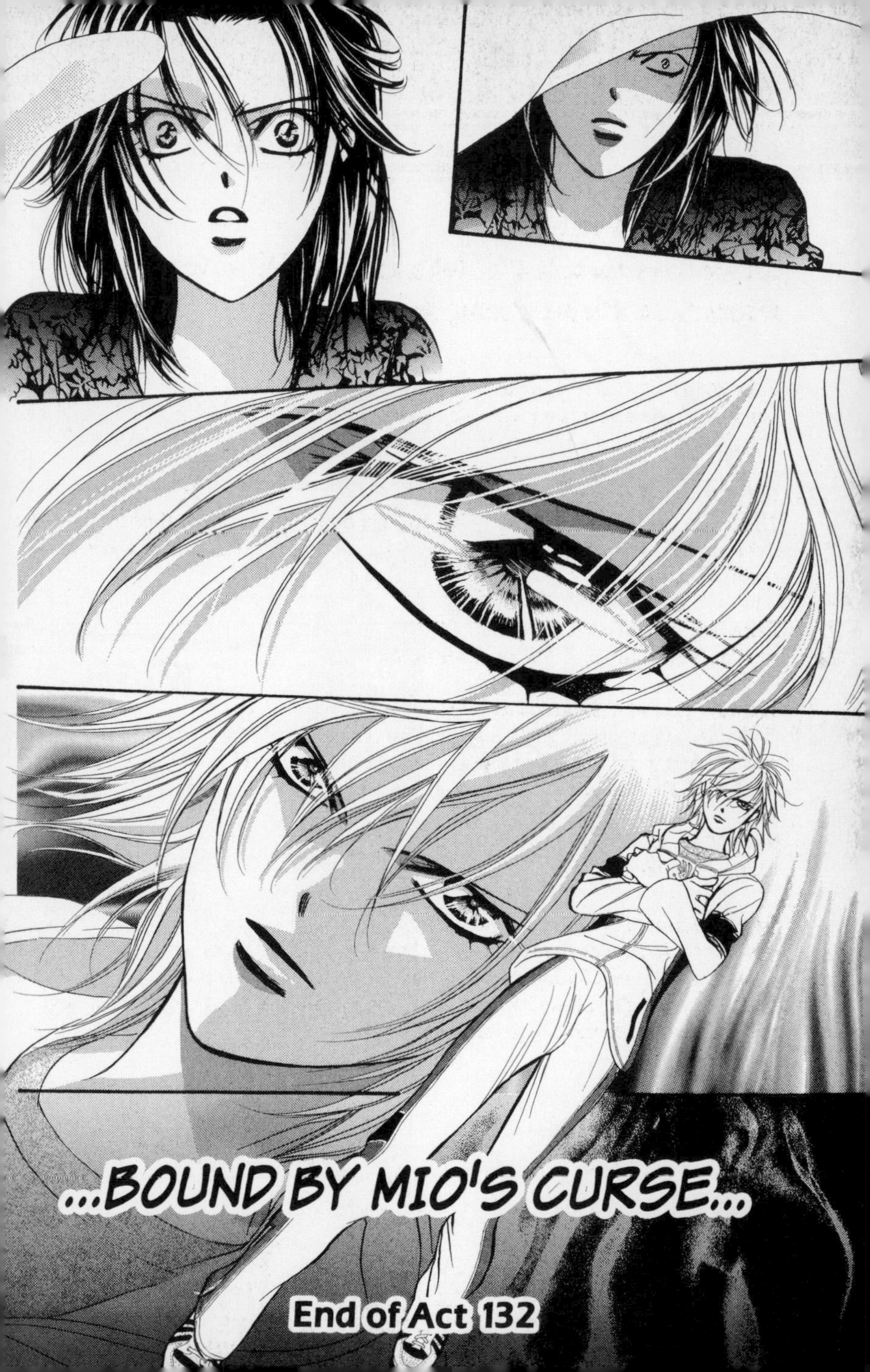
...BOUND BY MIO'S CURSE...
End of Act 132

# Skip-Beat! End Notes

Everyone knows how to be a fan, but sometimes cool things from other cultures need a little help crossing the language barrier.

**Page 26, panel 4: Corridor in an elementary school**
Some Japanese elementary schools mark a line in tape down the middle of their corridors so children know to walk to the right of the tape in each direction.

**Page 37, panel 5: Talento**
A "talento" in Japan usually appears on various TV shows and other mass media outlets. They often sing, star in commercials or movies, write for magazines, or publish books.

**Page 159, panel 5: V Cinema**
Similar to straight-to-DVD releases in the U.S.

**Page 173, panel 4: Bean paste bun**
Called *anpan* in Japanese, it's a typical bread bun filled with sweet red bean paste. Sweetened bean paste is most commonly made from red (azuki) beans, but it can also be made from black beans, mung beans, etc.

**Page 173, panel 8: Okonomi**
Means "whatever you like."

**Page 174, panel 1: Okonomiyaki**
A savory griddlecake made of a basic batter of flour, eggs and cabbage and topped with items of your choosing. Common toppings include seafood, meat, cheese and noodles. *Okonomi* has the same meaning as on page 173 (whatever you like), and *yaki* means "grilled."

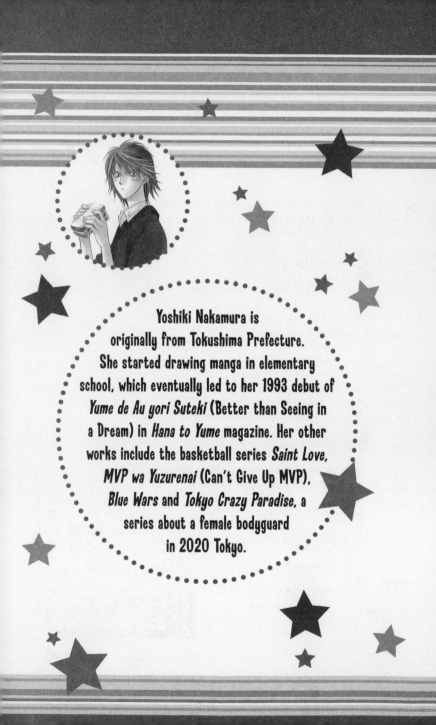

Yoshiki Nakamura is
originally from Tokushima Prefecture.
She started drawing manga in elementary
school, which eventually led to her 1993 debut of
*Yume de Au yori Suteki* (Better than Seeing in
a Dream) in *Hana to Yume* magazine. Her other
works include the basketball series *Saint Love*,
*MVP wa Yuzurenai* (Can't Give Up MVP),
*Blue Wars* and *Tokyo Crazy Paradise*, a
series about a female bodyguard
in 2020 Tokyo.

Shojo Beat

# SKIP·BEAT!

## Vol. 22

Shojo Beat Edition

STORY AND ART BY YOSHIKI NAKAMURA

English Translation & Adaptation/Tomo Kimura
Touch-up Art & Lettering/Sabrina Heep
Design/Ronnie Casson
Editor/Pancha Diaz



Printed in the U.S.A.

Published by VIZ Media, LLC
P.O. Box 77010
San Francisco, CA 94107

www.viz.com

www.shojobeat.com

10 9 8 7 6 5 4 3 2 1
First printing, December 2010

RATED T FOR TEEN

**PARENTAL ADVISORY**
SKIP·BEAT! is rated T for Teen and is recommended for ages 13 and up. This volume contains a grudge.
ratings.viz.com

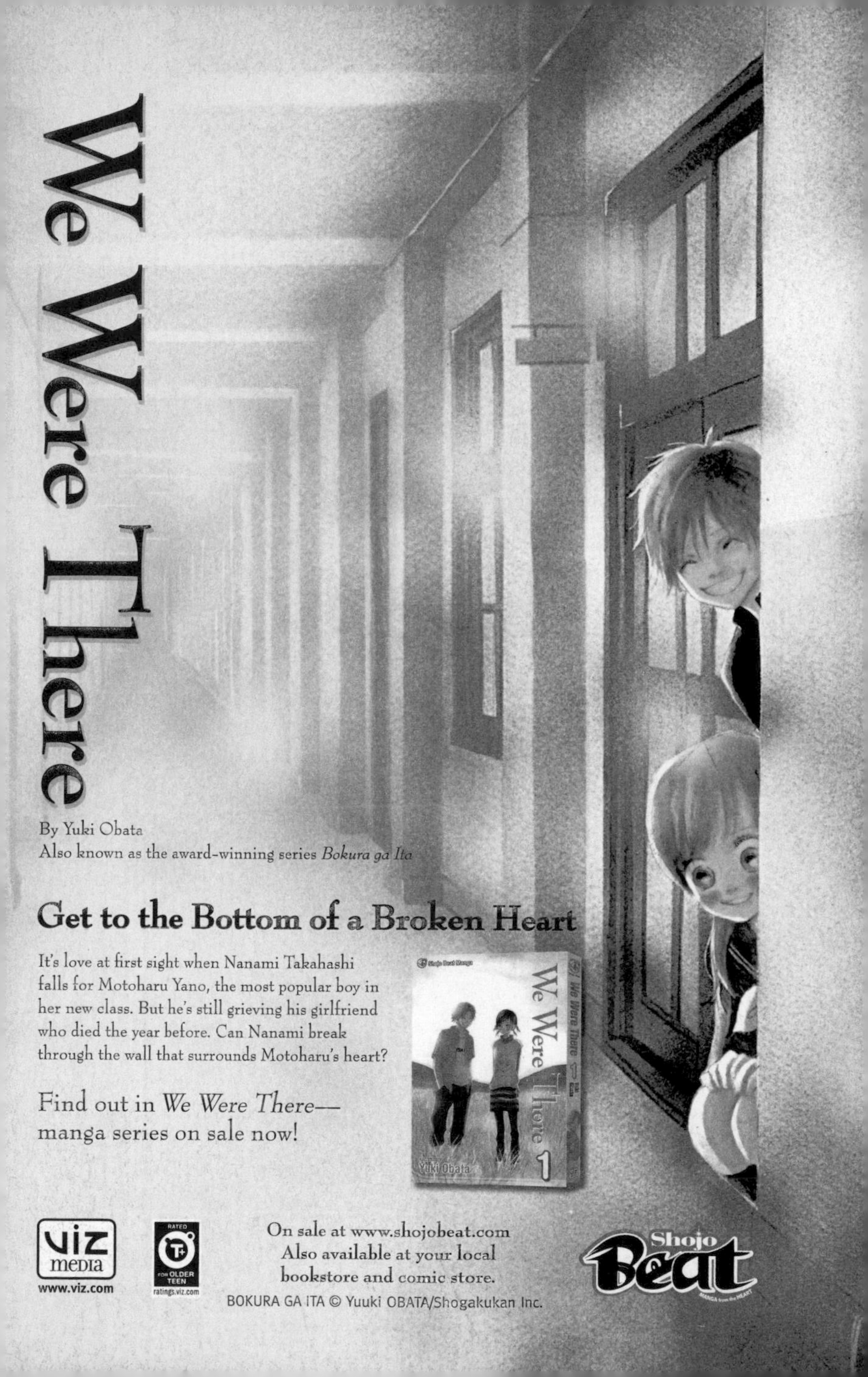
We Were There
By Yuki Obata
Also known as the award-winning series Bokura ga Ita
Get to the Bottom of a Broken Heart
It's love at first sight when Nanami Takahashi falls for Motoharu Yano, the most popular boy in her new class. But he's still grieving his girlfriend who died the year before. Can Nanami break through the wall that surrounds Motoharu's heart?
Find out in We Were There—manga series on sale now!
We Were There
Yuki Obata
1
viz media
www.viz.com
RATED T+ FOR OLDER TEEN
ratings.viz.com
On sale at www.shojobeat.com
Also available at your local bookstore and comic store.
BOKURA GA ITA © Yuuki OBATA/Shogakukan Inc.
Shojo Beat

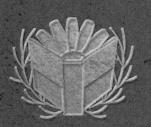
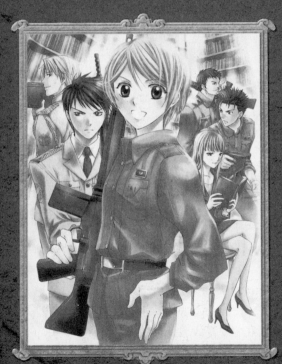
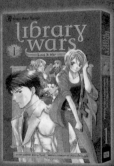

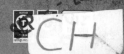

P9-DDM-507

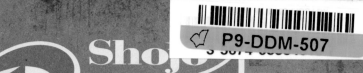

MANGA from the HEART

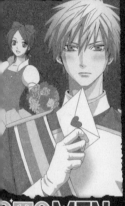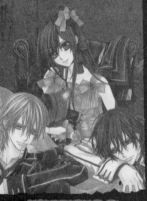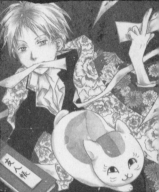

## OTOMEN

STORY AND ART BY
AYA KANNO

## VAMPIRE KNIGHT

STORY AND ART BY
MATSURI HINO

## Natsume's BOOK of FRIENDS

STORY AND ART BY
YUKI MIDORIKAWA

Want to see more of what you're looking for?

# Let your voice be heard!

# shojobeat.com/mangasurvey

Help us give you more manga from the heart!